Secret Yankees

War/Society/Culture
Michael Fellman, Series Editor

Secret Yankees

The Union Circle in Confederate Atlanta

THOMAS G. DYER

THE JOHNS HOPKINS UNIVERSITY PRESS
BALTIMORE AND LONDON

Endsheets: A panoramic photograph of Atlanta taken by George Barnard from the cupola of the Atlanta Female Institute, located less than half a mile west of where Cyrena and Amherst Stone lived. (Library of Congress.)

The Johns Hopkins University Press
2715 North Charles Street
Baltimore, Maryland 21218-4363
www.press.jhu.edu

LIBRARY OF CONGRESS CATALOGING-IN-PUBLICATION DATA

Dyer, Thomas G.
    Secret Yankees : the Union circle in Confederate Atlanta / Thomas G. Dyer.
        p.   cm. — (War, society, culture)
    Includes bibliographical references and index.
    ISBN 0-8018-6116-0 (alk. paper)
        1. Unionists (United States Civil War)—Georgia—Atlanta—History.
    2. Atlanta (Ga.)—History—19th century. 3. Georgia—History—Civil War,
    1861–1865. I. Title. II. Series.
    F294.A857D94   1999
    973.7′41—DC21   98-28165
                                                                CIP

A catalog record for this book is available from the British Library.

For Elizabeth and her mother

CONTENTS

Illustrations follow page 96.

This project began in 1979, when I first read "Miss Abby's Diary," a document written anonymously by a Unionist woman living in Atlanta during the Civil War. At that time, my understanding of wartime Atlanta was shaped in large measure by popular images that spring from fiction and film. For me, and I suspect for most people, Civil War Atlanta was a unified city, solidly secessionist and resolutely Confederate. I had no idea that strong Union sentiment existed in the city that has often been called the "second capital of the Confederacy." That is partly why "Miss Abby's Diary" appealed to me so much. It challenged my own stereotypes. It opened doors to a fuller understanding of the sad trauma of war on the home front. It made me curious about how Unionist sentiments like those of the diary's author could have endured in a city that was so unrelievedly Confederate.

Secret Yankees results from that curiosity. It is the story of a circle of Unionists in Atlanta of which the diarist, Cyrena Bailey Stone, was a member. Although the book presents a markedly different view of Atlanta than we have had before, it is not only about Unionists and Unionism. It is about loyalty as well and how issues of loyalty affected Atlantans of various political stripes. To a great extent, *Secret Yankees* is history that has been hidden since the Civil War and uncovered using research techniques that are presented in detail in appendix A. I hope readers interested in how the book's stories came to light will enjoy reading about the research paths I took as much as I enjoyed following them. The book has plenty of what are sometimes derisively called "scholarly appurtenances"; readers should be forewarned that there are notes with documentation here. First and foremost, however, I have tried to write a good story that is enjoyable for the general reader as well as for scholars. In keeping with that aim, the editors and I have agreed that we will eliminate as many intrusions as possible, in particular the use of the term *sic*. Deviations from standard spelling in quoted material should not be mistaken for editorial sloppiness. We have tried to be as true to the texts as possible.

BEFORE WRITING THE BOOK, I had an incomplete understanding of the collaborative nature of historical scholarship. In each of my research projects, I have benefited from the support of friends, colleagues, archivists, librarians, and other researchers, but in re-creating the story of Cyrena Stone and the Unionists of Civil War Atlanta I accumulated far more debts than ever before. To all the persons and institutions mentioned in this short space, I am profoundly grateful. I am equally grateful to many others who are not mentioned but who patiently listened to the story or graciously helped with the research.

I owe special thanks to colleagues in history at the University of Georgia and elsewhere who read the manuscript at various stages. John C. Inscoe listened to me talk about the project for a decade or more and never showed a trace of impatience. He advised me on research, introduced me to germane scholarship, asked probing questions, and gently criticized an early draft. We have always been friends, but in the process I also became his student.

Numan V. Bartley, a glutton for punishment, read the manuscript twice and gave me always candid advice about how to write a book that would have as broad an audience as possible. F. N. Boney and I talked about the project and "Miss Abby's Diary" over a span of many years. His knowledge of Civil War Georgia and his criticism of the manuscript were of inestimable importance. I am also grateful to Michael Fellman of Simon Fraser University, whose cogent reading of the manuscript helped me to focus on conceptual and organizational flaws. He will find many of his suggestions incorporated in these pages.

Clarence Mohr of the University of South Alabama, a friend and colleague since graduate school days at the University of Georgia, knows infinitely more about mid-nineteenth-century Georgia than I will ever know. As always, he freely shared his knowledge while prodding me to think more deeply about themes important to the era. James C. Cobb, recently returned to the University of Georgia from two decades of scholarly peregrinations, told me in unequivocal terms to dispose of a superfluous portion of the manuscript. I was incensed but followed his advice nonetheless. Rayburn Moore, professor emeritus of English, generously helped identify elusive literary passages. Lesley Gordon, formerly a graduate student at the University of Georgia and now a faculty member at the University of Akron, not only helped with the research but also instructed me in military history. I am also grateful to Albert Castel of Hillsdale, Michigan, who kindly provided information concerning the activities of Union soldiers in occupied Atlanta. Franklin Garrett of the Atlanta History Center spent many hours in conversation with me about the topic and invited me into his home so that I might have access to his necrology. I owe debts of friendship to William S. McFeely and Emory M. Thomas. Lester D. Stephens supported me, as he has since 1970 when I entered graduate school at Georgia. I also thank Robert J. Brugger of the Johns Hopkins University Press for his patience, persistence, and faith in this project.

The research for this book required extended stays in Vermont. On several occasions, I traveled throughout that marvelously beautiful state in search of fugitive historical characters and found help from virtually every Vermonter from whom I sought assistance. Barney Bloom and Michael Sherman of the Vermont Historical Society, Montpelier, were especially helpful. I owe a special debt to Jeffrey D. Marshall, university archivist, University of Vermont, for his help on a number of phases of the project but particularly for his willingness to share his own research with me. J. Kevin Graffagnino, formerly of the University of Vermont, was also quite kind, as was the staff of the Bennington Museum in Bennington, Vermont. I also thank Susan Burnor, town clerk and treasurer, Sheldon Vermont, and Larry and Betty Hopkins of Franklin, Vermont. In time, it became necessary to spend summer vacations at Caspian Lake in the Northeast Kingdom, a splendid place to think and write but far too beautiful to afford much time for either during brief summertime stays.

I revised the manuscript while teaching at the University of Heidelberg. I am deeply indebted to Lothar Tresp and Erich Pohl for the opportunity to teach at Heidelberg and to Erich and Heidrun Pohl for opening their hearts and their home in Dilsberg to our family.

The research for this project would have been much more difficult and far less thorough without the generous assistance of Marion Smith of the Andrew Johnson Papers, the University of Tennessee. Mr. Smith, a superb historian and noted spelunker, led me through numerous dark passages toward hidden research of great value. His careful research greatly enriched the story and saved me from numerous egregious errors. I am very grateful.

The staff of the libraries at the University of Georgia could not have been more helpful. I am indebted to Mary Ellen Brooks, Gilbert Head, the late Larry Gulley, and other members of the staff of the Hargrett Library. I also thank John C. Edwards of the Russell Library and Erwin Surrency, director emeritus of the Law Library.

Over the years, I have accumulated obligations to other colleagues and friends in the University of Georgia. Faculty, staff, and graduate students in the Institute of Higher Education have been helpful and kind. Ronald Simpson and Cameron Fincher provided collegial support, as did Edward G. Simpson, Melvin Hill, Libby Morris, and Larry Jones. James Hearn, now of the University of Minnesota, offered valuable sociological perspectives on the concept of loyalty. I also thank Susan Sheffield, Sheri Carter, Betty Warren, Catherine Finnegan, Ted Kalivoda, and Kristi Welch for their assistance. One of my most recent debts is to Claire Major, now of Samford University, who assisted me in research and helpfully criticized the manuscript. One of my oldest debts is to Diane Green Smathers, who while a graduate student in the Institute of Higher Education (more years ago than either of us cares to remember) did much of the early work that ultimately led to the identification of Cyrena Stone as the author of "Miss Abby's Diary."

I also thank Louise McBee, friend and vice president for academic affairs emerita of the University of Georgia, for her warm support of the project while I served as senior associate vice president. I am grateful to another friend and colleague, S. Eugene Younts, vice president for public service and outreach at the University, who let me labor in scholarly fields while I worked with him as associate vice president. Jeanette Stroer, a colleague and friend in Dr. Younts's office, helped enormously. My thanks also go to Al Ike, Nancy Cates, and Debbie Robinson, all colleagues in service. I also thank all my friends in Old College for their support while I served a brief term as interim provost of the University.

Financial support for the project in the form of fellowships came from the Vermont Historical Society through the Weston A. Cate Jr. Research

Fellowship and from the Center for the Humanities (now the Center for the Arts and Humanities) at the University of Georgia.

I have never liked lists in acknowledgments, but in the interest of space, I am reduced to listing numerous other persons who made the project much easier. I thank Aloha South, Michael Meier, and especially Michael P. Musick, of the National Archives; Edward Weldon and Jane Powers Weldon, of Atlanta; Colonel James Bogle, Atlanta; James Cassedy, of the Federal Records Center, Suitland, Maryland; Sally Sypher, county historian of Putnam County, New York; Anne P. Smith and Anthony Dees, formerly of the Georgia Historical Society; Lynda L. Crist, editor of the Papers of Jefferson Davis; Walter J. Fraser, of Georgia Southern University; Nancy Manley, of the Lake County Library, Leadville, Colorado; James M. Russell, of the University of Tennessee, Chattanooga; Stephen R. Wise, of the University of South Carolina; Jonathan Sarris, of Appalachian State University; Tom Peyton, of Golden, Colorado; Robert S. Davis, of Hanceville, Alabama; Mary Ann Hawkins, of the Federal Records Center, East Point, Georgia; Helen Matthews, of the Atlanta History Center; and Philip Lee Williams, Stanley W. Lindberg, Malcolm Call, Karen Orchard, A. J. Angulo, Jean Cleveland, Bernard Dauenhauer, and Betty Jean Craige, all of the University of Georgia. Thanks also go to Peter Strupp of Princeton Editorial Associates.

It is to my family that I owe the most. My work has always been one way I attempt to pay debts to my parents and other members of our family. While writing this book, I had the pleasure of the frequent companionship of my oldest brother, John. Although he is gone now, his wife, MaryLou, fills the void and is a cherished member of our circle. I am also grateful to Sam and Jim for being Sam and Jim, and for visits (usually wacky) with Peter and Jonathan, cooking with Michael and Sara, and New Hampshire sojourns with Bob and Sadie. Since 1971, I have lived in the same household with Anna Burns Dyer, and, to this day, I marvel at how lucky I was that she took me in. In 1984, the birth of Elizabeth Burns Dyer immeasurably enriched our family. During the last fourteen years, I have had the great good fortune to watch Elizabeth mature into a wonderful teenager—graceful, spirited, intelligent, and unfailingly kind. She is much like her mother, and it is to the two of them that this book is lovingly dedicated.

Introduction

Interstate 75 dives into Georgia from Tennessee and, for much of the 120-mile stretch between Chattanooga and Atlanta, follows the path of the Union army that marched through Georgia in 1864. Not long after it crosses into Atlanta and near the site of the Battle of Peachtree Creek, fought on July 20, 1864, I-75 merges with I-85, which comes into Atlanta from the northeast. The joined interstates are known to Atlantans as the Downtown Connector. The connector races to the west for a mile, bringing it near the outer limits of the 1864 city, then takes a sharp turn to the south for a half-mile before snapping back to the west through an area that lies between the old city and the site of the Battle of Atlanta, fought on July 22, 1864.

The traveler who takes exit 95 and drives east on John Wesley Dobbs Avenue comes quickly to the corner of Irwin and Hilliard Streets. To the north, next to the present A. T. Walden Middle School, a line of low trees parallels a no-longer-extant segment of Hilliard. Those trees mark the western boundary of fifteen acres of land, which, in 1864, were the home of Cyrena and Amherst Stone, Vermonters who moved to Atlanta in 1854 after having lived south of the city in Fayette County for four years (see map 1).

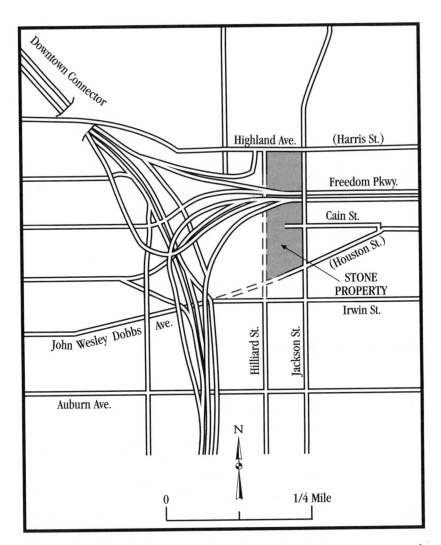

Map 1. Approximate location of property (shaded area) where Cyrena and Amherst Stone lived. Contemporary (1999) street names are used, with former names in parentheses. Dashed lines represent street segments that no longer exist.

In 1864, the property was partially wooded and partially open and had an imposing house, a walled garden, and several outbuildings. At that time, the property touched the city limits of Atlanta on its northeast side and was partially rural. Today it is a jumble of apartment buildings and businesses in the congested city center and is bisected by the "Freedom Parkway," which cuts a deep gash in the Stones' old property and rushes on toward the library of the only Georgian to become president of the United States.

Cyrena and Amherst Stone have been forgotten. They are as obscure as the occupant of the presidential library is prominent, and had not a traveling manuscript dealer paid a call on the University of Georgia Library in 1976, they might have remained totally lost to history. The dealer offered to sell a "diary" (see appendix A). The eighty-page document, spanning the period from January 1 through July 22, 1864, disclosed that a courageous Union woman who lived in Atlanta during the most dramatic days in the city's history had left a record of thoughts and deeds markedly different from those of the most famous woman in Civil War Atlanta, Scarlett O'Hara, the protagonist of Margaret Mitchell's fictional account of the Civil War city. The difficulty was that the diary's author, intent on obscuring her identity and those of others she mentioned in her narrative, did not give her name and referred to herself only as "Miss Abby." Many of those persons were members of a circle of loyal Unionists, entirely omitted from Mitchell's and other accounts, who lived in Atlanta during the war and whose wartime experiences, unknown until now, provide a strong counterweight to the Atlanta of Civil War literature and stereotype.

In time, Cyrena Bailey Stone would be discovered as the author of the diary. And in time, the hazy outline contained in the diary would sharpen into a clear but complex picture of a Union woman, wife of an ambitious lawyer and would-be blockade runner, living a mile from the center of Atlanta, part of a circle, white and black, male and female, who at great hazard maintained their loyalty to the Union in the "second capital" of the Confederacy. Identifying Cyrena required persistence and luck and obliged the researcher to find an assortment of sources overlooked by the novelists, journalists, and historians whose writings tell the story of Civil War Atlanta. The characters in *Secret Yankees,* both Union and Confederate, are neither legendary Civil War heroes nor fanciful creations of a writer's imagination. They are common people—citizens and slaves—transformed by war, both subtly and obviously, into loyalists and traitors.

From the perspective of hard-core, true-believing Confederates, the Unionists were execrable traitors. And from the standpoint of their neighbors who were die-hard true-believing Unionists, the Confederates were equally despicable, equally disloyal. There were, however, many shades of gray and blue—and many shades of loyalty. Slightly less committed Confederates and somewhat less unswerving Unionists, who were not as eager as the true believers to condemn their neighbors, found that the demands of national loyalty could be met without rupturing ties of community, friendship, and family. And, at the far end of the spectrum from the patriotic zealots, were those for whom national loyalty was irrelevant, a pliant abstraction whose practical meaning depended wholly upon circumstance and advantage.

LIKE PEOPLE EVERYWHERE and in all times, those who lived in Atlanta during the Civil War had multiple loyalties. Allegiances to family, home, friends, lodges, church, class, state, and region (among others) competed with or complemented national loyalty. Individual loyalties varied in intensity and scope over time, and when compared to other loyalties each varied in importance as well. In peacetime, societies normally allow for simultaneous competition and complementarity of loyalties, but during periods of great stress or great ambition, demands arise that national loyalty be paramount and controlling.[1]

Leaders in Confederate Atlanta believed that national survival required maximal loyalty on the part of each person, and that neither minimal loyalty nor the mere absence of disloyalty would suffice. National loyalty (construed variously as loyalty to the South, the Cause, or the Confederacy) was paramount. Yet in the decentralized Confederacy and perhaps especially in state-rights-oriented Georgia, loyalty would usually be a matter for local definition and inquisition. During the more than four years from secession to Appomattox, the sentiments of national loyalty in Atlanta rose and fell with hardship and deprivation, with victories and defeats, and with changing perceptions and comprehension of who was winning the war. But always the dimensions, proportions, and measurements of loyalty absorbed Atlantans and particularly those Confederate Atlantans for whom the preservation of the inchoate nation was paramount. For them, the heart of the Confederacy beat to the rhythm of a unifying and vigorous loyalty. Survival depended upon unity, and unity required complete loyalty with disaffection minimized and disloyalty rooted out.

All Northerners, all Yankees, and all Unionists were enemies. It had to be so. The conceptual integrity of a Southern republic depended upon separation from the corrupted North so that uncorrupted Southern civilization could be the foundation for something new. But Southerners still needed the North and Northerners in order to clarify their own identities.[2] And Atlanta's Confederates needed Atlanta's Unionists to define by negation what it meant to be a loyal Confederate. Internal enemies, imagined or real, thus contributed to the Confederate search for nationality and provided ready grist for propaganda mills. Suspicion and bluster traveled together. In the Atlanta newspapers, which played powerful roles in forming opinion, energetic reporting of suspected espionage and treason coexisted with incessant trumpeting of Confederate glory. Editors and correspondents sent out frequent appeals for the loyal to unearth the disloyal and for patriots to root out traitors. Loyalty tests became common features of everyday life, and the most readily visible Yankees, the Unionists, became frequent targets of street gossip, vigilante groups, Confederate officials, and the newspapers, which used barrels of expensive ink and reams of scarce paper to exploit fears of a dangerous fifth column in the city. Thus, the Confederates created an omnipresent foe, and from early in the national crisis throughout much of the war period, citizens suffered from a mild paranoia, discovering treason everywhere—from the Atlanta streets on which they lived to the halls of the Confederate Capitol in Richmond.

It is easy to dismiss such fears, but hindsight makes paranoia seem an almost reasonable response. Eventually, it would become evident that the disloyal were not a war-induced hallucination and that significant disloyalty to the Confederacy did exist in wartime Atlanta. Although Unionists did not present a constant menace to the city's survival, as have underground groups in other cities during other wars, their disruptive presence was a constant reminder that the political unity necessary to the construction of a Confederate nation might not be so easily achieved in the strategically important city often referred to as the "second capital of the Confederacy."

Many Unionists lived in pre–Civil War Atlanta, if by Unionists we mean those persons who placed a high value on the Union of states and who opposed secession. During 1860 and 1861, that number dramatically diminished; so much so that by the summer of 1861, after Fort Sumter and First Manassas, perhaps no more than a hundred families in the city could fairly be described as strict or unconditional Unionists. In a city of about eight thousand persons, this was a small, but significant minority, made more so because many of the key Unionists were among the influential and the wealthy with strong, long-established ties to the community.[3]

Like varieties of loyalty, the Unionists came in a variety of shapes and sizes. After the war, those Unionist men who survived were fond of recalling the perdurable works of a few dozen "Union men," and thus they defined Unionism along gender lines, although in their recollections they sometimes recognized the parts played by white Unionist women and blacks, men and women, who engaged in some of the most dangerous resistance activities, partially protected by gender and racial distinctions. In particular it is Atlanta's female Unionists who capture the imagination—women such as Emily Farnsworth, with her penchant for undertaking risky missions of mercy; Mary Summerlin, who repeatedly provided aid to a Union spy; and, of course, Cyrena Stone, whose diary has made it possible to reconstruct this hidden phase of Atlanta's history and to understand, at least to a significant extent, the role Unionist women played in the Confederate South.[4] There were intriguing black Unionists as well—men such as Prince Ponder, a black businessman, well known and trusted in Unionist circles, and Robert Webster, an enigmatic mulatto slave who lived in semifreedom, fully accepted by the white male Unionists as one of their own and reputedly the son of one of nineteenth-century America's greatest statesmen.

Other engrossing characters weave their way through the narrative of Unionism and into the web of conflicting loyalties in Civil War Atlanta: William Markham, leader of the Unionists and one of the city's wealthiest men; James Dunning, unbending Unionist and Reconstruction-era postmaster who led a movement to erect a statue of Abraham Lincoln in postwar Atlanta; "General" Alfred Austell, another of Atlanta's wealthiest, capable of being both Unionist and Confederate; Émile Bourlier, a French-born Union spy who passed in and out of the city for several years; Colonel George Washington Lee, an ambitious prewar saloonkeeper and wartime provost-marshal of Atlanta; and Cyrena's husband, Amherst Stone—Unionist, sometime blockade runner, alleged agent of the Confederacy, and, eventually, U.S. district judge.

SECRET YANKEES is the story of the Stones, but it is also the story of as many of Atlanta's wartime Unionists as can be coaxed out of the shadows of the Lost Cause mythology that has enshrouded them for generations. At times Cyrena and Amherst Stone are pushed from the narrative by the stories of the others, in part because of the paucity of sources available to reconstruct the Stones' lives and in part because of the conviction that an account of the activities of the entire Unionist group enlarges history and shows wartime Atlanta more nearly as it was—a city of considerable ideological diversity—and not unrelievedly pro-Confederate.

Only the most fleeting references to Atlanta's Unionists have found their way into the fiction and history that describe the Civil War city.[5] There are no Unionists in *Gone with the Wind.* There are no statues of the Unionists on Capitol Square in Atlanta, no visible manifestations of memory that remind us of this group of citizens and slaves whose beliefs and actions ran in countercurrent against the flood of Confederate ideology. Yet the inquisitive motorist who leaves Cyrena Stone's home place on old Houston Street (now Dobbs Avenue) and sets out to tour the modern city will discover a few unacknowledged, rarely recognized reminders of Atlanta Unionists in the place-names of the metropolis—in Markham, Dunning, Hayden, and Webster Streets; in Angier Avenue; in Lynches Alley; in the suburban towns of Austell and Norcross—each of which bears the name of one of Atlanta's secret Yankees.

CHAPTER ONE

The World of
Cyrena and Amherst Stone

Cyrena Bailey began life in the northwestern Vermont village of East
Berkshire, the daughter of a Yankee tinkerer and Congregationalist
minister, Phinehas Bailey. Reverend Bailey was born in Landaff, New
Hampshire, in 1787, one of seventeen children of Major Asa Bailey, a Revolutionary soldier who earned lasting infamy as an abuser of his wife and
children. After the major had been driven from New Hampshire, poverty
forced young Phinehas's destitute mother to send many of her children to
live in the houses of others. Phinehas was one of those sent out, and he
grew up in the household of an older sister. Apprenticed to a clockmaker,
he learned the trade and then emigrated to Vermont in his early twenties,
setting up there as a maker of brass clocks and jewelry. In 1810, he married Janette MacArthur, who lived in Chelsea, Vermont, where Phinehas
had settled. Religion absorbed Bailey, and following a period of intense intro-
spection, he began a long quest to become a Congregationalist minister.
After thirteen years of arduous independent study, he achieved his goal.
His first church was in Richmond, Vermont, where he spent less than a
year. Then in 1824, he accepted an offer from the Congregationalist
Church in East Berkshire in Franklin County (see map 2).

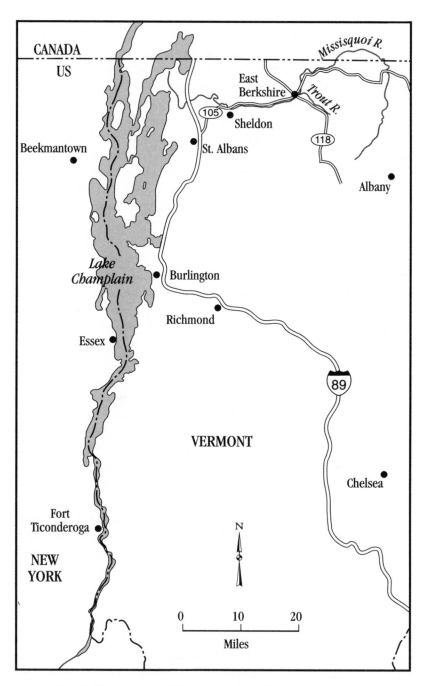

Map 2. Northwestern Vermont and northeastern New York.

Fewer than ten miles from the Canadian border, East Berkshire lies near the beautifully clear Missisquoi and Trout Rivers of northern Vermont, within sight of the Green Mountains. Situated amidst verdant, wooded hills the village was relatively prosperous, its prosperity resting upon farming. Bailey quickly built a reputation as a devout, hardworking, strong-minded pastor; "more Calvinistic than Calvin," one commentator noted. The area's natural beauty and arcadian setting made life pleasant enough (except, perhaps, during the fiercely cold Vermont winters), but the low salary Bailey earned kept his family on the edge of poverty both in East Berkshire and in later pastorates. Into this climate of piety and penury, Cyrena Ann Bailey was born in 1830, the fifth child of Phinehas and Janette MacArthur Bailey.[1]

Cyrena spent her childhood and early adult years in a succession of similarly neat, equally picturesque Vermont and New York villages, where her father held the pulpits of Congregationalist churches. Three years old when Phinehas decided, for reasons that are unclear, to leave East Berkshire, Cyrena and the family moved across Lake Champlain to Beekmantown, New York, where another sister was born. Phinehas Bailey soon rued the decision to leave East Berkshire. A deteriorating economy in the 1830s and an uncertain relationship with his congregation led him to move from Beekmantown after four years and to leave the active ministry to publish in Essex, New York, "The Berean Guide" a religious publication of the Berean Society, which Phinehas had evidently founded in East Berkshire. Meanwhile, the family endured a succession of difficulties including the death of one of the boys and the serious illness of two of the girls. Finally, in August, 1839, Janette MacArthur Bailey fell ill and died, leaving a penniless Phinehas to face the terrible prospect of subjecting the children to the trauma of his own childhood by breaking up his family.

They stayed together, however, and much of the grueling work necessary to keep the family intact fell on nine-year-old Cyrena. Years later, Bailey recalled in his memoirs that "we kept house about four weeks [after his wife's death] when some of the neighboring women said to me that my daughter Cyrena would shortly follow her mother unless we used great care to preserve her health." Bailey, too poor to hire any help, told Cyrena to "slight it all she could," in order to protect her health, but according to family recollections, the plucky child persisted in her work. In a few weeks, Bailey solved the problem by finding a new wife, thirty-five-year-old Betsey Fisk, the sister of a ministerial colleague. The second Mrs. Bailey quickly took charge, devotedly tended Bailey's children, and, within a few years, gave birth to three children of her own. Meanwhile, Bailey moved his family three more times, first to Ticonderoga, New York; then to Hebron, New York; and finally, in 1845, back to his old congregation in the familiar surroundings of East Berkshire.[2]

By the time Phinehas and Betsey Bailey and their brood returned to East Berkshire, Cyrena was fifteen. As might be expected, her childhood was filled with the elements of Bailey's religion—rigorous devotion to prayer, regular church attendance, frequent devotionals, Bible reading, and even regular family fasting—a practice Bailey probably adopted for pecuniary as well as theological reasons.[3] Little else is known about her early years. She was likely educated in the common schools of the villages in which she lived, but she also seems to have profited from the elder Bailey's emphasis on learning in the home. In later years, she would show a literary flair, writing with a skill that exceeded considerably the level of achievement associated with common schools. Possibly Cyrena took some advanced training to enable her to teach in the common schools after she had finished her own course of study, for there is some slight evidence that she was a teacher. Whether this is true or not, it is certain that she had strong literary interests and worked hard to hone her own skills as a writer. As an adult, she would publish a series of reflective essays centering on spiritual and natural topics and, to a lesser extent, on political considerations.[4] Cyrena and her siblings also benefited from her father's inventive turn of mind. The elder Bailey had designed and perfected a system of shorthand based on phonetics. The system would later enjoy some limited commercial success, but in the meantime he taught it to his children, who soon became adept at using it in their studies and for years afterward in personal correspondence and in diary keeping.[5]

In her teens, Cyrena Bailey became an attractive woman with dark eyes, dark hair, and a lively personality—if her half sister's partially fictionalized account of Cyrena's life is to be believed and if Cyrena bore resemblance to that half sister. Although Reverend Bailey's firm hand and well-known aversion to dances and other forms of riotous living precluded an extensive social life, Cyrena did take part in the round of activities common to the rural youth of northern Vermont during this time, including such well-chaperoned outings as picnics and excursions as well as the more ritualized home visits between families.[6]

It was likely that soon after Cyrena and the family returned to East Berkshire she met young Amherst Willoughby Stone, son of a local farmer, Mitchell Stone.[7] Named for a Berkshire physician, Amherst Stone showed clear signs of ambition, and in 1848, by the time he was twenty-two, he had been admitted to the Franklin County Bar.[8] There is no record that Stone attended any college in Vermont or, for that matter, any of the institutions in nearby New Hampshire or New York, although his grandfather, George Washington Stone, had attended Dartmouth. Young Stone apparently acquired his legal education by reading law in St. Albans with Judge Homer E. Royce, a native of nearby Berkshire and a lawyer of growing influence who would later become chief justice of the Supreme Court of Vermont.[9]

Like the Baileys, the Stones came to Vermont from New Hampshire and were part of the general westward migration to the Green Mountain state in the late eighteenth and early nineteenth century. Five Stone brothers, of whom one was George Washington Stone, left Piermont, New Hampshire, in the Connecticut River valley and arrived in the East Berkshire area about 1800. One brother settled in a western portion of Berkshire, while the other four established farms along the banks of the Missisquoi. The Stone family gradually grew in stature, and by the time Abby Hemenway published her remarkably detailed history of Vermont late in the nineteenth century, the Stones were thought of as one of the four or five most prominent families in early Berkshire. Hemenway regarded one of the Stone men as "plain, sensible, and solid"; another, who was a justice of the peace, was "ready at all things, a prompt and rapid, but impartial" justice, as well as a "busy and active merchant, in which business—to complete the illustration—he failed."[10] The Stone family was related to the family of Chester A. Arthur, who was born in rural Fairfield, Vermont, fewer than ten miles south of East Berkshire. Amherst was a first cousin of the future president. His aunt, Malvina Stone, a daughter of George Washington Stone, married Arthur's father and gave birth to Chester in 1829.[11]

In 1848, Amherst Stone decided to emigrate to Georgia, encouraged perhaps by the surfeit of lawyers in St. Albans and the abundance of siblings (five brothers and a sister) on his father's farm.[12] Like many young New Englanders who looked to the West or the South for opportunity, he clearly wanted to better himself and felt constrained by the lack of opportunities in rural Vermont. Why Stone decided on Georgia is not known, but by 1850, he had settled in Fayetteville, approximately twenty-five miles south of Atlanta. There he began a law practice and lived in a local boardinghouse. Within a short time, he had become active in civic affairs and helped found an academy.[13]

When is not clear, but sometime earlier Amherst had begun to court Cyrena, and in August 1850 the two married and started their domestic life together in Fayetteville. Within two years, Cyrena gave birth to a little girl, whom she and Amherst christened Jennie Arthur, perhaps after Cyrena's mother, perhaps in recognition of the Stone family's ties to Chester Arthur's family. Old Phinehas Bailey, having moved yet again (this time to Albany, Vermont), took pleasure in seeing his first grandchild during a trip the Stones and Jennie made from Georgia to Vermont when the child was eleven months old. The old man's happiness did not last long, for within a few months of the Stones' return to Fayetteville, Jennie died from consumption.[14]

The death of a child has profound effects upon parents, but because the Stones left no letters or diaries from the 1850s, it is difficult to determine how each was affected by the loss of Jennie, the only child they would ever have. For Cyrena and other nineteenth-century women, death and the loss of children were all too familiar; three of Cyrena's brothers and sisters as well as her mother and stepmother had already died. Cyrena obviously felt the loss of her daughter very deeply, and in the month of Jennie's death, she published anonymously in the Augusta *Chronicle and Sentinel* a twelve-hundred-word meditation on dying entitled "The Voice of the Pestilence," the first of a series of published essays on various topics. The essay adopted the voice of death and probed the dark universality of human experience with death and disease in the nineteenth century and in particular the swift suddenness with which they struck down the old and young. Like most of Cyrena Stone's essays, this one was written in a literary style that twentieth-century critics might characterize as "purple prose" but which in many ways was both richly descriptive and highly introspective, calling on metaphor and simile to explain human reaction to profound subjects. Most poignantly, it focused on the death of a child, the "sweet bud of infancy [plucked] from its parent stem ere yet its petals are unfolded to a lifetime of sunshine and storms."[15] Soon after Jennie's death, Cyrena and Amherst left Fayetteville for Atlanta, perhaps because of the greater opportunities awaiting a young lawyer there or perhaps in an attempt to leave behind the scene of their child's death. Sometime later, a handsome, four-foot-high marble obelisk appeared as a memorial to the child in the cemetery at the old church in East Berkshire. It bore only the simple inscription "Little Jennie Arthur."

THE MOVE TO ATLANTA brought great opportunity for Amherst, who eventually took office space in a building belonging to another Vermonter, E. E. Rawson, and began to build a legal practice in the active little city of approximately six thousand people.[16] Brash, confident, raw, and fluid, Atlanta had been literally hacked out of the wilderness during the previous fifteen years and had grown rapidly because of its pivotal location with respect to the railroads then being constructed across Georgia. Ambitious Atlanta, the nascent railroad center, soon gave birth to booming commercial and financial activity.

The urban boosterism of post–Civil War Atlanta had its roots in the decade of the 1850s as early residents, eager to present their town as a vigorous and lively place for business, energetically built railroads, worked to bring agricultural fairs to the city, and even tried to move the state capital from Milledgeville to what was becoming known as the "Gate City of the South."[17] Atlantans also concentrated on building churches and schools, and a vigorous variety of denominations vied for the souls of the city's residents. Presbyterians, Baptists, Episcopalians, Catholics, and Methodists all gathered congregations and built churches that played large roles in the lives of their parishioners and which promoted and sustained the intensity and commitment many Atlantans, like many Americans generally, felt to evangelical Christianity and to the nation.

Cyrena and Amherst joined the Presbyterian Church in Atlanta, the denomination doctrinally nearest to Cyrena's Congregationalist upbringing. As a youth, Amherst may have been a Baptist (at least one uncle was a Baptist minister); later, after he left Georgia, he became an Episcopalian. In Atlanta, Cyrena also found outlets for the sometimes religiously oriented essays she wrote, composing and revising them at home and publishing them under pseudonyms in the *Atlanta National American* and the *Commonwealth.* In the church, the couple also found friends and political soulmates such as William and Amanda Markham, whom the Stones had known in Fayette County.[18]

Markham, one of the wealthiest Atlantans, was born in 1811, the son of a Connecticut farmer. He migrated to the South in his early twenties, spending two years in North Carolina before coming to Georgia in 1835. At first a clock salesman, Markham lived briefly in Augusta before moving to McDonough in Henry County, where he farmed and ran a store and where he and Amherst Stone met. Booming Atlanta called, and he arrived there in 1853, when the town had only about thirty-eight hundred residents. Markham helped establish a savings and loan association and quickly entered the real estate and construction business. In the eight years after his arrival, he built as many as one hundred stores and other structures. By early 1857, a credit-rating company estimated his worth at around $40,000 and declared him to be "very indus[trious] & energetic." Three years later, Markham entered the rolling mill business with a New Jersey immigrant, Lewis Scofield, and produced iron rails for the rapidly expanding railroads of the South. By the end of the decade he was wealthy, and he built a handsome house on Marietta Street, not far from his extensive real estate holdings in the center of town.[19] A Whig and a strong Unionist, Markham served ably as mayor, clamping down on lawless elements in Atlanta and overseeing the construction of the new city hall on the site of the present state Capitol. He had married Amanda D. Berry while he resided in Henry County. She was the sister of Maxwell Berry, an Atlanta businessman, and the aunt of Carrie Berry, the ten-year-old diarist of the siege of Atlanta.[20]

Amherst Stone's status as a lawyer did not automatically guarantee that he would belong to the Atlanta elite. Attorneys were as plentiful as they were in Vermont with at least forty lawyers practicing in Atlanta toward the end of the 1850s, a sizable number for a town of six thousand.[21] Nevertheless, the resourceful Amherst ambitiously worked his way into the web of businessmen who controlled the city's enterprises and politics. Some attended Stone's church, some had backgrounds similar to Amherst's, and some would form the heart of Atlanta's circle of loyal Unionists when the trying days of secession and war appeared.

In fact, Stone moved with remarkable speed into some rarefied circles in Atlanta and by 1856 had taken part in the founding of two of the best-known, most expansive commercial ventures of that era. That year, he joined a group of influential Atlantans to form the Bank of Fulton, the first bank in the city organized and run by local citizens. Among the founders besides Stone were some of Atlanta's most prominent businessmen, including Jonathan Norcross, Greene B. Haygood, Jared I. Whitaker, and Clark Howell. The group chose Stone to become the bank's first president, and it was likely he who negotiated its sale to Alfred Austell, a wealthy Campbell County merchant, who moved to Atlanta in 1857. Austell put the bank on a firm footing and guided it into the war years.[22]

Also in 1856, Stone and fifteen other citizens combined to win a charter for the establishment of the Georgia Air Line Railroad. Jonathan Norcross, a principal figure in its establishment, saw the project as crucial to the economic future of the city. The railroad, when completed and connected with other prospective roads in North Carolina, South Carolina, and Virginia, would link New York City with Atlanta and the Deep South. A huge financial undertaking, the project, which ultimately failed, would have required in excess of $1.5 million. Stone probably acted as the group's attorney. Among the railroad's incorporators were a half-dozen other would-be railroad tycoons, including William Markham, Lemuel P. Grant, Richard Peters, Julius A. Hayden, Greene B. Haygood, and Jared I. Whitaker. Markham and Hayden, as well as Stone, would be active Unionists during the war, while Norcross, Peters, and Haygood each had strong connections to the Unionist Circle in Atlanta.[23]

In 1858, Stone became an educational promoter, just as he had done in Fayetteville, and he made friends with Alexander N. Wilson, an Atlanta schoolmaster who owned Wilson's Classical and English School. A native of Greeneville, Tennessee, the thirty-two-year-old Wilson had close ties to Andrew Johnson and would become an important link between Georgia Unionists and the new president in the aftermath of the war. Wilson had been the key figure in an attempt to organize a system of public schools in Atlanta, but the proposal failed in the Atlanta City Council, and in 1859 authorities evidently diverted $4,000 in city bonds from public schools to establishment of the Atlanta Female Institute.[24] Amherst Stone played a leading role in the founding of the institute, both as a stockholder and as a member of the citizens committee that raised the necessary funds to open it. He also served as secretary of the board of trustees. What role Alexander Wilson played in the formation of the college is unknown, but he and Amherst Stone were later to become close friends and political allies.[25]

Stone also seems to have had close connections with the mercantile firm of McNaught and Ormond, one of Atlanta's largest and most successful businesses. The young lawyer rented space in the same building with the two merchants and represented them in legal matters from time to time. Stone's connections in the business community also likely included Michael Myers, co-owner of the city's largest dry goods business, an operation that had twelve clerks and that took in over $300,000 in 1858. Myers, like many of Stone's other business associates, had a strong pro-Union orientation.[26]

Stone's increasing commercial and civic prominence extended into his religious life as well. When the governing body of the Presbyterian Church with authority over Atlanta decided that it was time to divide the Atlanta Presbyterian Church, Cyrena and Amherst Stone were among the thirty-nine founding members of the Central Presbyterian Church, which was established in February 1858. Stone became one of the three original trustees. By 1860, the congregation had erected a handsome house of worship in the center of the city across the street from city hall. It was to

this stately brick building with Corinthian columns and a tall spire that Cyrena and Amherst Stone regularly came to attend Sunday and midweek services.[27]

The Stones' business dealings and civic involvements clearly gave them prominence in Atlanta life during the late 1850s, but most of their activities, like those of many influential but relatively obscure persons, have gone unnoticed. Amherst's participation in the promotion of the Georgia Air Line, his role as a founder and first president of the Bank of Fulton, his involvement with the female institute, and his prominence in the Central Presbyterian Church obviously placed him among the most visible—and possibly the most influential—of Atlantans during the 1850s.

With prominence came prosperity and property. Where the Stones lived when they first came to Atlanta is not clear; perhaps they stayed in one of the city's boardinghouses or rented a house. In 1854, however, even before moving to Atlanta, Stone purchased acreage on the outskirts of town—just inside the city limits—and there constructed a large house with several outbuildings. The Stones built their house on property that faced Houston Street and was bordered by Jackson Street on the east, Hilliard Street on the west, and Harris Street on the north. At the time, the city limits of Atlanta radiated in a circle one mile from the center of town. The Stones were thus in close proximity to the bustle of the city and because their property had a high elevation, they could hear town noise—outdoor band concerts on summer evenings, unruly crowds on boisterous Saturday nights, and, in time, of course, the crash and tumult of a great battle. The house stood on a hill and commanded a good view of the center of Atlanta, which stretched along a spinelike ridge, running northeast and southwest, easily visible from the Stones' house. The valley between the house and the center of town was filling up with small, one-and-one-half-story cottages, interspersed occasionally with a more substantial house and a few imposing structures such as the female institute less than one-half mile west of the Stones, and the Atlanta Medical College, with its distinctive dome, located just to the south of the institute.

In the rural area to the northeast, about one and one-half miles away and also on a hill, Augustus Hurt, a wealthy plantation owner and businessman, had constructed a mansion with numerous outbuildings. About a mile east of the Stones, Hurt's brother, George Troup Hurt, owned property and was planning to build a mansion on another hill with a good view of the surrounding area. Augustus Hurt's dwelling was fated to become General Sherman's headquarters; Hurt's brother's house, unfinished, would become a famous focal point in the Battle of Atlanta. The Stones' neighbors also included a future mayor of Atlanta, Jared I. Whitaker, publisher of the *Atlanta Intelligencer,* a business associate of Amherst, and the man who had sold the Stones' property to them.[28]

Others of similar station lived in the community, but there were also some of more modest attainment—laborers, a distiller (Thomas Howard, whose name would be mistakenly attached to Augustus Hurt's house when it became Sherman's headquarters), slaves, and some blacks who lived between slavery and freedom, having purchased from their masters the privilege of hiring out their time and living more or less independent lives. Robert Webster and his wife, who fell into this category, owned and lived in a four-room house only a few hundred feet down Houston Street from the Stones. Before the war, the Stones had good relations with their neighbors, including future mayor Whitaker, but like most Atlanta Unionists, they would experience the painful sunderings of friendships that accompanied wartime divisions over loyalty.[29]

The precise size of the Stones' house is unknown, but given the couple's prosperity, it was likely ample. Cyrena's diary tells of a homey parlor with a fireplace, and her report of the presence of a piano and other possessions suggests the Stones lived in comfort like their neighbors, the Hurts. Nearly every house in the area had been built on a large lot. Some, like the Stones', had ten or more acres; others, like Augustus Hurt's, had larger tracts. Most had small outbuildings—smokehouses, storage sheds, slave quarters. Most would also have had quarters for animals as well—principally horses and a cow or two. Cyrena and Amherst's acreage provided plenty of space for a walled garden, fruit trees, berry bushes, and a small field in which they grew oats for their horses. There was also a "cotton house," where Amherst stored the heavy, compressed bales of the valuable fiber that he, like many of the more prosperous Atlantans, purchased on speculation. The grounds were well kept and neat; during the weeks just before the Battle of Atlanta, Cyrena oversaw the "turfing" of the lawn as two men who lived in the household sodded it with green grass. A shaded walk led from the house to the roadway. Some of the yards in the neighborhood were surrounded by neat picket fences that stood inside rows of trees planted streetside only a few years before, promising to provide shade for the lawns and the street in years to come. Most of the yards would have required fences of some kind to keep out strolling cattle and rooting swine, which sometimes wandered along the unpaved but graded roads that led up and down the rolling terrain between the Stone house and the more populous sections of town.[30]

Amherst Stone had other property as well, for by 1860 the Vermont native had acquired six slaves, or "servants," as he and Cyrena (and much of the rest of the South) called them. Because of Amherst's and Cyrena's backgrounds, owning other humans likely gave both of the Stones pause, although it appears to have given Cyrena greater concern. Her minister father had no truck with slavery, roundly condemning it and imbuing his family with biblical and moral arguments against the "peculiar institution." Slavery had reached into the Baileys' lives in a more direct way. Although a fierce opponent of chattel slavery, Phinehas Bailey did not embrace abolitionist arguments calling for immediate emancipation of slaves and refused to condemn some Northern religious organizations that did not subscribe to those tenets. These beliefs cost him the East Berkshire pastorate when his congregation adopted the more radical posture and found a pretext for firing the aging minister, who "felt that the liberation of the oppressed African race was but a part of the work awaiting Christian effort and that it was neither right nor wise, for the sake of this to oppose every other good enterprise."[31]

CLUES TO CYRENA'S MORAL DILEMMA and to Amherst Stone's views of slavery came from an unusual source, a novel of sorts written by Cyrena's half sister, Louisa Bailey Whitney, and based on Cyrena's life. Entitled *Goldie's Inheritance: A Story of the Siege of Atlanta,* and printed in Burlington, Vermont, in 1903, the novel has languished in obscurity since its publication, a literary oblivion deserved on artistic grounds. On historical grounds, however, it holds much value for it furnishes a strikingly different perspective on Civil War Atlanta from Margaret Mitchell's novel. Whereas Mitchell fixed her plot on heroic Confederates, Louisa Whitney crafted hers around a small group of loyal Unionists, equally heroic, who lived in the city during the war, enduring the wrath of Confederate citizenry and officialdom. The two novels contrast in many ways, but the most important distinction is that *Goldie's Inheritance,* unlike its famous successor, recounts to a large extent the experiences of real rather than fictional characters. It also provides extremely useful insights into the life of Cyrena Stone and into issues such as the Stones' ownership of slaves.[32]

Throughout her adult life, Louisa Whitney wrote occasionally for various religious publications but probably attempted no fiction until sometime around the turn of the century, when she started *Goldie's Inheritance.* By that time, she was nearly sixty years old and like many Americans who lived through the Civil War, she had powerful memories of the wartime experiences of family members and acquaintances that she wanted to record. Why she chose fiction instead of historical narrative likely bespoke the era's fondness for literary canonization of the wartime experiences of friends and family. The choice may also have reflected a concern for familial privacy, because not all of the family members upon whom the novel was based had acquitted themselves honorably during the war.[33] In writing her novel, Louisa Whitney had much more than memory to rely upon; she also clearly possessed the *full wartime diary* kept by her older half sister, Cyrena Bailey Stone. In a brief preface, Whitney disclosed that she had indeed based the story upon the real life experiences of Cyrena Stone, blended with her own fictional rendering of events and including some aspects of the life of another sister, Mary A. Bailey, a Vermont schoolteacher. "The long waiting, the terrors of the siege, and the rapture of triumph," Louisa Whitney wrote, "were experiences in her own [Cyrena's] life."[34]

Nearly half of *Goldie's Inheritance*'s 263 pages deals with the prewar years and encompasses the childhood and early adulthood of the protagonist, Goldie Hapgood (several of the novel's names are Bunyanesque), daughter of a virtuous Calvinist minister in New England. In this portion of the narrative, Goldie's character appears to be a composite of Cyrena Stone and Louisa Whitney, possibly also including elements of their sister, Mary. Another prominent but entirely fictional character, Arthur Hyland, is an orphaned boy who comes to live in the Hapgood household.[35]

As a child, Goldie is a star pupil, and after an education paid for by a benefactor (Louisa Whitney's education at Mount Holyoke was acquired in this way), she accepts an invitation to move to Georgia and teach (Cyrena Stone may have taught in Vermont). The invitation comes from a married couple, Egbert and Amy Fay, old New England friends, who have settled in Atlanta.[36]

Sometime around 1850, Goldie leaves Vermont and travels to New York City, where she sets sail for the South. She steps upon Southern soil for the first time in Charleston before traveling by railroad to Augusta and then on to Atlanta. In Atlanta, Goldie lives with the Fays, teaching school and taking part in the lively Atlanta social scene. She smoothly adjusts to Southern life and develops a fondness for the South and for some Southern customs, taking part in excursions to a plantation, witnessing a harvesting bee, and enjoying outings to Stone Mountain, approximately ten miles to the east, with the young people of Atlanta. She becomes popular and attracts the interest of suitors, but her heart is with Arthur Hyland, the orphan boy who lived with the Hapgood family and who has recently graduated from Dartmouth College.[37]

Fay is a lawyer, and his character draws much of its substance from Amherst Stone. Fay's wife takes bits of her character from Cyrena, but Louisa Whitney creates an unmarried Goldie in Cyrena's image, and in the process divorces her sister from Amherst, ascribing many of his less desirable traits to Egbert Fay. Thus, Whitney uses both Fays as foils to explain aspects of the Stones' lives of which she disapproved.[38]

For example, Louisa Whitney uses the Fays to explain why her half sister and her brother-in-law owned slaves. In the novel, Egbert Fay arrives in Georgia several years before he marries Amy Allen, who has remained in the North. Fay prospers in Georgia, as did Amherst Stone, enjoys a lucrative legal practice, and becomes a successful investor. Louisa Whitney emphasizes in the novel the revulsion the Bailey family felt concerning slavery and provides clues about the moral quandary Cyrena and Amherst may have felt at the prospect of owning human chattels. Before Egbert left Vermont, he and Amy together swore that they would never own slaves, resolving "to keep our hands clean of it [slavery] forever,—never to own a slave, come what would." Just as Amy is departing, however, she receives a letter from Egbert explaining that a client, a "religious woman of extreme old age," had asked him to arrange her business affairs and to dispose of her property, which consists of "three slaves for whose welfare she was very solicitous." The old woman could die peacefully, she told the lawyer, if only he would agree to buy the slaves at, what Egbert cheerily reports is, a "remarkably low" price.

Egbert leaves the choice to Amy, who seeks the advice of Goldie, fearing that a minister or some other "sage advisor" would offer only a "concoction of Northern prejudice, having no element of sympathy." Goldie presents an easy and quick solution. Amy should "do the most natural thing in the world, take a missionary view of it: you could do these slaves a great deal of good." "It looks right to me," Goldie goes on, "but it's queer isn't it? I would have said this morning that it was impossible to make you a slave-holder."[39] The accuracy of the fictive account of the Stones' transformation into slaveholders remains debatable, yet it comports with a hoary and widespread justification for slaveholding advanced by Southerners and transplanted Northerners alike. Still, it does not ring completely true. As the Civil War approached, the Baileys opposed slavery powerfully and Louisa wrote to her sister, Mary, in early 1861, concerning the issues of Union and slavery. "I have got completely tired of reading and hearing so much about 'Union,'" she declared. "*Slavery* [Louisa's emphasis] seems to be forgotten and even Republicans are willing to give up their principles to save the Union." Nothing good, she wrote, could come of "a union of slavery with freedom, of right with wrong." She wanted "to hear of somebody that was doing something for the 4 millions of slaves who are groaning in bondage."[40] No evidence suggests that old Phinehas Bailey ever learned that his son-in-law and daughter had become slave owners before he died in 1861. Although he was not abolitionist enough to satisfy his congregation, he would surely have strongly disapproved of members of his family owning human chattels.

In 1861, Amherst Stone decided to transfer ownership of the slaves to Cyrena with himself as trustee, a legal stratagem used by male Unionists who feared that their property might be taken from them through sequestration proceedings under Confederate law.[41] The Stone household included six slaves: a man, thirty-six years old; two women, twenty-four and twenty-five; and three children, a six-year-old girl, and two boys, one and three years old. The census taker who visited the Stones in 1860 categorized the man as black, the rest as mulatto. The little girl was doubtlessly "Poppy," who is mentioned in Cyrena's diary and the novel, and if the account in *Goldie's Inheritance* is correct, Cyrena "paid a ransom to give this poor child a home until the time of deliverance comes" and to "prepare her for freedom." The man may have been Jerry, referred to in the diary. One of the two women was named Margy (and perhaps was Jerry's wife). The two remaining children could have been theirs.[42]

The other woman gained her freedom in 1863. She "belonged" to Cyrena (likely as a result of Amherst's 1861 transfer of his slave property to her) and became free when her husband, whose name was Richard Mayes, bought her from the Stones for $1,000 in Confederate money. Richard Mayes was also known as Dick Cobb and was the slave of Sarah Cobb of Athens, mother of Howell Cobb, speaker of the U.S. House of Representatives and U.S. secretary of the treasury under James Buchanan. In 1857, Mayes persuaded the Cobbs to let him "buy his time"; that is, lease himself from his owners so that he could strike out on his own and attempt to survive as a quasi-free black man living in a slave society. That year, Mayes left Athens for Atlanta, where he found work as a porter on the state-owned Western & Atlantic Railroad. He also got a license to trade, and he sold fruit and other goods to passengers on the trains. Mayes paid the Cobbs $150 a year, about an 8 percent return for the wealthy Athenians if they valued their slave at the going rate for a healthy male. Mayes had a knack for business, scrimping along, living in puritanlike frugality and simplicity, working hard, saving his money. As the war approached, he sensed new opportunities and began to buy the time of young slaves whom he hired out to drive wagons or work in smithies. Richard Mayes made money. In his own words, he "became independent."[43]

Independence allowed him to think about establishing a home and family. Whether he was married to the female slave in the Stone household before coming to Atlanta is unknown. A good guess would be that the two married sometime between the census taking of 1860 and the beginning of the war. Sometime during that period, Mayes accumulated enough money to approach the Stones about buying his wife's time just as he had bought his own from the Cobbs. Amherst agreed to the proposition. Earlier, Stone had offered to carve out and sell to Richard a corner lot of their property in the block bounded by Willoughby Street on the north and Jackson Street on the east, approximately two hundred yards to the northeast of the Stones' house. Mayes liked the idea and agreed to pay Stone $500 for the property. The parties devised a payment plan, and by 1866 Mayes had paid for it in full.[44] Stone could have allowed the couple simply to reside on his property, but he chose an alternative route that permitted the slave to possess the land and to build his own house upon it with the expectation that it would become his legally in the future. After the war, Stone kept his portion of the bargain, as Mayes had kept his, and in 1866 deeded the property in fee simple to the former slave.[45]

Sometime in the early 1860s, Mayes built his house. By white standards, it was modest but infinitely more comfortable and spacious than the Cobb slave quarters he had known as a child and young man. Thirty by thirty-six feet with a front "verandah," it was well furnished and shingled. A four-and-one-half-foot picket fence graced the front of the lot, and a five-foot-high close board fence enclosed the rest of the property. The couple also built their own barn and smokehouse and acquired livestock including a cow and a few hogs. In time, they had a little girl, and years later Amherst Stone would see to it that she owned property in Atlanta as well.[46]

By 1864, the slave composition of the Stone household had changed slightly with the addition of a leased slave named Dan.[47] The household also included two white servants, Tom and Mary Lewis, and their son, Homer, born in 1859. One of Stone's brothers, Chester Able Stone, ten years younger than Amherst, also lived with Amherst and Cyrena and clerked in the firm of J. L. Cutting, who ran a general merchandise store. Within a few years, Chester had become a partner and enjoyed a good reputation in Atlanta where he was regarded as honorable, industrious, and high-minded.[48]

THUS IN 1860, the world of Cyrena and Amherst Stone was one of comfort and privilege that neither had known during youth. They were among the established in Atlanta, and Amherst was influential in the community. A shrewd businessman as well as a capable lawyer, his economic future was secure and bright. As immigrants to the South, neither Cyrena nor Amherst had nearby the extended families that both had known growing up, but at least young Chester Stone was there, and that pleased them both. Cyrena's circle of friends seemed wide, and her relationships with the servants and slaves who shared her household, and with Dick Mayes and his wife who shared the Stones' property, seem to have been free of conflict. The character of these relationships and the generosity that her diary discloses in dealing with poor whites suggest that Cyrena Stone actively practiced a social Christianity that grew out of the teachings of her father and her active involvement in the Central Presbyterian Church of Atlanta. In many ways, religion stood at the center of her existence, giving focus to her thoughts in every sector of her life.

The Stones' social life was sedate, genteel, and enjoyable, with regular visits among friends and occasional picnics and outings into the nearby countryside perhaps with neighbors such as the Whitakers or fellow Presbyterians such as the Markhams. As far as can be determined, they did not take part in the frivolous gaiety that characterized the social life of some Atlantans. Theirs was not a life of charades, tableaux, and charity balls. At home, their life seemed pleasant enough and was filled with music, books, writing, and friends.

Still, the Stones would never be treated in the same ways as native Southerners treated one another. As New Englanders, they were thought of by some Georgians as latecomers, regarded by others as nouveau riche, and assuredly stereotyped by most as Yankees. And from behind the practiced facade of Southern graciousness and hospitality would regularly emerge hard-edged questions about where they had come from, why they had come South, and what they thought about this or that political or racial question. Although Atlanta was a city of immigrants as well as natives, some Atlantans and many Georgians could barely conceal a choleric distaste for outsiders, for newcomers, and especially for those whose ideas might be incompatible with a Southern consensus that emphasized exclusivity, sectional identity, and ideological conformity. For persons like Cyrena Stone, a dissenter and an immigrant to the South, ardently patriotic and steadfast in the primacy and sanctity of Union, the years ahead would be a time of severe testing.

CHAPTER TWO

Loyalty under Fire

Unionists and the Secession Crisis

John Brown's raid on Harpers Ferry in 1859 raised a specter in Georgia that transformed talk over the future of the Union. From an on-again, off-again discussion of whether Southern rights were being sufficiently trampled upon to warrant disunion, the debate became infused with racial paranoia and fear of an approaching Armageddon. Throughout Georgia, and especially in those areas of heavy slave population, many whites became transfixed by the imminent and awful possibility of an abolitionist-driven slave revolt. Racial fears escalated the rhetoric of disunion as Georgians resolutely organized to thwart the menace through vigilance committees that would purge abolitionists and protect the community against incendiarism and revolt. This was no ordinary slave insurrection panic, and for those who cherished the Union and defended ideas of Union, there was the much enhanced prospect that they would themselves be labeled abolitionist enemies of the South and become victims of the purge.[1]

Despite the great civil uproar that was shaking the nation, Atlanta celebrated the advent of 1860 with festive enthusiasm at a public dance in Hayden's Hall on New Year's Eve. During the evening, however, the gaiety was interrupted when "a slight difficulty occurred between one of the managers of the celebration and parties who have been heretofore accused of giving expression to Abolition sentiments." Gunshots rang out, but no one was hurt. The *Atlanta Intelligencer* reported that the source of the unpleasantness was D. S. Newcomb, a native of New York and a clerk at a dry goods store owned by John Ryan, an Irish immigrant and merchant. Newcomb, it was said, had drunk toasts to "Old 'ossawattomie' Brown—calling him 'brave' and stating that he should not have been hung." A vigilance committee promptly formed and called upon Ryan (whose business associate Michael Myers would later be accused of militant Unionism), demanding that he get rid of Newcomb. The merchant fired the New Yorker and, according to the newspaper, declared that "no one guilty of savoring of abolition could 'clerk' for him." The hapless Newcomb hurriedly left the city, just ahead of a mob. There was a lesson to be learned. "To gentlemen of the abolitionist cloth," the newspaper adjured, "we would say that they had as well be chary of expressing such opinions and sympathies, for it is a noted fact that our climate invariably becomes unhealthy to such."[2]

Four days later, on January 5, the Georgia politician Alexander Stephens wrote to Atlanta newspaperman J. Henly Smith that he judged there was a lack of "excitement in the public mind upon public affairs in Georgia."[3] Atlanta must have been an exception to Stephens's generalization, for in the early months of 1860 the city seemed ready to burst with opinion on the great issues of Union and disunion, whether expressed in the none-too-genteel setting of a public dance or in the relatively sedate pages of the city's newspapers. The *Atlanta Intelligencer,* published by Amherst Stone's neighbor, business associate, and soon to be mayor Jared I. Whitaker, was the city's leading newspaper and provided the forum for a vigorous but increasingly rancorous debate on secession. No sterile disputation in political theory, the discussion took place in a context of grave agitation over the events of the preceding fall and the fear of militant abolitionism engendered by Brown's raid.

By 1860, *abolitionism* had become an elastic byword for a host of evils that Southern whites feared, the greatest of which was that militant Republicanism would converge with abolitionism to force the outright and immediate destruction of slavery. The intensity of fear that abolition generated throughout the South is hard to exaggerate. As Steven Channing has noted with respect to South Carolina, it created a vision of "unthinkable horror, attendant with boundless physical, economic, social and political disasters" that "darkly colored the attitude of South Carolinians toward northern society, and explained the frantic response to the rise of the Republican Party."[4]

Some Atlantans harbored comparable fears, and because there were few abolitionists or Republicans readily available, they projected their fears of incendiaries, abolitionists, abolitionist emissaries, and Northerners in general onto the city's Unionist population and particularly on those who were not of Southern origin. These militants favored secession and called for immediate redress of the South's grievances. Others, perhaps a majority of the city's residents in early 1860, did not so readily embrace such fears and hewed to a more moderate politics of cooperation with the North that called for preservation of the Union with secession acceptable only as a last resort. Thus, during most of 1860 Unionists and Unionist principles had places in the momentous debates occurring in Atlanta, but in a relatively clear progression Unionism virtually disappeared from public discussions, a victim of the radical politics of secession and of demands for absolute loyalty emanating from fire-eating secessionists.

In early 1860, most Atlantans were at least in part heirs to a tradition of Southern Unionism that stretched back to the early days of the republic. Indeed, in the first decades of the nineteenth century, the people of the South in general can be thought of as Unionist, if, as Carl Degler argues, they saw no "sharp difference" between sectional and national interests. Only gradually, after the Nullification Crisis of 1832, the Compromise of 1850, and the secession crisis itself, did the region and Georgia embrace disunion and then by no means unanimously. As Degler has also pointed out, there were always Southern Unionists whose views were so staunch as to be "unqualified, even when tested against loyalty to region."[5] The secession crisis and the war would reveal a small number of unconditional or strict Unionists who remained in the Confederacy and whose loyalty to the Union and affection for national values were strong enough to endure condemnation, ostracism, violence, and even death.

IT IS IMPOSSIBLE to know how many Atlantans may have regarded themselves as Unionists in the early days of 1860, but by the time the secession crisis had run its course and war had begun, the number had dramatically diminished, to the point that likely no more than one hundred families at most would commit themselves to strict or unconditional Unionism. "We have no *class* of tories or traitors among us," the editors of the *Atlanta Southern Confederacy* wrote, although they admitted that disloyal Atlantans did exist and should be "ferretted out, brought to public justice and properly dealt with."[6] The newspapermen accurately assayed the composition of the group of Atlantans who held on to their loyalty to the Union beyond the days of the secession crisis. These unconditional Unionists were not drawn from any particular class of citizens but included a variety of persons from different economic, social, and ethnic groups.

Atlanta had fewer than ten thousand residents in 1860, nearly two thousand of whom were blacks, almost all of them slaves.[7] Because of its smallness, Atlanta had an almost villagelike intimacy. Family, social, and business ties were complex and interwoven, binding together many of the citizens, Union and Confederate alike. Moreover, most Atlantans knew each other personally or at least knew who people were and something about their standing in the community. Citizens kept well informed about goings-on in the city through five newspapers (two of which were dailies) and especially through the active chains of conversation and gossip that characterize small places. Thus, when the *Southern Confederacy* and other newspapers discussed the nature and composition of the Unionist group in Atlanta, citizens were certain to pay attention and sure to add their own opinions, evidence, and embellishments to the newspaper accounts. Villagelike intimacy would diminish somewhat during the war as the town became a small city, seemingly ready to burst at its seams with tens of thousands of wartime travelers and soldiers in temporary residence at barracks, hotels, hospitals, and prisons. Nevertheless, old ties and acquaintances often lingered despite political differences of great gravity. And in spite of Atlanta's transformation, small-town habits persisted, although these were modified somewhat by the presence of so many strangers and newcomers.

James Dunning, one of the most vocal of the Atlanta Unionists, frequently said that only thirty-five or forty true "Union men" remained in the city for the entire course of the war. Dunning's estimate would have included only those men who he believed had followed an uncompromising Unionist line—never saying anything in support of the Confederacy, never uttering anything that could be construed as disloyal to the Union, doing business with the Confederate government only under compulsion, providing aid to young men escaping the Confederacy to evade military service, and avoiding if at all possible the rendering of any support whatsoever to the Confederate cause. Dunning mainly cited those members of the professional, merchant, and manufacturing classes in the city whom he knew well—people such as Amherst Stone—but he also clearly knew and likely included tradesmen, artisans, and mechanics who were active Unionists.

He completely omitted Unionist women, some of them wives, sisters, or daughters of the Unionist men, some with no family ties at all to Unionists. He also omitted a group of foreign-born Atlantans—natives of Ireland, Germany, Scotland, France, and England who resolutely refused to take up arms for the Confederacy and spent the war years trying to carry on business as usual while devising ways to stay out of Confederate service. And finally, he omitted all but one of a circle of black people who lived in Atlanta and who had powerful attachments to Unionism and Unionists.[8]

The most systematic exposure of the ideas of unconditional Unionism in Atlanta came from a correspondent to the *Intelligencer* who styled himself "Plebian" and who regularly delivered his columns to the *Intelligencer* office of publisher Whitaker. The *Intelligencer* commented that although it respectfully dissented from Plebian's arguments, it was "willing that the important questions of Disunion be fully ventilated—that both sides be heard—and if any practicable means can be suggested by which the rights and honor of the South can be preserved intact in the Union," the newspaper would "give it the aid of our feeble exertions." The rights of the South, however, would have to be fully taken into account in any such plan.[9] The editors, clearly uncomfortable with Plebian's ideas, repeatedly distanced themselves from his more radical views, all the while professing admiration for the solid citizen who wrote anonymously as Plebian.

Although it cannot be proven conclusively, Plebian appears to have been James A. Stewart, an Atlanta miller and businessman. Stewart was Unionism's most prominent literary exponent in Atlanta, its scrivener and ideological theorist, who crafted numerous letters to newspapers under his own name and pseudonymically expounded Unionism as he understood it and linked it to the major local and national issues of the day. Born about 1811 in east Tennessee, a hotbed of Unionism, Stewart resided in Robertson County, Tennessee, until only a few years before the secession crisis. With his partner, William Moore, Stewart owned and worked a small steam mill that produced flour. He appears to have been relatively prosperous (he was free of debt in 1860) and had won the respect of the local business community as well as that of a national credit concern that had "every confidence" in him and his partner. An active Democrat and, like several of the Unionists, a slave owner, Stewart built a wide circle of acquaintances, including future president Andrew Johnson and Alexander Stephens, the Georgia politician who would become vice president of the Confederacy. Stewart corresponded with both. Stephens referred to Stewart in his diary as his "old and true friend."[10]

Stewart had a good mind, but one that harbored highly iconoclastic ideas for a mid-nineteenth-century Southerner. For example, in a public lecture, "Sectarian Influence in Schools," given in the Atlanta city hall in 1859, he boldly declared himself a religious free-thinker whose liberal parents had "induced [him] to read the Bible as . . . any other book, with a spirit of investigation, adopting the good and rejecting the bad." Stewart told the Atlanta audience that he "adopted all the moral precepts, but found in them nothing superhuman—nothing but truths derived from the revelations of Nature through experience and observation—truths which had been taught and reduced to practice by heathen philosophers." Stewart also advocated the stunningly unconventional idea that schooling for children should be purely secular and that the reading of any sacred books, for instance, the Bible or the Koran, should not be required in schools.[11]

Stewart's political beliefs were less radical but strongly pro-Union and grew in unpopularity as the South edged ever closer to disunion. In pamphlets, in correspondence with Stephens, and in letters to the *Atlanta Intelligencer,* Stewart expounded a Unionist philosophy that totally rejected the idea of secession. During the first seven months of 1860, as Plebian, and in the spring of 1861, under his own name, he engaged in a running commentary on the great issues of the day, completely antagonizing the considerable population of non-Unionists in Atlanta and, finally, the newspaper that published his commentary.

Like many Americans of the Unionist stripe, in the North and the South, Stewart harbored a nearly mystic attachment to the concept of Union, stressing its God-given immutability. In mid-January 1860, Plebian noted that there was a "conservative power in existence which will ever preserve and perpetuate the Union" despite the "treasonable efforts of politicians North and South to destroy it." Common sense and common honesty, property of the common working people, would soon arise to defeat the treasonous designs of the elite. Common sense would manifest itself in an adherence to popular sovereignty. If the people of a state or territory should decide to establish slavery, so be it. No other state should interfere. Such a philosophy, Stewart believed, should be embodied in the Democratic platform of 1860, and the party should nominate either Andrew Johnson or Stephen Douglas to carry out these designs. "This done," Plebian concluded, "and our Union is safe."[12]

Soon Plebian extended his argument in defense of the Union to a passionate condemnation of disunion and secession. Although he was strongly critical of abolitionists who worked to destroy the Southern institution of slavery, he had equally harsh criticism for those who persistently advanced the ideas of disunion and secession. "Let not one desire for dissolution disturb our peace," Plebian wrote. Peaceable secession was the "language of deluded men" and could never take place. Boundary lines of secession could never be agreed upon, he argued, but if they were, foreign powers would soon intrude and prey upon the weaker states created by secession. If a Southern confederacy were established, a breakup into small and hostile localities would inevitably ensue. "What precautionary measures can they institute to prevent a dissolution of the Southern Confederacy?" Plebian asked.

> Will it not have a *North* and a *South?* and will not venal and ambitious men disturb its peace and destroy its nationality? Will not disaffected States secede and assume the self-importance of nations? And will not the separate and distinct nations of South Carolina, Georgia, Alabama, & c., get to logger heads with each other and appeal to arms as the arbiter? Would not citizens of the *great nation of Georgia* discover that there is a North and South within its *vast limits?* and might not the hardy mountaineers of the Cherokee country invade the soil of the fertile valleys, giving cause for another division and dissolution? Will not this dividing and subdividing, when once commenced, proceed unchecked, until all we hold dear is lost?[13]

Plebian's words angered the editors of another Atlanta newspaper, the *Southern Confederacy,* which criticized the *Intelligencer* for printing such objectionable opinion. "We think the communications of Plebian have proclivities that are not altogether applicable or proper at this time, and at no time to a Southern people," the paper declared.[14]

Nevertheless, the commentary continued to appear, and for a brief time in the early spring of 1860, Plebian was joined by another Unionist, who took the name Osceola and whose views were slightly more conservative. Osceola's identity cannot be determined, but he was a Virginia native whom the *Intelligencer* described as "one of Atlanta's most honored citizens." Osceola argued less from defined political positions than from a strongly emotional attachment to "this glorious heaven-born Union." Emphasizing the necessity to protect the rights of every section, Osceola identified his political views with those of figures such as former president Millard Fillmore and former speaker of the house Robert C. Winthrop, and he condemned the politics of strong antislavery advocates such as William Seward, William Lloyd Garrison, and Salmon P. Chase. Osceola called for a resurgence of patriotism and for a proper estimate of the "immense value of [the] National Union" to "collective and individual happiness." If the Union were dissolved, Osceola argued, then liberty would perish and Americans would "hear the wail of dying liberty and catch the requiem of mourning millions."

But Osceola soon departed, leaving the field to Plebian, who, in a series of communications to the *Intelligencer,* increasingly analyzed the crisis in a class context. True to his pen name, he emphasized the values of working people as a means for solving the national dilemma and fastened guilt for the impending crisis on the slave-owning elite and on Northern elites who agitated the slavery question. "Emboldened by the prospects of a political revolution growing out of the slavery question," the wealthy aristocracy would cast aside democracy for their own enrichment and benefit. "They have conceived the idea that they themselves are not people," Plebian declared, "but are a privileged order of gentlemen, having a divine, or some other supernatural right" to rule in politics and society. "Of course, they desire class legislation," Plebian wrote, "and hence, the people, or poor folks, must be deprived of a voice in law-making assemblies." As enemies of popular sovereignty (and thereby democracy), they had seized upon the Harpers Ferry incident "as a favorable pretext on which to precipitate a dissolution" of the Union.[15]

While Stewart was defining a class-oriented, strict Unionism, there was no shortage of rhetoric that just as vigorously propounded secessionism. Numerous authors of letters to the *Intelligencer,* as well as the journalists themselves, repeated well-rehearsed justifications for secession, defended slavery, condemned Northern tyranny, and celebrated all things Southern. They also eagerly embraced romantic schemes presented as essential to the Southern cause. Such was the case in early March 1860, when febrile representatives of the Knights of the Golden Circle arrived in Atlanta promoting a Southern expansionist scheme that James A. Stewart and others in the Atlanta Unionist circle found absurd, but also feared.

The Knights were the creation of "General" George Bickley, a Cincinnati filibusterer and skillful liar with the good fortune to have married a wealthy widow willing to finance his fantasies. In Bickley's mind, the Knights were a secret society whose purpose would be to conquer Mexico and the countries of the Caribbean rim and introduce Anglo-American civilization into that area. Bickley gained the interest of some Southerners, who saw in his scheme the prospects for a territorial outlet for slavery, and in the early spring of 1860 he went south looking for support, hunting dues-paying members for the Knights of the Golden Circle.[16]

After a brief stay in New Orleans, "General" Bickley and a retinue arrived in Atlanta. Local secessionists were eager to hear about the filibustering schemes and had orchestrated a well-attended meeting in the city hall on a Monday evening in mid-March 1860. A persuasive speaker, Bickley convinced his audience that he was a veteran of the principal battles of both the Mexican War and the Crimean War and that he was an expert on military affairs, bearing "upon his bosom," according to the *Intelligencer,* "the emblem of his valorous deeds in that [the Crimean] war." Bickley had brought with him "Major" Henry Castellanos, who "enchained the audience with the most finished, classic and thrilling strains of refined eloquence ever listened to." "The people of Atlanta are devoted to Southern interests and Southern rights," the *Intelligencer* gushed, "and whenever questions involving this subject are the topic of discussion, the people of Atlanta always give an attentive hearing." The *Intelligencer* declared the meeting a grand success.[17] Another meeting on the next evening, under the chairmanship of Alexander M. Wallace, an Atlanta insurance man and a prominent secessionist, brought forth a set of resolutions endorsing Bickley's scheme. The *Intelligencer* explained how citizens could, for five dollars each, become Knights of the Golden Circle. Some of the most prominent of Atlanta's citizens, including Wallace, formed a committee to receive the donations and enroll new Knights.[18]

If Bickley's swing through Atlanta had all the trappings of a medicine show, it was clearly taken seriously by Unionists as well as secessionists. Invitations went out to pro-Union members of the community to assemble for a meeting to discuss the Knights. Unfortunately, one of the invitations fell into the hands of a secessionist who took grim delight in sending it to the *Intelligencer* with a derisive accompanying letter declaring that Unionists "And their beloved 'Union' may go to the Deuce together."[19]

Despite the ridicule, the Unionist meeting took place. James A. Stewart was one of two orators who spoke against the Knights; James L. Dunning, a native of Connecticut and a partner in an Atlanta foundry, presided. Forty-six years old, Dunning lived in Rome, New York, before emigrating to Georgia and settling in Cassville sometime in the late 1840s. He moved to Atlanta in about 1852 and, with two partners, owned and operated the Atlanta Machine Works. Three years later, credit reporters declared that the three owners of the business were "wealthy men." Dunning was regarded as honest, careful, and prudent, as well as a shrewd businessman.[20] He was also one of the most uncompromising and outspoken Unionists, quite likely to take a role in publicly denouncing the Knights. The *Intelligencer* derided the event as a "Union meeting" and reported that only thirty or forty persons, a "small portion" of the citizens of Atlanta, had attended. In the end, Dunning, Stewart, and the Unionists proved to be fully correct in their suspicions concerning the Knights, who were soon exposed as a sham, General Bickley having succeeded too well in fund-raising and too little in filibustering.[21]

After the Knights had departed, Stewart continued to hammer away at secessionism with his Unionist rhetoric. Moreover, the *Intelligencer* published his arguments well into the summer months, but as the secession crisis deepened, Atlantans became increasingly intolerant of dissent—and of Plebian. In May, when Stewart left the city for several weeks, another citizen managed to publish a letter in the *Intelligencer* that squarely and cynically condemned the principal elements in Plebian's political philosophy and in addition signed the name Plebian to the column.[22] Whether the newspaper was complicitous in the ruse is unknown, but when Stewart returned to Atlanta and discovered what had happened, he composed a long answer, incidentally condemning the writer who used his pen name, but couching his most powerful antisecessionist rhetoric in fiery metaphor.

"We have had enough of the low mutterings of disunion fires," Stewart wrote, and in apocalyptic terms he adjured secessionists to

give vent to the pent up flames—scatter your firebrands over this fair earth—make bonfires of our temples of liberty—run the dividing line which shall cause kindred and friends, now inhabitants of a common country, hereafter to meet as foreigners, perhaps in hostile array, to shed each other's blood. Clip the telegraph wires—pull up your iron rails—stop the transportation of our mails—compel non-intercourse between the North and South—involve our now peaceful inhabitants in civil war—close up our workshops and factories—abandon our plantations and farms—neglect the education of our children, and let famine and pestilence ensue to complete the sum of horrors which must inevitably result from the consummation of your frenzied schemes. Let us know the full measure of your strength. If powerful for destruction, and bent on mischief, why procrastinate the evil day? . . . Let us at once know the worst. But remember the lovers of the Union are not men of straw. Deeply imbued with a silent, though patriotic, devotion to their common country, its bond of union can never be dissolved whilst there is a man of us left to wield an arm in its defense. "By the Eternal this Union shall never be dissolved."[23]

This column proved to be Plebian's, but not James A. Stewart's, last in the Atlanta newspaper. After the incident involving the ersatz Plebian and Stewart's impassioned response, public pressure mounted on the newspaper to rid itself of its correspondent. Soon, the *Intelligencer* revealed a contempt for Plebian, stating that he had been "boring the Georgia press and disgusting readers long enough." "Afflicted with a swelled head" and "the perfection of self-conceit," he had "imbued his articles *usque ad nauseam* with that foul and odious doctrine": popular sovereignty. Plebian sent a response, but it was dismissed as a "sickening effusion" and never published.[24]

The dismissal of Plebian from the *Intelligencer* marked the end of significant dissent in the newspaper. By late July, when Plebian made his final attempt to respond in the *Intelligencer,* the path of dissent had narrowed to the point that it was no longer possible to advance unpopular views without significant risk. Free speech, always fragile and never complete, was disappearing for Atlanta Unionists.

STEWART AND DUNNING were among the most outspoken of Atlanta Unionists in 1860, but they did not stand alone. As the presidential campaign of that year warmed, Unionists met occasionally in public but more often furtively to draw strength from each other and to discuss ways to stem the tide of secessionist sentiment in Atlanta. Throughout the year, as antagonism had grown toward Northerners and things Northern, the Unionists, a great deal of whom were born outside the region, were treated coolly by old friends and neighbors who sensed the strength of their commitments to the Union. In many instances, the coolness turned to heated hostility, with the condemnation of Yankees and Yankee ways increasingly pointed toward Northerners and Northern transplants in the city. Exactly when the Union men of the city began to meet secretly is unclear, but probably by early summer a core group of twelve to fifteen loyal merchants and professional men had begun to congregate regularly. The office of New Hampshire–born Nedom L. Angier, an Atlanta physician and real estate investor, was the most frequent gathering place for the Union Association, as the men sometimes called themselves. "An association of us here met frequently at his office," one wealthy Unionist later recalled, "[and] we met there for the purpose of discussing the best means of preventing secession." Because of the growing hostility toward them, the men would leave the meetings individually or in twos or threes so as not to attract attention, some going out the front of Angier's office, others taking the back stairs out to the street.[25]

Nedom Angier had been in Atlanta since 1847. Educated in his home state, Angier taught for a few years while he studied medicine in the East. He moved to Georgia in 1839 and taught school for four years in Coweta County. Then in 1843, Angier decided to complete his medical studies and attended lectures in medicine at New York University, returning to Georgia in 1844 and beginning a medical practice in Randolph County. He remained there for three years and then moved to Atlanta, where he practiced medicine, ran a drugstore, and opened an academy. After a year-long gold-hunting trip to California in 1850, Angier returned to Atlanta, became a real estate speculator, and between 1850 and 1860 amassed considerable wealth. During this time, he developed Angier's Springs, which became a popular spa and a spot for picnics and holiday outings. Angier also was an incorporator and stockholder in the Atlanta Bank, which was the town's first financial institution and which had had a brief, volatile life before it closed in 1855. His political activities before 1860 are not documented, but he was a Douglas Democrat in 1860 and an ardent anti-secessionist. In that year, he also became a member of the Atlanta City Council. He would later be credited with having suggested the name for Fulton County.[26]

Amherst Stone frequently attended meetings at Angier's office and other locations. Stone emphasized that the Unionists met not only to discuss issues and plan strategies but also "To sympathize with each other all we could." "Confidential friends," they gathered as a group and would meet with each other individually, "very privately often at night." Ultimately, they would help each other plan how to evade service in the Confederate army. Stone and William Markham met at Markham's office, at Stone's home, at Stone's office, and at the houses of their friends, including that of schoolmaster Alexander N. Wilson, a native of east Tennessee, "a mutual friend of ours, who was a very strong Union man and a member of Mr. Markham's church." William Markham said that they were often joined by James Dunning, Thomas G. Healey, William Farnsworth, and Alfred Austell, "among others."[27]

Thomas G. Healey, a partner in a brick making and construction firm, was born near Hartford, Connecticut, in 1818. As a youth, he apprenticed with a mechanic; later, he became a contractor, doing business in Hartford.

In 1846, Healey moved to Georgia, settling first in Savannah and later moving to McDonough, where William Markham had also lived. Healey married Markham's sister, Olive, and the two moved to Atlanta in 1852, a few months before Markham arrived. Like his brother-in-law, Healey was a Presbyterian. Unlike Markham, he was not active politically before the war.[28] William T. Farnsworth, a native of Massachusetts, was among the most active Unionists. Thirty-nine years old in 1860 and a foreman at Pitts and Cook's ironworks, Farnsworth also worked as a contractor and skilled craftsman, doing interior woodwork on buildings. His wife, Emily, also a Massachusetts native, was perhaps the most active of the Unionist women.[29]

Alfred Austell was among the wealthiest of antebellum Atlantans. Born on a farm near Dandridge in Jefferson County, Tennessee, in 1814, Austell had limited education but was highly ambitious and left the farm at an early age to clerk in his brother's store in Spartanburg, South Carolina. When he was twenty-two, Austell moved to Campbell County, Georgia, opening his own store there. Within a few years, he had become prosperous and then wealthy. Austell acquired several plantations, and by the time he moved to Atlanta in 1858 he owned about three thousand acres and more than fifty slaves. The year before, he and a partner bought the Bank of Fulton, which had been founded in 1856 and whose president was Amherst Stone. When the war began, Austell's wealth exceeded considerably the $100,000 minimum estimated by the R. G. Dun Company in 1858. The value of his real estate in Atlanta alone amounted to more than $40,000 in 1861, and his slaves would have been worth at least $50,000. Before the war, Austell had been a member of the local branch of the Georgia state militia and had risen to the rank of brigadier general in that organization.[30]

Among the others who met in Markham's office was C. T. C. Deake, schoolmaster and native of east Tennessee; Thomas G. Simms, a local businessman and brother-in-law of Austell; and John Boutell, an architect.[31] When people on the street saw the men entering Markham's office, they began to whisper that a Union meeting was under way or that the men were "getting up a Union League." As a result, the Markham group gathered and departed surreptitiously, just as those meeting in Angier's office did.[32] A broad cross section of Unionist men also met regularly in the Lynch brothers' store at Whitehall and Alabama Streets, one of the busiest corners in Atlanta. Michael Bloomfield, an Irish immigrant and stonecutter, reported that the store was a well-known "stopping place" for Unionists and "headquarters for Union men to go to for their news."[33]

For the Atlanta Unionists who met in Lynch's store or in one of the other locations, the paramount issue remained the preservation of the Union, but that issue, of course, became inextricably bound to the presidential campaign of 1860. Schisms occurred in the national Democratic party over sectional issues, and three presidential candidates were produced from the party's wreckage. Illinois senator Stephen A. Douglas emerged as the candidate of the national Democrats and those who favored popular sovereignty. Vice President John C. Breckinridge became the candidate with greatest appeal to secessionists. John Bell of Tennessee won the nomination of the Constitutional Union party and appealed to Southern voters who favored compromise to preserve the Union.

As far as can be determined, Atlanta Unionists divided their support between Douglas and Bell, with perhaps more favoring Douglas. Dunning and Stewart both supported Douglas. So apparently did Austell, who at one time styled himself "a Duglas Democrat" and on another occasion described himself as a "constitutional Union man provided slavery and all its rights could be preserved and not without." Julius Hayden, the president of the Atlanta Gas Light Company, endorsed Douglas and did everything he could "to get the State to go for him." John Lynch, one of the five Lynch brothers who had emigrated to Atlanta in the 1840s and now a very prosperous merchant, also supported Douglas. Henry C. Holcombe, the Atlanta city clerk and a native of South Carolina, supported Bell.[34]

The Republican party, putting forward only its second national ticket, made no effort to get its candidates on the ballot in Georgia and other Southern states. The party's identification in the South with abolition contributed to its image as a party of mad radicals who intended to destroy slavery and the South through immediate emancipation of the slaves. The public agitation about so-called Black Republicans grew from a feverish pitch to a sustained frenzy that lasted long after the election of Abraham Lincoln. Labeling Unionists as Lincolnites or abolitionists became routine in Atlanta. It was more than mere name-calling and represented yet another of the pressures that slowly accumulated against those in the city who departed most radically from the community's political norms. There are a few hints that some Atlanta Unionists sympathized with Lincoln's candidacy. It does not appear that much pro-Lincoln sentiment existed among the merchants and professional men who composed the Union Association, but there is evidence to suggest that Cyrena Stone, unlike some other Northern women living in Atlanta, greatly admired his presidency and perhaps his candidacy. Such thoughts could not be expressed publicly without great risk, of course, and it is likely that she confined her expressions of support for Lincoln to close friends and perhaps to the male Unionists who met secretly from time to time in her home.[35]

Even a neutral mention of Lincoln's name could produce public outrage, and when rumors swept Atlanta that several Atlantans had written to the Lincoln Executive Committee in New York expressing interest in the Atlanta postmastership if Lincoln were elected, the *Intelligencer* unsuccessfully demanded their names.[36] Outright expressions of sympathy for the Lincoln candidacy brought even more drastic consequences. Benjamin Franklin Longley, a carpenter and native of Maine who had recently arrived in Atlanta, enraged secessionists with a public declaration of support for Lincoln. "Helper" reported to the *Intelligencer* that Longley "is very pious, [and] loves Lincoln and the 'niggers' by his own declaration." Community pressure drove Longley from Atlanta, Helper reported, before "his *friends* [could] see him off." The newspaper obligingly printed Helper's detailed description of the fugitive in the hope that he might be intercepted.[37]

Osborne Burson, a rural Atlantan, was overheard saying that if Lincoln had been on the ballot he would have voted for him. Perhaps just as damning, Burson declared his belief that "negroes were as free as he was . . . and if he had a chance he would assist in freeing them." The *Intelligencer* accused Burson of "tampering with negroes" and complained when area residents decided to let Burson go without punishment, "attributing his language to ignorance." That was not good enough for the newspaper, which urged that the authorities deal with Burson summarily. Ultimately, Burson paid a high price. Enrolled in the Confederate army in the summer of 1861, the twenty-seven-year-old laborer was killed at the Battle of Seven Pines in Virginia the next spring, leaving a wife and a five-year-old daughter.[38]

Lincoln's candidacy was not the only factor that aroused strong passions during the campaign. Breckinridge partisans roundly condemned supporters of the other two candidates and particularly those who supported Douglas, because of his stance on popular sovereignty. Richard M. Wall, a thirty-four-year-old secessionist merchant, stomped into the Lynches' store late one evening and began to declare vociferously for Breckinridge. John Lynch quickly tired of Wall's rhetoric and stepped from behind his desk on an elevation at the rear of the store, declaring just as vociferously that Wall should not advocate Breckinridge's election in *his* store and that if the Kentuckian were elected it would mean that "the Union would be desolved." Stephen Douglas, Lynch concluded, would save the Union.

Put off by Lynch's abrupt manner, Wall told Lynch that "he ought to stand up for his Section of the Country" and that "Douglas was a more dangerous man than Lincoln."[39]

As the election approached and tensions grew, such arguments occurred countless times in Atlanta. The *Intelligencer* echoed Richard Wall's sentiments about Breckinridge and condemned "Douglassites and Bellites" who were "loud in their denunciations of Breckinridge and Lane [the vice presidential candidate]." Supporters of Douglas and Bell knew full well, the *Intelligencer* commented, that nothing in Breckinridge's history indicated that he favored secession. Those arguments were specious, of course, as the newspaper seemed to acknowledge in the same column. "Away with this nonsense about dissolving the Union," the *Intelligencer* fumed. "The Democracy of the South will cling to it as long as it is worth preserving."[40]

The secessionist antipathy toward Douglas and his supporters accelerated when the "Little Giant" decided to visit Atlanta on a campaign swing through the South less than two weeks before the election. An earlier trip had been intended to garner votes and perhaps help bring about a fusion of the Douglas and Bell tickets, but by the time of the second trip it had become clear that Georgia would go for Breckinridge. Douglas apparently came to the state at Alexander H. Stephens's behest "to carry the cause of the Union into the heart of the south." Stephens favored holding the Union together and told Douglas that if he came to Georgia, his visit would change the views of thousands of Georgians who did not understand Douglas's position. Stephens knew there was no hope of carrying the state, but hoped that appearances by Douglas would maintain "sound principles and sound national organization."[41]

A correspondent to the *Intelligencer* thought differently. "Atlanta" wrote that a "gentleman of Northern birth, who is deeply interested in saving the Union," had made a lead contribution of fifty dollars to send James P. Hambleton, the editor of a rival newspaper, the *Southern Confederacy*, to Chicago, where he had met with Douglas and persuaded him to come to Georgia "to enlighten the people of Georgia on Squatter Sovereignty." Hambleton returned with the news that Douglas would visit Atlanta on October 30.[42]

Prior to Douglas's arrival, the Georgia politician Robert Toombs, a fire-eating secessionist, had threatened that Douglas would not be allowed publicly to discuss the principles of his "Norfolk Doctrine," which had been widely denounced for favoring the use of coercion against a seceded South. Alexander Stephens introduced Douglas when he made his Atlanta speech and called for the large crowd to let intellect and not passion rule their response to Douglas's speech. Douglas did repeat the "Norfolk Doctrine" despite Toombs's threat and won the admiration of at least some of the crowd for his courage in the face of such threats.[43]

The Unionists who supported Douglas did so with commitment and enthusiasm. "I voted for Douglas and did everything I could to get the State to go for him," said one. Another voted for Douglas because he was a "national man" and opposed Lincoln and Breckinridge because he saw them as purely sectional candidates whose success "would produce a war."[44] Some courage was also necessary to vote for Douglas at the polls. Before the age of secret ballots, voters either declared their preferences orally or wrote out their ballots and handed them to election officials, who immediately knew for whom the ballot had been cast. Unionists, and especially those branded as Northerners, knew that they could be subjected to harassment at the polls. When the votes were counted on November 5, 1860, the Atlanta precinct cast 1,070 votes for Bell, 835 for Breckinridge, and 335 for Douglas. Thus, 1,405 voters, or 63 percent of Atlanta's voters, favored the more moderate Bell and Douglas.[45]

BUT ABRAHAM LINCOLN and the "Black Republicans" had been elected, giving a powerful boost to the cause of radical secessionists. In Atlanta, the five months between the election of Lincoln and the outbreak of war were a time of frenetic activity, as the state moved toward secession and the city succumbed to the fever of Southern independence sweeping the region. For the Unionists, those months provided a few final opportunities to plead the case against disunion, but in general it was a time of tightening proscriptions against those who showed any signs of behavior disloyal to the South.

South Carolina's rapid movement toward secession after the election greatly accelerated the trend toward disunion in Georgia. Despite the appeals of moderates for delay, a statewide election was called for January 2 to elect delegates to a convention on January 16 that would decide the fateful issue. Postelection political alignments in Atlanta reflected the community's attitudes on secession. The succinct perspective of one Unionist, Henry Holcombe, outlined the situation. He said that there were two parties: the secession party and the cooperation party. The secession party was for "immediate and separate State action" on secession. The cooperation party sought "to prevent such action, preferring if such action should come for all the States to act together," that is, secede together. There were many persons "opposed to secession in any form," and they "when acting at all, acted with the co-operation party."[46]

During the interim of almost two months between the presidential election and the election of delegates to the secession convention, Atlanta Unionists, who had fought secession since early in the year, continued to oppose the radical course, referring to themselves as conservatives dedicated to preservation of the Union. Amherst Stone, for example, made numerous public speeches against secession as "hundreds of Union citizens of the state of Georgia can testify," he recalled three years later.[47]

Others, such as Julius Hayden, president of the Atlanta Gas Light Company, had not been deeply involved in politics before the secession crisis but now became openly Unionist and took a "very active part[,] more so than . . . [he] had ever done before." Hayden was a native of Connecticut, born in 1811, perhaps near Hartford. When he emigrated to Georgia is uncertain, but he had settled in Atlanta soon after the town was founded, and he became a member of the city council in 1849. For the remainder of the prewar period, Hayden maintained an active civic life, serving as justice of the Inferior Court of DeKalb and Fulton Counties, helping to plan Atlanta's first agricultural fair and continuing to serve on the city council throughout much of the period. A large slaveholder, Hayden clearly had an interest in the expansion of slavery and backed an effort in Atlanta to raise cash for the support of colonists who would go from Georgia to Kansas in the mid-1850s to secure that territory for slavery. By 1855, Hayden had become a wealthy man; a credit firm estimated his net wealth at $75,000, probably a low estimate. His primary venture was in construction and brick making, a business he owned in partnership with Thomas G. Healey, a boyhood friend from Connecticut. Throughout the 1850s, Hayden participated in nearly every important commercial venture in Atlanta, joining with Angier and others to charter the Atlanta Bank; taking part with William Markham and others in chartering the Georgia Western Rail Road Company in 1854; joining with Markham, Norcross, Stone, and others in the Georgia Air Line Railroad scheme; and serving as incorporator and president of the Atlanta Gas Light Company. Hayden also married well, taking as his wife the daughter of one of the wealthy founders of Atlanta, Reuben Cone. In addition to his house in Atlanta, he owned a farm just outside the city and a plantation in southwest Georgia. In 1860, Hayden owned fifteen slaves in Fulton County and dozens more in southwest Georgia.[48]

When the influential Hayden began to attend antisecession meetings, his stature in the community made him a frequent choice to chair the assemblies. Although presiding brought him out of the political shadows, it also made him the target of persistent verbal abuse on the Atlanta streets. Rabid secessionists who reveled in disrupting Unionist meetings also attacked Hayden. On one occasion, Atlanta physician B. D. Smith, who was considered a "violent secessionist," went to city hall, where an antisecession meeting was in progress, threw open the door to the meeting room, fired a series of epithets at Hayden, and demanded to know what "a damned Yankee was doing in the chair."[49]

In late autumn of 1860, Hayden's Unionism typified that of many Atlantans who continued to resist the idea of secession, and he joined others of like mind in signing a petition that called for a county meeting to discuss whether the legislature should call a state convention to consider "the state of our National relations, and the necessity of providing *new guards* for our future safety."[50] After secession, Hayden would become a strict Unionist, but it was apparent in the fall that he believed that serious political rearrangements between the North and the South were necessary if the Union were to be preserved. In December, in the midst of spiraling secessionist radicalism, Hayden and a small group of moderates, which included Jonathan Norcross and George W. Adair, sent a telegram to Senators Stephen A. Douglas and John J. Crittenden. The Atlantans sought advice on what political course to follow and asked the politicians whether sectional compromise could be achieved. They were "for the Union as our fathers made it, if we can preserve the rights of the South." If not, they might consider secession. Was there "any hope for the rights of the South in the Union?" they asked. The two politicians had little to offer except encouragement. "Don't give up the ship! Don't despair of the Republic," Douglas and Crittenden replied. Other Unionists also sought counsel and comfort from Northern friends. Nedom Angier, physician and businessman, "spent a good deal of money sending telegrams to Union friends North for advice what to do." Pharmacist and Methodist minister David Young wrote to Northern business contacts expressing his dismay "at the course of the South."[51]

Some Northern-born Unionists visited the North during 1860, perhaps considering whether caution dictated a permanent return. Cyrena Stone, who regularly returned to Vermont in the summer, went home in 1860 to visit her aging father and other members of the family after an unexplained stay of several weeks in a medical institution in New York City.[52] Vermonters Henry Huntington, a physician and dentist, and his wife Martha traveled north in the fall of 1860 to see old friends who urged the Huntingtons to stay and hinted that if war came, they would regret returning south. One man told Mrs. Huntington, "in laughing bravado" that "if you go back, we will go down there and destroy you, burn your houses, demolish your gardens, and drive you back in fear and trembling." "You cannot do it," Martha Huntington replied, "You do not know the southern people." "Oh yes," he answered, "I know they are pluckey, but we are too many for them." The Huntingtons decided to stay in the South but would ruefully recall the friend's "prophecy" many times.[53]

When the Huntingtons returned to Georgia they found the excitement "even more intense" than in the North. And, to be sure, as time for election of delegates to the secession convention drew near, mass hysteria gripped Georgia and the South. With the ascending tensions, the Lynch brothers prepared to shut down their businesses if Georgia seceded. Both James and John Lynch told John T. Cunningham, whose house was not far from the store, that "if the Confederate govt. was established they would not be willing to live in it[;] they would move away." Seventeen-year-old Marcellus Markham was caught up in secessionist fever despite his father's prominence among the Unionists. Young Markham, who boarded and studied at the Georgia Military Institute in Marietta, rushed down to Atlanta during the excitement to witness a torchlight parade and hear speakers who celebrated the dismantlement of the Union. Marcellus wanted to go out and join the fiery parade, but before he could leave his father's house on Marietta Street, the elder Markham calmly took him aside and told him that he wanted him to hear his views on the crisis and the future of the South. If secession occurred, Markham bluntly said, there would inevitably be war. "The South will be overrun, our property will be confiscated, and we will be ruined," he prophesied. William Markham had "no confidence in the success of the South, in case of a war." He was, his son said in later years, "thoroughly loyal to the Union . . . opposed to a division of the country, and a breaking up of the Union. He was loyal to the Government and to the flag."[54]

Although the cause seemed increasingly hopeless, Atlanta Unionists electioneered among friends and acquaintances to send a moderate slate of delegates to the convention, including George W. Adair, publisher of the *Southern Confederacy,* and James M. Calhoun, soon to be mayor of the city. Philip McIntire, a laborer, took his friend Joab Jenkins to the Atlanta city hall to vote against secession. McIntire, who ran a woodlot for Atlanta financier Richard Peters, told Jenkins that he would die rather than fight against the Union. George Edwards, a Scottish immigrant, also election-eered, as did Thomas Jordan, a Unionist farmer who lived just outside Atlanta. "I took the Union side & pretty nigh every body knowed it in this country," Jordan said. "I argued & talked & electioneered with my friends for the Union & did all I could against secession, & voted against it." When Thomas Healey went to the polls to vote against secession, he was cursed and called a sneak and a traitor by the prosecessionists. William L. Hub-bard, a cooperationist who later served in the Confederate army, overheard William Markham say that he thought Georgia was pursuing a "suicidal course." Thomas Crussell, a contractor and staunch Unionist who worked against secession, believed that had the secession question been submit-ted to the people of the state, "Georgia never would have gone out. That is my opinion. I am confident she never would have."[55]

But Georgia did secede after a favorable convention vote for secession on January 19, 1861, which some historians believe did not accurately reflect the state's sentiments. However that may be, the act of secession had profound, immediate consequences: literally overnight, the ranks of Unionists and cooperationists throughout the state dissolved. Thousands of moderate Georgians, when faced with a choice between loyalty to the United States and loyalty to Georgia, chose the latter course. James M. Clay, an illiterate thirty-eight-year-old Atlanta stonemason, judged that the state was "about equally divided" on secession at the first agitation of the question and at about the time the vote was taken. After secession itself, that distribution dramatically changed, Clay recalled, "the great body of the people [then] being in favor of the separation." Some Atlantans, who had once espoused strong Union views, moved toward a more neutral stance. Jonathan Norcross, an early settler in the area and one of the wealthiest businessmen in the city, remained a Unionist, at least in Confederate eyes, but became largely silent about his views. An Atlanta contractor and brother-in-law of two of the more prominent Unionists, Madison Berry fol-lowed Norcross's example and seems not to have been actively involved in later Unionist activities.[56]

According to Julius Hayden, there were excellent reasons for Union-ists to keep their views to themselves—especially after the decision to secede. "After the ordinance of secession was passed every Union man was muzzled," Hayden said, and "he could not express any opinion at all unless he expressed it in favor of secession." The more radical elements in the city now dominated and tried to eliminate dissent and to impose a single, correct view of the conflict between the North and South. "Regulators or investigating committees" quickly came into being, Hayden recalled, with the charge "to see how every man stood. . . . Every Union man they could find who expressed Union sentiments was ordered to leave the State and a good many were whipped or lynched."[57]

AS COMMUNITY PRESSURES accumulated and as the drift toward war continued, almost no one spoke out publicly on issues related to disunion. However, James A. Stewart was bold at a mass meeting on February 7, 1861, when Atlantans considered the Virginia resolutions that called for each slaveholding state to send commissioners to a meeting that would "devise and recommend such system of common measures as in their judgment may be advisable for defense, and the redress and prevention of wrongs." The Atlantans, eager always to attract conventions, enthusiastically drafted a report that would "offer the hospitalities of the city to the convention or conference" and that supported the resolutions. Stewart objected strongly to the report because he thought that the conference "might result in a dissolution of the Union, a measure to which he was utterly opposed." Alexander M. Wallace, the secessionist insurance man and by then an officer of a recently organized military unit, ridiculed Stewart's discussion of the matter because there was "then in progress on the public square an important public sale, which was of greater importance than Stewart's objections." According to the Atlanta historian Wallace P. Reed, Stewart delivered a speech characterized as "the usual fanfaronade about the Union, which had so often been declaimed by sophomorical Fourth of July orators."[58]

Although still prevented from publishing his views in local newspapers, Stewart carried his personal crusade against disunion to out-of-state newspapers. On March 4, 1861, the *Intelligencer* published an extract from the *Nashville Democrat,* which it denounced as "bristling with rank treason" for its denunciation of Jefferson Davis and its declaration that Davis would lead the South into war and destruction. In the view of the *Democrat,* Davis was a traitor and should be hanged. Moreover, the editor wrote on, "We know hundreds of men in the seceding cottonocracy who are ready to tie the rope for the hangman." Such talk itself amounted to treason and led the *Intelligencer* to call for a close scrutiny of the homefront to be sure that traitors in Atlanta were dealt with under the laws of treason and that local officials did their duty in ferreting them out. "If the Greek horse is among us, let us cast him into the sea," wrote the editor.[59]

James A. Stewart saw the report in the *Intelligencer* and the next day sat down at his desk to write a pro-Union letter to the Nashville paper. "I may be coerced to obey," the courageous Stewart wrote, "but I will never acknowledge or recognize the Government de facto of the seceding States": "I will never cease to honor and love the old Stars and Stripes; and no hostile power on earth can absolve me from allegiance thereto. Yet I hope the incoming administration will not countenance or recommend war against the erring people of the South. If let alone, I think the Union men, at the *ballot-box,* will effectually put down the revolution." The Union men of the South, Stewart wrote, pleaded that President Lincoln "Attempt no coercion," and give the "seceders a peaceful opportunity to test their Utopian and visionary schemes, and trust us at the ballot-box, and on the stump to fight the battles for the preservation of the Union and we will achieve a peaceful and permanent victory without the expenditure of treasure, or the shedding of blood." And, in words strongly reminiscent of the prose of the banished Plebian, Stewart wrote that Union men should forget "old party lines" and join hands "in opposition to Disunionists—North and South—to abolition fanatics North, and aristocracy, monarchy, and despotism South."

For Stewart, military preparations under way in the South (and notably in Atlanta as well) amounted to a "stupendous farce. The seizure of forts and arsenals is simply ridiculous, as no war has been waged against the South, by the General Government." No sensible person would "for a moment believe that Lincoln ever contemplated the invasion of the Cotton States." The Knights of the Golden Circle and other military organizations, Stewart believed, had as their "chief object" the "coercion of Union men into support of their revolution." The proof lay in the threat of Robert Toombs "with sword in hand, to put Georgia out of the Union against the voice of the people."

In less than a week, the *Intelligencer* secured a copy of the *Nashville Democrat* in which Stewart's article appeared and reprinted it for all of Atlanta to read. The reaction was predictable. The newspaper itself (once more reminiscent of the Plebian episode) allowed that it thought Stewart an honest man, but went on to proclaim that "a more dangerous man never lived in a slaveholding community." The law would have to protect Atlanta and Atlantans against such "traitors and midnight assassins." "The fact of it is this, all such men as this Stewart is," the *Intelligencer* concluded, "must leave this community 'peaceably if they may, forcibly if we must.'" J. A. Stewart must be "expelled."

His presence is highly dangerous. He is a traitor in our camp. He not only writes treason in our midst, and furnishes weapons to our enemies, but he disseminates treason, and scatters incendiary documents in the shape of Nashville *Democrats* among our population. We have done our duty, in this man's case, unpleasant though it may be. We now call upon the proper authorities to do their duty and that promptly. Let treason and traitors be expelled from our community, now, or we will soon be a ruined and servile people.[60]

Two days later the mayor, "at the invitation of a highly respectable Committee of gentlemen," called on Stewart in the afternoon with the result that Stewart was persuaded to make a public statement in which he declared fealty to the Confederacy. The statement had the ring of a loyalty oath with its promise to "abide by all the laws of the Confederate States, and support with all my power any war measure necessary to resist coercion, by the Federal Government, or the invasion, by any other power, against the Confederate States of America" and was likely composed by the "Committee of gentlemen." What threats may have been made against Stewart will probably never be known, but the result was that he was forced to admit political error publicly. As far as can be determined, he published nothing else on the topic of disunion until the war was over. In the end, the punishment for Stewart's public expressions seems relatively mild, for unlike Osborne Burson or Benjamin Longley he was allowed to remain in Atlanta (a reflection perhaps of his social and economic standing), although he, like all other Unionists, would suffer in other ways as the era wore on.[61]

But Stewart could not remain entirely quiet and sought to influence the course of events in private correspondence with Alexander Stephens, the vice president of the new Confederacy. In mid-March 1861, he wrote Stephens that he hoped for a "reconstruction" of the Union and argued that the people should be given a chance to cast ballots directly on the question of secession "untrammeled by fear, unbiased by falsehood, and uncontrolled by self-constituted committees." Blunt and outspoken, Stewart sternly warned Vice President Stephens that "If your government does not suppress the mob spirit that prevails in our unhappy country, . . . we will, erelong, be deluged in blood." A people used to freedom would not easily "submit to a despotism that deprives them of . . . freedom of speech, and threatens their hearthstones with violence, and their houses with unreasonable searches and seizures." And amazingly, despite his public confession and the threats made against him in Atlanta, he asked permission to publish an open letter to Stephens—one that scathingly denounced the Confederacy and sharply criticized Stephens himself.[62]

Much of Stewart's criticism emphasized the authoritarian character of the new government, its abandonment of constitutional liberties, and its reliance upon "secret vigilance committees" to destroy freedom of the press and freedom of speech. Stewart complained in particular about the suppression of civil liberties by "self-constituted vigilance committee[s], incident to revolutionary times, which . . . [Stephens's] new government has not had time to suppress," but which, more ominously, might be a part of the character of the government itself. His Unionist views had made him "an object of vengeance" and put him at risk of violence "at the hands of maddened factions."

Stewart charged Stephens with caving in to many of the changes since secession, radical changes that Stewart said were "infinitely for the worse." He strongly criticized his old friend, whose conduct could not be considered as error free. "You will perceive that I am speaking very frankly," Stewart told Stephens, "and you will concede that I have a right to thus address you, as you are a leading supporter of measures, the [i]nauguration of which has incidentally, if not directly, endangered life and deprived men of civil liberty, and the enjoyment of that peace, safety and happiness which, for near three-quarters of a century, have been enjoyed under the old Government." Stewart unfavorably compared Stephens with "the noble and patriotic" Stephen A. Douglas, whom, in fact, Stephens had invited to canvass the South during the presidential election campaign of 1860. Douglas had been true to the idea of preserving the conservative principles of Union; Stephens, on the other hand, had forsaken them and sanctioned secession.

"The noble hearted Douglas," had "planted himself between the leaders of the maddened political factions, North and South" to prevent war. "The eloquent Stephens," had taken up with the "revolutionists of the South." Douglas sought to save the country from "maddened destroyers"; Stephens was "Vice-President of the most stupendous revolution ever recorded in the annals of history." Stewart described Douglas as one who "nobly battles," Stephens as one who "abandons the holy cause." Douglas appealed to "reason and patriotism"; Stephens sanctioned "extensive military organizations." The nation had "looked to the wisdom of a Douglas, and the thoughtful eloquence of a Stephens, to save our sinking ship." Douglas stood firm "amidst the raging storm"; Stephens was "afloat, on a fragment of the old vessel, giving vent to his feelings of gratification, at being released from the 'shackles of the old government.'" Stephens, Stewart prophesied, would yet return "to the old Confederacy," because he was an honest man.[63]

Stephens's reaction to the criticism is unknown, and Stewart's letter was evidently not published until after the war. It was remarkable, nonetheless, for its stinging candor and for Stewart's bravura in seeking to publish it when he had already come under the sanction of a vigilance committee. It was also remarkable that Stewart felt his relationship with Stephens strong enough to permit such criticism of the Georgia politician privately and, potentially, in public.

Meanwhile, another Atlantan had published in the *Commonwealth,* the city's "lively evening paper," a pro-Union essay bewailing the destruction of the Union. Using the pseudonym "Holly" the writer entitled the essay "The Spring of 1861" and contrasted the beauty and harmony of nature with the disharmony of human affairs. "With so much brightness and beauty, and harmony in the natural world, how sad to look upon the world of humanity—the world of political strife and wild commotion," wrote Holly. "Our country," the essayist continued, "so long the boast of every one proud to call himself American! her beautiful banner now trailing in the dust, and *Ichabod* written upon her altars!" In direct reference to secession, Holly wrote that "Some of the 'Stars' that were so bright . . . have 'gone out.'"

> We read of the "late United States" which tells the world "the sad trouble" that the nation was "no more!" Just as she reached the proud period of matured beauty and greatness, she fell "and great is the fall thereof! The fair corse still "lies in State," for it is yet unknown whether her burial shall be as her baptism—in the crimson life-blood of thousands—or whether they shall wrap around her the flag of Columbia—the Stars and Stripes that have waved so long over our Washington's grave—as fitting drapery for the death-sleep of the fairest, the noblest Republic upon which ever shined the Sun.

In the agitated atmosphere of Atlanta during the spring of 1861, when even slightly favorable references to the United States would draw severe criticism, the short essay could only have been interpreted as disloyal. Perhaps it brought pressure upon Josiah Peterson, editor of the *Commonwealth,* to reveal Holly's identity, just as pressure had been exerted against the *Intelligencer* in the Plebian affair. On the other hand, the writings of Holly had appeared intermittently in the Atlanta newspapers for several years. It may have been common knowledge that Holly was the pseudonym of Cyrena Stone.[64]

BY THE END OF MARCH 1861, less than two weeks before war began, Unionist voices, except for James A. Stewart and Cyrena Stone, had fallen silent. Public debates over Union and disunion, which had gradually diminished during 1860 and 1861, disappeared altogether. Only private correspondence, such as Stewart's letters to Alexander Stephens, showed that arguments with old friends, now adversaries, could continue. Unionists clandestinely discussed politics and the calamity of disunion only with trusted friends inside the small band of diehards who remained after the winnowing of the secession crisis, or occasionally with new acquaintances—but only after subtle, searching inquiries into trustworthiness. As well, Unionists were in large measure cut off from friends and relatives in the North, who feared to correspond lest their letters be intercepted and the recipients punished. In Vermont, old Phinehas Bailey—pensioned, retired, and nearing death—wanted desperately to write to Cyrena and Amherst but "dare[d] not for fear of endangering their safety."[65] As war approached, Atlanta Unionists began to learn how to live under conditions of silence, isolation, and pressure unlike anything they had ever known.

CHAPTER THREE

"The Knell of All Our Bright Hopes"

On April 13, 1861, Atlantans who included Henry and Martha Huntington went to a nearby mineral springs (perhaps the spa owned by Nedom Angier or nearby Ponce de Leon Springs) to spend the warm spring afternoon. Many in the group, but not all, were Northern born. They had enjoyed the outing away from the increasingly tense atmosphere of the city, but toward evening the pleasant interlude snapped when a friend of the Huntingtons, also a Northerner, suddenly appeared and breathlessly announced that Confederates had attacked Fort Sumter and that the Union fort had fallen. A sharp wave of fear and dread rolled over all the group but one, "an enthusiastic little southern girl," who clapped her hands, delivered a hurrah or two, and then glanced self-consciously at the "sober faces" of her companions. "Oh," she said disgustedly, "I forgot you all were Yankees."[1]

Sumter was the final signal that war would not be averted. It also told Unionists that an already precarious situation could quickly become much more dangerous. In remaining "at the South," some had wagered that war would not come and that they could continue life much as before. The attack on the federal fort in South Carolina showed the folly of that wager.

For the transplanted Vermonters, Martha Huntington, her husband, and two small children, the fall of Fort Sumter signaled "the knell of all our bright hopes."[2]

In the wake of the attack, the fictional Cyrena Stone heard rumors of a new harshness on the part of local Confederate officials toward Unionists. It was said that a man had been "dragged off to prison" for declaring "that he didn't think that it took a great deal of courage for a force of seven thousand men to seize a fort defended by seventy soldiers." Cyrena reacted to probings concerning her own loyalty with what would become a well-practiced circumspection. A Confederate woman visitor to the household had not been satisfied that the South Carolinians had been thorough enough in their attack on Sumter and pronounced it "a perfect shame that Beauregard let Major Anderson live a moment." Anderson, in her judgment, should "have been taken out and hung right up." During the next four years, Cyrena would repeatedly search for words that would provide a response to such remarks but stop short of treason. This time, she accomplished her purpose by proffering a backhanded compliment to the Confederate general who led the attack. "It seems to me," she said, "that Beauregard took the wiser course."[3]

The fall of Fort Sumter intensified the acrimony between loyal Southerners and disloyal Unionists, many of whom were Northerners. "Northerners were everywhere looked upon with distrust," Mrs. Huntington wrote, and friendly relations with neighbors broke apart under the strain of wartime. Years later, Mrs. Huntington would recall the atmosphere of hatred and the high level of suspicion that Confederates had of Unionists. They knew, she recalled, that loyal Unionists would have a great deal of difficulty entering "into a course that would bring us into direct opposition to our flesh and blood and all the teachings of our childhood."[4]

Mrs. Huntington alluded to the intensively patriotic education and acculturation common in the North, where schools, the primary molders of patriotic sentiment, were much more numerous and advanced. In prewar days, Southern schools may not have had a comparable impact upon the fostering of patriotism, particularly after the development of self-conscious sectionalism. Atlanta, like virtually all of the South, did not have publicly supported common schools, relying instead on a variety of privately run institutions, many one-woman or one-man operations. There is only scattered evidence concerning these schools, and thus little is known about whether schoolmasters and mistresses were as assiduous as their non-Southern counterparts in cultivating American patriotic values. Neither do we know much about how intensely patriotic antebellum Atlanta or for that matter, the entire South, may have been in the years before secession: the historical record is largely silent about the practice of national rituals in the antebellum South. We know far more about patriotic observances outside the South—the enthusiasm, the pride, the religious atmosphere that suffused observances such as Washington's Birthday and the Fourth of July.[5]

IN *CONFEDERATE* ATLANTA, however, the record is much clearer. The schools quickly moved to increase the storehouse of Southern patriotism required for a successful prosecution of the war and for the reinforcement of loyalty. Even children had to demonstrate loyalty and, equally important, show an enthusiastic contempt for the United States. In early May, just weeks after the attack on Fort Sumter, a large crowd of Atlantans (Cyrena and Amherst Stone likely among them) attended an "entertainment" at the female institute, which Amherst had helped to found. Like other Unionists, they would have been mortified at the finale of the evening's exercises, when the young ladies of the institute mounted a mock bombardment of Fort Sumter. The scene began with the raising of the American flag, followed quickly by the hurling of floral "bombs" at the great symbol of the United States "with a jest and spite which caused the house to ring with cheers and loud hurrahs." The force of the bombardment soon brought Old Glory to the floor of the stage. The banner was replaced "in a twinkling [by] the usurper, and the house [shook] with the stamping of feet, and . . . wild shoutings and cheers."[6]

Attacking the symbol of Union was the mid-nineteenth-century equivalent of flag burning, calculated to shock and to demonstrate that nothing associated with the United States was any longer inviolable. The Atlanta school girls' destruction of the once-sacred symbol fed the pent-up hatred of the most militant Confederates and reinforced the will of those prepared to sacrifice for the Confederacy, but it also brought more than a twinge of sorrow and perhaps guilt to those who only months before had occupied the middle ground of Atlanta politics and who had expressed grave doubts about the dismemberment of the United States.

In 1861, perhaps no Atlantan loyal to the Southern cause seriously believed that the city would ever be threatened by Union forces. After all, Atlanta was hundreds of miles from the Northern states and a safe distance from the coast. It was well nigh unthinkable that Union soldiers would ever march down Whitehall or Peachtree Street. Still, there were plenty of enemies to be guarded against. Propagandists railed at Yankees—those in the North and those at home. The newspapers, concerned about abolitionist agents in 1860, warned of spies in 1861. "Foreign" ideas also posed a threat to the patriotic task of solidifying loyalty to the new nation. The Northern press could no longer be read in safety, and the home press had to be made secure from patriotic impieties. No Atlanta newspaper could print dissenting views as had been expressed in the pages of the *Intelligencer* and the *Commonwealth* in 1860. War had come. Unity had to be forged. In short, a patriotic orthodoxy was to be formed locally and maintained locally through ritual, the press, the churches, and, if necessary, by coercion. Orthodoxy would be enforced under the watchful gaze of local officials and by citizens who pledged undying loyalty to the South—and promised to keep a watchful eye on each other as well.

If the fall of Fort Sumter created an instant mythology of invincibility and brought a surge of patriotism to Confederate Atlanta, President Lincoln's call three days later for 75,000 volunteers to quell the revolt in South Carolina produced an equal outpouring of rage. Together the two events sparked a sudden increase in fears about outsiders and especially about spies and incendiaries. One diligent correspondent to the *Southern Confederacy* reported that he had frequently seen the names of Northerners on the city's hotel registers and urged that these persons should be closely watched by a citizens' committee that would probe the loyalty of suspect Atlantans. If any should hesitate to prove their loyalty, they should be tarred, feathered, and driven out. "In times of such immense excitement," the correspondent wrote, "we cannot be too particular."[7]

Citizens were also warned to look out for persons who merely appeared to be suspicious. A bartender at the Trout House, one of the city's leading hotels, reported that Frank H. Nichols, a New Yorker of "known Abolition principles" who had been driven out of Cumming, forty miles to the north in Forsyth County, had been sighted in Atlanta. Men such as Nichols should not be allowed to remain in the state even for an hour, a correspondent to the *Southern Confederacy* wrote.[8] Other citizens cautioned Atlantans about a sudden increase in the population of beggars, suggesting that mendicants could be disguised spies or incendiaries. "They are not Georgians," he wrote. "Where did they come from?" Atlantans should not cultivate a false sense of security lest "a volcano . . . bursts forth in its fury."[9] The same day, the *Intelligencer* issued a general warning to "Look out for Spies." There was good reason, the newspaper observed, to believe that the "Black Republican Government" had dispatched agents to the South and that the region was "swarming with Yankee spies who are in direct communication with our Northern enemies." Hotel keepers, boarding house proprietors, and restaurant owners were warned to be especially vigilant and keep a "bright look out as to the character of their guests." All citizens, the newspaper concluded, should practice watchfulness: "Eternal vigilance is the price of liberty."[10] One Atlanta newspaper concluded that it was doubtlessly true that there were spies *and* traitors in Atlanta who were intent on arousing discontent among the slaves. Atlantans should "keep a sharp look-out on all strangers" and particularly on those who had no apparent business in the city.[11]

The concern about strangers and spies continued throughout the late spring of 1861 and by summer seemed close to full-blown paranoia. On May 22, a "supposed spy" was arrested, but after the authorities determined that he was merely a New Orleans merchant "of good standing," he was released.[12] Within a few weeks, however, Atlanta officials had a better candidate for espionage and arrested William H. Hurlburt, a New York journalist. Hurlburt had been denounced in Richmond, Charleston, and other cities as a "bold, daring, and accomplished spy," although his exact accomplishments in espionage seemed modest. Warned by the mayor of Augusta that Hurlburt had entrained for Atlanta, the city marshal arrested the New Yorker at the Atlanta depot and took him to a hotel, Washington Hall, where he was put under guard. A "committee of investigation," including Benjamin C. Yancey and James M. Calhoun, took charge, looked into the matter, prudently decided that the case could best be handled by higher authorities in Richmond, and recommended Hurlburt's transfer to the Confederate capital.

The charges against Hurlburt appear to have been vague, alleging only that he was an abolitionist agent and a purveyor of anti-Southern journalism. But he certainly bore the markings of what Atlanta *imagined* a spy to be. In fact, the *Southern Confederacy* was quite taken with Hurlburt's appearance and demeanor ("He is well educated, and has remarkable conversational powers—has traveled extensively and is well posted on almost everything afloat in the world"), and it thought the committee acted judiciously in deciding to transfer him to Richmond. Plenty had been learned in interrogating Hurlburt, the newspaper assured its readers, but the editors believed it "prudent to suppress" much of that.[13]

Yet another committee transported Hurlburt to Richmond; delivered him to Confederate authorities; and laid the case before Jefferson Davis, Robert Toombs, and Judah P. Benjamin, among others. Reports later reached

Atlanta that Hurlburt had been turned over to Virginia officials for a preliminary examination and possible extradition to South Carolina. Meanwhile, William H. Browne, assistant secretary of state for the Confederacy, apparently intervened in the matter and returned the spy to the North through a prisoner exchange, a decision that produced outrage in the Atlanta newspapers.[14]

The Hurlburt incident fed both the fear and the sense of excitement Atlantans felt at the prospect of spies in the city. The fear of spies also threw more suspicion on Unionists, who were thought of as natural contacts for espionage agents making their way into Atlanta. For the moment, however, the fear of spies worked mainly to agitate the imagination of loyal Confederates and to increase the level of "watchfulness" under which Unionists lived.

Foreign ideas portended as much danger as foreign agents for many Atlantans, and in the late spring and summer of 1861 worries about "incendiary and treasonable sheets" competed with fears of espionage for dominance in the popular mind. Unionists, especially those born outside the South, came under increasing pressure, as Confederates purged the city of dangerous ideas. The *New York Herald,* because of its abolitionist bent, was particularly repellent to Atlantans, and when Michael Lynch, bookseller and Unionist, was reported to have "rejected that vile incendiary sheet . . . from his counter," the *Intelligencer* beamed approval. The next day, however, Lynch's newsboys sold the paper in the streets as usual, prompting an inspection of his newsstand by representatives of the *Intelligencer.* "We visited Mr. Lynch's store in the evening," the paper reported, "and we found large piles of the *Herald* exposed for sale on his counter."[15] With no apparent sense of hyperbole, the *Intelligencer* declared that reading such newspapers constituted as dire a threat to the community as harboring a "secret agent of Abe Lincoln" or refusing to take up arms for the South. Correspondents to the *Intelligencer* soon linked the issue to Unionists who had emigrated to the South. "There are men in Atlanta who came here poor from 'Abe Lincoln's land,'" one correspondent wrote, "and they have grown rich from the labor of the slave, and now unless they show a desire to protect that interest, they are no longer suitable men to inhabit slave territory." Moreover, he went on, there were also plenty who subscribed to New York newspapers of an abolitionist bent. "Let us have all such looked after, and allow no man to remain among us who would, in *any way,* give comfort to the enemy."[16]

The local newspapers agreed with the correspondent and published lists of objectionable publications that should be banned. They included the *Herald,* the *New York Observer, Harper's Weekly,* the *Louisville Journal,* and *Brownlow's Whig,* the publication of Knoxville, Tennessee, Unionist "Parson" William Brownlow. These and others like them should be "suppressed," the *Intelligencer* argued, as it offered the vain hope that Atlanta had "seen the last of Northern journals—secular, religious, literary and political."[17] Such powerful sentiments did make it much more difficult for Northern publications to circulate in the city, but throughout the war Atlanta Unionists managed to acquire them and surreptitiously circulated tattered but highly prized copies of *Harper's* and other banned publications.[18]

The hunt for spies, the suppression of dissent, and the enforcement of a patriotic consensus—much of it led by the press—took a different twist when Josiah Peterson, the editor of the *Commonwealth* who published Cyrena Stone's columns, came under scrutiny for having made anti-Southern remarks and for writing unpatriotic columns. A native of Rhode Island and the son of Danish immigrants, Peterson had resided in Atlanta only a few years, earning his living as a journalist after some uneven successes in business.[19] Atlanta historian Wallace P. Reed, who was a teenager in Atlanta during the war, thought Peterson's newspaper a lively journal, perhaps because it offered a wider array of materials than some of the city's other newspapers.[20] Peterson had strong Unionist sentiments and had reportedly made very strong anti-Southern statements. "Do you suppose that I am going to fight against my friends and relations in the North? Never, while the sun shines in the heavens—I would have my hand cut off first," he reportedly said to friends in the reading room of the *Southern Confederacy.* Peterson also allegedly said that he hoped that intransigent South Carolina would have a "brush" with the federal government "and get the worst of it." He concluded with the dangerous declaration that "Such men as [Robert] Toombs and [William Lowndes] Yancey were TRAITORS and ought to be HUNG!"

Peterson's remarks aroused the anger of John H. Rice, a native Atlantan, probably a banker, who claimed to have overheard the remarks. Rice also heard the curious rumor that Peterson was involved in organizing a militia unit, and he threatened to fire any of his employees who joined the group since *"it was being gotten up by an abolitionist."* Rice told the men that he would have nothing to do with any of them who "followed the lead of an Abolition Scoundrel!" When Rice heard that one of Peterson's editorials had been reprinted in a Kentucky newspaper (a "Coercion-Union-Lincoln" sheet) and that Peterson's views were interpreted as evidence that Unionist sentiment persisted in Georgia, he renewed his attack on Peterson in the *Southern Confederacy*.[21] Peterson, stung and probably frightened by the attack, used a column in his own newspaper to deny all that had been alleged. He declared publicly what seemed to be an unswerving loyalty to the Confederacy. "My only recourse," Peterson wrote, "is to denounce any direct or indirect charge, accusation or allegation on any insinuation that I sympathize with Abolitionists as a base, infamous and malicious LIE; and I further denounce as a liar, John H. Rice, and any and every other man who accuses, or charges, or insinuates, even, that I am an Abolitionist, or sympathize with, or that I sympathize with the Lincoln government and movements or am in the slightest degree disloyal to the government of the Confederate States of America or to the institutions of the South."[22]

Peterson's public confession of loyalty resembled James A. Stewart's coerced recantation of his political views. Whether a committee also paid a call on Peterson to compel his statement is unknown, but the short-term effects were clear: after the May attack little appeared in the *Commonwealth* that could even remotely be construed as disloyal. In the long run, however, Peterson privately continued to profess strong Unionist sentiments and after the war swore that he had remained a faithful Union man throughout the conflict.[23]

The craving to stamp out dissent, if only temporarily, turned away from the Unionists and toward Atlantans of seemingly impeccable Southern credentials. Two men, neither of whom was a Unionist, had their loyalty publicly questioned, and, as with Stewart and Peterson, community pressure led to public statements concerning their "soundness" on issues. S. D. Niles, an Atlanta merchant, was rumored to have been "unsound" on the slavery issue and had to defend himself in the press.[24] Similarly, the standing "as a southern man" of J. N. Beach came into question in connection with trips abroad. Beach, a wealthy merchant who was traveling at the time in Europe, found a defender in the strongly pro-Confederate Joseph P. Logan, an Atlanta physician, who assured the public that Beach was honorably carrying out a mission to build trade with European countries, likely an allusion to talk that Beach was less interested in diplomacy than in feathering his own nest. Soon, however, the focus returned to Unionists and other disreputable Southerners, but the brief detour into questioning the purity of undivided loyalties to the South surely made many Confederate Atlantans jittery.[25]

Up until this point the concerns over loyalty were vigorously stoked by the newspapers, which took it upon themselves to act as patriotic conscience and arbiter for the community. The enforcement of codes of loyal behavior appear to have been undertaken largely by ad hoc vigilance committees, likely with the complicity of the newspapers. While this practice would continue throughout the war years, community worries about disloyalty in the summer of 1861 led to a citizens' meeting at city hall and the establishment of a broad-based committee, composed in part of the city's leading ministers, which would deal with the increasingly complex matter. At the meeting, which occurred a few days after the Confederate victory at First Manassas, the citizenry resolved that "the time has now come when every member of this community should demonstrate his loyalty to the South whether of native or foreign birth." Anyone who did not espouse the cause of the South was perforce "a secret enemy" who was "admonished quietly, peaceably, but promptly to leave our community and the State." A Committee of Public Safety would be responsible for determining who was loyal and, presumably, for enforcement of the resolution.

Although enthusiastic and broad support existed for the committee's establishment, one person attending the meeting raised strong objections. Reverend William Clark, a Methodist minister, said that he was opposed to the establishment of any committee that had no precisely defined duties. Clark argued that the committee would likely be "irresponsible" and declared that "the laws of the land was amply sufficient for the public safety." In other cities, Clark warned, the history of such committees "showed that the weak man, without friends, was often punished, while the bad, bold, and defiant man was allowed to go scot free." Clark's impassioned arguments were shoved aside, and the committee was established, but whether it supplanted or merely augmented the ad hoc vigilance committees is unclear.[26] The formation of this committee raises the question of whether members of the Atlanta establishment may have worried that self-appointed enforcers of loyal behavior had gone too far in accusing S. D. Niles and J. N. Beach of disloyalty. The idea of an official, community-based committee on disloyalty (complete with the city's clergy) may have reflected a concern that ad hoc vigilantes should be restrained and that the process of creating and maintaining a culture of loyalty properly belonged in the hands of the city's elite and not under the control of vigilante groups or ragtag army units composed of the lower orders of white society.

Oddly enough, the *Atlanta Intelligencer* objected to the formation of such a group, for in addition to exposing the disloyal, it was charged with ensuring that all Atlantans contribute generously to the support of troops and of their families left at home in the city. Despite the stinginess of a few, the newspaper argued, Atlantans made solid contributions of troops and support funds. The committee therefore had no business *assessing* citizens for support of troops and their families. Not only did such an action strike "directly at the foundation of all freedom"; it also violated "every principle of republican government" and was a "dangerous doctrine" under which no one's property or life would be safe. On the other hand, the newspaper praised the action of the citizens' group to discover and expel the disloyal. Disloyal or suspicious persons should be sought out both by individuals and by committees and then "punished according to the laws of the land or banished from the country."[27] The newspaper's objections to the committee on constitutional grounds appeared disingenuous at best. Calling for continued pressure against the internal foes by both organized committees and individuals likely indicated that the editors preferred the status quo of newspaper-directed opinion and vigilante-enforced loyalty as opposed to public management of the problem of disloyalty.

Indeed, throughout 1861 and into 1862, groups of citizens and self-appointed watchdogs continued to seek out the disloyal, relying less upon the laws of the lands than upon violence, ostracism, coercion, and simple harassment to enforce the will of the community where disloyalty was concerned. The role and fate of the formally organized group are unknown. The activities of all the vigilance committees, or "committees of safety," as they were sometimes called, are largely confined to the shadows of Civil War Atlanta's history. If such committees kept detailed records or membership lists, they have not survived. Such committees received occasional mention in the Atlanta press or in the various records that cast light on the Union Circle in Atlanta, but these disclose only the general claim that vigilance committees drove the disloyal from the city, pressured men to join the Confederate army, and as in the cases of James A. Stewart and Josiah Peterson, coerced recantations of "disloyal" speech or extracted professions of loyalty to the Confederacy.

One detailed account has survived, however, that hints at the efficiency and the effect of vigilance committees in dealing with disloyalists. James R. Matthews was a native Georgian, a son of Newton County, which lies to the southeast of Atlanta. A tinner, born in 1828, with a wife and several children, Matthews was poorly educated and of very modest means. But he ardently opposed secession, convinced that civil war would be the outcome. "I was a poor man," he wrote to Andrew Johnson in 1865, "my intreates availed nothing. . . . In the hast and rapid spread of this mania of rebellion I saw the dear old flag go down to the dust by the hands of those whom slavery had brutalized."

Matthews claimed, "love of country made me forget the dangers around me and I would not abandon my principles for the mere sake of property or the security of my person." Matthews was evidently outspoken, as his language implies, and in March 1862 he and his family received notice from a committee of safety "that we sympathized with the enemies of the Confederate States—and tharefore we would have to leve the county or be errested and imprisoned." Matthews was convinced that the committee meant business and that failure to comply would bring imprisonment for his family or even death. "I shuffled the cards to my liking," he said, "and under grate privations safely reached the Union lines." Eventually, he settled his family in Cincinnati, and there the displaced Georgian joined the Union army. "I loved my country too well to stand edley by, and see it insulted without linding my ade in its support. So I sholdered my gun and went foth to meet the cowards who had run me away from my native home be cause of my attachment to the government of my fathers." Matthews concluded that he "was the first and probably the only native Georgian who represented that state in the grate contest for freedom and equal rights."[28]

Loyalty and disloyalty were not always easily defined, and opinions varied in the first years of the war concerning both the seriousness of the threat posed by disloyal persons and what constituted disloyalty. Throughout much of 1861, both of the leading newspapers, the *Intelligencer* and the *Southern Confederacy,* took pains at one time or another to deny that any significant threat from disloyal persons existed in Atlanta. Soon after Fort Sumter, the *Intelligencer* announced that virtually all of the citizens of the city were loyal, although it acknowledged there had been "divisions on minor political subjects" that had died out. Just in case the traitors remained in the city, however, they should be dealt with to the full extent of the laws of treason. Three months later, the *Intelligencer* noted that Unionist sentiment had been "crushed out by the arrogance and domineering spirit of the Lincoln Government."[29]

At bottom, however, the *Intelligencer's* denial of a threat rang hollow, for the newspaper steadily commented on evidence of disloyal behavior and grew particularly strident in its condemnations of "neutral Yankees," that is, Southerners of Northern birth whose patriotism was frequently called into question. Neutral Yankees could be smoked out, the *Intelligencer* sardonically observed, by asking them certain political questions and listening closely for answers that would inevitably emanate from the "Puritanical carcass" of the "desciple of Plymouth Rock."[30]

The *Southern Confederacy* took a more liberal view and offered a rather sprightly defense of persons of Northern birth, arguing that they should be judged individually and not condemned as a class. The newspaper chastised the *Intelligencer* for its intolerance, and soon the entire matter became a war of the columns, with the *Intelligencer* striking the lowest blow when it implied that J. Henly Smith and George W. Adair, the editors of the *Southern Confederacy,* were themselves unpatriotic. Of course the *Confederacy* was overly sensitive on the issue of neutral Yankees, the *Intelligencer* complained. "How long have the proprietors of that print been secessionists?" And was it not true that one of the editors was a "Union candidate for the Georgia Convention [Adair] and the other [Smith] was a Douglas correspondent of the Atlanta *Southern Confederacy*[?]"[31]

If loyalty was a complex matter for Confederates, it was doubly so for the Unionists. For both those of Northern and Southern birth, loyalty often collided with other strongly held values and particularly with family loyalties. Several of the leading Unionists confronted emotion-fraught situations involving family members who supported the Confederacy. Their reactions ranged from the contemptuous disgust of John Silvey, an Atlanta merchant and native Georgian who refused to aid three nephews who served in the Confederate army, to the painful anguish of Nedom and Elizabeth Angier, who could not prevent their seventeen-year-old son from joining the Confederate army. Even James Dunning, a most vociferous Unionist, had to live with the knowledge that his son was a Confederate volunteer.[32] In the early days of the war, Cyrena and Amherst Stone also experienced such a conflict, when loyalty to family clashed with national loyalty. The conflict involved Amherst's brother, Chester Able Stone, who had arrived in Atlanta sometime in the mid-1850s, probably in 1856. Like his brother, Stone entered into civic life in Atlanta, becoming in 1857 a charter member of the local militia unit: the Gate City Guard. Membership in the unit ultimately caused the Stones to address complicated, intertwined questions of family and national loyalty, for Chester Stone decided to side with the Confederacy.

Beginning as a private, Chester Stone rose through the ranks of the Gate City Guard, and by the time the unit disbanded in the spring of 1862, the Vermont native had become its captain and commanding officer. Early on, his duties with the guard were more ceremonial and social than military, although he did take part in the group's occasional encampments.

In early 1860, he spoke for the unit in a ceremony in which it received a flag from one of the young women of Atlanta. During the secession crisis, far more serious matters occupied the guard as it debated its proper course. When some members proposed that the U.S. flag continue to fly over the unit's armory, a bitter debate ensued, resulting in a decision not to fly the Stars and Stripes. Nearly half of the unit's membership resigned in protest, but Chester Stone remained, choosing not to depart with those of stronger attachment to the flag. Not long thereafter, the unit "place[d] itself on a war footing," offered its services to Governor Joseph E. Brown, and elected new officers to fill the vacancies created by the exodus. Chester Stone was elected third lieutenant.[33]

In mid-March 1861, the guard received orders to report to Macon, and on March 31 and April 1, a cheering Atlanta turned out for sermons and elaborate ceremonies to send the guard to meet the Yankees. Whether Amherst and Cyrena Stone were in the applauding crowds that sent the military unit on its way from the Atlanta depot is not known, but the Stones were a closely knit family and they were likely there. The closeness of the two brothers was apparent. They had both decided to leave Vermont and to live with each other in Georgia. Over the years, Amherst and Chester Stone would often live near each other and in time would become business partners. Cyrena Stone also was fond of Chester, regarded him as her own brother, missed him during his wartime absences from the Stone household, and was obviously pleased when he returned for visits.[34]

THROUGHOUT THE WAR, Cyrena Stone would remain as staunch and unremitting a Unionist as there was in Atlanta, and her responses to Chester Stone's decision to go with the Confederacy were no doubt anguished and emotional. Although there is no direct documentary evidence for gauging her reactions, several sections in the novel based upon Cyrena's journal hint at the despair she felt when her brother-in-law decided to join in "the gay pageant of treason" and at the emotion-laden departure of the younger Stone with his unit. It would have been hard enough merely to say good-bye to the younger brother who was going to war, "bad enough just to see him going to face danger and possible death; but the deeper pain to which neither . . . could be reconciled was to know that he was going to fight against the land of their birth, perhaps their own kindred." A "great shadow" spread over the household. When evening came and the troops departed the depot, the eyes of the novel's protagonist "were blinded with tears," and "there was a scene of wild excitement—fathers, mothers and sisters hanging upon the necks of those they loved, some screaming and some fainting. There were waving of handkerchiefs and 'God bless you's; and, as the train moved off, shouts long and loud rent the air."[35]

The troops went to Macon, where, within days, Chester Stone was elevated to second lieutenant. Then the guard moved on to Pensacola, Florida, where it was to participate in an assault on Fort Pickens and the nearby federal navy yard. Atlantans anxiously waited for news of the soldiers. One of the first reports that circulated in the city came from Chester Stone, who wrote to Amherst from Florida. The younger Stone's letter brimmed with enthusiasm for the Confederate effort and reflected the naive ardor for military adventures of one who had not yet seen the misery and carnage of war.[36]

Pensacola was beautiful in the spring, Chester Stone wrote, with "magnolias and flowers of all kinds in full bloom." The soldiers of the Gate City Guard were all in good health "and enjoying ourselves merrily," but the brave men of the unit were "ready, at a moment's notice, to meet the armies of the Rail-Splitter, and split them worse than he ever did rails." Seven thousand Confederate troops had been massed near the fort, young Stone reported, while five federal war ships lurked off the coast ready to protect the troops inside the fort.[37]

Within a few days, Chester Stone's letter found its way onto the pages of the *Southern Confederacy,* Amherst permitting its publication. Whether Amherst Stone sought to have the letter published or whether he had merely shown it to friends or to the publishers of the newspaper is not known. If he desired that the letter be published, his reasons for so doing can only be supposed. But Stone could not have been unaware that Atlantans would have interpreted the action as signifying some loyalty to the Confederacy on his part. Publication of the letter indicated at the least that he may have wished to give an impression of being loyal to the South.

Chester Stone and the Gate City Guard remained near Pensacola until early June, when they were ordered to the Virginia theater, which proved to be a chilling contrast to balmy Florida. The guard traveled by rail to Richmond and from there over the Allegheny Mountains to Laurel Hill. Wet weather and the change in climate brought much sickness to the soldiers, who soon came under strong attack from Union forces. For three days and nights fierce fighting followed, and on the fourth day, a blunder in the Confederate command resulted in the guard and five other companies' being cut off from the main force. With no chance of rejoining the main body of troops, the officers voted to try and find their way through uncharted wilderness back to the Valley of Virginia. In constant rain and with little food, the troops wandered in the wilderness for days, sick, wounded, and delirious. The experience so traumatized the Atlantans that some became "permanently deranged." Others died of illnesses contracted during the ordeal. Finally, the group encountered a hunter who agreed to guide the soldiers out of the wilderness.[38]

Chester Stone survived the retreat, participated in several other actions, and late in 1861 became the elected captain of the Gate City Guard. By early autumn, however, he had had enough of war and wrote to Amherst and Cyrena that he and his men were "weary and heart-sick, praying for the time to come when we can go home once more." Now in command, Stone led the Gate City Guard back to Atlanta sometime in the late winter or early spring of 1862. Having completed their one-year terms of enlistment, the entire group was mustered out of the service. Although some reenlisted in other units, Stone apparently returned to his brother's home in Atlanta and took up arms again only when Sherman threatened the city.[39]

While Chester Stone wandered in the Virginia wilderness, Cyrena and Amherst Stone returned to Vermont in June for what would be their last visit for several years. Within months, it would become much more difficult to leave the South, especially after the establishment of a passport system that worked against free movement throughout the region. Cyrena had apparently gone ahead of Amherst and spent some time in New York City, including several weeks at a medical institution, although the nature of her illness is unknown. She then went on to visit her father in Albany, Vermont, and on the same trip returned to her childhood home in nearby East Berkshire, where Amherst joined her. Before preparing for the return trip to Georgia, the two no doubt visited relatives, including Amherst's parents and another brother, Charles Birney Stone, who would soon join the Union army. They also visited some old friends, Aldis O. Brainerd, a St. Albans merchant, and his wife. In later years, Brainerd would recall that during the visit he had grown suspicious of Amherst's loyalty to the Union, because Stone had advised his friend to stay out of the war, warning him that "they [the rebels] mean business there. I tell you; they are going in for killing, and you had better keep out of it."[40]

The journey back to the South began with a twenty-two-mile ride on the mail coach from East Berkshire across Franklin County to St. Albans, just a few miles below the Canadian boundary near the shore of Lake Champlain. Along the way, the open coach bounced along on a road that ran beside the Missisquoi River and passed through some of the other villages that dotted the Vermont countryside between East Berkshire and St. Albans. By the time the Stones began the trip, the ordeal in the Virginia wilderness was over for Chester Stone, although it is likely that neither Cyrena nor Amherst yet knew details of the Laurel Hill episode. The Battle of Bull Run had also just occurred, and the Southern victory on that Virginia battlefield created euphoria throughout the South and profound shock in the entire North. Word of the Confederate victory reached East Berkshire the day before Cyrena and Amherst boarded the mail coach. Bull Run dominated conversation in the crossroads village.[41]

Only two other persons, the driver and a young man whose name was William Clapp, were on the coach. Clapp later recalled that the effect of the defeat "was every where noticeable" in northern Vermont and that "it overspread the faces of all with gloom." He climbed on the coach after the Stones boarded and was introduced by the driver. Clapp sat with the driver, the Stones on a seat behind them. Amherst Stone surely recognized young Clapp as the nephew of another William Clapp, with whom the Stone family had a long-standing feud. The elder Clapp had in earlier years been a clever merchant in East Berkshire and had become wealthy running a store and stage station before moving on to the more cosmopolitan town of Burlington. Clapp sold his store to James and Franklin Stone, Amherst Stone's uncle and cousin, in exchange for real estate, likely the Stone family farm. James Stone was not an able businessman, and he soon had to sell the store. Without his farm and having lost his store, Stone began to keep a public house and to manage the local stage station. The feud persisted for years and probably grew out of the terms of the business arrangement, which the shrewd Clapp had arranged.[42]

On the mail coach, Amherst Stone suddenly emitted a string of pro-Southern statements. Shocked and irritated, Clapp said that Amherst spoke "treasonable sentiments" and muttered that "he [Amherst] had a good mind to wave a Confederate flag," which young Clapp concluded was packed in one of the Stones' trunks. Amherst's statement horrified Cyrena, and she "tried to check him indeed during the whole journey." Clapp remembered that "her manner toward him [Amherst] was expostulatory," whereas Stone "was evidently in the best of spirits as though he had got rid of some kind of restraint and was running over with desire to give vent to some kind of inward glee."

Young Clapp naively speculated that Stone was a Confederate agent but concluded that if he was "an authentic agent of the southern Confederacy he did not reflect much credit upon the sagacity of his principles."

As the coach rolled on, the voluble Stone continued to "talk about the news" and wagered that Washington would fall in a matter of days. Cyrena was "earnestly pleading" with her husband to be quiet. She began to cry. Stone kept talking. Not only would Washington fall, he announced, but a hundred days would be all that was required for the South to win the war. This declaration caused Clapp to be seized with a "fever of patriotic indignation," and he resolved to swear out a warrant against Stone. Later, however, he decided that it would be a "quixotic" undertaking and temporarily dropped the matter.[43]

Before the war had ended, the affair on the Vermont mail stage would cause Amherst Stone profound difficulties. For the moment, however, it mainly served to compound the clash of loyalties that Cyrena Stone felt. The loyalty of her brother-in-law to the Confederacy and her husband's behavior in Vermont must have put wrenching emotional pressures on her and made the maintenance of her resolute Unionism extremely difficult, especially if, in private, Amherst Stone's loyalties were as fragile as his behavior in Vermont suggested. But Cyrena Stone persisted in her adherence to the Unionist values she espoused and, as time would show, became even more aggressively Unionist, her political sentiments unaffected by the disloyalty of her brother-in-law and the dubious behavior of her husband.

Within a few weeks of the Stones' return to Atlanta, Cyrena published another column in the *Commonwealth*. Perhaps inspired by Laurel Hill, it was written from the perspective of a soldier dying on a battlefield and comported perfectly with published sentiments that began to fill Southern newspapers, as lengthening casualty lists tempered enthusiasm for war. The essay recounted battle scenes and focused on a soldier comforted by the knowledge that his mother prayed for him. Superficially, the essay had nothing to set it apart from many similar efforts, but a close reading reveals that the column was decidedly different in its complete absence of references to the South, the Confederacy, or the "Cause." Cyrena Stone wrote about all soldiers who died on the battlefields of the Civil War, not just about Confederate soldiers. Perhaps the artful deception escaped many of the *Commonwealth*'s readers, or perhaps it added to the nettlesome awareness among Confederate Atlantans of the strongly Unionist sentiments of Cyrena Stone.[44]

Cyrena's column appeared at a time when the Atlanta press was strongly condemning attempts to "reconstruct" the Union. The newspapers fretted about rumors of efforts to reunify the seceded states with the North and thus restore the old Union. Confederate Atlantans saw a Unionist plot in the reconstruction effort. One correspondent, "Secession," wrote to the *Intelligencer* that there was renewed danger from "the foes in our midst" and declared "Reconstructionists" to be "as dangerous as the Yankees." "Secession" also implied that the rich and the well-off led the reconstructionists: "Wealth and position are not to be coverings for such now. . . . It is the rich that have their all at stake." Another correspondent, "Secessionist," thought that a secret organization existed to create a "Reorganization" party in Georgia and that its members permeated every level of government. They were mysteriously known as the "C & S."[45]

Reconstruction sentiments did exist among Atlanta Unionists, and possibly those who were wealthy did display that interest—thus giving credence to "Secession's" claims. Although prevented from expressing his views on this and other matters in the newspapers, the tenacious James Stewart argued strongly for reconstruction as late as November 1861 in additional private correspondence with his friend Alexander Stephens. A secessionist friend had just returned from a visit to his brother in the Confederate army in Richmond, and Stewart had been greatly moved by the views of this man, who was convinced that the war might drag on interminably with horrendous loss of life. Stewart's friend had been converted to the idea of reconstruction and called for reestablishment of commercial relations with the North as a beginning. Put simply, Stewart's friend concluded that secession simply would not work, even if secured by war. Permanent separation from the North would result "in a labyrinth of evils and calamities," including standing armies placed in the border states between the two nations, where they would obstruct trade, collide constantly, and engage in "robbery and plunder." It would be better, Stewart's friend thought, to return immediately to the Constitution and the old Union.[46]

Of course Stewart agreed, and he penned a set of dire warnings for Stephens to contemplate. From Stewart's stout Union perspective, there was an antisecessionist "revolution in public sentiment" brewing. Formerly only a "murmur of discontent," it now grew "audible, and the fear is, that, without some wise and prudent council it will become formidable for mischief." Perhaps fearing for his own economic position, Stewart also saw a spreading panic "in relation to bread stuffs and other necessaries which threatens mob violence upon speculators and merchants." The Atlanta miller reported that Memphis, Tennessee, mills were about to stop operations because of a lack of grain and that supplies of flour in Atlanta were "very limited." Moreover, Stewart told Stephens, the "country people" displayed a growing resentment at increasing taxes. In addition, a shortage of money from a constricted cotton market meant that slaves would not be well clothed and fed, thus inciting discontent among the bondsmen.

In short, Stewart predicted that a "gathering storm of discontent betokens a counter revolution." It was, he told the vice president of the Confederacy, "the legitimate result of rash, unjustifiable and precipitate secession." Only the reconstruction of the Union and the reestablishment of free trade would head off calamity. "I am fully satisfied," Stewart declared with startling prescience, "that unless some provision is made for reunion or reconstruction, that the South is doomed to witness scenes of carnage and desolation not paralleled in the annals of history."

Stewart urged that the basis for reunion be the settlement of the slavery question under the principles of the Compromise of 1850 and the Kansas-Nebraska Act. He was, of course, overly sanguine that this approach would be acceptable to the North and that it could lead to an honorable settlement, making it unnecessary to resort to "the necessity of hanging men or enforcing the penalties for treason," a none-too-opaque reference to Stephens's role in the rebellion. Everyone "in possession of his reason and with a share of common sense," Stewart observed, knew that secession and disunion had brought calamity. The "only escape" would be immediately to "renounce secession as no remedy for any evils of which the South has complained; but on the contrary as having produced evils of a thousand times greater magnitude than ever could have resulted in the union from the fanatical raids of abolitionists." In a closing personal word to his friend Stephens, Stewart wrote that he did not wish "the destruction of our leading southern men: but I am seeking for them an honorable release from the terrible dilemma in which they have placed themselves by their rashness and folly."

Whether Stephens answered Stewart is not known, but there is little doubt that events in the South had moved too far to permit the reunification Stewart urged. The reconstruction movement, slight and ephemeral, appears to have petered out in Atlanta very quickly and had little effect throughout the South. It was important, however, as an indicator of persistent Unionist sentiment and of the continual tension that Confederate Atlantans felt concerning the "traitors" in their midst.

The concerns of the Confederacy about the presence of Northerners and disloyal persons in the South soon led the government to cast eyes on the considerable property that belonged to persons who were styled "alien enemies." As a consequence, the Confederate Congress in 1861 enacted deportation and sequestration laws designed to deal with alien enemies and their property. The Confederate district courts, successors to the U.S. district courts, administered the sequestration laws and held concurrent jurisdiction with the state courts in the deportation law.[47]

The deportation law appears to have had little or no effect upon the Atlanta Unionists. Some records of the Confederate District Court for the Northern District of Georgia exist, but they contain little information on the deportation law's administration. Under the law, alien enemies were required to leave the Confederacy within forty days after the law had taken force or to face imprisonment or deportation. At least some Unionists thought the law laughable. John M. Trimble, from nearby Fayette County, said that he did not believe Jefferson Davis had "any right to make me leave my home" and that he knew of no man who left the South because of the law.[48]

The sequestration laws had more force. Soon after their passage, James T. Nisbet became receiver for the Northern District under the laws and quickly took out an advertisement in the Atlanta papers announcing that he was prepared to begin his duties. All citizens, he declared, must provide him with information concerning property owned by alien enemies. A few days later, "Atlanta," one of the ubiquitous correspondents to the *Southern Confederacy,* criticized Nisbet for inaction, reporting that many Northerners had already left with the proceeds from their property and that "*two Yankees* left here this morning," while every day others made preparations to leave. "What is our Sequestration Agent doing?" "Atlanta" asked.[49]

Nisbet was busily working with the district court to implement the sequestration and garnishment portions of the laws that allowed officials to identify and dispose of property owned in whole or part by alien enemies. Ninety-eight writs of garnishment were issued against residents of Fulton County in the first (and largest) wave of proceedings under the law, and approximately twenty to twenty-five of these were against members of the Unionist community in Atlanta—including virtually every Unionist merchant and substantial property owner. Because the records are fragmentary, however, it cannot be said with certainty that Unionists had been singled out for special attention, but it is noteworthy that nearly all the Unionist merchants or substantial property owners were caught in the first net cast by Receiver Nisbet.[50]

Amherst Stone's law practice received a hearty boost from the proceedings, as he was the attorney of record in a number of the cases against

Unionists and others. He was also one of those whose property came under the court's scrutiny. Stone owned a house in Marietta (in partnership with L. O. Wilson of New York), which he reported to the court when he, like others thought to have business connections with Northerners, received an open-ended notice of garnishment on October 31, 1861. Within a short time, the court ordered the house sold at public auction, where it brought $777.25. Under the law, the proceeds from such sales were paid to the receiver for the Confederate government. In this instance, however, only half the proceeds went to the receiver; the other half went to Stone, indicating at the least that he was not considered an alien enemy by the district court. In fact, Stone appeared to be in good standing with the court, where he had a large practice and where, in order to continue his practice, he took an oath to the Confederate government, an oath, he later said, that he took with a mental reservation. Stone argued that he had been compelled to take the oath and that he would have lost his property and been immediately conscripted had he refused. He secretly vowed not to abide by the oath, believing it "as all intelligent persons must believe, to be a nullity." From his point of view he had incurred no moral obligation, because the oath was involuntary, illegal, and required of him as a result of the "unholy cause of rebellion."[51]

If the records of the Confederate district courts were fuller, we might more confidently judge the effectiveness of the deportation and sequestration laws. It does seem safe to conclude that the enforcement of these national laws had the approval of the vast majority of the city's citizens. The revenues went to the central government, but locals could get bargains at auction when confiscated properties were sold. The records do not tell us enough to gauge the effects of property loss on Unionists. If Amherst Stone's experience is typical, not much was lost. The significance of the sequestration laws for Atlanta Unionists lay in bringing to bear the added weight of the Confederate government in the formula that determined loyalty. Atlanta officialdom and the unofficial vigilantes who swore to enforce loyalty thus had a useful ally.

AS 1861 DREW TO A CLOSE, Confederate Atlanta resonated with a vigorous patriotism strengthened by distant battles, reinforced by home front vigilance, and supported by central authority. On the whole, loyal citizens seemed confident in this patriotism and confident that no reconstruction would occur. But the questions surrounding who should be responsible for the maintenance of loyalty (and thereby unity) must have troubled some citizens, particularly those Confederates who were themselves accused of disloyalty when the requirements of loyalty became too stringent and the enforcers of loyalty too enthusiastic. The newspapers continued their powerful roles in ensuring orthodoxy, and an occasional if mistaken thrust at a patriotic Confederate might be forgiven in the context of the zealous pursuit of enemies—internal and external.

For Cyrena Stone, loyalty took on a much more personal dimension with her brother-in-law's defection to the Confederate cause and Amherst's disquieting, dangerous behavior on the stagecoach in Vermont. We can likely never know exactly how Cyrena judged Amherst's patriotism and loyalty, but every scrap of evidence that throws light on her life suggests that agony was her companion so long as Amherst's loyalty to the Union remained conditional. Perhaps she accepted the fact that her husband had to play the dangerous game of mollifying Confederates in Atlanta while continuing as a member of the Unionist group and that his permission to publish Chester Stone's letter was part of that game. And perhaps she interpreted his behavior on the Vermont stagecoach as braggadocio begat of an anticipated Southern victory in a brief war. Oddly, and despite these bits of evidence, doubts concerning Amherst's loyalty never arose in the Unionist circle in Atlanta; there is no hint that any of the leading Unionists ever questioned his loyalty.

Cyrena Stone believed that in acting faithfully to the Union she was acting morally. Loyalty to her husband, to family, friends, slaves, neighbors, and nation each required a separate duty from her, and each offered something in return. Loyalty to any one of these could never be total or complete. To some uncertain extent, each competed with the others. Thus Cyrena Stone, like all of the Atlanta Unionists, could not avoid encounters with conflicting loyalties, each with limits, each demanding something, and each requiring either a choice or a reconciliation.[52]

CHAPTER FOUR

The Limits of Loyalty

Throughout the first months of the war, Confederate morale remained buoyant on the home front, with patriotic fever cresting after the victory at Bull Run. Indeed, spirits stayed relatively high throughout most of 1861, but as casualty lists lengthened, war fever subsided and a chilling recognition seeped into the Southern consciousness that the conflict would be a long one. By early 1862, Atlantans heard no more easy assertions of Southern victory.

Union victories at Forts Henry and Donelson in Tennessee had an electric effect in both the North and the South. The fictional Cyrena Stone rejoiced at the news of the fall of the two forts, but she like all of the Unionists had to conceal her excitement. The Unionists knew that Ulysses S. Grant's victory at Donelson provided Abraham Lincoln with a decisive, highly significant victory, easily the most important in the ten months of fighting, and that it also greatly raised Grant's standing in the Northern armies. The victories secured Kentucky for the Union and opened the way for Northern invasion into the heart of Tennessee. Combined with the absence of any significant Confederate military successes since Bull Run and with the loss of Missouri, New Mexico, West Virginia, and a large part of Tennessee, a "gathering gloom" settled in on the South.[1]

LOYALTY HAD LIMITS throughout most of 1862; those who professed a strict Unionism encountered repeated challenges from Confederates to demonstrate that they were not disloyal. At the same time, they searched their own consciences for room to compromise the principles of strict Unionism when circumstances, or even survival, demanded it. Some of the challenges became almost routine; for example, all women in Confederate Atlanta—Unionists most certainly included—were expected to provide aid to the Confederate wounded transported to the city and its hospitals. Similarly, all men had to contribute money and supplies to the Confederate cause, or, if they owned businesses critical to war needs, they had to give full cooperation in support of the war effort. The Atlanta Unionists constituted a tiny minority of the population, and, for the most part, it would have been foolhardy to overtly resist these demands. But the Unionists soon found covert forms of resistance that irritated and vexed Confederate Atlantans, especially the local military police.

In 1862, for the first time in the war, the Confederate army began to send wounded soldiers to Atlanta, which was becoming a hospital center as well as a rail and industrial hub. The existing hospitals were insufficient to care for the nearly three thousand soldiers who arrived in the city by early March 1862, and workmen swiftly converted other buildings into hospitals and began construction of new facilities.[2] In time, the city would have more than twenty hospitals and thousands of wounded and sick soldiers. When there was overflow, the authorities expected Atlantans to take the wounded into their homes.

Unionists in particular felt pressure to prove their Southern loyalty by caring for the Confederate wounded. Thomas Healey took in two Confederates after the fight at Fort Donelson, and they stayed in his home for several weeks. Healey later recalled that he had been "personally called upon" to care for the prisoners by "the rebel authorities" and yielded to the pressure "to save myself from being cried down." A wounded soldier from Virginia spent several weeks in the fictional Stone household, where he was cared for until he was strong enough to desert the Confederate army.[3]

Unionist women also experienced pressure to become members of hospital aid committees and other groups that rolled bandages, worked in the Confederate hospitals, or provided support to the families of absent Confederate soldiers. When the Hospital Association was formed in Atlanta in

March 1862, no women with Unionist connections appeared on the initial list. Eventually, however, the names of a few appeared on the rosters of such organizations, including Mrs. Henry Holcombe and Mrs. Alfred Austell. Cyrena Stone's name was notably absent from such lists.[4]

Intense pressure fell on Unionist men of Northern origin to contribute financially to the war effort, and, because they were suspected of disloyalty, "requisitions" were made of them with greater frequency than of Confederates. According to the testimony of R. H. McCroskey, one of the more militant Unionists, virtually all the Unionist men had to contribute money to the Confederate cause. McCroskey himself did so, believing that he would have been imprisoned had he failed to donate. Prominent men with Unionist ties seem to have been singled out and pressed especially hard. McCroskey thought it would have been particularly difficult for a man of William Markham's stature and wealth to have declined. Markham's business partner, Lewis Scofield, remembered that Markham refused to contribute for "as long as he could do so with safety." When Scofield made a contribution in the name of their firm, it angered his partner. Finally, however, after repeated harassment from the provost marshal of Atlanta, Markham yielded "in order to protect his person and property."[5] The relatively small contributions of cash extracted from Markham amounted to little when compared to the high stakes involved for the Confederacy in the operation of the partnership with Scofield. The two men owned and operated one of the largest rolling mills in the South, and although accounts differ concerning its profitability before the war, it became evident soon after hostilities started that the mill would be of immense importance to the Confederacy because it was one of only two such mills in the South large enough to produce the steel plate required for armored naval vessels.[6]

Markham and Scofield faced a serious dilemma. If they refused to produce steel plate for the Confederacy, they likely would face seizure of their property or perhaps imprisonment. On the other hand, compliance with Confederate demands would mean they were aiding the enemies of the United States by producing a vital commodity. Both men felt an intense allegiance to the United States, but they were also fully exposed to Confederate charges of disloyalty or even treason.

The mill also provided opportunities for a sizable number of foundrymen of Northern and foreign birth to escape service in the Confederate forces. Just before the war commenced, the Atlanta Rolling Mill employed fifty-six persons who were listed in the city directory. Of these, only six can be definitely shown to have served in the rebel army. Those who did serve were unskilled laborers; those who held skilled positions such as machinist, rail straightener, heater, boilermaker, shearsman, or blacksmith did not serve. There is no doubt that the mill provided a refuge from Confederate service for skilled laborers.[7]

The pressure began early in the war, when Nelson Tift, a Georgian managing construction of the Confederate gunboat *Mississippi,* came to Atlanta to contract with Scofield and Markham for the production of plating for the ship. The circumstances surrounding this episode are not completely clear. Markham and Scofield apparently refused at first but in the end yielded to Tift's pressure and entered into a contract to produce the steel plate.[8] The *Mississippi* contract was for a relatively small amount of plate, but by the following spring, with the war effort greatly intensified, the Confederate Department of the Navy was determined to contract with Scofield and Markham for five thousand tons of rolled iron for various military purposes and the construction of naval vessels. The secretary of the navy assigned James G. Minor, who was a general agent for the Navy Department, to deal with the two men. Minor came to Atlanta and brought with him the authority to seize the mill if its owners refused to comply with the Navy Department's demands. Apparently they did refuse, and Minor, uncertain of what course to follow, went back to Richmond to consult with the government. When he returned to Georgia, in about three weeks, he threatened immediate seizure of the mill. According to Scofield, Minor declared that if the two men continued to refuse the requests, the government "would seize the mill and run it themselves, for they were compelled to have the iron." Markham feared that if government officials operated the mill, they would damage or wear out the installation's expensive machinery, and his entire investment would be lost.[9]

Faced with the prospective loss of their investment, the two men again yielded to the Confederate request and began to refit the mill in order to produce the huge amount of iron. At about the same time, they asked the secretary of the navy for exemptions from service for twenty-seven men and also asked that several others be detailed for work in the rolling mill. Mallory sought and received approval for the action from G. W. Randolph, the secretary of war.

Simultaneously, Scofield and Markham decided to sell the enterprise and thereby escape both the dilemma of loyalty and the dangers of noncompliance. Almost immediately, Markham went to Richmond with the plan of selling the mill to the Confederate government. He met a complete rebuff from Secretary of the Navy Stephen Mallory. Produce the iron according to the contract, Mallory said, or the government would seize the property *and* sue the two men for breach of contract. Nervous and disappointed, Markham returned to Atlanta still determined to sell and offered the firm to a group of businessmen in Richmond (possibly the owners of the Tredegar Iron Works) and to the Georgia Railroad Company. Ultimately, Markham and Scofield offered the mill a second time to the government and finally, as Scofield recalled, "to every one else that we thought would buy." There were no takers.

Meanwhile, the two men decided on a risky strategy, conspiring to keep production low and to operate the mill at minimum capacity. "While we were running the mill for the Confederate government," Scofield recalled, "we could have increased the capacity of the mill nearly double at small expense." Instead, the two men determined that they "would make as little iron as possible in the operation so as to excuse ourselves with the Government," a likely reference to their hope that once the war was over they might be judged as having compromised their loyalty only under duress. They also decided that Scofield, whose technical skills were essential to the running of the operation, would feign illness, claim that he could no longer run the mill, and thereby induce the Confederate government to purchase the operation. James Minor saw through the ruse and notified Secretary Mallory, who once again threatened seizure.[10]

Throughout 1862, the troubles of Scofield and Markham multiplied. As Atlantans became ever more vengeful toward suspected Unionists, an especially abusive vigilance committee threatened the two men with expulsion from the South. At some point, Markham was shot at as he drove at night through the Atlanta streets, although it is not clear that it was during this period.[11] Alarmed at the prospective loss of the two businessmen, Minor intervened to protect them, threatening to have members of the vigilance committee "arrested, put in irons, and sent to Richmond," so valuable was the work of the Atlanta Rolling Mill to the Confederacy—even, it would seem, at minimum capacity. National exigency and power thus took precedence over local concerns with loyalty.

Minor also seems to have drawn closer to Markham and Scofield, and when the two men decided to "sell the mill at all hazards," he agreed to help them dispose of it. He was eminently successful and arranged a deal that culminated in the sale of the mill in mid-1863, relieving the two businessmen of their entrepreneurial albatross and also relieving them of $100,000, which was the commission Minor charged on the sale price of $600,000. No documentation survives to indicate that anyone thought that Minor acted improperly or that the payment could have been in the nature of a bribe.[12]

Most of the Unionists agreed that Markham and Scofield took the only course open to them without endangering their lives and property, and after the war Markham would be regarded as the most prominent, perhaps even the leader, of the Atlanta Unionists. James Dunning, easily the most rigorous of the Unionists when it came to judging who had been loyal, always identified both men as being among the thirty-five or so truly loyal men in Atlanta. Dunning's judgment about those who professed Unionism could often be harsh, and even though he unreservedly characterized both Markham and Scofield as loyal, he speculated that "intelligent men" could differ over whether the two men made the right choice in operating the mill. Jonathan Norcross, an astute businessman and marginal Unionist, saw the matter in a slightly different light. "My opinion is," Norcross said, "that [Markham] rolled iron for the Government for the purpose of making money and saving himself and not out of any good will for the Confederacy."[13]

Not every Unionist suffered from the wartime economy or had to deal with predatory officials. Christian Kontz, a German immigrant bootmaker, saw an opportunity when Northern supplies of beer were shut off and opened a brewery that won the warm endorsement of the *Atlanta Intelligencer* for its cleanliness and its contribution to homegrown industry. ("Lager beer has become a favorite beverage of our people.") Peter Huge, a French immigrant and grocer, opened a soap factory in response to the same dynamic and also won the approbation of the *Intelligencer*. ("We have seen a specimen of Mr. Huge's Soap, and according to our judgment it is not only good, but very good. Patronize home industry.") Charles Bohnefeld, another German immigrant, found that his skills were more and more in demand. Bohnefeld, a cabinetmaker, quickly converted to the production of coffins, an item that seemed to have nearly unlimited demand during the war years. Robert Webster, a slave who hired his time from his master, Benjamin C. Yancey, continued to prosper as he operated two Atlanta barber shops. So did Prince Ponder, another slave, who carried on several enterprises and operated his store on Decatur Street. Both men also speculated in currency.[14]

By 1862, nearly all of the Unionists had learned to compromise in order to survive in the increasingly hostile environment in Atlanta, whether by contributing to relief and hospital committees, taking in wounded Confederate soldiers, or doing business with the Confederacy. Loyalty thus had boundaries. On the one hand, Atlanta Unionists complied with some Con-

federate demands that seemed unavoidable compromises with unconditional loyalty and represented minimal compromises with loyalty to the
Union. In these regards, Unionist disloyalty to the Confederacy could thus
be minimal and afford fewer causes for retribution. Loyalty had other limits as well. Individual Unionists had to decide how far they were willing
to go toward overt or covert resistance that would constitute treason or
espionage and thus invite severe retribution—possibly even death. Some
were mulishly militant and vocal in their opposition to the Confederacy.
Outspoken, even foolhardy, Dunning railed against the government. All of
the Unionists regarded Dunning as the most outspoken of their group and
repeatedly wondered at his courage in tempting the authorities with his
outspokenness. Dunning himself frequently observed that it was extremely
dangerous for men "to express Union sentiments during the war" and that
there were "few men in this community who had the moral courage to face
public sentiment." The Connecticut native did not seem to have close
friends among the Unionists, but he earned their respect and the affectionate
nickname of "Old Man Dunning."[15] Unlike Scofield and Markham, James
Dunning refused to put his business in the service of the Confederacy, a
decision that in part led to his arrest later in the year.[16]

R. H. McCroskey faced an equally difficult predicament. The outspoken, irascible McCroskey had moved to Atlanta in 1861 from LaGrange,
Georgia, seventy miles to the southwest in Troup County. There, McCroskey
had been accused of being an abolitionist—despite being a slave owner—
and had endured a series of threats and intimidations followed by a visit
from a vigilance committee. After the mayor and city council had served
him with "official notice," to leave the town, he was run out. McCroskey
opened a store in Atlanta, continued his outspoken opposition to the Confederacy, and earned a reputation for being an uncompromising Unionist.
He particularly resented the taxes imposed for the war effort, and refused
to pay "Gov. Brown's war tax." The local tax collector accordingly declared
McCroskey disloyal and threatened to close his store if the taxes were not
paid. The obdurate McCroskey refused, the collector closed the store, and
the sheriff sold the entire stock to pay the tax. After the loss of his business, McCroskey eventually found work as a clerk at one of Atlanta's
hotels.[17]

James A. Stewart also could not contain his opinions and risked phys-
ical violence in resistance to the Confederate cause. In the spring of 1862,
Stewart got into an argument at the "car-shed" and once more vented his
Unionist sentiments. A crowd quickly gathered and threatened to lynch

Stewart, but they beat him instead. Philip McIntire, who worked as gardener and stock tender for the wealthy Richard Peters, had a confrontation with Colonel Alexander M. Wallace on an Atlanta street in 1862 soon after the Yankees had taken Nashville. Wallace, one of Atlanta's most ardent secessionists, had been in the city raising troops and renewing his contempt for Unionists. Wallace overheard McIntire make a remark that was "exceedingly disloyal to the South." McIntire apparently boasted about the Yankees having taken Nashville and predicted that they would soon be in Atlanta. I am "too good a Union man to go into the rebel army," McIntire declared. A furious Wallace cursed McIntire and said that "such talk was unworthy of a Southern man." McIntire then offered to fight Wallace "outside the corporate limits." Wallace said that the two could settle it on the spot, but according to Wallace, McIntire "walked off & that was the end of it."[18]

David Young, the pharmacist and Methodist preacher, "made himself very obnoxious" by repeatedly voicing his Unionist sentiments and, more particularly, by preaching the Gospel to Atlanta blacks. For his preaching, Young earned the nickname "Nigger Young," and, according to the black tinner Austin Wright, Young created a sensation by telling blacks that "a white man was just as good as a nigger provided he behaved himself." Atlantans also believed that Young preached to blacks about their prospects for freedom, but Young denied that he had gone that far. He did acknowledge that his preaching and his Unionism had put him in danger from time to time and that it had separated him from other Methodists in Atlanta. Young was especially critical of another Methodist clergyman, a "very rabid secessionist" who had "dropped" him, despite Young's sizable contributions to the minister's church. As word of Young's disloyalty and preaching to blacks spread, he soon found that he was no longer called upon to participate in any Methodist services and that he was thoroughly shunned by his coreligionists.[19]

WHILE THESE UNIONISTS risked danger because of their outspokenness, they and many others in the Union Circle found a more effective way to resist the Confederate authorities and to lend support to the Union cause. Beginning after the Battle of Shiloh in April 1862 and continuing until the end of the war, Atlanta Unionists devoted great energy to relieving the condition of Union prisoners in Atlanta. Prisoners did not arrive in Atlanta in significant numbers until the late spring and early summer of 1862. In mid-May, the *Intelligencer* announced that six Yankee officers, prisoners of war captured below Savannah, had arrived in the city. Twelve enlisted men in the same group were evidently left at Macon. The presence of these and subsequent groups of Yankee prisoners produced a strong effect among Atlantans. Confederates young and old, accustomed to constant propaganda that painted Yankees as menacing monsters, clamored to lay eyes on the prisoners in the streets as they were being transported to and from the jails or visited the jails in the hope of viewing them there. Men and women pushed and shoved to glimpse the devils, who, only months before, had been their fellow citizens. Even children found ways to sneak satisfying looks at the prisoners, though, upon close inspection, they did not seem so menacing after all.[20]

The presence of the prisoners also excited the Unionists. Anderson L. Scott, a Massachusetts-born physician who had arrived in Atlanta in 1858, saw "great curiosity" among the citizens when the first prisoners of war came into the city. Scott himself joined a throng bound for the railroad station to get a look at the Yankees. When he reached the station, he was greatly moved and on impulse tucked some money inside a newspaper and dropped the paper through an open window onto the floor of a railroad car where federal prisoners could reach it. A friend did the same thing. From that time forward until he left Atlanta in January 1864, Scott remained a ready friend, at considerable risk, to dozens of prisoners of war who passed through or were imprisoned in Atlanta.[21]

The fictional Cyrena Stone heard from a friend that there had been "quite a sensation" in the city with the arrival of some Yankee prisoners. "Six Union officers, and they are splendid men," her friend reported. He also said that he had gotten a pass to see the prisoners and would take Cyrena along. For the remainder of the war, Cyrena Stone frequently managed either to visit Union prisoners or to send food or money to them. Among Atlanta Unionists and among Yankee prisoners, she was recognized along with her friends William and Emily Farnsworth as the most intrepid of those who gave aid and comfort to imprisoned Union soldiers. Women who regularly visited the hospitals and prisons—successfully delivering money, food, and wine to Union prisoners—included Emily Farnsworth, Massachusetts born, and her daughter, Helen, who risked much to relieve the suffering of Union prisoners; Bridget Doyle, who had been in Atlanta since 1852, operating a small store on Decatur Street next door to the Masonic Hall; Martha Huntington, whose stirring narrative of escape from Atlanta revealed the conditions of fear and intimidation under which Unionists lived; Mary Summerlin, a seamstress who aided Union prisoners and helped a

Union spy who tarried in Atlanta; Ann Packard, also one of those who brought relief to Union prisoners but about whom nothing is known except that she was the sister-in-law of Lewis Scofield; Harriet Stansel, Massachusetts born and the sister of William Manning, who would be imprisoned for his Unionist beliefs; Mary Hinton, the sister of Martin Hinton, also imprisoned; and a pseudonymous friend of Cyrena Stone's, "Mrs. Frank," whose very identity, like that of several other Unionist women mentioned in Cyrena's diary, cannot be established with certainty.

Children took part in these dangerous mercy missions as well, including Helen Farnsworth and six-year-old Ella Summerlin, who lived with her widowed mother across the street from the Empire Hospital. The novel, *Goldie's Inheritance,* recounts how little Ella "was employed constantly, taking wine and money" to the prisoners that had been given her by Cyrena and some of the other women, including a Mrs. Reed, perhaps the mother of young Wallace P. Reed, the teenager whose journalistic recording of events in Civil War Atlanta provided much of the substance for one of Atlanta's first histories. "These were the persons who communicated with me and gave me money which my little daughter would put in her bosom and carry over to the wounded," recalled Mary Summerlin in 1864.[22] It is clear that Mary Summerlin is the character Mrs. Waincloss, who repeatedly appears in the novel. Mrs. Waincloss is described initially as "a poor widow who took in sewing, living very near one of the prison hospitals." She is "both shrewd and kind, and she had a seven-year-old daughter who partook of both of these qualities." The little girl "was allowed to run about at will in the hospital, and she would often carry things in her pockets or under her apron, and learned to watch her opportunities to distribute them to the unfortunate men."[23] Several of the Unionist women, including Mrs. Farnsworth and Cyrena, also gathered money for the prisoners from those members of the Union Circle who could keep the secret. At one time or another, most of the Unionists contributed.[24]

The Confederates seemed unprepared for the fact that the Unionists would be clever enough or brazen enough to find ways to give aid to the prisoners, and they were particularly unprepared for the complicity of women in the activity. During the two weeks after the arrival of the six Union officers, Unionist support for the prisoners may have been lost in the general public curiosity about the Yankees, which brought literally scores and perhaps hundreds of Atlantans to the jail to peer at the visitors. Lost in the crowd, Cyrena Stone visited the prisoners on several occasions.

The fictional Cyrena also did so, winning entrance to the prison in the escort of a male friend and taking "strawberries, or flowers, or something to cheer the captives." On one occasion, she provided a prisoner with a city directory and a map as an aid for a successful escape. Whether the real Cyrena Stone actually aided in an escape cannot be proved, but it is certain that she was among those who soon would be attacked in the *Intelligencer* for aiding and comforting the federal prisoners.[25]

The proof was in the strawberries. On May 28, 1862, a correspondent to the *Intelligencer,* "Verbum Sat.," reported to the community that he "was not a little surprised, a day or two since, on being informed that several ladies of this city, of respectability, had been to visit the Yankee prisoners." Moreover, he went on, "some of them had sent the prisoners bouquets, and others had treated them to strawberrys." "Verbum Sat." was shocked. "Is it possible this can be true?" he asked. "If so, by what motives could the ladies have been thus influenced?" The writer deduced that they were "influenced by curiosity or sympathy." Curiosity might have led them to the prison, "if they merely wished to get a sight of a live Yankee; but it hardly would have caused them to send the prisoners boquets and strawberrys."[26]

"Verbum Sat." seemed unable to grasp that support for the prisoners could be linked to the presence of Unionists, but others quickly linked loyalists to prisoner aid. "A Southern Woman" thought what had occurred was either treason or the attention-getting acts of "individuals [who] belong to that class of officious persons, who are ever ready to do something (no matter what) to bring themselves into notice." Both traitors and "officious persons," however, had taken shelter behind scriptural adjurations to "visit those who are sick and in prison." The writer thought it "curious . . . to see the ingenuity with which human nature can pervert the plainest teachings of Holy Writ to its own purposes," because the scriptures clearly did not intend that Christians should give aid to "insolent and haughty foes" who were "provided with every thing that is needful" and were "better lodged and fed than hundreds of soldiers, now standing as a wall of fire between us and our enemies." "Would it not be well," she concluded, "to inquire if these people are really Southern born men and women, or only Yankees whom we have permitted to remain among us?"[27]

This was one of many times when the actions of the real Cyrena Stone conformed to those of her fictional reflection, when the currents of the novel written about her flow parallel to the real occurrences in Civil War Atlanta. But the novelist's sources were more limited than the historian's, and the fictional account of Cyrena Stone's loyal Unionism reveals only a part of the complex relationships that developed between Unionists and Union prisoners in Atlanta.

Unionist men and women, black and white, were beginning a steady, increasingly silent program of aid to the thousands of federal prisoners brought to Atlanta during the war. Although the early encounters were largely in the open and received the attention of Confederate Atlanta, the Unionists would later use stealth and subterfuge to bring aid to prisoners in the jails and the hospitals. Assisting the federals became a project of great importance for the Unionists, whose small numbers among the overwhelmingly Confederate population of Atlanta made other forms of resistance to the Southern cause futile if not impossible. As a result, the prisoners became the focus of much Unionist energy and in return provided precious tidbits of uncensored information about life in the North and the progress of the war. James Dunning later recalled that "all the assistance rendered [to the prisoners] was done in a clandestine manner and through agencies not understood by those who stood guard over the prison." Dunning said that he often aided the prisoners privately and that he had done so publicly on two occasions.[28]

The identity of all six of the first Union officers who reached Atlanta is not clear, but they were federal soldiers captured at Shiloh, not below Savannah as the *Intelligencer* reported, and included two Union generals, Benjamin M. Prentiss and Thomas L. Crittenden. Prentiss and Crittenden had been captured at Shiloh and taken to Savannah before being brought to Atlanta with the other officers. They were likely the ones who received the strawberries and flowers that created the public storm. James Crew, an Atlanta railroad official, noted that on the same afternoon that General Prentiss arrived, eighty-six more Union prisoners came into the city as well as one thousand sick Confederates. "This place is to be the great Hospital," Crew told his wife.[29]

Atlantans poured vitriol on Prentiss. The Missouri general, audacious even after capture, offered sharp-edged criticism of Southern military prowess. A Georgia officer thought Prentiss "one of the most violent enemies of the South and an unprincipled scoundrel." The *Intelligencer* called him a "creature" whose "vanity" was "intolerable." It was time to halt visits to such despicable prisoners, the newspaper argued, because the Union prisoners obviously made statements "so utterly at war with the truth" that they could have a negative effect upon Confederate citizens. Moreover, should such statements "reach the ears of disloyal men and spies," they would be "used for only treacherous purposes." "However much our citizens may desire to gratify curiosity in visiting these prisoners," the *Intelligencer* declared, "a stop should at once be put to it."[30]

PRENTISS AND HIS COMRADES not only received support from the white Unionists of Atlanta but also were cared for by Robert Webster, a mulatto barber. Webster, also known as Robert Yancey, had bought his time from his master, Benjamin C. Yancey, an Athens merchant, plantation owner, secessionist, and brother of the fire-eating secessionist politician, William Lowdnes Yancey. In the mid-1850s, Benjamin Yancey moved to Atlanta, and shortly thereafter he permitted Webster to open a barber shop, helping him secure the funds to open the business. By the beginning of the war, Webster had achieved remarkable success, owning two barber shops and employing nine barbers. In 1861, Robert Webster was likely worth in excess of five thousand dollars—barbering, making risky loans to white gamblers, and buying and selling produce. He lived with his wife in a four-room house that he owned (although title resided with Yancey) down Houston Street, a short distance from Cyrena and Amherst Stone. Webster regularly paid his master the monthly sum required for him to continue his entrepreneurial activities.[31]

After the war, it would be reported that Webster was, in fact, the son of Benjamin Yancey. Yancey told a different story, however, relating how Webster had been brought from Virginia when he was a youth and sold to one of Yancey's uncles in South Carolina, from whom Yancey bought both Webster and Webster's wife. Webster, Yancey recalled, "was a very intelligent and accomplished House servant; a fair cook, meat & pastry; a fine maker of Preserves & Pickles—a good barber." He was, Yancey went on, "truthful, sober, affectionate, honest." Yancey and his slave seem to have been personally quite close, sharing a strong bond of affection. After the war, when Yancey was financially ruined, Robert Webster was prosperous enough to lend his old master enough money to get on his feet again.[32]

Other speculation about Robert Webster's patrimony centers upon the seemingly implausible, if not fantastic, rumor that he was the son of Daniel Webster, the Massachusetts politician and giant of the U.S. Senate. Frederick Ayer, an American Missionary Association official in postwar Atlanta, commented to a Northern colleague on the close relationship between Yancey and Webster, passing along the information that Yancey frequently stayed overnight with his former slave, who lived across the street from Ayer. Ayer also mentioned, in an almost offhanded way, that Robert Webster was the "putative son of Daniel Webster."[33]

To be sure, Daniel Webster was for decades the subject of rumors in Marshfield, Massachusetts, where he lived, that he had fathered children by his cook, a slave woman whom he bought in Virginia sometime in the 1820s and later freed. The rumors had wide circulation and may have been the product of abolitionist propagandists who detested Webster for his part in forging the Compromise of 1850. Although Webster had a powerful reputation as a womanizer, there is little hard evidence to support the claim that he fathered children by his cook, and no evidence that Robert Webster claimed to be the offspring of the famous senator. Neither is there clear evidence about when Robert became known as Robert Yancey and when he became known as Robert Webster. It is certain, however, that Robert Webster was a mulatto and that he claimed to have been born in Washington, D.C.[34]

Webster had entreé to the jails during the war because of his trade and perhaps because Confederate officials might have thought a black man incapable of giving material assistance to the prisoners. He would arrive at the prison carrying his barbering tools and bundles of towels and would freely pass in and out of the barracks, where he was permitted to shave the prisoners. Webster may have initially gained entry into the prison stockades in the company of William Lewis, a slave who served in the Confederate army as a barber and drummer. Lewis, who lived at West Point, Georgia, before the war, spent the war years in Atlanta.[35]

Webster used his access not only to assist Union prisoners, but also to turn a profit by illegally dealing in the currency black market, an extremely dangerous activity. A man of means, he would get much-desired greenbacks from the prisoners and then sell them to other members of the Atlanta Unionist group. He used the Confederate money he received from the Unionists to buy various items, including tobacco and other commodities that held their value. Thomas Crussell recalled that he had purchased greenbacks from Webster for as many as three hundred Confederate dollars to one greenback. E. T. Hunnicutt, who worked for the Confederate provost marshal, testified after the war that he knew that Webster had bought greenbacks "though it was a dangerous thing for a man to do."[36]

Later in the war, Webster took even greater risks. In his visits to the prisons, he came to know many of the prisoners, including a "Colonel Cliff," an east Tennessean. "Colonel Cliff" was actually William D. Clift, a Unionist whose imprisonment in Atlanta resulted from unusual circumstances. Seventy years old, Clift had been a prominent leader in the antisecessionist movement in Tennessee. Wealthy and with extensive landholdings in Tennessee, he was a leader in the Greeneville Convention of 1861, which tried to carve a separate, loyal state out of east Tennessee. As the Confederates ascended in Tennessee, Clift, who had been a prewar militia colonel, led much of the opposition in the Chattanooga area. When a series of local conflicts broke out between Union and Confederate sympathizers in the area, it became known as "Clift's war." Confederate troops were introduced into the region in an attempt at pacification, but Clift and his troops took to the mountains and continued their resistance from there. Later in the war, when Union forces came into the area in large numbers, Clift came out of hiding and became a courier for General William S. Rosecrans. On a mission to Knoxville in the autumn of 1863, however, he was arrested by a Confederate officer and handed over to rebel authorities, who shipped the aging man to the military prison in Atlanta. The man who arrested Clift was his own son, Moses H. Clift, a captain in the Confederate cavalry.[37]

In prison in Atlanta, Clift asked Robert Webster to help him escape. After the war, Webster recounted their conversation.

"Bob, I want to get out of this place," Clift said.

Webster demurred. "Captain, you know I can do nothing for you."

"Yes, you can," Clift insisted.

"Now, you want to get me into a scrape and then tell Wash Lee [Col. George W. Lee] about it, and he will hang me."

"I will die before," Clift replied. "This fellow out here will pull me over the fences if you will bring me a line."

Webster provided the rope and apparently rejected the twenty dollars in greenbacks the Union colonel offered him in gratitude. Webster never knew who in Atlanta agreed to help Clift, but there were several east Tennesseans among the Unionists, including James A. Stewart and Alexander N. Wilson.[38]

It was nearly winter, sometime after December 6, 1863, when Clift escaped, scaling the prison wall with the help of the outside person, threading his way through Atlanta streets until he reached the outskirts of the city, and then making his way to familiar, hilly terrain in north Georgia, where he dodged Confederate patrols until he was finally hiding in the relative safety of the east Tennessee mountains. The tough old Tennessean survived the cross-country escape but suffered considerably in the freezing weather, losing some toes to severe frostbite.[39]

Confederate authorities, incensed at the escape, pounced upon Robert Webster and charged that he had helped Clift. Although Webster was arrested for questioning, he was held only a short time before being released, perhaps for lack of evidence. Or possibly Webster bribed his way out of jail, a common enough occurrence in Civil War Atlanta and not an impossible feat for a well-off black man to accomplish.[40]

OTHER UNIONISTS ALSO endangered themselves to help Union prisoners, and women sometimes ran greater risks than men because they may have believed, as did Mary Hinton, that the Confederates would not hang a woman. Hinton, her mother, and her two sisters devised ingenious ways to help the prisoners, putting money in the "spring backs of books" and even secreting it in pies. Once, Mary Hinton recalled, she lost twenty dollars when a prison matron found the money tucked "between the crust and the pie."[41]

The well-off Hinton family also gave money directly to Union prisoners. Samuel B. Houts was a Union surgeon from Missouri who cared for the swelling numbers of prisoners in Atlanta in the early summer of 1862. Houts, who had also been taken prisoner at Shiloh, became acquainted with Martin Hinton, Mary Hinton's brother, within a week after arriving. Hinton immediately let him know that he was a Union man and that all the members of his family were Unionists. He then volunteered to assist in any way he could the wounded federal soldiers in the hospitals under Houts's charge. Every day for a week, according to Houts, the Hinton family sent provisions to the wounded and sick soldiers until "they were peremptorily prohibited by the rebel authorities from furnishing any more." Hinton also regularly provided money for medicine and medical supplies and over time secretly sent the Yankee surgeon Confederate bills equivalent to about four hundred U.S. dollars.[42]

Houts and Hinton became fast friends. Hinton visited the federal surgeon when he could, and Houts admired the Atlanta photographer for his great loyalty to the Union. "I formed a strong attachment for him," the surgeon said, "because of his earnest devotion to our cause and the anxiety displayed for the welfare of the sick and wounded federal soldiers." Hinton was "entirely open and unreserved in the expressions of his political sentiments to me; . . . he was intensely loyal." Houts also met some of the other Unionists, who "each and every one, desired the success of the Union cause and wished the destruction of the so-called Confederacy."[43] They included the Harvard-trained physician Anderson Scott, who sought out Houts soon after he arrived in Atlanta. As a doctor, Scott cited professional reasons for visiting Houts, and when the two met, Scott promised to do everything he could to aid the prisoners. Scott managed to introduce Houts to a number of Union people who contributed "quite a large sum" for the relief of prisoners. Eventually, however, Confederate suspicions grew, and Houts was closely guarded, making it much more difficult to gain access to the surgeon and his patients.[44]

The most celebrated group of prisoners with whom the Unionists had contact during 1862 were the men who participated in the daring and audacious raid on Big Shanty (Kennesaw), Georgia, and commandeered a locomotive, the General. The raid shocked Atlantans, who had not believed that the war could be brought so close to home. Commanded by James J. Andrews, the raiders planned to steal the locomotive, take it northward, and destroy key bridges along the railroad in Georgia and Tennessee. In March 1862, Andrews and eight men slipped into Atlanta to begin the mission. Andrews had apparently secured the services of an Atlanta-based engineer who worked for the Western and Atlantic railroad, but when he and his men arrived in the city they could not locate the man, and they returned to Tennessee. Planning a second attempt, Andrews expanded the mission's objectives and this time took along his own engineers. The group of twenty-one volunteers rendezvoused in Marietta and went to Big Shanty, where they seized the locomotive and began the run toward Chattanooga, pursued by Georgians in another locomotive. Ultimately, Andrews and his band fled overland, but they were captured and imprisoned at Chattanooga. After sentences of death in court-martial trials and abortive escape attempts, Andrews and eight men were brought to Atlanta on June 7, 1862. A few days later, Confederate officials transported twelve more of the party to the city.

Confederate officials carried out the death sentences. On the same day that he arrived in Atlanta, Andrews was hanged. Eleven days later, seven more of the raiders died in a particularly grisly hanging, during which two of the men had to be twice hanged before they were pronounced dead. The remaining fourteen (another group of the raiders arrived later) stayed in Atlanta prisons for months, fearful that they would also be killed.[45] Anderson L. Scott charged that Oliver H. Jones, the livery stable owner and sometime city marshal, seemed to take special glee in the hanging of Andrews. Jones, Scott said, was a "violent rebel," "clamorous for the execution of Union citizens and prisoners." According to Scott, Jones drove the condemned men to the place of hanging and "while Andrews was suspended by the neck, removed the earth from under his feet that he might clear the ground."[46] James R. Crew, the Atlanta railroad official, reported the hanging in a letter to his wife. "Seven more of the bridge burners were hung here this morning," Crew wrote, "But the rope broke [and] let two of them to the ground." After a new rope was hastily procured, the two were hanged again, this time successfully. "Is this not awful," Crew wrote. "Would to God I was out of this town until the war was over."[47]

The hangings powerfully frightened the Unionists into believing that if the Confederates would hang prisoners of war, they would also hang disloyal Unionists who committed "treasonable acts." In the novel *Goldie's Inheritance,* anxious Unionists heard detailed accounts of the brutality of the executions and of the suddenness with which they were carried out, denying the raiders an additional day so that "they might prepare for eternity."[48] Despite fears and the great risks involved, the Unionists furtively contacted the surviving raiders and lent them the same kinds of support they gave to other Yankee prisoners. While in the Fulton County jail—a closely guarded, brick, two-story building—William Pittenger, one of the captured raiders, discovered "that there were many lovers of the old Union" in the city. "These visited us, and, although always in the presence of guards, managed to express their kindness in very tangible ways." "They told us much of their hopes," Pittenger went on, "and of the strength they numbered."[49]

Pittenger singled out Anderson L. Scott for giving special help to the raiders, recalling that the thirty-one-year-old physician had made "liberal contributions" to the prisoners' needs. How Scott and the others succeeded in aiding the closely guarded prisoners remains a mystery. In the autumn of 1862, Pittenger and seven of the remaining raiders made a daring escape from the Fulton County Jail and found their way back to the North. Whether Scott or the other Unionists may have aided in the escape is not known, but an account of an escape in *Goldie's Inheritance* at approximately the same time contains details similar to those of the escape of Pittenger and his fellow prisoners. In that escape, the fictional Cyrena Stone had a key role. Anderson Scott also later fled the city, made his way through the Confederate lines to the North, and arrived "destitute" in Ohio, where he was aided by the grateful Pittenger.[50] It is possible, of course, that Louisa Whitney had read one of Pittenger's accounts of his escapes and adapted it for her book.

Multiple threats plagued Atlanta Unionists, and in the spring of 1862 yet another was added with the passage of the first Confederate conscription act. Prior to the act's passage, the Unionists faced intense community pressures to serve Georgia and the Confederacy. The conscription act joined the force of law to community pressures. Perhaps even more than those who merely sought to evade service, Unionists were subjected to the hounding of the enrollment officers.

The first conscription act, passed in April, applied to men between the ages of eighteen and thirty-five and obligated them to three years' service, or less if the war ended before the three years expired. When the Confederate Congress considered exemptions, it decided to exclude certain occupations, including "national and state officers, railroad employees, druggists, professors, schoolteachers, miners, ministers, pilots, nurses, and iron-furnace and foundry laborers."[51]

Some of the Unionists could claim exemption by virtue of age. William Markham, Alfred Austell, and Amherst Stone, for example, were all over the age of thirty-five, although Stone barely so. Occupational deferments rescued others. Pharmacists such as David Young, teachers such as Alexander Wilson and C. T. C. Deake, and railroad workers such as William Dyer could all claim exemptions. And, of course, the foundry workers, some of whom were Unionists (Luther Faught, for example) were already exempted by the action of Secretary of War Randolph. A greater threat for most of these men would come in October 1862 with the passage of the second conscription act, which raised the eligibility age to forty-five and thus included most of the male Unionists in the city. Younger members of the Unionist families were not exempt from the first law. William Markham's son, Marcellus, became a prime target for enrolling officers, and Markham decided to do all he could to keep his son from being conscripted. Ultimately, he would expend extraordinary effort in order to ensure that young Marcellus would not be forced into Confederate service.[52]

The upheavals of the late winter and spring of 1862 had caused numerous dislocations in Atlanta society. The arrival en masse of the Confederate sick and wounded spread disease (including smallpox) to the civilian population, and the appearance of the hated Yankee prisoners of war conditioned Confederate Atlantans to be ever more vigilant about the disloyalist threat. Equally important was the continued emphasis on the rooting out of spies who, according to popular belief, roamed in and out of the city at will, reporting the city's strategically important activities to Yankee generals, who were now less than two hundred miles away, in Tennessee. These three classes of "Yankees"—Unionists, federal prisoners, and spies—were all persistent reminders of Atlanta's increasing sense of vulnerability to the lengthening war's bloody horrors. Spies must be smoked out. Yankee prisoners must be sequestered. And the Unionists in the midst of Atlanta must be carefully watched, constantly harassed, and strictly prevented from carrying out acts of disloyalty that could harm the city and the Southern cause. Talk was plentiful and rumors abounded about the secret activities of the Unionists and the presence of other Yankee threats in the spring and summer of 1862.

The *Daily Intelligencer* renewed its warnings about spies in early April, only a few weeks after James Andrews and his men had visited the city the first time and just a few days before the actual theft of the General. The newspaper reported a recent arrest of three suspected spies, two of whom were released on lack of evidence and one of whom remained in custody, soon to be sent to Confederate military headquarters in Tennessee. The newspaper told its readers that it knew the secret details of the spy's arrest and the means by which the proof was obtained but that it would not reveal any information because there were likely other agents in the city who would be discovered if citizens and authorities remained vigilant. "Hear them *talk,* and then *search* their persons, and *search* their trunks," the newspaper urged. The work of the local military authorities had been effective in uncovering espionage, the newspaper declared, and "if the officer [Colonel George W. Lee] who directs it is not soon ordered away," others would soon be arrested.[53]

In the summer, the tempo of warnings escalated. A citizen in a nearby town wrote to the *Intelligencer,* complaining that Atlantans were not "sufficiently on their guard respecting enemies in our midst." "Who can tell," he wrote, "but a conspiracy may be on foot all through the Confederacy, fomented by the Yankees and perhaps a few traitorous Union men, who are sneakingly silent in our midst." The *Intelligencer* agreed, and in a lengthy exposition on the subject of disloyalty warned the "traitors in our midst" that when the war closed, there would be a reckoning with the disloyal. Retribution would be both "just and terrible," and it would be conducted in the courts of law and in private. The treatment of Tories in the American Revolution provided a perfect model. The "open and armed traitor" would "suffer the severest penalties." The "secret traitor, when convicted, must pay the same tribute to our Independence." The merely disloyal could not remain in the South or "breathe the same air" as those who were loyal. The South would be "purged of the presence of all upon whom treachery and disloyalty to her can be fastened." Every patriotic citizen was duty bound to point out the disloyal and the courts were duty bound to convict them. Those who sought neutrality in the conflict would be regarded as having been against the South and must "prepare for the judgment that will be pronounced upon them."[54]

During the summer, readers of Atlanta newspapers also saw long expositions of the meaning of the term *Yankee* and attachments to that term of powerfully pejorative, politically charged adjectives. The newspapers concluded that the most dangerous Yankees were no longer the abolitionists of the North or the "avowed enemies" who lived in the Northern states, but rather those secret Yankees who remained in the South—those who adhered clandestinely to their "vagaries, fanaticism, and puritanism." They should "pull up stakes at once." They should leave. Failing that, they should be identified and forced out; "Every Southern community should be made too hot for them."[55]

Atlantans also took seriously reports from other areas of the South that the city was a hotbed of Yankee sentiment. A correspondent of the *Mobile Advertiser and Register* found "a strong Yankee element" in the city and told of an Atlantan who, while traveling in the North, divulged valuable information concerning the position and morale of Southern armies. The same Atlantan reportedly stated that "a large number of persons in Atlanta were Union men, being of Northern birth and but for their present interest and situation, they would be with the North." The reporter complained that numerous Atlanta citizens were "Lincolnites" who were "still permitted to remain there, and give information to the enemy whenever it is in their power to do so." The *Intelligencer* was horrified by the damage done to Atlanta's image as a patriotic city but equally convinced that the allegations were true. The newspaper recommended that the authorities look into the identity of the traveling Atlantan. "There is no doubt at all," the newspaper concluded, "but traitors and spies have been often in our midst."[56]

BY MID-1862, many of the Unionists had crossed the line between disloyalty and treason. The limits of Unionist disloyalty to the Confederacy had expanded beyond dissent into active, definitional treason. Aid and comfort regularly went to Yankee prisoners of war, including the hated soldiers who shocked the entire Confederacy with the hijacking of the *General*. Women, children, and men, black and white, took part. The Unionists could not doubt the growing danger. The public's temper, always hostile toward Yankees, now grew even more so, reinforced by daily threats in the press, the streets, and the neighborhoods. Added to the mixture was the growing influence and power of the Confederate provost guard in Atlanta, a presence that would soon intimidate virtually all members of the Union Circle in the city. Thus, the Unionists tightened their circle. Ostracized from much of the society in which they lived, they drew strength from each other's company, from aiding the Yankee prisoners, and from the practice of patriotic traditions in which they had been steeped as children and adults. But the "old flag" would now have to be hidden and revered in private; its mere possession was a crime. And patriotic holidays could be observed only in secret or at a distance from the city.

It was in this context that Martin Hinton, his mother, and three sisters went to Stone Mountain to observe the Fourth of July in 1862. There the Hintons met James Dunning and his family, and the two families celebrated the holiday. "We went up the mountain together," Dunning said, and sang "some national airs." Then the Dunnings and the Hintons talked about the war, its injustices, and its tragedies. They agreed that it was terribly unnecessary and "fruitful of evil to us nationally." James Dunning later recalled that Martin Hinton's words that day were those of a man "who felt a love & attachment for the Government of the United States." The same could have been said for the members of each family.[57]

There were others at Stone Mountain on July 4, and they heard the singing and the patriotic declarations. That would come back to haunt both families.

A bird's-eye view of Civil War–era Atlanta, taken from a painting by the Atlanta artist and historian Wilbur Kurtz. (Atlanta History Center)

Alexander M. Wallace, Atlanta insurance man, ardent secessionist, and Confederate colonel. (Atlanta History Center)

(Left) William Markham, wealthy businessman, leading Unionist, and mayor of Atlanta, 1853–54. James M. Calhoun *(right)*, wartime mayor of Atlanta. (Atlanta History Center)

The office of the *Atlanta Intelligencer,* located near the railroad station. (Library of Congress)

Looking down Decatur Street with a view of the Masonic Hall, the large building with a peaked roof, located next door to the Trout House, with its distinctive ironwork. Unionist Bridget Doyle operated her store in the wooden structure nearest the Masonic Hall. (Library of Congress)

(Left) Louisa Bailey Whitney, half sister of Cyrena Stone and author of *Goldie's Inheritance,* the novel drawn from Cyrena's diary and based on her life. (The Mount Holyoke College Archives and Special Collections) *(Right)* The only known likeness of Amherst W. Stone, taken from an issue of the Denver *Rocky Mountain News* and probably reproduced from a photograph of Stone when he was in his early forties. (*Rocky Mountain News*)

View of the Confederate defenses, which is quite similar to what Cyrena Stone would have seen from her home. The unidentified house in the background was located at approximately the same distance from these defenses as was the Stone house from the emplacements nearest to it. (Library of Congress)

The railroad depot where Atlantans boarded boxcars before leaving Atlanta during the fall 1864 evacuation. Note the baggage and other goods piled on the tops of the cars. (Library of Congress)

General William Tecumseh Sherman sits stoically in one of the Confederate forts that surrounded Atlanta. (Library of Congress)

A view looking down Marietta Street during the Union occupation. The flagpole in the foreground may have been the one to which Unionist James Dunning attached the American flag during the first day of the occupation. (Library of Congress)

The Atlanta city hall, located on the site of today's state capitol. The Central Presbyterian Church, which Cyrena and Amherst Stone attended, is in the background. The wooden "tents" were constructed for Union soldiers, using lumber from dismantled fences and buildings in the city. (Library of Congress)

Nedom L. Angier, Atlanta businessman, Unionist, and Reconstruction-era state treasurer. (Atlanta History Center)

Depiction in *Harper's Weekly* of the Abraham Lincoln memorial service in Savannah, April 22, 1865, at which Amherst Stone spoke. (Georgia Historical Society and University of Georgia Libraries)

Unionists fled Georgia throughout the autumn of 1864. *Harper's Weekly* used this engraving for the cover of its December 10, 1864, issue. (University of Georgia Libraries)

"A Perfect Reign of Terror"

Atlanta had changed from a relatively tranquil antebellum town into a rapidly growing wartime city with serious problems of crime and violence. Many Atlanta citizens blamed the sharp and sudden increase in the city's crime rate on the "secret enemies" they saw lurking in every corner—the Unionists, spies, even the "shirkers" who evaded military service. They also fixed blame on Atlanta's population of slaves, free blacks, blacks who hired out their labor, and an increased population of runaways in the city. Prostitution, disease, robbery, murder, and a persistent, unnerving rowdyism worried Atlantans and added to the disruption and havoc that the war brought. Throughout 1862, Atlanta verged on chaos.[1]

NONE OF THE VARIOUS committees of safety and other vigilante groups (including briefly a force of secret police) could deal with the problem of rising criminality, and the "public" demanded a force of military police to deal with the situation. As a result, in May 1862, Atlanta became a military post under a Confederate officer with expansive powers. Guards, sentinels, and military police soon became much more visible in the city as they protected government installations, helped to maintain civil order, and boarded trains to "examine and arrest all suspicious persons pointed out to them." In addition, new military regulations sought to eliminate liquor sales to soldiers, control public drunkenness, restrict access of Confederate soldiers to the city, and prevent unaccompanied slaves and free blacks from being on Atlanta streets after 9:00 P.M.[2]

The man with responsibility for the enforcement of law and order in Atlanta was George Washington Lee, whose rank in May 1862 was colonel but who held various ranks at various times and who would soon become the provost marshal of the city. In a relatively brief period, Lee became a man of importance and power in Atlanta with as strong a commitment to eliminating disloyalty as he had to controlling crime. A native Georgian, Lee was thirty-two years old in 1862. Although the record of his life and service in the Confederate forces is fragmentary, ample evidence survives to indicate that he was cunning and an accomplished self-promoter adept at survival in military life. For Lee, the war provided an opportunity to advance himself and to win a measure of power and respect.

Before the war, Lee was a saloonkeeper, the coproprietor of the Senate Saloon on Alabama Street in Atlanta.[3] Soon after secession, however, he left the barroom and joined a company of Atlanta soldiers who elected him captain. Lee then sought a commission for himself and acceptance of the unit into state service with the help of some prominent Atlantans including Jared I. Whitaker and Alexander M. Wallace, each of whom endorsed the raising of the company and recommended it to Governor Brown. The Atlantans told Brown that the prospective soldiers came from the "nerve and sinew of the county," not an especially precise metaphor, but added that many of them were "out of work with no hopes of getting anything to do," undoubtedly a more forthcoming assessment of the group who were likely young as well as unemployed.[4]

Brown refused to accept the unit. His reasons are unknown, but he appears to have been suspicious of Lee and perhaps concerned about the quality of the men who composed the company. Lee then turned to the Confederate War Department, which was not so discriminating and accepted the troop, ordering it to Pensacola in the spring of 1861. In Pensacola, the soldiers came under the command of General Braxton Bragg, who very shortly formed a highly negative impression of George Lee. The War Department's decision to accept Lee and his troops annoyed Bragg, who knew of Governor Brown's refusal and ascribed it to Brown's knowledge of Lee's bad reputation. For Bragg, Lee was "A man without education or character." "You will observe," he told General Joseph E. Johnston in early 1863, that "he never signs his own name."

In Pensacola, Lee quickly fell into difficulty and was arrested and charged with "stealing the clothing money off his men, then in his hands." Lee seems to have escaped punishment by resigning his commission in August 1861.[5] He then returned to Atlanta, where he constructed an entirely different personal image and attracted the attention of the bellicose *Intelligencer,* which was always glad to enthuse over the return of a warrior. Under the headline, "Capt. G. W. Lee," the newspaper commented on the pleasure of shaking hands with "the above named gallant Georgian," ventured the unwitting observation that Lee had "made considerable reputation during his service," and added the extraordinarily erroneous report that Lee was "a great favorite" of General Bragg. The gallant Lee was home on furlough, the paper reported, and would be happy to take letters and packages back to the troops serving in Pensacola.[6]

By the autumn of 1861, Lee was more or less permanently ensconced in Atlanta and resumed his military career as the elected lieutenant colonel of another unit. It was from this base that he would emerge as a colonel in charge of the military post in the city. By the spring of 1862, Lee had assembled a large group of men who served under him. Although the unit operated within the geographical command of Braxton Bragg, it did so independently of Bragg's oversight, and George Lee thus succeeded in keeping out of the way of his old commander. Bragg seemed powerless to thwart Lee, but he complained bitterly to General Johnston about the man who ran the Atlanta military post. "By misrepresentation and downright falsehood, and by evading and misconstruing orders," Bragg wrote, "he has raised a force of nearly 500 men in Atlanta, more than half conscripts, [and] 'home guards.'" The Confederate general fumed over Lee's handling of the military apparatus of the city. "The state of affairs at Atlanta is disgraceful," Bragg wrote to Johnston in a letter full of complaints. Prisoners were "confined for months" without being charged. Lee had employees, "by the dozen, able-bodied and without occupation." And there were "expenditures most lavish." These matters did not offend Bragg half as much, however, as the galling, seemingly inalterable decision by Richmond to leave Lee free of Bragg's command and to continue the assignment of Bragg's wounded and sick to Lee when they were in the military hospitals of the city. "I am compelled to leave this man in command of 2,000 sick men of my army," Bragg raged, "and intrust their lives, funds and safety to him."[7]

Some in Atlanta agreed with Bragg's assessment of Lee, but they seemed less exercised over behavior than breeding. Thomas S. Garner recalled after the war that "There was a second class set of cow bred Confederate officers" in Atlanta who were extremely hostile to Unionists, possibly a reference to Lee and his associates. G. G. Hull asked a military friend in mid-1863 to have Lee removed from command in Atlanta. "Although a very clever man," he wrote, Lee should not continue in authority. "Unfortunately," Hull sniffed, the colonel could not, "on account of his social position, command public confidence and respect, sufficiently to insure the enrollment of the better portion of the citizens."[8]

But Lee commanded five hundred men and the warm admiration of the *Atlanta Intelligencer.* When it appeared that Lee would be transferred from the city (probably at Bragg's urging) in June 1862, the *Intelligencer* lamented his impending departure and heaped praise upon him for his "energy, firmness and spirit" in restoring the city to "quiet, peace, and security." The newspaper also hinted that Lee had been especially effective in controlling disloyalists. No transfer materialized, however, and the wily Lee stayed on in Atlanta, where he frustrated Braxton Bragg, consolidated power, and became provost marshal of the city, with sweeping authority to maintain order.[9]

In August 1862, Bragg countered with a declaration that Atlanta would henceforth be under martial law. The order, initially welcomed in the city, likely stemmed as much from Bragg's frustrations with Lee as from his desire to protect the city's strategic assets, maintain order among troops in transit, and deal with civil disorder. Martial law lasted only a month, however, as a dispute quickly arose between Bragg and local authorities, who were confused by the general's appointment of Mayor James M. Calhoun as "civil governor." The locals appealed to Alexander Stephens, who, along with Governor Brown and Robert Toombs, succeeded in having martial law lifted. Martial law could have made a great deal of difference to Lee if he had come under Bragg's direct command, but once again he survived intact and independent.[10]

AT ABOUT THE SAME TIME, Lee decided to move against the Unionists and deal decisively with the secret enemies and traitors within the city. Given the mood of Atlanta—its concerns over disorder, its apprehension about spies, and the continuing nervousness about security that was brought on by Andrews's raid—Lee's timing was superb and clearly calculated to strengthen his position with an increasingly uneasy population. Since the opening of the war, Unionists had been constantly watched by the authorities and by other Atlantans. Persistent shadowing, observation, verbal abuse, social ostracism, and the continuing, general threat that Unionists should be hanged or banished exacted a severe psychological toll. In addition, of course, there had been the occasional beatings and forced departures from Atlanta. Now, however, George Lee and his associates embarked upon a concerted policy of intimidation and retribution against the Atlanta Unionists. The decision to attack the Unionist problem opened what Amherst Stone referred to as a "perfect reign of terror."[11]

Some men who held official or semiofficial positions seemed to take special pleasure in sniffing out disloyal persons. Oliver H. Jones, who owned a livery stable and may have briefly served as provost marshal, won a special reputation for his diligent pursuit of Unionists and was known for being "Among the most notorious of persecutors of Union men." Jones also took on a responsibility to keep an eye on Union women, and he trailed female Unionists around Atlanta. In addition, he appeared to enjoy harassing Prince Ponder, the slave-businessman with close ties to the Unionists.[12]

E. T. Hunnicutt, an Atlanta merchant, a first lieutenant in George Lee's battalion, and, for a time, supervisor of Atlanta jails, had specific responsibility for being sure the Unionists were watched. Hunnicutt himself was responsible for keeping an eye on a dozen or so suspected disloyalists, including Alfred Austell, E. W. Munday, Thomas Crussell, James Dunning, John Dohme, Holmes Sells, and Julius Hayden. Lee issued broad general orders to Hunnicutt and his men, directing them to shadow the Unionists and "arrest them if they did anything to be arrested for."[13]

By early August, George Lee seemed almost frantic. An attempt to burn a munitions laboratory in Atlanta caused him particular concern. Fires had been set around the building, and only through the alertness of his men, Lee declared, had disaster been averted. He sought help from Richmond, asking permission to raise more troops, and in correspondence with the secretary of war, he pronounced the Atlanta post to be the most important under the supervision of the secretary. It took all his vigilance, Lee asserted, to oversee a city that experienced twenty-fours hours a day a "moving mass of people passing and repassing in every direction." He worried especially about the "Yankees and foreign population," who were, in Lee's view, the most dangerous enemies "because, like the assassin they strike in the dark." Since the beginning of the "revolution," Atlanta had been particularly afflicted with such "debris." The city was, he said, "a point of rendezvous for traitors-Swindlers-extortioners-and counterfeiters" and had a dangerous population of "Jews, New England Yankees, and refugees shirking military duties." But he reassured Richmond that he was up to the task and promised that he would "untiringly . . . watch direct and consign to suitable punishment these miscreants."[14]

Lee kept his word. He soon decided to strike at the heart of the "Union Circle," an organization, he described as "extremely pernicious in its views and considered of a dangerous character."[15] Suddenly, without warning on a Thursday in late August, Lee and his men arrested at least eight, and as many as twelve, prominent Unionists. In the secretive fashion common to newspaper coverage of such matters, the *Southern Confederacy* initially reported only that "five men and three women—residents of this city— all of Northern birth and of suspected Northern proclivities, were arrested by the Provost Marshal on suspicion of being dangerously unfriendly to us." An item the same day in the second edition of the newspaper, perhaps added just before publication, reported that the arrests were "quite numerous— something over a dozen persons having been taken into custody." Typically, the newspaper would "give no particulars," and offered the opinion that "everything connected with the affair is very properly withheld from the public."[16] Because of the silence of the newspapers and because huge caches of Confederate records were later lost or destroyed, it has been difficult to determine the details of this episode, even the identity of those arrested.

Nevertheless, by drawing upon long unexamined documentary sources and by carefully scrutinizing *Goldie's Inheritance,* a fairly complete version of this story can be reconstructed. A total of six men and three women were arrested in the sweep through the city. Among the men was James Dunning, who believed his adamant refusal to operate his foundry and machine shop in support of the war effort accounted for his arrest. Various Confederate officials had "importuned" Dunning to produce shot and shell for the army, but he held to his refusal and thus incurred the enmity of the officials and the wrath of those Atlanta citizens who despised the crusty, outspoken Dunning for his repeated professions of loyalty to the Union. On the day of his arrest, Dunning had once again refused orders from the local ordnance chief, Moses H. Wright, to convert the foundry to munitions production. Taken to the same Fulton County Jail that still housed some of Andrews's raiders, Dunning discovered that the Fourth of July celebration he and his family had enjoyed with the Martin Hinton family on Stone Mountain was also cited, along with a general allegation of disloyalty, as a cause for his arrest.[17]

Dr. Anderson L. Scott, who had taken a leading role in helping the imprisoned Andrews's raiders, also was arrested. Scott had become the object of a great deal of calumny in Atlanta and was attacked for his Unionism by locals who reviled him as "the little Yankee Scott, who calls himself an M.D." The Harvard-educated Scott attributed his arrest to the aid that he had given Union prisoners and to his repeated contacts with Samuel B. Houts, the Missouri surgeon assigned to the federal prisoners. Scott was arrested by the sheriff of Fulton County, Thomas Shivers, and by Captain J. W. Conway, whom Scott described as a "detective." According to Scott, the officers took him to George Lee's headquarters, and Lee ordered him taken to the "barracks," where he was "placed in a room with all the rebel 'rough-scuff,' the dirtiest, filthiest set I ever saw." Later, some of George Lee's men went to Scott's office, broke into his trunks, examined his personal papers, and "destroyed many of them, and left the contents of the trunks lying promiscuously around."[18] The details relating to the charges against three more of the men are sketchy. Alexander N. Wilson, the schoolmaster and close friend of Amherst Stone, was also among those taken to jail. Wilson had become one of the most visible Unionists in the city, and he and his wife appear to have been deeply involved in providing aid to Union prisoners. Another man arrested was William B. Manning, a blacksmith who had only recently emigrated to Atlanta from New Jersey. The fifth man was James Sturges, an Atlanta resident about whom almost nothing is known except that he was an acquaintance of Samuel P. Richards, the English-born bookseller who had moved to Atlanta in 1861, and was a member of the same volunteer fire company as Amherst Stone.[19]

The sixth man arrested was Michael Myers, the wealthy Irish immigrant and dry goods merchant. Myers had been involved in Unionist activity from the beginning and had contributed significant sums of money for the relief of Union prisoners. Earlier in 1862, he had been publicly attacked for disloyalty, in particular for having refused to accept Confederate money in the dry goods store that he owned in partnership with John Ryan. Like James A. Stewart, Josiah Peterson, and others, the thirty-nine year-old Myers felt compelled to make a public statement that seemed to confirm his loyalty to the Confederacy, denying an allegation that he had refused to take Confederate money. To reinforce the image of loyalty he wanted to project, Myers declared that he owned ten thousand dollars in "Treasury Notes" (presumably Confederate but not explicitly stated as such) and that his only brother was a Confederate officer. In the ambiguous language often used by the Unionists, Myers declared that "Everything dear to me, and all I have or own are in and of the Confederate States."[20]

The public confession did Myers no good, for he remained under suspicion, and Lee had him arrested. Then, on the day after his arrest, Atlantans learned that the well-off merchant had died while in custody. Arrested, "on suspicion of belonging to a Union organization in this city," Myers had been "severely attacked at the Barracks, where he was under guard," the *Southern Confederacy* reported. Colonel Lee ordered that the critically injured man be taken to a nearby hospital, where two local physicians "did all in their power to save his life." According to the newspaper, Lee then "allowed" Myers's friends to take him home, where he died after suffering convulsions and paralysis, "which caused an eruption of the blood vessels in the brain."[21]

The newspaper's account did not stand the test of time. The next day's edition reported that a postmortem examination of Myers revealed that there was indeed "an extensive fracture of the skull," but the newspaper now speculated that there had been no attack by the guards. "Convulsions" came upon Myers, causing him to hit "his head against the wall." Within a few more days, the newspaper published the results of an autopsy, allegedly carried out by three physicians. No external evidence of violence existed, the doctors reported, "save some tumefaction over the region of the fracture." A blood clot had been discovered on the right side of the brain, "and extensive effusion of blood," as well as lacerations of the brain on the left side, directly opposite the fracture." After careful consideration of the injury, the physicians concluded that Myers's death resulted from "a fall upon the floor of the room in which he was confined." Moreover, the three "deem[ed] it proper, furthermore, to state, that we believe the casualty resulted from the peculiar condition of his system at the time, consequent upon his habits, and was not at all attributable to the carelessness or negligence, on the part of any one."[22] In other words, the physicians concluded (perhaps with the encouragement of George Lee) that Myers was drunk.

Not everyone agreed. A friend of Myers, Joseph Harford, wrote to the *Intelligencer* commenting on the circumstances of the incident, defending Myers's loyalty to the Confederacy, and calling for an investigation. The paper printed the defense of loyalty but refused to print Harford's comments concerning the circumstances of Myers's death. After the postmortem, the newspaper noted, there could be no further doubt. Moreover, there would be no additional journalistic commentary until authorized "by *all parties* concerned."[23]

Harford continued to agitate, however, and within a few weeks, Lee arrested and jailed him. While in jail (and probably with the aid of someone on the outside), Harford wrote to Jefferson Davis, complaining of his arrest and of the attempt to cover up Myers's death. When he wrote to Davis, Harford had been jailed for five weeks without being charged. Although told that he had been arrested for violation of the liquor laws, he believed his confinement resulted from his call for an investigation into Myers's death. Harford did manage to contact an attorney, who advised him that there was no legal basis for his retention and that George Lee's only authority was "at the point of the bayonets placed at his command." Harford believed that Myers had been arrested less for his Unionist activities than as a result of "private enmity" on the part of a vengeful provost marshal.[24]

Davis's staff sent the letter on to G. W. Randolph, the Confederate secretary of war. Almost immediately, Randolph asked for an explanation from Lee. Lee claimed that Harford was a chronic bad character and had been arrested for violating liquor laws. Not only had he sold bad liquor to soldiers, Lee said, he had also sold it to slaves and was always engaged in illicit sales of whiskey in the train station. Just recently, Lee boasted, one of the "lynx-eyed guard[s]" under his command had "detect[ed] such villainy."

As for Myers, Lee declared that his arrest stemmed only from membership in the "Union Circle" and from suspicion of possessing counterfeit Confederate notes. Myers, "a decided victim of inebriety," had been "scarcely ever sober, and had been drinking very hard for months before he was taken up in the excitement of drinking." What had caused his death? Lee stated that "A fear of the probable consequences of his misdemeanors produced drunken fits, in one of which he fell, and being a large & heavy man, and his head coming in direct contact with the floor of the room in which [he] was at the time confined, produced a fracture of the skull of which he died soon after." Lee had "immediately ordered an investigation," and the committee of surgeons had reached their conclusion. As for Harford's complaint to Davis, Lee believed that it was the work of a lawyer. Randolph apparently accepted Lee's account of Myers's death, but the Unionists in Atlanta did not, and for decades thereafter pointed to Michael Myers as the martyred victim of a brutish George W. Lee, who was bent on finishing off a relatively defenseless victim who had been hounded for months.[25]

Certainly Lee's explanation was lame, but it seems at least conceivable that Myers may have become obstreperous and that Lee's overzealous teenaged guards administered the fatal beating, primed by months of anti-Unionist propaganda, filled with an easily acquired hatred for the Yankees in Atlanta, and confident there would be no retribution from their commander.

THE STORY OF THE ARREST of the three women is even more difficult to piece together, but there is evidence to suggest that they were Mary

Summerlin, the widowed seamstress who is the character Mrs. Waincloss in *Goldie's Inheritance,* Mary Hinton, and Cyrena Stone. In the novel, Mrs. Waincloss is betrayed by a "pretended helper," threatened with arrest "toward the end of August [1862]," and then arrested two days later. Mrs. Waincloss fears being imprisoned or hanged, and, in a passage from the novel almost certainly based upon a missing portion of Cyrena Stone's diary, her terrified child cries out, "O Mamma, will they hurt you, Will they hang you?"[26]

Mary Hinton had moved from Montgomery, Alabama, to Atlanta in May 1861 with her two younger sisters; her mother; and her brother, Martin Hinton. From the beginning, the Unionist family endured more than its share of abuse from Confederate officials, who constantly pressured Martin Hinton to join the Confederate army. Like James Dunning, Hinton wore his Unionism on his sleeve and left no doubt with Confederate officials about where his loyalty lay. On one occasion, according to his sister, Hinton declared that he would rather be blown to atoms before serving against his country, and on another he proclaimed that he "would have his arm torn from its socket, before he would raise his arm against his country."

Hinton's temerity had few bounds, and when he declared publicly that "a just God would rain down a shower of fire upon the Confederacy," Confederate officials "seemed never to get over" Hinton's remark. Hinton despised the Confederacy and resisted attempts to coerce him into Confederate service with a resolve that drew on his contempt for the seceded states and their officials. "He hates well," Mary Hinton later recalled. "He would have given his life to injure that cause. He was a mule all over, and would have died—been chopped into mince meat before he would have ever surrendered to them, and aided them."[27]

But with the passage of the conscription laws, evasion of service became much more difficult, and Martin Hinton began to move around. Finally, in May 1862, he left his photographic business in the hands of an employee and went into hiding in Rome, Georgia. Planning to escape from the Confederacy, Hinton got word to his sister that he needed money. Mary Hinton went from Atlanta to Rome and took funds to Hinton, knowing that if her brother returned to Atlanta, he faced sure arrest. Mary did not know, however, that she was being shadowed by a Confederate detective. Shortly after she left Rome to return to Atlanta, the detective recruited a volunteer to aid him in arresting Hinton, who must have been forewarned, because he left Rome in a buggy apparently bound for Memphis, Tennessee. "In hot haste" the detective and his companion followed and captured Hinton ten miles outside Rome.[28] The detective brought Hinton back to Atlanta "hand-cuffed, chained down, and accused of being a spy." The *Rome Southerner* reported that Hinton was in fact an agent and that he had informed Union general Don Carlos Buell of the movements of Braxton Bragg's army. The detective predicted that Hinton's guilt would be established "beyond a doubt." Hinton, the *Intelligencer* noted, would be tried by the military courts.[29]

Confined in a jail in central Atlanta, Hinton was in constant danger of being taken out and hanged. His frightened family lived nearby and feared constantly for his life. "If we heard any noise we would rush out at night to the gate, thinking that the mob had taken him," Mary Hinton recalled. "We could hear the noises. They made threats to hang him, and they did so with others. We didn't know when they might hang him." The Hinton women were terrified, especially Martin Hinton's mother and his two younger sisters. "You can never guess how much we suffered," Mary Hinton recalled. "From the beginning to the end we had no peace," she added. "We would hear a noise and spring up startled as if called from sleep by bells announcing our doom." The pressures from the community became so intense that the Hinton women moved around the city furtively. "I got like a shadow," Mary Hinton recalled.

At the same time, they decided to do what they could to lessen the danger for Martin Hinton. "We all tried to take upon ourselves suspicion and relieve our brother. We knew they would not hang us, but our brother was liable to be hung or shot any hour. He was in imminent danger all the time." The decision to take risks that could have imperiled their own lives, despite the belief that they would not be hanged, may not have seemed wise from hindsight, because Mary Hinton was herself arrested and taken before courts-martial three times. Her two younger sisters (the elder was sixteen) also were arrested and had to appear before the military courts as well. "My sisters cried and were terrified," Mary Hinton recalled: "I was a little defiant."

Mary Hinton's defiance could be seen in her recollection of appearing before the military court:

I was examined under oath, in regard to contributions to those poor half naked, diseased starving Federal prisoners. I was being examined as a prisoner, but under oath. There were thirteen Confederate officers who formed the court martial. The examination was taken down in writing. I can only remember to give an outline. They asked me if I knew of contributions to the Union prisoners of clothing, provisions and money. I told them I did. They asked if I gave it all myself. I said a good deal. They wanted to know if other parties gave me money for them. I told them that was information they could not drag from me. They asked me if I knew the penalty. I said that they could imprison or blow me to pieces but they could not compel my lips to betray a trust.

It would be fruitless for them to bring her before the court again, Mary Hinton concluded, because she would "do the same thing again if opportunity offered." When told that her property would be confiscated if she did not cooperate, she replied that that could only be a temporary measure, implying that once Union victory had been secured, the property would be returned. After her first arrest, Mary Hinton was never formally released and was arrested at least twice more during the course of the war. Whether she or the other arrested women were actually imprisoned is unknown.[30]

Rumors ran through Atlanta, however, that there were women who had been arrested and imprisoned, including the fictional Cyrena Stone, whose fate, according to "wild reports in circulation," was either imprisonment or hanging. The exact nature of Cyrena's detention is unknown. About a year later, Amherst Stone stated that his wife had been arrested for Unionist activities and sentiments, but the fictional Cyrena Stone was only summoned as a witness to appear in a "grand investigation" into the rumored existence of a Union organization of three hundred men and of "a plot for the negroes to rise, the prisoners to emerge from their confinement, and all to unite in a rebellion against the Southern Confederacy."[31]

Once again the novel *Goldie's Inheritance* provides a credible explanation for events in Civil War Atlanta, particularly those that affected the Stones and other Atlanta Unionists. The prospects for an organized revolt of slaves and Union prisoners led by white Unionist men would have been believable to Confederate Atlantans already frightened about the direction of the war and well conditioned to believe in plots, intrigue, and slave revolts. The portion of the "grand investigation" involving the fictional Cyrena took place in an Atlanta hotel and corroborates much of what Mary Hinton related about her arrests. Cyrena was summoned by a "very polite note" from the provost marshal (perhaps written by George Lee's amanuensis), saying that she was under suspicion.

"I suppose," Cyrena told an advisor, probably Amherst, "I shall be obliged to tell everything that I have done or thought in opposition to the 'holy cause.'"

"No, you need not tell anything. They have really no right, moral or legal, to arraign you," he replied.

The two were frightened, and Cyrena "felt almost as if her hour had come." When they arrived at the hotel, several women sat in the parlor awaiting the call to appear before the military tribunal, among them probably the Hinton sisters. One young woman, perhaps one of the Hintons, reached out and took Cyrena's hand and in a tremulous voice asked plaintively, "What is all this for? What do they want of me?"

Amherst sought to reassure Cyrena, but both he and she would have been anxious about the proceedings. Cyrena was the first to be summoned from the parlor and, accompanied by Amherst, followed a soldier to an upstairs room where the military court was in session. The hotel room—furnished with a washstand, a few chairs, and two, high-posted, cheaply clad beds—seemed to the fictional Cyrena to be an unlikely place for a military court to convene. But there was a curious compatibility between the room and the officers of the court. Cyrena's reaction to George Lee, who presided, recalled Braxton Bragg's assessment. "Colonel L. the Provost Marshal, seemed illiterate and uncommanding in appearance," the fictional Cyrena observed. On one side of Lee was "a tall man in a coarse suit with small pinched-up eyes, and with hatred of the Yankees written on every feature." On the other was a youth, perhaps one of the unemployed teenagers who constituted much of the provost guard, "trying to put on manly dignity by cultivating a moustache—a 'blessed scattered hair or two' giving evidence of his success." Several other men crowded into the room, among them a reporter from one of the newspapers. They all stood when Cyrena entered.

Then an embarrassment occurred; no Bible could be found for swearing. When one did arrive, Cyrena refused to swear, citing scripture that forbade oathtaking. The men in the room stared at her in disbelief. Amherst interceded: "She will affirm," he said. By this time, Cyrena had lost her fear: "The room was so unlike the typical courtroom, and the court so lacking in real dignity, that fear vanished, and a sense of the ludicrous took its place." In the novel, her answers to the court's questions verged on nonchalance.

"Will you tell the truth?" asked one of the "dignataries."

"I usually try to," Cyrena answered.

"You affirm that you will tell the truth, the whole truth and nothing but the truth—" said the colonel adding the usual ending of an
oath.

"She neither lifted her hand nor bowed her head, and the investigation, upon which the destiny of a nation seemed to depend, proceeded. Colonel L—— and the man in gray whispered some time,
then the latter asked,"

"[Mrs. Stone], do you know of any Union organization existing
in this city?"

"I do not."

(Whispering again.)

"Do you know of any meetings being held in this city calculated
to work against the Southern Confederacy?"

"I do not, sir."

(More whispering.)

"Have you heard of any secret Union meetings being held here?"

"Before the war began, I heard of many being held publicly—I have
heard of none since then."

"Have you ever heard any one say anything against the South?"

"No." She thought she could put her own interpretation on that
word "against."

More questions followed from Colonel Lee's "medium," and then
there were some from "a man of some sixteen summers who stood leaning against the bed in an artistic attitude." He closely quizzed Cyrena about
her fictional friend, Mrs. Waincloss (in real life, Mary Summerlin), in whom
the sixteen-year-old inquisitor took special interest, asking whether Cyrena
considered her to be a poor woman, whether she was "supported by any
society or association," and whether Cyrena herself helped to support
her. Later, it would become evident that Confederate authorities strongly
suspected the real-life Mary Summerlin of espionage. After those questions,
the court suddenly dismissed Cyrena. She and Amherst returned to the
parlor of the hotel, where Cyrena tried to cheer the other women waiting
to be called by telling them about her refusal to take the oath.[32]

If the version in *Goldie's Inheritance* is correct, Cyrena Stone's treatment at the hands of the court of inquiry appears to have been more benign
than that accorded Mary Hinton. Hinton described aggressive, probing questioning about Unionist activities, whereas the questions put to Cyrena were
more deferential. The court badly frightened Mary Hinton and her sisters,

but Cyrena Stone found Colonel Lee and his court of inquiry to be almost ludicrous, emboldening her in her refusal to take the oath and in her answers to the questions put to her.

Both accounts may have been accurate. Mary Hinton and her sisters did not have the same social standing as Cyrena. Despite his Unionist identification, Amherst Stone remained an important and powerful man in Atlanta. George Lee would have been careful around the Stones, if only because of Stone's connections to the social and business elite of the city. Mary Hinton, on the other hand, had just moved to Atlanta, and as a young, single woman she had few ties of substance that might afford protection from the peril posed by the court. In addition, she had the added burden of being Martin Hinton's sister, and Hinton, one of the "vilest" of the Yankees in Atlanta, was now formally charged with being a spy. Both women had ample supplies of courage, and as events would show, Cyrena Stone could not be easily intimidated and was quite capable of acting courageously in difficult, threatening situations. Mary Hinton remained technically under arrest for the remainder of the war, but it appears that Cyrena Stone and Mary Summerlin received "paroles" of a sort and returned to life as usual in wartime Atlanta—and to their Unionist activities.

MEANWHILE, SIX UNIONIST men (Dunning, Wilson, Manning, Sturges, Scott, and Hinton) remained in jail. After Michael Myers's death, Anderson Scott reported that "communication was sent to the mayor remonstrating against our being kept in such a filthy place." Mayor Calhoun promptly went to the barracks and arranged for the prisoners to be moved to better quarters and away from the rabble Scott had earlier described.[33] Nathaniel J. Hammond, a well-known Atlanta lawyer, was hired to prosecute five of the men (Dunning, Wilson, Manning, Sturges, and Scott) for disloyalty. In addition, Hammond resisted the discharge of Dr. Scott on habeas corpus, claiming that Scott had tried to bribe him "not to appear against him."[34] Trials may have been held for Dunning, Wilson, Manning, and Sturges, but without the prisoners being present. James Dunning said that during his imprisonment he was told that there had been a trial in his case. If so, he said, it was ex parte, for he was "neither present in person or by counsel," and did not have "any notice that a trial was proceeding." Moreover, Dunning claimed that he had never received notice of any specific charges.[35] No evidence survives concerning the nature of these trials or how they were conducted. Hammond said that he spent a total of about four days in preparation and in court, so it seems likely that all five were tried as a group in absentia before a military court constituted by George W. Lee. The legal outcome of the proceedings is also unknown, but within a few weeks some of the men had been released. James Dunning stated that he stayed in jail for a period of only two to three weeks, although later accounts would relate that he had spent most of the remainder of the war in prison.[36]

Anderson Scott remained in prison longer than the other five and was formally charged before a military court with being disloyal and with giving aid and comfort to the enemy. The specific charges against Scott claimed that he had belonged to a secret Union organization in Atlanta "called the Circle, whose professed intention was to give aid and comfort to the enemy." Scott's alleged anti-Confederate remarks in the wake of the Union victory at Fort Donelson were cited as evidence of his treason along with allegations that he had collected money for the Union prisoners, provided them with clothing, and secretly carried "letters of importance" to them.

Scott's trial opened at ten in the morning on November 17, 1862. The accused traitor was represented by a local attorney, Amos Hammond, who immediately moved to dismiss the charges for want of jurisdiction. The judge advocate "demurred" and asked Hammond and Scott to leave the room while he conferred with the other members of the court. A few hours passed. The court then ordered Scott and his attorney to return the next morning to resume the trial. At seven o'clock that night, however, Scott was suddenly released from prison by an order from "the commandant of the post." Years later, when asked to explain why he had suddenly been released, Scott said that he owed his good fortune to the fact that two members of the court and the post commandant were fellow lodge members in the Independent Order of Odd Fellows. As extraordinary as this explanation may have been, it could well have been accurate given the bizarre and very often personal nature of relations between Unionists and Confederates in Civil War Atlanta and given the high importance attached by mid-nineteenth-century American males to the mysteries and fraternal bonds that characterized such lodges.[37]

Meanwhile, Martin Hinton remained in prison awaiting trial for espionage. The incarceration was apparently arduous for Hinton; his sister would later claim that the trauma had turned the twenty-seven-year-old man's hair white. Hinton was also freed in November. The order for his court-martial had been issued at Knoxville, Tennessee, and called for trials of Hinton and any others who might be brought before the court on treason charges. The military tribunal, unlike the one that interrogated the fictional Cyrena Stone, was made up of regular Confederate officers. Hinton was acquitted of espionage and set free—but put on parole, confined to the states of Georgia and Alabama, and required to report to either George Lee or his counterpart in Mobile, where Hinton had business interests.[38]

Several possible explanations exist for the release of the Unionists. One is that the military courts found all of them innocent, an unlikely outcome because James Dunning later said that he was never told what brought about his release. Another is that the entire campaign of terror and intimidation started by George Lee had begun to spin out of control with the death of Michael Myers. The apparent murder, together with the subsequent imprisonments, interrogations, and trials may have aroused powerful members of the Atlanta community with ties to the Unionists to pressure Lee to bring the matter to a close. Or, it may be that Lee's incompetence and the inept conduct of the military inquiries, as described by Cyrena Stone, may have ended the entire affair.

IT WAS MUCH MORE DIFFICULT to enforce loyalty in Atlanta than the Confederates or George Lee imagined. There is also some evidence that the government at Richmond intervened (perhaps at the behest of powerful Atlantans) and ordered the release of the Unionists. Lee himself blamed Richmond for the failure of the purge. Some further indication, albeit minor, of the difficulty Lee had in managing the process came to light when he and N. J. Hammond fell into a dispute over how much Hammond should be paid for his legal services, Lee claiming that he could get no answer from Confederate authorities concerning Hammond's bill, while at the same time telling Secretary of War James Seddon that he considered the amount excessive.[39]

Mayor Calhoun's visit to the jail to arrange for more comfortable quarters for the Unionist prisoners, the deferential attitude of the military court toward Cyrena, and the concern among upper-class Atlantans about too much power resting in the hands of George Lee and his army of the youthful unemployed collectively suggest that class differences and solidarity played a significant role in the affair. From presecession days through the first two years of the war, it was evident that the Unionists, particularly the affluent ones, retained ties with the Atlanta elite, many of whom were doubtful about secession and harbored serious concerns about the Confederate enterprise throughout the war. Mayor Calhoun was only one— but an important example—of those who remained friendly with Unionists, and he may have been instrumental in preventing the arrest of leading Unionists such as William Markham, Nedom Angier, and Julius Hayden. The mayor would have had little interest in George Lee's type of law and order (and probably not much interest in social contact either) given the multifaceted conflict over whether Atlanta would be a city under martial law. On the other hand, the *Intelligencer* liked Lee and supported him, but exactly who was in charge of the newspaper during this period is unclear. Jared Whitaker, the owner and publisher, was away from the city on military assignment. It is abundantly clear that we do not have the full story of this "reign of terror" in Atlanta and likely never will have, but we should not be tempted from hindsight to minimize the seriousness of the episode because it resulted in only one death. Amherst Stone's characterization of the period as a "perfect reign of terror" may be simple exaggeration when compared to other terrible events, particularly in revolutionary settings. But for the Atlanta Unionists, 1862 was filled with constant threats of disaster and death and with quiet, yet frantic, efforts to work with moderates such as James Calhoun to thwart the ambitious George Lee and his troop of postadolescent enforcers of law and order in chaotic Atlanta.

Whichever explanation comes closest to the mark, the murder, arrests, and trials clearly served to intimidate and frighten the Unionists and not only those arrested. Within the next few months, several of those who had been imprisoned escaped from Georgia or had put escape plans into operation. In addition, other Unionists also searched for ways out of the Confederacy, seeking relief from the heightened pressure against loyalists and from the relentless pursuit of conscript officers.

Thus, by early 1863 the Unionist circle in Atlanta would begin to shrink, as key members of the group departed and others kept more and more to themselves. The "reign of terror" that George W. Lee began no doubt provided the catalyst for some of the departures and also gave impetus to the plans of others who were looking for ways safely to escape the South and preserve as much of their wealth as possible. Amherst Stone was among those.

CHAPTER SIX

Amherst Stone's Mission

In October 1862, the Confederate Congress extended the age limits of the previous spring's conscription legislation to include all males up to age forty-five. Exempted under the earlier act, Amherst Stone, thirty-six years old, stood more vulnerable than ever to service in the Confederate cause. Fearful of this prospect and shaken by the "reign of terror" unleashed against the Union loyalists in Atlanta, he wrestled with the dilemma of remaining in Atlanta (with the threat of impressment into Confederate service) and the prospect of departure with all that it meant: leaving his wife, leaving his wealth, and making what could be a danger-fraught escape from the South.[1]

Sometime in the autumn of 1862, spurred on by the threat of arrest for disloyalty and the virtual certainty of conscription, Stone made up his mind to leave. He thought carefully, worked quietly, and quickly devised a plan that would enable him to leave the city without appearing to escape. Once safely away from Atlanta, he would then try to make his way out of the Confederacy to a safe haven in the North.

STONE'S REASONS for leaving centered on his fear of conscription into the Confederate forces, but he had other motives as well. One was to find a way for Cyrena and possibly a "servant" or two to leave the region. (Stone would later say that removing his family had been his main objective.) Although it was possible for men to leave the South, it was much more difficult for them to escape with families. It was also quite difficult to take wealth out of the region. Stone decided that as a part of *his* escape, however, he would try and salvage his considerable personal wealth, and, in the bargain, make whatever profit he could.

By late 1862, Stone had discreetly converted much of his wealth into cotton. Like many others in the South and North, he had believed that the war would not last long and that by acquiring cotton at a time when the international prices of the commodity were escalating, he would be advantageously positioned, perhaps even wealthy, when the war did end. The lengthening war and the threat of conscription made it much more urgent for Stone to find a means to get himself and his cotton out of the South, but he had to do so in a way that would arouse as little suspicion as possible in Atlanta. Stone was an intelligent, creative businessman, and in his mind he turned over all the options he could think of, weighing the personal and financial risks, knowing that danger and perhaps death awaited those who sought to make their escapes through hostile territory. Then Stone learned that substantial amounts of cotton were being shipped out of Union-occupied New Orleans and sent to the North with the permission of General Benjamin Butler, who had been in command of the city since late April. Stone hastily conveyed this information, which came to him by way of a Tennessee businessman with interests in Georgia, to several of the leading Unionists, including William Markham and John Lynch. The Tennessean had said that the U.S. government wanted to get all the cotton out of the South that it could. He was right; President Lincoln and others in the executive branch strongly favored the idea of Southern cotton being brought out of the Confederacy. "Upon this information," Stone wrote, "a company was gotten up in Atlanta. I had some cotton; Mr. Markham had considerable cotton; the Lynches and other parties had some cotton."

When Stone used the word *company,* he meant, of course, *blockade* company. "Almost everybody [in Atlanta] who had any money was anxious to go into a blockade company," Stone wrote. "We wanted to get what money we could; it was pretty hard to convert confederate money into something we could use." By running the Union blockade, Southerners hoped to get goods out (usually cotton) and to take those goods to a neutral port where they could be sold for cash or traded for other products that would then be brought back to the South through the blockade. Besides offering a prospect of conserving wealth, blockade running also held the lure of vast profits, and it was widely believed that great fortunes could be made in this hazardous game.[2]

Stone planned that his blockade company would be decidedly different from others. The Wyly-Markham Company, as it was to be called, would secretly seek permission from the U.S. government to bring cotton out of the South and to sell it in a Northern port. Stone would also ask for a guarantee that if the cotton were seized by U.S. vessels it would be returned to him and the other Unionists who were members of the company and party to the plan. "Every Union man felt a deep anxiety to get out something . . . so as to have something left when the war closed. We were satisfied that the war would be a failure to the South and that everything we had there would be used up, and it was thought if we could get out cotton through the arrangement proposed we might save something," Stone said.

Membership in blockade companies not only gave the Unionists some prospect of preserving wealth; it also provided a measure of protective coloration to those Confederates suspected of disloyalty. It was ludicrous to believe, of course, that a blockade company could be made up only of Atlanta Union men. So the newly formed company (which carried Markham's name because he was among the wealthiest Atlantans and despite his not purchasing shares) also included a number of loyal Confederates, although a majority of stock was owned by Unionists. The Confederate members of the company were not to be told of the proposed arrangement with the U.S. government; neither were they to be told that the company did not contemplate returning any other commodities to the South. "There were some men who subscribed something who did not know this fact," Stone said. "We would not let them know it. . . . We were afraid of them. They belonged to the rebel side and I have no doubt they thought it was a regular blockade company."

Funds realized from the sale of the cotton would be converted to silver or gold and deposited safely in Northern banks. The Unionist members of the company agreed that if permission of the U.S. government could not be obtained, then the effort would be aborted. The stockholders chose Stone to be the treasurer and agent of the company, and William C. Lawshe, an Atlanta merchant, became the president. Lawshe, strongly pro-Confederate, evidently had no inkling that he was a member of a Unionist-led and -controlled blockade company.[3]

Neither did Atlanta bookseller Samuel P. Richards, who planned to buy stock. British born and only lately moved from Macon to Atlanta, Richards displayed Unionist leanings during the secession crisis but with the coming of war became staunchly pro-Confederate. The bookseller learned that Stone was the agent of "a company of our citizens who have *formed* [Richards's emphasis] for the purpose of running the blockade at Charleston with Cotton and mdze." "We have some idea of risking a thousand or two in it," Richards confided to his diary late in March 1863.[4]

To increase the company's chances of succeeding, Stone began thinking in other directions. The Davis government had discussed the possibility of seizing all cotton held privately in the Confederacy, and that sent a ripple of fear through the considerable ranks of Southerners who had put their money in the commodity. And when the belief spread that the Confederate Congress would pass a bill to that effect, Stone decided to seek the permission of the *Confederate* government as well as the U.S. government to take the cotton out of the country. "I conceived the idea," he said, "thinking that the Govt. could not with any show of consistency seize cotton it had granted permission to ship." Stone then called for help from Benjamin H. Hill, a prewar Unionist, a personal friend, and a Confederate senator from Georgia. Hill secured the desired permission from the Confederate government for Stone, but only after representing that the company would ship its cotton to a neutral port and then return goods to the Confederacy.[5]

The groundwork had now all been laid. When the sale of shares in the company brought in a large sum of money, Stone began to seek a vessel to take the cotton out. In the search for a ship, he looked to the port of Charleston, South Carolina, and negotiated an arrangement with, H. L. P. McCormick, owner of the *General Clinch*. McCormick's boat was an ancient steam-powered vessel built in 1839 that had participated in the events leading to the occupation of Fort Moultrie in December 1860, when Major Robert Anderson abandoned it and moved his men to Fort Sumter. Since the beginning of the war the *General Clinch,* with its two brass guns, had performed various duties in and around Charleston Harbor and become what one scholar has called the "handy man" of the harbor.[6]

The *General Clinch* was under contract to the Confederate government for approximately $7,500 per month, so Stone likely offered the owner much more. Little is known about the final phase of the negotiation between Stone and McCormick, but the Atlanta lawyer turned blockade runner was sufficiently encouraged to ask the Confederate government to release the *General Clinch* for participation in the blockade-running scheme. On January 31, 1863, and on a number of other occasions, Stone tried to convince Confederate military authorities to release the vessel from service and allow him to run the blockade with it—but to no avail.[7]

Stone gave up on the *General Clinch,* which continued to putter around in Charleston Harbor. He then shifted his thinking about his quest for a vessel. Instead of hiring a ship in the South, he concluded that he would hire a Northern vessel. With permissions to run the blockade from both the U.S. and the Confederate governments, the chances for success would be greatly enhanced, and the venture would be as secure as possible in the risky blockade-running business. At least that is how Stone would have presented his plan to the Unionist investors in the company. As he later recalled the chain of events, the investors looked to him, because of his connections in the North, to go there and undertake both the political errand of securing permission from the U.S. government and the commercial task of finding a Northern vessel that could come to the South and take out the company's cotton. Thus, the stockholders laid out Amherst Stone's mission and simultaneously provided him the opportunity to make his escape from the region and the conscript officers.

Stone agreed to go, but he waited until winter had passed before leaving Atlanta. In the meantime, because he planned not to return to the city while the war lasted, he did what he could to bring his legal practice to a close without arousing too much suspicion. He also continued quietly to convert real estate into convertible securities or cotton in an effort to take as much of his wealth out of the South as he could but also to leave enough behind to provide for Cyrena, who would have to remain in Atlanta for the foreseeable future. In addition, he tended to the business of the blockade company, working surreptitiously with Markham, John Lynch, and the other Unionists in the company to complete the plan for effecting an arrangement with the U.S. government while simultaneously acting out a charade with William Lawshe, the company's president, and the other Confederate members of the group, who expected him to locate a vessel and make the necessary commercial arrangements to sell the cotton in a neutral port and return goods to the South and great profits to the investors.[8]

By late March, warm weather had arrived in Atlanta, and Stone prepared to leave the city. He made no effort to conceal his departure; it was common knowledge that he was leaving in connection with the business of the Wyly-Markham Company. Stone's Unionist reputation appears not to have impeded his plan, perhaps because it was widely assumed that he was trustworthy in financial matters and that he would return to the South because his wife, his brother, and the other members of the household remained in the city. Samuel Richards, the bookseller and diarist, betrayed no concern about Stone's motives and, in fact, asked him to take a letter to his brother who was living in New York. "As Col. Stone of our city is expecting to go North this week I have just finished a letter to Add. [Addison] to send by him to Yankee Land," the bookseller wrote. On April 4, Richards noted in his diary that he had written the letter and it was on its way "*if* Colonel Stone went as expected."[9]

HE HAD GONE. Amherst Stone left Atlanta on April 3 and began what had been for many a dangerous journey from the Deep South to the North. Little is known about the details of his journey. He later would refer to it as having been hazardous, and undoubtedly it was, especially given the circumstances surrounding his trip and the fact that he was carrying with him a very large amount of currency, bank drafts, and negotiable bonds. The exact amount of money that had been subscribed is not certain, but it was likely about $100,000 in a mixture of instruments drawn on Northern banks and probably including some Confederate currency as well. Before leaving Atlanta, Stone and members of the company had decided that it would be inadvisable for one man to try and get through the lines carrying all of the funds of the company. In effect, the group took out an insurance policy against the prospect that one man might not get through or, conceivably, that he might decide to abscond with the money that had been raised. Consequently, the group had selected a young man, George Briggs, who would take half the money out by a different route than the one Stone was taking. The plan called for the two to meet in New York City and for Briggs to turn over all of the money to Stone, who would then make the necessary financial arrangements.

George Briggs has simply disappeared from the historical record. Briggs appears neither in the 1860 census of Georgia nor in the *Atlanta City Directory* for 1859 nor in any of the primary records that are the foundation of this book. There is, however, evidence to suggest that William Markham distrusted Briggs and that Markham cited Briggs's involvement for his decision not to invest funds in the blockade company.[10] However that may be, the two men left Atlanta on different routes to the North in early April. Stone went first to Richmond, likely to confer with Ben Hill about the permission from the Confederate government to take out the cotton. Leaving Richmond, he picked his way through the Confederate and Union lines lying between that city and Washington, D.C. He traveled under his own name, rode a stage when he could, and walked when he couldn't.

Perhaps he traveled at night as the novel *Goldie's Inheritance* suggests. He crossed the Rappahannock River about fifteen miles below Fredericksburg and the Potomac about one hundred miles below Washington. From that point, he rode both stage and "private conveyance" to Washington, passing through the Union lines without incident, likely being quizzed by the federal authorities who permitted him to spend the night in a Washington hotel before reporting to the Union provost marshal the next morning, where his identity and story were verified and he was allowed to go free.[11] Stone registered at the hotel and gave his residence as Vermont, relieved to be safely out of the Confederate States and undoubtedly anxious not to call unnecessary attention to the fact that he was from Georgia. He remained in Washington only briefly, inquiring about possible meetings with federal officials before going on to New York and Vermont. He was anxious to see his parents (both of whom were still living) and other members of the family who lived in and around East Berkshire.

Stone stopped over in New York and checked in at the St. Nicholas Hotel, which would be his headquarters during various stays in the city over the next several years. Second only to the Astor among New York hotels, the St. Nicholas reposed grandly on a corner of Spring Street in the middle of the theater district and attracted a wide range of prominent guests, many of them politicians and expatriate Southerners. Built in 1854, the opulent hotel stood six stories high, with more than six hundred rooms, impressive chandeliers, candelabra, and mirrors. The St. Nicholas had three hundred employees, three dining rooms, and a huge lobby, sixty feet wide and two hundred feet long, fitted with a massive oak staircase situated in the middle. Stone would have paid a hefty tariff at the St. Nicholas, but he likely could have afforded it because he had made it through the lines with the money he was carrying and had deposited $50,000, it appears, in a New York bank.[12]

While in New York, Stone made the political rounds and forged business connections. In addition, he paid visits to Cyrena's brother and sister, Keyes and Mary Bailey, and called on personal friends. Although it is pure speculation, he may have sought out his cousin, Chester Arthur, then serving in the Union army and headquartered in New York. Or he may have called upon Henry Raymond, editor of the *New York Times* and a Republican politician with close ties to Abraham Lincoln. Raymond had ties to Vermont and may have known Stone in his youth.

Stone stayed in New York for a week and then left for Vermont and a ten-day visit with his family. Nearly two years had passed since he had seen any of his Vermont relatives, and because of the difficulty in getting mail to and from the North, little communication passed between them. Until he arrived in East Berkshire, he may not have known that a younger brother, Charles Birney Stone, had enlisted in the Union army the year before and recently had been captured in fighting around Dranesville, Virginia. Briefly imprisoned in Richmond, Charles Stone had been exchanged the same day Amherst left Atlanta.[13]

Stone continued to tend to business while in Vermont, sending telegrams and letters to parties in Boston and New York, working out arrangements for getting a steamer to run the blockade. Apparently close to a deal, he left East Berkshire for New York to arrange the final details. Retracing the route he and Cyrena had taken from East Berkshire two years earlier, he went to St. Albans on the first leg of his journey. But by the time he arrived in the handsome village near the Canadian border, Stone's activities had aroused the suspicions of Rolla Gleason, the Union provost marshal in Burlington, twenty miles south of St. Albans on the banks of Lake Champlain. Gleason had learned of Stone's telegrams to New York and Boston from Stone's old enemy, William Clapp, by then the director of the customs house in Burlington and eager to tell the story of Stone's "treason" on the stage from East Berkshire in 1861. Some evidence suggests that Clapp was in league with Aldis O. Brainerd, the St. Albans merchant who suspected Stone of disloyalty in 1861. In later years, Brainerd claimed that he had intercepted Stone's correspondence concerning the blockade-running scheme and played a part in alerting the authorities. It is also possible that Stone may have repeated his performance of two years earlier when he had bragged to Clapp's nephew about the Confederate victory at Manassas, for it was alleged now that he had "indulged in conversation of a disloyal character—rejoicing at our defeats & rebel successes." At the very least, Stone had displayed remarkably poor judgment in sending telegrams related to his prospective blockade running, a recklessness that contrasted greatly with his careful behavior in Atlanta throughout the war years. When Stone went to Vermont both in 1861 and 1863, it appears that he underwent a transformation from a man of prudence into a careless braggart.

It cost him. While in St. Albans, Amherst Stone was arrested by Rolla Gleason and charged with being a rebel emissary and smuggler. A surprised, chagrined Stone readily admitted that he had planned to run the blockade, expecting perhaps that Gleason would be sympathetic to his mission and the complex Unionist scheme. Decidedly unsympathetic, Gleason turned

Stone over to a deputy provost marshal from New York, who had been look-ing for Stone in connection with the funds he had deposited in New York city—reported by Rolla Gleason to be $50,000.[14]

Stone was arrested scarcely a month after he had left Atlanta and less than three weeks after he had safely crossed the Confederate lines into Union territory. The *Burlington Free Press* gleefully reported the arrest of "A secessionist named Stone," who, the paper admitted, was a "Vermonter by birth" but who had two years before in Franklin County "provoked loyal men greatly by his outspoken treason." Avoiding arrest and imprisonment in Atlanta and successfully fleeing the South may have made Stone over-confident and indiscreet. Now, he found himself horribly embarrassed and ignominiously transported across Lake Champlain and down through New York State to Fort Lafayette, a federal military prison located in the New York Harbor. Stunned, shocked, perhaps even bewildered, Amherst Stone was in an exceedingly dangerous position, having been charged with being an agent of the Confederate government at a time when the writ of habeas corpus had been suspended.[15]

Fort Lafayette squatted on a small island in the narrows between Staten Island and Long Island, only several hundred yards from the shore of the latter. A relatively small octagonal fort, with walls 50 feet long and an inte-rior space of about 120 feet across, the fort had been used since early in the war primarily to house Northern political prisoners accused of disloyalty to the Union.[16] Accustomed to comfort, Stone would have been completely unprepared for prison life and for the conditions at Fort Lafayette—which although stark, crowded, tense, and filthy—were still vastly superior to conditions in the hellhole prisons of the North and the South. Crews of blockade-running ships also took up involuntary residence in Fort Lafayette, as did a few prisoners of war, some of whom were of high rank. In all, about 120 men were confined in the fort. One prisoner reported that, "a gloomier-looking place than Fort Lafayette, both within and without" would have been hard to find anywhere. Stone was held with several dozen other pris-oners in a dank, poorly lit casemate about fourteen feet long and twenty-four feet wide, with a vaulted ceiling reaching eight feet at its highest point. Only tiny slivers of light entered the cell from three small loopholes, each ten inches wide. The prisoners had beds, but conditions were so crowded that there was no room between them.[17] There were four casemates. Among the prisoners in "Number Three" were at least eight Confederate officers, including Brigadier General W. H. F. "Rooney" Lee, the son of Robert E. Lee.

Undoubtedly to his horror, Amherst Stone became a cellmate of the son of the great Confederate general and the other Confederate officers in "Number Three." To his undoubted credit, he proved eminently adaptable and led a double life in the prison, never arousing suspicion among the Confederates of his Unionist leanings while, at the same time, insinuating his way into their group by portraying himself as a Southerner victimized by Yankees.

Rooney Lee and the other Confederate officers had begun a prison news sheet that they secretly passed among the Southern prisoners in Fort Lafayette and hid in ratholes or coal buckets when guards conducted their periodic searches of the cells. Published immediately after the war in book form as *"Fort-La-Fayette Life," 1863–64 in extracts from the "Right Flanker," a manuscript sheet circulating among the southern prisoners in Fort-Lafayette, in 1863–64,* the eighty-page document began with an introduction of the members of the circle who inhabited "Number Three."[18] Among the half-dozen prisoners profiled was Amherst Stone. The contents of his profile reveal how he introduced himself to his fellow prisoners:

> Another case of Yankee victimizing is in a Georgian, to whom a New Yorker by adoption, but Yankee by birth, having held the position of a confidential friend in the South, and came from there with him, was intrusted with the care of a considerable amount of money. After reaching New York, the result was, that not only did the Yankee practice the 'cute trick' (it is not usual to use a harsher term in Yankeedom in respect of operations of this kind) of holding on to all the money, but reporting that it was intended for purchasing contraband of war, had him, who had often befriended him in Georgia, locked up here.[19]

Obviously, Stone had told his cellmates that George Briggs, the other Atlantan sent north by the blockade company, had stolen the funds of the company and caused Stone's arrest and imprisonment. The traitorous Briggs had, according to Stone, robbed him of $30,000 in state bank notes, bonds, and drafts as well as a draft on a Chicago bank for $4,000, which he had entrusted to him to bring through the lines. Briggs had then forged Stone's endorsement and reported to Union authorities that Stone was "an agent of the rebel government," thus bringing about his arrest. Briggs had then left for Canada.[20]

Stone remained in "Number Three" for a little more than a month. He immediately began an effort to win release, but since basic civil rights had been suspended for prisoners such as himself, he was prohibited from seeking the help of an attorney, a fact he doubtlessly learned soon after arrival.[21] Continuing to walk a tightrope stretched between professions of loyalty made to his Union captors and the acute discomfiture brought on by living in a cell full of rebel officers, Stone decided to write secretly to Edwin M. Stanton, the secretary of war, asking for help. So far as can be determined, Stone wrote to Stanton without any prior connection with the Department of War, although there is the possibility that he may have had contact with officials of the department when he had visited Washington earlier. He gave the secretary the full details of his predicament.

Stone told everything about the plan to bring cotton out of the South and the idea to seek Union approval for its removal. After insisting upon his patriotism and asserting his lawyerly belief that the American system would allow him to petition Stanton, he complained that throughout the months of his confinement at the fort, he had not been informed of precisely why he had been arrested. Stone then reviewed his past in detail, beginning with his birth in Vermont and proceeding through his decision to move to Georgia in 1848. He related how, when the war broke out, he had been unable to sell his property "without immense loss" and declared that he felt a "duty to my family to take such course as would secure to them the earnings of years." To have left the South at that time, would have been to "sacrifice it all," he told Stanton. Stone also forthrightly declared that he had "some servants I would not sell & could not bring them away." In the end he had concluded to stay in the South if he could avoid military service. For two years he had done so and had "anxiously looked for relief" from the Union army. "I had hoped and [had] hope defered," Stone wrote. "I had suffered some pecuniarily & much mentally in consequence of my love for the Union as it was & as I hope to see it again." Stone then referred to Cyrena and her situation in Atlanta:

My wife an enthusiastic Union woman, sick at heart, separated from the friends of her early years & her relations with few around to sympathize with her and discouraged in hope of relief, freedom & protection under the flag she loves, begged me to take some measures to get her North. I felt that her health & safety required it & I tried to get permission for her & our servant to come by Truce Boats from City Point, but was informed that it was not permitted without permission from your Honor.

Stone recounted the details of the blockade-running plan, including the involvement of Benjamin Hill, and he assured Stanton that the group had no desire to return goods to the South. He concluded the lengthy letter with an appeal for release. Acknowledging that he understood the need for summary arrest during wartime, Stone nevertheless concluded with a strong argument for due process.

> I only complain that I have not been permitted a hearing in the manner guaranteed to all citizens under the Constitution & laws. I love the Great Charter of our liberties. I love its proud banner. It would rejoice my heart to see it again float from every Dome the length & breadth of the land. I have never in thought word or deed forfeited my right to its protection. I now claim it. As my right I demand it.[22]

Soon after sending the letter to Stanton, Stone was transferred from Fort Lafayette to the prison at Fort Warren in Boston Harbor and remained there for about a month. Then, on about July 12, Philip B. Marsh, an employee of provost marshal Simeon Draper of New York, arrived at Fort Warren. Before the war, Marsh had been a traveling salesman and had frequently done business in Atlanta and had gotten to know some of the city's businessmen. Whether he and Stone knew each other before the war is unknown, but the two clearly had become acquainted—or reacquainted— in recent weeks. General John Wool, commander of the Department of the East of the U.S. Army, had sent Marsh to Fort Warren with an order to transport Stone to New York for an appearance before Wool at the St. Nicholas Hotel. From what transpired later, it is evident that Marsh engineered the order himself and that Stone bribed Marsh to secure his release.

On July 14, in the midst of the bloody New York draft riots of 1863, Stone appeared before the aging general at the St. Nicholas. Four days later, Wool ordered him released on parole with the provision that he not leave New York. Wool also directed that Simeon Draper deliver to Marsh "the package of money belonging to A. Stone" that had been confiscated at the time of Stone's arrest. The busy old general later divulged that he relied entirely upon Marsh's recommendation in releasing Stone and that he had never personally examined the documents in Stone's case. Wool later claimed that Stone paid Marsh $2,000 to obtain his release "by false representations." Another Union general thought the bribe amounted to only $300 and a gold watch. Whatever the amount involved, a liberated Stone was soon back in the comfortable surroundings of the St. Nicholas and apparently once again in possession of the money he had brought with him from Atlanta, minus, of course, the amount of the bribe paid to Philip Marsh.[23]

SOON STONE WAS ABLE to evade the provisions of his parole and won permission to leave New York. He went to Washington, D.C., staying there for a few weeks. The permission to leave New York may have been obtained through the influence of L. C. Turner, the judge advocate in the War Department with whom Stone had become acquainted when Turner visited Fort Lafayette to interrogate Stone and other prisoners in the fort. Although he recommended against Stone's release at that time, the two exchanged letters several times over the next few months. While in Washington, Stone claimed to have visited Abraham Lincoln and Edwin Stanton, apparently seeking permission to pass through the lines and return to Georgia. Why Stone might have wished to return is something of a mystery. He told Turner that he intended to "return to my family . . . & then for my wife & two servants to come North."[24] If Stone had returned to Atlanta, he would have, at the very least, made himself susceptible to the draft. Equally as important, he would have had to explain both to Unionist and Confederate stockholders in the blockade company what had happened to the funds they had sent north. Although it is only speculation, it is entirely possible that, after his release, Stone may have succeeded in making the necessary arrangements to run the blockade and that he was returning in order to put the scheme into operation and to bring Cyrena out as part of the bargain.

While there is no corroborating evidence to suggest that the audacious Stone made contact with either the president or the secretary of war, he did see L. C. Turner, who evidently offered a permit for Stone to return to the South. Meanwhile, Stone returned to New York and the St. Nicholas and wrote to Turner on August 24, thanking him for his efforts on his behalf and enclosing a letter to Cyrena, which he asked the judge advocate to forward through the lines to Atlanta. Stone said he was reluctant to make the request, "yet I know you can appreciate the anxiety of a wife to hear of her absent husband separated by what at present appears an impassable gulf." Stone reinforced his request for a pass by declaring that he could "accumulate testimony mountains high" of his loyalty. "And," Stone went on, "I cannot see why I might not be permitted to return to my family. Here I can do no good. There I might relieve the suffering of some poor Union prisoner, as I have heretofor done—and administer some comfort to my family." A week later, with no answer from Turner, an anxious Stone wrote again. This time he said that he had received word from someone in Atlanta that Cyrena was "sick & distressed on account of my absence." If Turner would "aid me in getting to her," Stone continued, he "will have the enduring gratitude of a good Union woman." No matter what, Stone concluded, he could not "remain away from my family much longer."[25]

Stone received his pass. On September 12, Turner wrote to Major General William S. Rosecrans giving permission for Stone to traverse the lines and return to the South. The same day, he sent Stone an apology for the delay, noting that he had been away from Washington for two weeks.[26] A grateful Stone quickly responded, offering the hope that when the war concluded the two men might meet and "congratulate each other on the result." However, Stone included more than thanks in the letter. "I am in receipt of information from Atlanta & Dixie generally up to the 4th September," he told Turner, from "a reliable gentlemen" who had left the South to avoid conscription. The information concerned Confederate military movements. Stone asked that Turner "in no event" connect his name to the intelligence. Stone's source informed him that

> the forces of the Confederacy are being massed under Jo Johnston at and about Dalton Georgia, 38 miles below Chattanooga, with a view of "wiping Rosecrans out." That all the militia of Ga. have been sent to that point & that many reinforcements are being forwarded from all parts of the Confederacy to that point.
>
> This gentlemen came via Richmond & on his way met three Divisions of Lees Army under Longstreet, Hood & Ewell on the way to reinforce Jo Johnston in Ga. That the impression South was that Charleston would soon be given up & Beauregard with his forces would also move toward Dalton. That forces from all parts of the Confederacy are moving in that direction. That it is understood that the great struggle for supremacy is to take place at that point & if possible Rosecrans is to be annihilated.

Stone repeated the plea that he not be connected with the intelligence and included the hope that it would be "of some interest & possibly advantage to the Govt."[27] Turner later declared that Stone's information "proved valuable and reliable."[28]

Stone soon left for Nashville, apparently intending to return to Atlanta. When he arrived in Tennessee, he went to the headquarters of General Rosecrans, identified himself, and presented his pass. Then or slightly later, Stone learned that his name was on a list of Atlanta Union men who had been identified by Rosecrans's commanders in preparation for a possible campaign against the city. Still later, while he was preparing to go through the lines, Stone claimed to have received a letter from Cyrena warning him against returning to Atlanta "as there was much indignation against me there in consequence of my Union Sentiment and that I would be immediately forced into the rebel service." That information, Stone recalled, "detered me from going through the lines and in the month of November I returned to the City of New York and stopped at the St. Nicholas Hotel."[29]

Once again comfortably ensconced at the St. Nicholas, Stone said that he spent the next two or three months preparing to go into business, a reference perhaps to the blockading scheme or to his intention to begin the practice of law in New York.[30] As the winter wore on, the preparations had nearly been completed, when on January 30 he was suddenly arrested again and returned to Fort Lafayette, where he was reimprisoned—this time in cell number two. Word of Stone's return to the fort circulated among the prison population and was duly noted by the authors of the "Right Flanker": "The addition to our neighbours in No. 2 is a young Georgia gentleman, who was paroled here some months since, and brought back under the late retaliatory order from Washington."[31] In fact, Stone appears to have been returned to Fort Lafayette as a result of his bribing Philip Marsh and the energetic vendetta of his old Vermont enemy, William Clapp, the customs collector in Burlington. Rolla Gleason, the man who had arrested Stone in May, had complained in early September of Stone's release and of the return of his funds. Gleason alleged that he had further information against Stone from Clapp and reason to believe that Stone's release resulted from "collusion between Stone & subordinate officers of Govt in N.Y." Gleason urged the rearrest of Stone, the reseizure of his funds, and a full investigation of the case.[32]

Gleason and Clapp's complaints reached General John Dix, then commanding the Department of the East. About the time that Stone returned to New York, Dix wrote to L. C. Turner asking for details of Turner's involvement in securing permission for Stone to return south. Turner replied that he had had no involvement other than carrying out the order of the secretary of war that Stone be permitted to return. Turner implied that Stone had presented petitions to Lincoln and Stanton and that these had resulted in the permission, a statement at some variance from his earlier remarks to Stone.[33]

Meanwhile, Amherst Stone languished once again in Fort Lafayette. Back in Atlanta, Cyrena learned somehow that Amherst had again been arrested, and in cryptic entries to her diary referred to his imprisonment and to the grim prison walls she saw in her mind's eye when she thought of her husband and his detention.[34] During this imprisonment, Stone had more difficulty getting the attention of military or civilian authorities concerning his predicament. Throughout February and March 1864, he seems not to have been able to establish contact with anyone in power who could help him. In fact, when a military commission arrived at the fort sometime in March to investigate the cases of various prisoners, Stone's luck took a turn for the worse, the commission recommending that he be "turned over for indictment and trial by civil authorities," on charges of disloyalty and blockade running. One official in the judge advocate general's office commented that "a more aggravated case of violation of the laws of war . . . has not been presented to this office." Nothing came of the recommendation for indictment, however, and Stone remained in jail, still charged with no crime. Meanwhile, Philip Marsh had also become a prisoner in Fort Lafayette, arrested by General Dix "in consequence of disclosures" made in Stone's examination, a reference to Marsh having taken a bribe from Stone for gaining his release in 1863 from General John Wool.[35]

In late April 1864, Stone appealed for help to Charles A. Dana, the assistant secretary of war. Dana, the second in command in the War Department, would have been a logical person with whom to lodge such an appeal because he was in charge of the day-to-day affairs of the department while his chief, Edwin Stanton, busied himself with the management of the war effort. Dana had already been informed of Stone's imprisonment (possibly by L. C. Turner), and he asked for the papers in the case from Colonel Martin Burke, commander of Fort Lafayette. Burke sent the documents he had, but none went to the substance of the charges against Stone or the details leading to his arrest. Burke, who had formed a positive opinion of Stone the prisoner, told him that Dana had made the inquiry. Stone immediately wrote to Dana with a resume of his case, charging that the government had "inadvisedly [been] made the instrument to gratify the pique of a personal enemy of mine." Stone told Dana that he had unsuccessfully sought permission to make his case before General Dix and that he had "suffered arrest at the South on account of my love for the Union & relief furnished Union prisoners," either an exaggeration on Stone's part or possible confirmation that he was among those arrested in Atlanta during George W. Lee's "reign of terror."[36]

Something in Stone's letter or someone interceding on his behalf moved Charles Dana to take an active interest in the case of this Vermonter-turned-Southerner now imprisoned in a federal military prison, and a few days after Stone had written to him, Dana requested the papers in the case from General Dix and asked why Stone was being held.[37] Dana had a demanding job, however, and his interest appears to have waned for a time. Meanwhile, Stone remained in Fort Lafayette prison through the spring and into the summer. By late June 1864, having heard nothing more from Dana, Stone decided to write a letter jointly to General Dix and the War Department in Washington. In this letter, Stone revisited the details of his upbringing, his migration to Georgia, his mission to the North during the war, and the facts of his arrests and imprisonments. The letter was an impassioned defense of his loyalty and an equally passionate demand for his release. He included in the letter a signed oath of loyalty to the United States and boldly offered to release the government and its officials from any liability in connection with his "illegal" arrests and imprisonments. "To conclude," Stone said,

> I am in prison with no prospects, except on my own application, for relief. My family in the rebellious States—myself in Fort Layfayette—my property South destroyed by rebel tyranny, and my property North squandered by sharpers—My family destitute there, Myself almost penniless here—I desire as a Citizen of the United States (unconscious of being guilty of any crime against my country) to be free.

Martin Burke subscribed Stone's oath to the loyalty statement and added in his own handwriting and peculiar spelling, "The Prison caharacter of Mr. Stone is excelent."[38]

On July 1, Dix forwarded Stone's letter to the War Department, where it was referred to L. C. Turner for investigation. Turner recapitulated the details of Stone's background and arrests in a report to Edwin Stanton. Turner bluntly criticized Dix for making no recommendation on Stone, and argued that Stone should be tried promptly or released on oath. Apparently the case was referred to yet another military commission for trial, but before the trial could begin, Stone made contact with a lawyer who took his case and pushed for his release.[39]

The lawyer was Benjamin Baily of Putnam County, New York, approximately fifty miles north of New York City. Perhaps a distant relative of Cyrena's, although there is no documentation to prove it, Baily had been prominent in local politics and a member of the New York State Assembly. Now he took on the task of winning Amherst Stone's freedom and traveled to Washington to undertake it. Baily apparently had valuable political connections, and in August 1864 he succeeded in procuring presidential support for his effort to examine War Department documents that related to Stone. "Mr. Lincoln on Tuesday gave me a line to the War Department requesting to see Major Turner's report," Baily told a department official on August 19, probably Charles A. Dana. Baily had already met with the official and insisted that he had "abundant evidence that Mr. Stone is the victim of a wicked conspiracy, and that he is a loyal man."[40]

The next day, August 20, Dana renewed his order to General Dix to forward Stone's file from New York. He also sent Dix a blunt telegram: "Has A. W. Stone been tried? or is he now being tried? or will he soon be tried?" Dix's answer is not known, but Stone's file soon arrived from New York City. On September 12, apparently still dissatisfied with Dix's response, Dana wrote to John Sedgwick, an officer in the Department of the East asking on what charge Stone was being held, but before Sedgwick could reply, Dana wired Dix that Stone could be released from Fort Lafayette on bail. The next day Amherst Stone left Fort Lafayette, free on bail. Once again, he took up residence at the St. Nicholas.[41]

WHY AMHERST STONE was twice arrested and twice imprisoned for lengthy periods cannot be determined with certainty. It is surely true that William Clapp played a prominent role in seeing to it that Amherst's indiscretions were brought to the attention of the federal authorities, who, like their counterparts in the South, feared domestic enemies nearly as much as organized military forces. In this regard, Stone's experience as a prisoner as well as his detention without formal charges or trial resembled that of hundreds, perhaps thousands of civilians, in the North and the South, who were imprisoned during the war with virtually no civil protections and little recourse except to do what they could, by whatever means, to win release from prison.

In the end, the length of Amherst Stone's imprisonment resulted from bureaucratic delays and the press of much more important business in the War Department and in the Department of the East, where officials seemed quite content to see Stone remain in jail and were singularly uninterested in doing anything that would have worked to Stone's advantage. When John Sedgwick finally investigated the case in August 1864, he concluded that "far too much importance" had been attached to it "in consequence of the injudicious conduct of Stone himself & more especially of his agents," a likely reference to Briggs and Marsh. Sedgwick concluded that Stone had stayed in prison long enough and that the only charge that could be made against him that would have a reasonable chance of success in court would be that he had crossed into the North illegally. Because of the "long confinement," however, Sedgwick had recommended to General Dix, several days before Dana's last inquiry, that Stone be freed on bail. Had Stone been convicted, Sedgwick went on, his sentence would likely have been suspended because of the length of his incarceration. "Probably the whole of the case is, that he is a man without strength of principle," Sedgwick concluded. "He has taken the oath of allegiance to the South & would to the North. He has given to Genl Rosecrans in Tenn. important information & would do the same to the South. He only wanted to make as much money as he could."[42] Stone's release infuriated William Clapp, who tried once more to have his adversary arrested, this time writing a long letter to a Union officer in which he recounted his nephew's testimony about Stone's disloyalty. Clapp's letter went unheeded.[43]

Meanwhile, Amherst Stone plunged into the life of a free man with vigor and characteristic cunning, renewing his efforts to meet influential men— and succeeding. Stone attracted the attention and interest, among others, of Henry J. Raymond, editor of the *New York Times* and chairman of the National Union Executive Committee, Abraham Lincoln's 1864 reelection organization. Perhaps they had met years before; Raymond had lived in Vermont and attended the University of Vermont in the 1840s. Stone volunteered to campaign for Lincoln and to speak for Union causes. Raymond had evidently heard him orate and thought him a "good speaker who can aid us essentially." The editor-politician wrote to General Dix, asking that Stone's bail money be returned if there was "no strong reason" for not doing so. "He wants to take the stump for the Union cause," Raymond wrote, "but wants these bonds discharged first."[44]

If Stone campaigned for Lincoln, it is not hard to imagine that in his political rhetoric he would have identified himself as an exiled Southerner who, having escaped from the South and having remained true to the Union, at last had the opportunity to support freely the reelection of the president of the United States and to add his voice publicly to the preservation of the Union and the destruction of the Confederacy. That is how he saw himself in later life and that is how he presented himself to others after the war was over.[45] At bottom, however, Stone's arrests and the treatment of his case resulted from a systemic difference between the Union and the Confederacy when it came to efficiency in such matters. The Confederate apparatus for dealing with disloyalty was decentralized, disconnected, inefficient, and without clear lines of authority. Atlanta under George W. Lee's authority illustrates well the confusion and conflict. The Northern system, however, was comparatively efficient with better communication and clearer lines of authority, though it, like the Southern system, presented ample opportunity for corruption. The offenses that constituted Stone's disloyalty in the North strongly resembled the disloyalty associated with Unionism in Atlanta. Fundamentally, his offense was that he spoke indiscreetly about a Southern victory in the war. From the standpoint of his accusers—his former neighbors in Vermont, the Burlington newspaper, local officials—that was treasonous behavior.[46]

In the popular mind, disloyal speech was equated with treason. If Stone had predicted Union victory in the Gate City, Confederate Atlantans would have reacted similarly. Southerners felt just as strongly that such speech was treasonous. The federal bureaucracy, in keeping with the American legal tradition of rarely charging persons with treason, preferred to allege that Stone was a Confederate agent, a catchall charge that could be used to hold him (and other prisoners like him) for as long as necessary during wartime while his case was investigated. On both Northern and Southern home fronts, citizens deplored disloyalty, repeatedly and resolutely crying out against the traitor and the disloyalist. But in both sections, disloyalty and treason were dealt with mildly when compared to the draconian responses in other civil wars then and now. Perhaps, as the American historian Merle Curti has observed, defeatism and covert treason were "gently dealt with because of [the great] extent [to which they occurred] no less than because of the American tradition of civil liberties."[47]

Amherst Stone likely benefited from widespread doubts about the war among the civilian populations in both the North and the South and also, despite his imprisonment, from the American tradition of civil liberties. In other nations at other times, he would not have had access to the federal bureaucracy that ultimately freed him. More than likely, he would have faced a much longer imprisonment or possibly summary execution. For Amherst Stone, as for other Americans on both home fronts, loyalty could be provisional, adaptable, contingent, and a medium of exchange for survival.

CHAPTER SEVEN

Exit and Espionage

Amherst Stone was not the only Atlantan who sought to escape the city. The "reign of terror" heightened the personal insecurity that most Unionists felt and lessened the likelihood that wealth and property could be made portable and taken out of the South. At the same time it motivated frightened Unionists to seek escape. The weight of Confederate authority; the threat of arrest or conviction; and the difficulty of subjecting small children, women, and the elderly to hazardous flight from the South all worked to deter Unionists from hasty decisions to flee. By early 1864, however, a steady stream of Atlantans fled the city. "Now, to escape is the question," Cyrena Stone wrote in her diary, "with rebels as Unionists. The former rush to Europe from the pleasant land their folly has turned into a Sodom;—they hasten from the flames their own hands have kindled."[1]

Some Unionists and Northerners had left Atlanta even before the war began and had been largely free to take their wealth with them. Others waited, unwilling to divest themselves of their property or to uproot their families, hoping that the war would be brief. Once the sequestration and conscription laws had been enacted, however, it became much more difficult to make the decision to leave the region. In addition, the institution of a passport system and the close surveillance of suspected Unionists made the task of leaving the South even more daunting. Male Unionists who contemplated departure also had to consider whether to go alone and leave families behind, for it was virtually impossible to straightforwardly convert property to negotiable instruments *and* take family out.

THESE WERE ALWAYS terrible decisions for the Unionist families to face. Principle and loyalty to the Union influenced the outcome, but so did the dread of forced service in the Confederate army. Most powerfully, perhaps, men and women had to consider the consequences for family members who stayed behind and who could easily become victims of another wave of terror or casualties of a closer war. Fundamentally, they had to decide if conscription and death were so likely for the men that the only chance to preserve a family would be for the men to flee, in the hope that the war might end quickly and all could then be reunited. In the end, it was mainly the men who sought to escape—singly, in pairs, or in small groups—although an occasional family left, but only after the most careful planning.

Even those who left early in the war had to take great risks in order to pass through or around the Confederate lines. Daniel Chaffee, a forty-six-year-old furniture dealer and native of Pennsylvania had lived in the South for at least twenty-five years but decided to leave in the late spring of 1861 after the battle of Pensacola. Chaffee, who was single, made his way to Nashville mostly on foot and went on to Indiana and finally to New York City by mule wagon and stage. Once in New York, Chaffee worked in the furniture business and ultimately found part-time employment as a "general agent," a sort of domestic spy, for General John A. Dix.[2] Other Atlantans who sought to escape were not so fortunate. William Ray, a painter and friend of Unionist Thomas G. W. Crussell, tried to get out sometime in early 1861 by passing through the mountains of north Georgia and east Tennessee. By that time, the treacherous mountains brimmed with guerrillas and bushwhackers who preyed on travelers and refugees. Ray was robbed, shot, and killed.[3]

Crussell himself wanted to leave Atlanta and devised an elaborate ruse in order to escape. In the late summer of 1861, the contractor-builder began to lay plans to raise a company of sappers and miners and take them to Skidaway Island near Savannah, from which he would then escape to the Union fleet that lay offshore. The company of sappers and miners was to assist in the building of fortifications around Savannah but would not actually be mustered into Confederate service. The need to build defenses promised reasonable wages and offered workmen an opportunity to avoid service as foot soldiers.[4]

Crussell needed help in carrying out the plan, and he began to cast about among Atlanta Unionists for men who would help him raise the company, participate in the escape, and keep secret the escape plan from the workmen who would constitute the company. Such secrecy was necessary in order to avoid arousing suspicion among Confederate officials. Crussell approached C. T. C. Deake, an Atlanta schoolmaster and native of New York, whose school was near a site where Crussell was building a house. Neither man knew the other well, and they assessed each other warily. Over several months, as the two got to know each other better, their confidence grew. Initially, the men engaged in small talk. Then, when conversation inevitably drifted to the topic of the war, they spoke tentatively. Next, as a cautious signal to each other, the two men agreed that the war would be "a serious matter, that it was not a sixty day matter as [was] first supposed—and the result would be that every one, within military age— between 20 and 45, would have to go into the military service." The mutual acknowledgment that the war would be protracted then led them to admit that each would like to have a "soft place" that would enable them to escape the dangers of infantry service. Perhaps, Crussell ventured to Deake, there could also be a way to make some money out of the war through the raising of the company of sappers and miners. Finally, after three or four months the two men developed enough confidence in each other to confess that neither really wanted a "soft place," or had moneymaking as their primary object, but that they wanted first and foremost, "to get through the lines and get out of the fight."

The two then began to plan a way in which they could raise the company of sappers and miners and decided that they would have to take in another partner with good connections to the local mechanics who would make up the company. Deake approached a neighbor of his, a carpenter named Grady, but in conversation with him became dubious about where his loyalties lay. Meanwhile, Crussell had conversations with Dr. Holmes Sells, a dentist of Unionist loyalties, and told Deake that they should include him in the plan. The three would then "make a tool of this man Grady, to help raise the company because he knows the Mechanics better than we do."

The next night the three men met secretly in the counting room of David Young's drugstore. After Crussell had assured Deake that Sells could be trusted, they decided to proceed with the plan. The recruitment of mechanics did not go as smoothly as they had hoped, but within a few weeks twenty men had agreed to join the company. All were impatient to be out of Atlanta, fearing that by remaining in the city they would soon be coerced into joining state troops. As a result, Crussell left Atlanta with the twenty, heading for Savannah and Skidaway Island. A few days later, Deake and Sells followed with another three or four men.

Because the group was too small to constitute a military company, the colonel commanding the post on Skidaway refused to receive them. Overnight, however, Sells arranged with the colonel for the men to be taken on as civilian laborers at forty dollars a month each, with Crussell and Deake serving as foremen. Sells became frightened, however, and returned to Atlanta. Deake, Crussell, and Crussell's father-in-law, Frank Rice, remained on Skidaway. It soon became apparent that escape was going to be much more difficult than they had imagined. "It is a damned sight tighter here than I thought it was," Crussell reported to Deake and told his associate that the Union fleet was farther out than he had thought earlier. Moreover, nearly all boats along the shore had been taken up by the Confederate forces to Savannah, presumably to discourage escape attempts.[5]

Meanwhile, Crussell decided to try to make his way to the fleet without Deake and Rice. To do so, he enlisted the aid of Pat Connor, an Irish oysterman from Savannah with connections to Confederate authorities. Connor owned a boat, and the two men took it out to the mouth of Oyster Creek and waited there, planning to escape once the tide was high enough. When the tide rose, they floated down the tributary toward the ocean. All went well at first, but suddenly Confederate soldiers on the shore spotted them and yelled for them to stop. Crussell and Connor kept going, and the troop opened fire. The two evaded the rifle shots and got away, but soon encountered still more soldiers. This time, Connor guided the boat to the shore. Crussell thought surely the Confederates would arrest them, but the troops were led by an officer who had employed Connor and was, according to Crussell, "disarmed entirely of any intention to hurt us or to imprison us" by Connor's jovial banter and Crussell's declaration that the two men had been out oystering. "Well, Captain," Crussell said, "you know me very well; we were loaded with oyster & were doing the best we could to make the Foot." Crussell said that the officer smiled and let the two men go, largely because of his friendship with Connor. Although Crussell made one other attempt to reach the Union fleet, he failed. All the while, he felt that he was closely watched, and soon he was sent back from the shore to Fort Jackson, which lay between Skidaway and Savannah. Within two or three months after leaving Atlanta, Crussell and Deake returned to the city, discouraged and apprehensive about their safety and that of their families.[6]

Martin Hinton also soon departed Atlanta, leaving his mother and sisters and going to Mobile. When he reached Mobile, however, Hinton found that he was persona non grata, forbidden to leave the city or, for that matter, to remain in it. So, he took up residence for a period of seven weeks near Mobile bay in a rowboat with an awning for a roof. Repeatedly arrested and held for periods ranging from a few hours to a few days, the harassed Hinton decided to try to leave the Confederacy. With three companions, he waded through the south Alabama swamps toward the Union-held position at Barancas, Florida, but was captured and returned to Mobile handcuffed, bound, and dragged through the streets "like a dead dog." Imprisoned again for an indeterminate period, the indefatigable Hinton then planned an escape by sea.

Hinton was well off, and he purchased two boats as speculative ventures, planning to leave the country in one of them. Both proved to be too small to navigate the ocean, however, so Hinton sold them and purchased a larger boat, *Wild Pigeon*, with the intention of running cotton through the blockade and going to New York by way of Havana. Captured once again, he was imprisoned for three weeks before bribing Confederate officials for his release. Shortly thereafter, determined as ever, he finally made it out of the Confederacy to New York on the ship *Donegal*, possibly in disguise as a clerk.[7]

Meanwhile, in early 1863 Nedom Angier had also decided that the risks of remaining in Atlanta were too high, and he hatched a complicated scheme to get out. Unlike Hinton, Angier planned to take his entire family out, including his son, Alton, who had entered Confederate service two years before at age seventeen. The family planned that Alton, now discharged from Confederate service, would try to get through to the Union lines in Tennessee and join the family in the North after they had escaped through Florida. In preparation for carrying out the plan the elder Angier decided to go to Washington, D.C., and there make arrangements for his family to get out. He also planned to seek assurances from federal officials that any assets he succeeded in getting out of the Confederacy would not be seized by the government. As a test, he took with him some gold, a gold watch, and "other valuables," including about $30,000 in cash.[8]

Angier went into the North confident in his ability to persuade U.S. officials that he was loyal but also secure in the knowledge that a relative,

L. C. Turner, was an important official in the War Department, where he served as associate judge advocate. Angier was prudent, wealthy, and physically fit, well prepared for a difficult overland trip through the nearby north Georgia mountains, but he decided to travel instead to Memphis, Tennessee, and go from there to Union territory. He had a traveling companion, James P. Hambleton, the physician who had been editor of the *Southern Confederacy* during a controversy over the blacklisting of Northern merchants in 1860 and who had been instrumental in bringing Stephen A. Douglas to the city during the 1860 presidential campaign. Soon after the beginning of the war, Hambleton had joined a Georgia regiment as its surgeon ("from the dictates of humanity *only,* and from the fear of conscription and confiscation," he said) and had remained in service for more than a year, resigning his commission in December 1862. He had joined the Confederate army under duress, he later recalled, and, "Like the majority of those who composed the Rebel army, I was compelled to enter the service or flee the country deprived of all property." Hambleton's health had apparently broken during his service; he suffered from a lung ailment, likely tuberculosis. The journalist-physician would appear to have been a certifiably loyal Confederate, but he wanted to leave, he declared, for his health and also because he had become disaffected and wanted to escape the "excitement, turmoil, and distressing scenes at the South." He also claimed to be on an errand of mercy, taking money to destitute relatives who lived in the Memphis area. His wife and children remained in Atlanta.[9]

The two men left the city in early April 1863. Although Angier apparently had no difficulty crossing the lines, Hambleton was briefly detained in Memphis and took an oath of loyalty to the United States in order to receive a passport allowing him to travel in the North. He had plenty of money, over $11,000 in bills of exchange, but only one-third of the amount that the wealthy Angier carried. The two headed for New York City but took a circuitous route, going from Memphis to Cairo, Illinois, then to Detroit, Michigan, and Albany, New York, before finally arriving in New York City, where they registered at the Metropolitan Hotel.

At the Metropolitan they ran into very bad luck. Hambleton was recognized by Philip Marsh, the detective who had aided Amherst Stone. Marsh and Hambleton, it turned out, had known each other for years. Before the war, Marsh had been a salesman with a New York mercantile firm and probably met the Atlantan on regular visits to the city. Marsh arrested both men, but no specific charges were brought. Such arrests were relatively common in the North as well as the South, vague allegations of disloyalty being all that was necessary for detention. Angier was quickly released because of his kinship with L. C. Turner, or so Hambleton believed. At some point, Marsh demanded a bribe of $300 from Hambleton. Hambleton paid but was nevertheless sent to the U.S. prison at Fort Lafayette in New York Harbor.

Hambleton believed his misfortune stemmed from his role in the blacklisting of "a few malignant abolition merchants of N.Y.," a belief confirmed by Turner and Lafayette C. Baker, chief of the Secret Service.[10] Imprisoned on May 23, Hambleton stayed at Fort Lafayette until June 30, when Turner ordered his release, stating that the government had no case against him. He remained in New York City until September 1, then went to Washington, D.C., having secured a pass from the office of General John A. Dix. Hambleton asked permission from Turner to return to the South and his family. Turner told him that there would be a delay.

In the meantime, Hambleton and a companion traveled to the Eastern Shore of Maryland, perhaps to visit relatives, but also probably seeking to escape to the South with goods illegally acquired in the North. Twice arrested while on this sojourn, Hambleton managed to evade detention and acquired a pass from Secretary of War Edwin Stanton to return to New York, where he was to report to General Dix. Meanwhile, the nefarious Philip Marsh had trailed Hambleton to Washington, hounding him for another $300 and threatening to supply the authorities with information that would result in Hambleton's being returned to prison. Hambleton refused and complained about Marsh to Lafayette Baker, but the secret service chief showed no sympathy and merely confiscated Hambleton's pass. Marsh took his revenge and made good on his threat; James Hambleton was rearrested and confined to the notorious Old Capitol Prison in Washington.[11]

The conditions in Old Capitol were hideous. Hambleton's health worsened, and he plaintively complained to Turner that "every day is a year to me in this prison." He also sought help from President Lincoln, and in a long letter he recounted the details of his experience, protesting the conditions and the governmental bureaucracy that kept him in confinement. "Red tape," as well as "circumlocution and customary ceremonies" accounted in part for his continued confinement. "I have *ever been* and ever expect to be true & loyal to the Government of the U.S.," Hambleton pleaded; "I am forced to die by piecemeal in prison walls."[12]

Kept in the main part of Old Capitol only briefly, Hambleton was transferred to Carroll Prison, the annex of Old Capitol, on October 14, 1863, where he continued his efforts to be released, sending out a freshet of letters that eventually tested the patience of prison authorities, who thought that

Hambleton did little except pester officials about his release. In mid-November, Hambleton wrote to Turner with a sharp complaint about the federal official's failure to keep faith with him. "Why is it *you will not deal candidly with me?*" he wrote. "Why make statements and promises to me you never carry out?" Hambleton also complained about the favorable treatment shown Angier and Amherst Stone. He complained again about Philip Marsh and renewed a complaint to Turner that Lafayette Baker had taken $17,000 in Confederate money from him. Although Baker may have turned the money over to the government, he also had a reputation for venality. It was "the custom" to confiscate such funds, Turner apparently said in response.[13]

Hambleton was willing to try anything that might get him out of Carroll Prison. He would exchange himself for any Northern journalist held in Richmond. He would take part in a planned exchange of surgeons. He would stay in the North if need be and report to a provost marshal twice a day. Or he would post a $50,000 bond to achieve his freedom.[14] By the early spring, Hambleton had won his release, but which stratagem succeeded for him is unknown. He had paid dearly for his sojourn into the North, however, spending nearly a year in close confinement in some of the most unpleasant federal prisons, all the while suffering from his lung ailment and weighing only a little more than one hundred pounds when released. In the end, he was a victim of bureaucratic delay, an unscrupulous federal officer, and his own inability to understand why a former Confederate surgeon and editor of a prosecession newspaper would have been questioned and detained by federal officials.

Nedom Angier had a decidedly better time of it. Once released in New York, he had also gone to Washington, where he established valuable contacts with prominent federal officials, likely as the result of Turner's influence. Angier had audiences with Secretary of State William Seward, Secretary of the Treasury Salmon P. Chase, Secretary of War Edwin Stanton, and Secretary of the Navy Gideon Welles. Like Amherst Stone, Angier owned a large amount of cotton and sought permission from the federal officials to run the blockade and bring the cotton into the North. He also wanted assurance that the property would not be seized once it was on federal soil. Most important, he wanted to bring his entire family out of the Confederacy. None of the four powerful men would give written assurances to Angier, but all agreed that if Angier came to the North with his family and remained there, then his "property would not be violated." Chase suggested that it would be safer if Angier bought a schooner for the trip, but when Angier told him that he could not get Confederate clearance for the purchase, Chase assured the Atlantan that he and his family would be protected if they came out on a blockade runner. With these assurances in hand, Angier prepared to return to Atlanta. He took a truce ship, which Turner had outfitted for the transport of women and children back and forth between the United States and the Confederacy, and he arrived at City Point, Virginia, in the late spring of 1863, intent upon completing the plan to bring both family and wealth out of the South.

Back in Atlanta, Angier quietly set about converting his assets into portable wealth. After he completed the task, he went to Florida on the pretext of going into the salt production business. Before leaving he had arranged with his wife that he would telegraph the family to signal them when to join him. Also before leaving, Angier had discreetly met with Unionist John Erskine, a Newnan, Georgia, lawyer who had moved to Atlanta and who adroitly maintained connections with Confederate military and political figures. Erskine wrote on Angier's behalf to a Confederate general, who issued a pass to the Atlantan enabling him to remain in Florida and making it easier to get space on one of the blockade-running vessels. In addition, Angier took letters of reference from Atlanta mayor James M. Calhoun and Atlanta city clerk Henry C. Holcombe.[15]

When Angier arrived in Florida, he quickly purchased Sea Island cotton and booked passage on a blockade-running steamer leaving from Mayport. He then sent the summoning telegram to his family, doubtlessly with a prearranged message, signaling them to come to Florida. Angier next authorized the loading of his cotton on the steamer, but the family was delayed and did not arrive in Mayport until the steamer had already left—with some of Angier's valuable cotton on board.

After seemingly interminable delays, Angier and the family made another attempt to escape. The Atlantan had heard of a blockade runner located on Black Creek near the Saint John's River, and he arranged to put both cotton and family on the ship for the hazardous trip through the blockade. When the steamer began the journey down the wide river toward the ocean, it almost immediately ran into a much more extensive blockade than anticipated and quickly returned to port. In the confusion that followed, Angier once again lost cotton. The Angiers made a third effort. This time, with the help of a contact made by fellow Unionist William Markham, they found a steamer that made it through the blockade and steamed safely on to Havana. From there, the Angier family went to New York, where they disembarked before proceeding to Massachusetts and refuge.

Soon after arriving in New York City, however, Angier's fears that he might be arrested or his property confiscated were realized. Jailed, though only for one night, he won release "as soon as his character was ascertained." However, $10,000 worth of land warrants that Angier had brought with him were confiscated, despite the assurances that he had received from William Seward and others. In time, the warrants were returned, and in the end Angier apparently lost none of his property to federal confiscation. He commented later, however, that he had lost fully two-thirds of his personal wealth in carrying out the escape, which brought his family and him to safety in the North.[16]

Meanwhile, Angier's nineteen-year-old son, Alton, also made his escape from Atlanta but by a different route. Young Angier had enthusiastically joined the Confederate army in June 1861 and took part in the Laurel Hill disaster with Chester Stone and the other Atlantans. Like the others, Angier received a discharge soon thereafter and began to work on the Western and Atlantic Railroad to avoid being forced back into the army. He continued with the railroad until just after New Year's Day 1864, after which he concocted a pretext and left Atlanta, going by rail to Dalton. From there he struck out across mountainous north Georgia, crossed the Hiawassee River, and entered the Union lines in Tennessee, where he supplied intelligence officers with a valuable description of the fortifications and estimates of the condition of rebel forces around the city.[17]

Alton Angier's escape from the South came after youthful enthusiasm led him into Confederate service. For Marcellus O. Markham, son of the wealthy William Markham, escape from the South would be the only alternative to military service. Two years of avoiding military service with the help of his powerful father worked relatively well, but as hostility toward Unionists increased and manpower demands swelled, Markham became ever more vulnerable to service. Avoiding conscription was difficult, and although young Markham had been declared unfit for service by a Confederate surgeon, he had at one point been "carried off [conscripted] because of his father's loyalty." The elder Markham promptly went to the capital in Richmond and, through the exertions of an officer of the rebel army "who was obligated to him," procured a release of his son. It was then that Markham decided that young Marcellus had to leave the South.[18]

On September 2, 1863, Marcellus Markham stole away from Atlanta, taking an eastern route through the lower South. The seventeen-year-old left well prepared, with a carpetbag full of clothes and plenty of money, at least $15,000 in a mixture of gold, greenbacks, and bank notes, all provided by his father. He went first to Richmond; then to Port Royal on the Rappahannock, where he forded the river; and then on to the Potomac, which he crossed by boat near Mathias Point. From there, he traveled to Leeber in Maryland and on September 11 took the stage from Port Tobacco for Washington, D.C.[19]

While the stage rolled toward Washington, two detectives under the command of the captain and provost marshal of the District of Columbia were on duty in the eastern part of the district, searching for draft evaders and deserters. Edward Shanley and Joseph Scott had been ordered to the Anacostia Bridge to wait for the stage from Port Tobacco, which was lumbering toward them when the two men arrived at the bridge in the early evening. The two officers halted the stage and questioned the passengers. Scott became immediately suspicious of Marcellus Markham.

When the detective asked the young Georgian where he had come from, the frightened Markham lied, but he soon reversed himself and confessed that he was a refugee from Atlanta. Then the two officers ordered Markham and another passenger off the stage, taking both into custody. What was in the carpetbag? the detectives asked Markham. Clothing and money was the answer. What sorts of money? they inquired. Gold, greenbacks, and bank bills was the youth's reply.

All four men then climbed into a carriage and started for the city. Within a matter of minutes, however, the detectives released the other man. The three remaining passengers—Scott, Shanley, and young Markham—went on into Washington. By then it was abundantly clear that the two officers had little interest in Markham as draft evader, deserter, or refugee; they were interested primarily in the contents of his carpetbag. Shanley and Scott took Markham to a "drinking place" near the Capitol, where they urged him to join them in a drink. The youthful Markham refused the drink, but he did smoke a manly cigar. The two officers drank a while and then decided that Shanley would take charge of Markham for the purpose of fleecing him and that Scott would tend to other business.[20]

Shanley then hailed another carriage and drove away with Markham. The detective told young Marcellus that he was in a great deal of trouble indeed, that he would likely "be shut up in prison a long time," and that his money would all be confiscated by the government. Six months could pass, Shanley reported to the fearful youth, before he might be accorded a hearing. On the other hand, the officer ventured, a way out of the dilemma might be found. "You go to the Metropolitan Hotel in the carriage," Shanley said, "and I will get out & go up in the cars, there might be suspicion if I was seen with you as I am a Detective." Shanley then stopped the carriage on Pennsylvania Avenue and told the driver to take his passenger to the Metropolitan.

Markham proceeded dutifully to the hotel. When he arrived, Shanley was already there. The detective told him to sign the register and give a New York address. The two then went to Markham's room, where Shanley immediately emptied the carpetbag and lovingly counted its contents. The government, Shanley announced, allowed him a 10 percent commission on any money he confiscated. Pay the 10 percent directly to him, Shanley suggested to Markham, and he would let the youth go. Thoroughly frightened by the possibility of arrest, imprisonment, and confiscation of his father's money, Markham agreed. Remarkably, the two then went to dinner and to the theater, with Markham paying the bill. Afterward they spent the night together in Markham's hotel room.

The next morning, Markham counted out $1,430 and paid off the officer. Given the circumstances, Shanley was not a particularly greedy man. He might easily have had all of Markham's money, but he was apparently disinclined to violence and decided that sending Markham on his way out of the city would end the matter. Before escorting the youth to the railroad station, however, he demanded that Markham give him his watch and chain. Markham refused, but when Shanley pressed, he gave him his diamond stickpin. At 6:30 A.M., by prearrangement, Scott was waiting at the railroad station when Shanley arrived with Markham. The two men put the youth on the train with the understanding that Markham would go to New York. As the cars pulled out of the station, Shanley shared the proceeds with Scott, giving him $250, telling the other policeman that he had only gotten $500.[21]

Relieved, but still badly shaken, Markham got off the train in Baltimore and contacted friends of his father, who urged him to return to Washington and complain to the authorities. Two detectives from Baltimore accompanied him back to the capital and took him for an interview with Lafayette Baker, who ordered Shanley and Scott arrested. Federal officers soon arrested the hapless extortioners, who were tried by a military court and sentenced to prison at hard labor. Marcellus Markham spent the remainder of the war safely in the North, far away from the impending catastrophe in Atlanta.[22]

BACK IN ATLANTA, the most immediate threat to Unionist men continued to be the conscription officers, who, with steady thoroughness and the cooperation of the press, persisted in the ferreting out of the disloyal who evaded service in the manpower-hungry Confederate forces. During the summer and fall of 1863, conscript officers kept up their campaigns to increase the Confederate ranks and made the public aware through the newspapers of the names of those who had been called to serve. On the lists were several Unionists who had been successful in evading service to that point, including Charles Bohnefeld, the German immigrant coffin maker; Dr. Holmes Sells; and Dr. Anderson L. Scott. Bohnefeld creatively relied upon his craft to win exemption from service, arguing in a petition to Governor Joseph E. Brown that coffin making was a vital occupation and that he should be exempted because he was the only private citizen engaged in the business, the other coffin operation in Atlanta being a government shop "not intended to supply the citizens." Already under contract to supply coffins to the city, Bohnefeld noted that his production now ran from seven to ten per week. Demand would soon escalate.[23]

Other Unionists adopted alternate strategies to avoid conscription. Thomas Jordan, the Fulton County farmer who had moved into Atlanta in 1862, now began to move around the countryside from place to place in attempts to outwit the conscription officers. Jordan and his wife had been caught by rebel officers trying to "slip things" in to Yankee prisoners in the city, and he was thus in double jeopardy. Philip McIntire, stock tender for Richard Peters, was arrested after midnight one evening during the fall of 1863 by E. T. Hunnicutt, the deputy provost marshal, and taken to Decatur to be put into service. "Surrounded by guards and bayonets," McIntire took an oath to the Confederacy but somehow succeeded in avoiding service, perhaps using a medical excuse procured for him by Peters—a tactic he would use when arrested once again in early 1864. When the pressure increased, McIntire fled the city altogether and sneaked through the Confederate lines, making it safely to Nashville.[24]

C. T. C. Deake, the east Tennessean schoolmaster who had gone to the Georgia coast with Thomas Crussell and Holmes Sells in the fall of 1862, succeeded in keeping out of the Confederate army until the late summer of 1863. Like many of the Unionists, Deake had been under constant pressure from citizens committees to enlist, but he made friends with conscript officers and bribed them to keep him out of the service. When this no longer worked, he took a job traveling through the rural areas of Georgia and Alabama, buying up gum shellac for use by the Confederate ordnance department. Finally, when he saw that there was no way left to evade conscription, he made his way through the guerrilla country in the treacherous highlands of north Georgia to the Union lines in east Tennessee, first taking his wife out and then, after a brief return to Atlanta, returning to Tennessee himself.[25]

Tom Crussell never did succeed in escaping Atlanta but called on friends to help him stay out of the rebel forces, first winning an assignment to keep the public cisterns full of water (work considered critical to the war effort) and later, when this ruse no longer worked, accepting the offer of a close friend, William Rustin, master mechanic of the Georgia Railroad, to take a railroad job that would keep him safe from service. Alexander N. Wilson, one of the most visible of the Unionists, had already gone through the lines to Nashville, leaving his wife and three small children in the city, while he began to explore ways the embattled Unionists might eventually profit from their records of loyalty to the United States.[26]

By early 1864, still more Unionists and other Atlantans suspected of disloyalty escaped northward from the city and provided valuable information to Union officials. John C. Peck fled Atlanta shortly after the first of the year. A carpenter and architect, Peck described in detail the fortifications encircling the city to Union intelligence officers and reported that he and many other citizens thought the city poorly defended. He also disclosed the location of ammunition magazines and stressed that they were very poorly guarded—"*sometimes not at all.*" Peck said that a raid on the city might easily destroy the magazines because no more than 1,200 men "could be mustered in the city to prevent it." Atlanta had little coal, Peck said, and most of the machine shops, so vital to the Confederate war effort, had ceased operating because of the lack of coal. According to Peck, no shop in Atlanta except the arsenal had more than a two weeks' supply of the valuable commodity.[27]

Escaping from Atlanta in 1864 could clearly be hazardous. Not only was the countryside full of vicious characters and roving, scavenging bands with no loyalty to either side, but also there were men who took grim delight in finding, arresting, and summarily punishing those of questionable loyalty to the South during its hour of greatest need. In the early days of July 1864, James S. Thomas, an Indiana sergeant in the field near Atlanta, reported a chilling example of the treatment that could await those considered disloyal. "I have heard of the barbarities of the rebels a great many times," he wrote, "but never saw them until yesterday." Thomas had stumbled upon four rotted human carcasses hanging from trees. "These men were Hung for the sin of being Union Men," he wrote to his family. It had been reported that nine more had been hung "further up the river."

These men were "All conscripts" who had been caught trying to get through to Union lines.[28]

In addition to Peck, Anderson L. Scott left in early 1864. So did James A. Stewart, who made it through to the Union lines at about the same time. Later in the year, Thomas Healey, the contractor, and Henry Huntington, the Vermont-born dentist, also safely left the South. Julius Hayden took refuge in his rural residence and, as much as possible, kept out of sight. Thus, Atlanta's population of Unionist men had declined steadily, with only a handful of the most active still in the city by early 1864.[29]

For the most part, however, the women remained. And by and large, as the war stretched out, they came under increasing suspicion. Carrie King, a Columbus, Georgia, woman who had been recruited to spy for the Union army, made occasional forays into Atlanta and reported in early 1864 that the rebels had become "very strict regarding persons passing through the lines—Especially women," who they believed "were doing them more Injury than any one else."[30]

Female complicity in intelligence gathering did occur in Atlanta, and the activities of women such as Mary Summerlin amply confirmed Confederate fears. Mary Summerlin was a Virginia native in her mid-twenties when the war broke out. While still a child, she and her family had moved to Athens, Georgia, but at age eight, Mary was sent to Vermont to be educated. She had relatives there; her paternal great-grandfather was General John Stark, and her father was a first cousin of Zachary Taylor. In 1855 Mary returned at age eighteen to Athens and married storekeeper W. T. Summerlin. The married couple lived in Henry County, Georgia, but when Summerlin died in 1858, Mary suddenly had to support herself. She settled in Atlanta where she opened a dressmaking shop in her home directly across the street from the Empire Hospital. Mary frequently visited the hospital with the other Unionist women, and she was clearly one of the women arrested in August 1862 during the "reign of terror."[31]

The arrest did not inhibit her anti-Confederate work. Between five and six o'clock one winter evening, just before Christmas 1862, a man came to her door. He had heard of her from Union prisoners across the street who told him that she could be trusted and would help him. The man was a Union agent who called himself Tommy. He said that he would tell her his full name and more about himself if she wanted to know. Mary Summerlin "told him to hush." She said she would aid him in his work but wanted to know as little as possible about him. "Knowledge was dangerous," she said. Tommy did let her know that she was "not the only friend he had here," but judging from their subsequent activities, she must have been one of the best. Mary decided to pass Tommy off as her cousin and invited the man to stay with her and her young daughter. Sometime later, when a "Mrs. Hewson," who was a matron of a Confederate hospital in Chattanooga, invited Mary to accompany her on a supply-gathering trip to Charleston and Augusta, Mary persuaded the matron that her "cousin" should accompany them. Mrs. "Hewson" was undoubtedly Mrs. Ella K. Newsom, the so-called Florence Nightingale of the Southern Army, a famous Confederate nurse who served as matron of hospitals in Chattanooga and Atlanta, among other places. Ella Newsom liked the idea of having a man along, and the three departed—the hospital matron being completely unaware that her traveling companion's cousin was a Union spy. Tommy used the trip to great advantage and while in Charleston, according to Mary, he "was all through the forts and harbors and works." In Charleston, the three met Confederate general D. H. Hill, with whom Mary was acquainted. Who was Tommy, the general wanted to know. Mary quickly gave the spy a surname and introduced him to Hill as "Cousin Tommy Burton." Hill seemed satisfied.[32]

Soon after the three returned to Atlanta, Tommy took leave of Mary and the city, evidently returning north. Some months later, however, as the Union armies approached Chattanooga, Mary received a letter from him. Although obscurely phrased, the letter seemed to say that Mary could expect to see him soon. Sure enough, Tommy reappeared in Atlanta in the summer of 1863, shortly after the Yankees took Tullahoma, Tennessee. He once again took up residence with Mary and her daughter. Soon, however, some Atlantans became suspicious, and when Tommy left the Summerlin residence to take a room at the Trout House when Mary had overnight guests, "detectives were soon after him." Tommy needed help quickly and persuaded a black man who worked at the Trout House to go to Mary with the message that he was about to be arrested. Mary sent back one of her dresses. Tommy put it on. He then left the hotel, heading for Mary's house.[33]

It was only a few blocks from the hotel to the Summerlin house, and Tommy was not followed. Mary took him in, and for two weeks she hid him when necessary in a "goods box," which had previously contained fabric she used in her business. Now it served as a table upon which she stored her kitchen utensils. During the two-week period, agents searched her house, perhaps more than once, but they did not find the man. Finally Mary and Tommy decided that he must leave, and he again donned a dress (this one with a hoopskirt). Late one night, Mary led him to the outskirts of the city.

There he changed into a pair of gray jeans that she had made for him and slipped quietly away. About two weeks later, Mary was arrested again and charged with "suspicion of harboring spies." Kept under arrest for six months, she became ill while in confinement and was eventually paroled. She returned to her home, where she remained until the city was occupied by Union forces.[34]

Carrie King came to Atlanta on several occasions, and her presence and that of a few other Union spies such as Tommy, who left traces of their sojourns in Atlanta, confirmed the fear of Confederate inhabitants that Union spies frequently moved about the city, gathering information. Once in the early spring of 1864, Carrie King visited Atlanta and stayed several nights with an aunt who lived about one and one-half miles outside the city. Whether Carrie had any direct contact with the Unionist group in Atlanta is not known, but she did make contact with Henry G. Cole, a staunch Unionist from nearby Marietta. Cole, a New Yorker and engineer by profession, was well known in Atlanta and had lived in the South for decades. His militant Unionism brought him into contact with more than one Union agent passing through the city and led him to volunteer for hazardous operations inside the Confederate lines. For example, he told Carrie King that "any time the Federal Authorities wished the Rail Road Bridge over the Chattahoochie burned he could do so that the man who was formerly the watchman of the Bridge was still living in a House near the Bridge and that he could burn it at any time he [Cole] wished & that the arrangement had been made for some time." Cole also said that he knew "a very intelligent negro boy who was a servant for Genl Cheatham and that he kept him [Cole] posted in regard to the movements of the Army." Cole passed information on military movements to King on two other occasions. In time Cole was discovered, arrested, and imprisoned in Atlanta along with three other prisoners also charged with spying: J. N. Cobb, G. W. Sherman, and John Moran. Confederate authorities took the three to Macon, leaving Cole in Atlanta.[35]

Henry Cole was clearly a prime contact for Union agents operating around Atlanta. Spies also had regular contact with Robert McCroskey, the Atlanta Unionist who in 1862 had refused to pay his war tax. McCroskey now ran a boardinghouse on Whitehall Street, and by the time Union troops had begun their descent into Georgia, he had a reputation for being "perfectly reliable" as a contact for Union spies and as a conduit to J. P. McWilliam, an official in the Confederate Commissary Department who was also an agent. McWilliam had to be approached through McCroskey,

Union agent James G. Brown reported. "Mention Thomas A. Calloway's name & he [McCroskey] will send for or procure any information from the latter agent."[36]

Perhaps the most effective and certainly the most colorful spy who came to Atlanta was Émile Bourlier, a Frenchman who had lived for some time in New Orleans. Bourlier, articulate and sophisticated, visited the city at least twice during the late summer and early autumn of 1863 as part of a more general assignment to assess military and civilian conditions in a large swath of the South from Mobile to Richmond. The engaging Bourlier seemed able to win the confidence of Confederate officials and citizens as he gathered his information. He also had a valuable knack for survival. Arrested or conscripted several times during his mission, the wily Frenchman always escaped to move on to the next phase of his espionage.

Bourlier came to Atlanta on September 9, 1863, in search of information concerning Confederate movements and strategy. While there, he had contact with Colonel James C. Nisbet of the 61st Georgia Regiment and Major Thomas C. Glover of the 21st Georgia Regiment, and he reported that he had extracted information from both concerning the arrival of D. H. Hill's and James Longstreet's forces to reinforce Braxton Bragg's army in northwest Georgia. Although Bourlier's skill as a spy often put him into position to garner useful information, sometimes he was simply lucky. Once, while talking with a room clerk at the Trout House in Atlanta, Bourlier had an extraordinary bit of good fortune. A Colonel Thompson arrived at the hotel and asked to see General Howell Cobb, sending his card up to Cobb, who was a guest. Soon the rotund general appeared in the lobby, and the two began a conversation on different subjects but discussed primarily the fact that a battle near Chattanooga was imminent. They then reviewed details of what the Confederate strategy should be. Bourlier took in every word. "I managed to seat myself behind them," the spy reported, "pretending to devour the contents of divers newspapers which turn by turn I took from my pocket."

While in Atlanta, Bourlier also gathered extensive information concerning Confederate morale ("there seemed to be great despondency and no little uneasiness for the safety of Atlanta") and many details concerning the near panic that seized Atlantans when they mistook large groups of deserters being marched through the city as being Bragg's army in full retreat. Stores and houses were closed and preparations made to leave the city. Bourlier also sent valuable information concerning the city's defenses.[37]

Bourlier's thoroughness probably brought him into contact with Unionists in the city as well, although he made no such comments in the one surviving report of his visits to the city. However, intriguing evidence suggests that Bourlier (or another spy in the city at precisely the same time) had contact with the Unionists and actually spent time in the household of Cyrena Stone. The evidence lies in *Goldie's Inheritance.* In the novel, the fictional Cyrena Stone, together with several other Unionists, plays host to a spy who is visiting Atlanta at a time that coincides precisely with Bourlier's visits to the city in September 1863. The spy, however, is not a Frenchman, but the fictional Cyrena's childhood friend from Vermont. The language of the pages dealing with the spy's visit is clearly a mixture of Cyrena's language (likely taken from the missing portions of the diary) and that of the author, her half sister. The dialogue in the pertinent sections was no doubt written by the half sister; the narrative passages contain hallmarks of Cyrena's literary style.

In the novel, the spy's appearance comes a short time before the Battle of Chickamauga, which occurred on September 19 to 20. Bourlier first arrived in Atlanta on September 9 and returned just after Chickamauga. Part of the spy's mission is to determine how much Union sentiment exists in Atlanta, and after finding his way to the fictional Cyrena's household, he meets with some of the Unionists and discusses various aspects of the war with them. After conversation, the group quietly sings patriotic songs, while others keep watch outside to be sure that they are not overheard or observed. Meanwhile, the fictional Cyrena has quietly left the room. Soon she returns with a small package. She unwraps it and unfurls an American flag, which is then draped over the piano. After the singing, the spy relates some of his experiences to the Unionist group. Whether Émile Bourlier was the spy who visited the Stone household may never be known, but it seems possible from a close reading of *Goldie's Inheritance* that Cyrena Stone had contact with one and perhaps more Union agents. Later, she would herself be accused of transmitting information to the federal armies, a charge she would deny in the privacy of her diary.[38]

SO FRAGMENTARY is the historical record left by Civil War Atlantans—even more so Atlanta Unionists and federal spies—that it is impossible to know the extent of connections with and support of Union agents. Clearly, Henry Cole had extensive contacts, and so did R. H. McCroskey. And the evidence in the novel indicates that Cyrena Stone and her circle of Unionist friends may have as well. The courage shown by many of the Unionists, particularly by the women, suggests that such contacts became frequent and perhaps regular as more and more agents visited the city, and as the Union forces began their descent from southern Tennessee into the heart of Georgia. The Unionists took hope and encouragement from the presence of other Yankees in Atlanta, whether prisoners or spies, and looked expectantly to the day when a fourth group of Yankees, scarcely 120 miles to the north, would join them in the Georgia city. In the meantime, the longing for the appearance of Union soldiers in the streets of the city was complemented by the patriotic rituals the Unionists followed—secret viewings of the American flag in Cyrena's parlor, quiet singing of patriotic songs, and whispered discussions of the symbolism of hope for the Union bound up in the off-season blooming of a white lily.

CHAPTER EIGHT

"The Red Waves of War"

While Amherst Stone shuttled between the St. Nicholas Hotel in New York City and the lesser accommodations of Forts Lafayette and Warren, Cyrena remained in Atlanta. Life in her home remained remarkably calm, considering the havoc that would ensue once the Yankees drew nearer to Atlanta. Cyrena ran the household with a light hand, enjoying the company of the slaves, the servants, and the variety of pets she kept and loved. Her diary, however, reflects relatively little of the details of home life during this time. Occasionally, she referred to some domestic project—like the turfing of the yard—or complained about the inflated prices of food and clothing, but by and large she focused on the great struggle, already under way in January 1864, for control of Georgia and the city of Atlanta, increasingly seen as critical to Abraham Lincoln's chances for reelection and the outcome of the war. The nearness of the gargantuan contest being waged between Confederate and Union armies less than 120 miles from Atlanta and the pressures of being a Unionist in a rebel city controlled her actions and her mind.

Despite Amherst's absence, loneliness rarely gripped Cyrena during her seven months of journal keeping in 1864. When it did, she apparently kept it to herself or consigned it to the privacy of her diary. She took comfort in the presence of "kind servants" and, after the rest of the household had gone to sleep, she would remain awake, writing in her diary, reflecting on the dramatic conflict around her, coping with loneliness when she did feel it, being always careful to keep "the eye . . . calm—the lips silent," and exercising close control of her own emotions, so much so that she would sometimes try to repress emotion-filled thoughts of the natural beauty of the rural New England she loved. Occasionally, though, she did let her thoughts wander to Vermont and the comforting majesty of its natural environment, wishing that she might "see those lofty mountains sweeping against the sky." Once, she recalled the portion of her childhood spent in nearby New York State, remembering a girlish romp through the old battlefield at Ticonderoga.[1]

On rare occasions, the loneliness included specific reference to Amherst or brother-in-law Chester, but always in cryptic camouflage, never by name. As the conflict around Atlanta intensified, she referred to herself as "alone on the hill" where the Stone house stood, alone with "no husband or brother near." And once, she referred to "Welcome letter again from H——," a reference to communications from her husband secretly transported to her from the North. There are a few other implied references to the absent Amherst but only very few. Perhaps Cyrena feared that if her diary somehow fell into Confederate hands and there were specific references to Amherst, the document might be decoded and endanger her. Yet because the diary was almost certainly kept in the obscure shorthand that her father had taught her, this seems unlikely. Whatever the answer, the surviving fragment of the diary that Cyrena Stone kept does not reveal a person who dwelled upon loneliness or isolation. Instead, it discloses a woman almost always able to deal effectively and confidently with a situation of great peril and difficulty. In short, Cyrena Stone showed great courage and self-reliance in the face of cataclysm.[2]

Throughout the war, Cyrena led a life governed by her ardent patriotism and her passionate commitment to the Union. Life for her in the months before Atlanta's destruction was a daily mixture of risk taking, a routine that blended the remnants of a comfortable existence with fast-increasing privation and an unwavering longing for the appearance of the Union armies. Even if she coped effectively with the challenges of everyday life in the Confederate city, she had more difficulty in dealing with the suffocating political atmosphere of a region she believed had steeped itself in treason. For Cyrena Stone, the Confederacy was a confining, stifling sarcophagus. She and the other Unionists longed for the coming of the Union army to "roll away the stone from the tomb into which Secession has consigned us—without any embalming." Unionists, she said, wanted to "step forth free men & women, and live as we have never lived in this land before." For this woman of commitment, the Union and loyalty to it had a mystical, religious quality that went beyond mere patriotism. Those who remained loyal to the Union did so with a "true loyalty of Soul." Those who embraced treason (and there was absolutely no doubt in her mind that Confederates had done so) "dwarf[ed] the Soul, so that the body may exist." Life and its "earthly possessions," Cyrena Stone believed, were worthless "without a *Goverment* to cling to." In her prayers she "longed to clasp the hand of the merciful One, and tell him *why* we asked that our Goverment might triumph. It was for this;—that Truth & Right & Liberty had long been in chains—bound by this soul-crushing despotism, beneath which so many were languishing."[3]

For more than three years, Cyrena's longing for the coming of the Union army had steadily intensified, and in the last months before William T. Sherman and his armies actually appeared in Atlanta, the longing became her passion. Throughout the seven months before the Battle of Atlanta, her diary brimmed with hope for deliverance from the Confederates by the Yankee army. That hope, she believed, was shared by "three classes who are looking anxiously for the coming of the victors." First, of course, there were the Unionists: "Those who love their Country and their Goverment with true loyalty of Soul." Then there were "the poor who are suffering for the commonest comforts of life." And finally, there was "this nation of negroes who have patiently waited through long years for their deliverance to come."[4]

CYRENA HAD EXTENSIVE TIES, of course, with the Unionist community in Atlanta, but she also had contacts with poor whites and with blacks, and these helped shape her views about the extent of disaffection within the Confederacy. Poor whites regularly visited the Stone household, sometimes coming with wares to sell, at other times with favors to ask. Over the years, Cyrena had evidently gained a reputation as a helpful person with few pretensions of class, for a stream of visitors came to her home to ask favors or to sell wares or both. Unlike some Confederate women, Cyrena was clearly at ease with persons of lower social standing. Some of these were poor whites, and by early 1864 they had begun to complain vitriolically about the Confederacy.

One was a middle-aged farmer, "Farmer T" (or "Mr. T——") as he is identified in the diary, who had sold produce to the Stones for years. He stopped by the house one morning in late January 1864 with a load of fodder for sale. "You'd better take it—I reckon its the last fodder or any thing else I shall ever bring you," Farmer T declared.

"Why so?" Cyrena asked.

"Well, I'm ordered off to Virginy. They've got me in this war at last. I didn't want to have any thing to do with it any how. *I* didn't vote for Secession—but them are the ones who have to go & fight now—and those who were so fast for war, stay out. I thought I was old enough, and had worked hard enough to stay at home the balance of my life . . . but they've got me now, and I spose there's no getting away from them. I don't want to fight the Northern folks, they've always treated me well enough. Where shall I put this fodder?"[5]

Cyrena was deeply moved by the man's plight and by his plaintive resignation "to go & get killed, and try to kill somebody—though he didn't know what for." Indeed, Farmer T did go off to Virginia to fight, and there he fell ill. Whether he survived is unknown. His wife, left at home with several children, returned to the Stone household in the late spring with her teenaged son to sell butter and eggs. While talking to Cyrena, she lost control and "burst into tears." Two of her children had died since her husband had gone, she reported, "and now," she told Cyrena, "they're going to take this boy away from me." "What will become of me?" she went on. "I can't work my farm myself." The distraught woman turned and gestured toward an impressive house nearby: "Why don't Mr. Newman go to the war?" she asked. "He was mighty fierce for it and a great secessioner." The woman prepared to leave and in saying good-bye commented that Cyrena must be "powerful glad your husband aint here to be dragged off and killed all for nothing." "Poor woman!" Cyrena wrote in her diary, "my heart ached for her—but I could only extend my hand, and give her as tearful a good bye as she gave me."[6]

Another visitor was an unnamed country woman who lived with her husband and five children two miles out from Atlanta. She also broke down, telling Cyrena that her husband could no longer evade service and that he had "been published as a deserter." Her eldest daughter, aged sixteen and with a "bad cough," walked daily to the city to get sewing work, and because the material was so heavy the frail girl stopped at the Stone house to rest on her way home. She had been sewing for months, Cyrena reported, in order to save enough to buy one pair of shoes, which she displayed with great pride. In a time of skyrocketing prices, her wages were pitifully low, and Cyrena wondered whether the girl would not be forced to turn to prostitution for survival. "Is it any wonder that crime and prostitution are so common?" she wrote. "This girl is intelligent and refined in her feelings, and she often cries when she tells me of the insults she receives from the men who deal out the work." The girl's mother prayed for the coming of the federal army. "O, I wish these Yankees would ever get here," she said, "before we are all murdered and starve to death."[7]

Such visits to Cyrena were common. In the space of one afternoon, three more women, all poor whites, came to visit, one of whom was "in tears as usual—her husband gone—she sick—and the same cry—'How *can* I get bread for my children!'" Two more soon appeared, one whose husband had already been killed; the other's spouse was "sick & wounded." Both complained that "rich neighbors had persuaded their husbands to volunteer in the first [of the] war, promising that their families should never suffer." "But the promise was forgotten, & the little sewing they could get, hardly kept them alive. This class of women know nothing about work, save of the coarsest kind; they could make a flour sack, sweep a cabin, & bake a 'hoecake,' and this is about all—so it is less trouble to give to them, than to employ them." The blacks in the Stone household took a less charitable view, condemning the poor whites as "no-count" and lazy. "It always excites the ire of negroes to see charities bestowed upon 'Ole poah white folks,'" Cyrena wrote, "no matter how sick or helpless they may be."[8]

The slaves, however, looked for the coming of the Yankees as avidly or more so than the poor whites and the Unionists. At the beginning of the war, Cyrena wrote, "the fear was universal, that there would be 'risings' & 'insurrections' without number. But nothing of the kind." Cyrena explained the absence of widespread slave insurrections in her own racial terms, believing that blacks as a race were submissive and pointing to the relative absence of difficulties with slaves on the plantations as further evidence. "There are isolated cases of insubordination & murders," she wrote, "but they are no more frequent than in times of peace."

After the Emancipation Proclamation, she went on, similar apprehension had swelled among the whites that there would be uprisings. Virtually every slave had heard of the edict, she wrote, and all understood its significance. "Yet no change was visible; though who can tell of the wild joy that thrilled their hearts, when they felt that their chains were at last broken." Although Cyrena Stone may have relied upon racial explanations for the absence of widespread black uprisings during the war, she also clearly understood that the strictly enforced regulations of a slave society made resistance exceedingly difficult. "If negroes are found out after nine o'clock in the evening, even with passes from their owners," she observed, "they are carried off to the 'Caliboose.'" The authorities also prevented any "social 'pleasuring'—and long before their [the blacks'] church was taken for a hospital, no meetings were held without a force of policemen being present, with their clubs in readiness."[9]

Cyrena thought the close regulating of blacks to be impolitic, "for there is no surer way to convince them that the whole thing [slavery] is wrong, and a consciousness of power is thus forced upon them—should they choose to use it." She found confirmation for these views in conversation with a "Southern lady," who ascribed the absence of active black resistance to "a grand faith in their final freedom," which had "given them patience" and determination "to wait & see what this war would do for them." The "worst calamity that could befall the South," this woman continued, would be for the war to bring Southern independence. Then, the slaves would have "all hope cut off, and no North to look to" for help. A great uprising would follow, the woman went on, slaves would no longer "submit to their masters, and we should witness scenes never dreamed of before." From her point of view, such a prospect provided ample reason to hope for a failure of the Confederacy. The arming of slaves to resist a Northern invasion had been discussed widely in the Confederacy, in both official and unofficial circles. This prospect, Cyrena commented, "amuses them [the slaves] exceedingly." She pointed to her visitor's "waiting man" as an example of how blacks might react if that decision were made. "Missus," he said, "they better keep them guns out of our folks hands—cause they dun'no *which way we going to shoot!*"[10]

The relationships with the Unionist community that had done much to sustain Cyrena throughout the war seemed to take on a slightly different character in 1864. Many of the men were gone now, having escaped through the lines, and Unionist contacts were almost always with the women who remained. Gatherings of the "Union Circle" in her home certainly contained fewer men than in years past. The symbols of national loyalty took on even greater importance as the war progressed and as the Union army approached. All during the conflict, Cyrena had kept in her possession a small American flag, secreting it in a variety of hiding places, at one time in a jar of preserved fruit, at another in her sugar canister. Atlantans with sympathies for the Union would regularly visit the Stone household and ask to see the flag, which was illegal to possess in the Confederacy. One

woman came furtively; she did not want her husband to know of her interest "in the advance of the Federals." Cyrena had previously sent her a "wee
picture" of a U.S. flag, and the woman, on a pilgrimage to restore faith and
hope, now wanted to see Cyrena's real flag. When Cyrena retrieved the hidden banner, the tearful woman kissed it "reverently." Before she left, she
said that she was very worried about the danger to Cyrena in keeping
the flag in her possession. "I have heard such bitter threats," the woman
warned.[11]

Other visits by individual persons or small groups to the Stone home
often culminated in the practice of patriotic rituals—principally the
singing (in softened voices) of the "Star-Spangled Banner" or "Hail Columbia." These were emotionally charged, often tearful, meetings for the Unionists, who, for nearly four years, had experienced the escalating strain of
dissidents trapped within the confines of a despotic state. Contact with other
Unionists remained a necessity, both as a way to exchange information and
to provide psychological support in a situation where ubiquitous danger
was mixed with passionate hope for early liberation by the Union armies.
Caution had always to be exercised, however, especially when someone
of unknown loyalties asked to see the flag or tried to engage Cyrena in political discussions.[12]

LIKE ALL THE UNIONISTS, Cyrena had altered her behavior in order
to cope with the constant probings and tauntings by Confederates who
hoped to entrap her in a seditious act that could be interpreted as treason. She learned to control her emotions and her behavior in these settings just as she hid her emotions from those who lived in her household.
In social settings—and contact did continue with loyal Confederates—war
news would invariably be interpreted in the best possible light for the rebel
cause. Confederate loyalists would, of course, show enthusiasm. Downcast
Unionists, sometimes shocked by the Confederate claims, would try to react
in ways that would minimize suspicion. A May outing into the woods around
Atlanta included a "pleasant little party of the fair, the young, the brave—
and some that were not fair nor young nor brave; some too were of Union
and some disunion proclivities." Conversation inevitably turned to the war.
The news had just been received that a great Confederate victory had been
scored around Chattanooga and that Joseph Johnston's Confederate army
had pushed General Sherman's troops back past Chattanooga. Cyrena and
a young woman had been sitting apart from the larger group when the "victory" was being discussed. The young woman, possibly William Farnsworth's

daughter, became distraught and started to cry. Cyrena hastily led her far-ther away from the group so that her tears could not be seen. By the time the party decided to return to Atlanta, the young girl had recovered her composure and gaily rejoined the group. "We have learned our lessons well,—can cry when we would laugh—and laugh when we would cry," Cyrena wrote.[13]

Emotions had to be controlled at all times when in the presence of Con-federates, whether there was a direct challenge to loyalty or not. At times, Cyrena would fight against normal reactions to wartime news, biting her lips to keep the color in them, holding her hands tightly together to keep from using them to express herself, fighting back a blush: "The face must keep its color—white or red—though the heart stops beating or flames up in scorching pain." When Unionists met unexpectedly on the street, they greeted each other properly, without seeming overly friendly, in order not to arouse suspicion. After receiving some good news about the progress of the war, Cyrena encountered a Unionist man ("staunch & true") walk-ing with a Confederate officer. "Very slightly and sedately," the Unionist bowed toward her, but after he had passed "something, which often impels us to look back, made me turn my head; at that instant, his head turned too, & his face was covered with smiles." Intuition, Cyrena concluded, "schooled as it has been these years—tells us where to laugh & when not to."[14]

Practiced, furtive behavior also became second nature when Cyrena and the other Union women visited the hospitals. In the early days, when Union prisoners began to arrive in Atlanta, it had been much easier to slip food, money, and mail to them. By 1864, officials had tightened security and made it much more difficult to bring aid to wounded and sick Union prisoners, who were sometimes kept in the same hospitals as Confeder-ates. Thus, in an attempt to divert suspicion, the women routinely visited wounded Confederate soldiers first, listening patiently to their complaints and requests. When the visits to the Confederates ended, and the baskets they had brought with them were apparently empty, a casual remark would open the way for a visit to the ward where Union soldiers were held under guard: "We have a few biscuits left—guess we'll give them to the Yan-kees," one of the women said.

"You going in there? Well, I'll go with you," the guard replied in an almost careless way.[15]

Emily Farnsworth continued to be the most active of the Union women in visiting the hospitals, and constantly took risks to gain access to Union prisoners, who were treated worse than the wounded Confederates, themselves fed irregularly and cared for under primitive medical and sanitary conditions. According to Cyrena, Mrs. Farnsworth's companion, Mollie, an attractive young woman, had become so accomplished a "secessionist" that she had little trouble gaining entreé to the wounded and had acquired a coterie of admirers among the Confederates. One guard, a widower, was particularly attracted to the young woman. Emily Farnsworth, Cyrena, Mollie, and Nelly, another young woman, would work together to distract the guards and slip food to Union prisoners. As Cyrena recounted it:

> Mrs. F—— whispered as we stepped into the door—You & Nelly go on—Mollie & I will take care of our *guard.*" So she talked pleasantly . . . about our bright prospects—recent defeats of the Federals, and Mollie interested the widower in her own peculiar way—while Nellie was slyly hiding things under pillows besides the "few biscuits"— and pockets were emptied of more contraband articles."

What the contraband may have been is impossible to determine, but it was likely money or some article useful to a prisoner contemplating escape. "Contraband" also may have included letters—perhaps to Amherst or others in the North—which prisoners took out with them, sewn in their clothes, when they were exchanged or escaped.

Cyrena deeply admired Emily Farnsworth for her commitment to the risky business of helping Union prisoners and Confederate deserters. There were sixty deserters in the Confederate prison hospital and a few Union prisoners. Mrs. Farnsworth went there at least once a week—sometimes more often. "She has a sincere compassion for them [the deserters]," Cyrena wrote, and "she can thus gain access to the few remaining prisoners, who seem dependent upon her for almost life itself." Cyrena discounted her own involvement in the prison visitations, giving credit to Mrs. Farnsworth: "No fitful impulsive charity here is hers—gushing forth at first sight of suffering, then subsiding—but earnest continuing in well doing—consulting never self interest or ease. It is no holiday freak with her, as with the rest of us, who occasionally get our courage up enough to challenge watching eyes and bitter threats."[16]

Religious beliefs as well as Unionist loyalty impelled Cyrena and the other women to take the risks associated with the prison visits, and although Christian beliefs remained a dominant and central part of Cyrena's character and makeup, she frequently found the conduct of church services devoid of comfort and sometimes totally unsatisfactory. She and Amherst had been founding members of the Central Presbyterian Church, and Cyrena continued to attend after Amherst went north. Some members of the church shunned her, refusing to speak or acknowledge her presence. She had come to expect this treatment and though it was hurtful and wounding, she endured it. She had less patience for the ways the ministers at Central Presbyterian used the pulpit to advance the objectives of the Confederacy. Sometimes she remained away from services altogether. "If I attend," she wrote, "I am like the woman who spent her all upon physicians and was 'nothing better, but rather grew worse.' I become only more & more embittered, by hearing from the pulpit such vile aspersions continually cast upon the [U.S.] Goverment—such prayers for its destruction—such assertions that 'our cause is just, and a just God *will* crown it with success.'"[17]

On one Sunday, Cyrena thought the message at Central Presbyterian sound until "it was spoiled by the last word, which was Confederacy, instead of Heaven." The two words were "once thought synonomous by some," she confided to her diary, but one would judge it was not so now, for the eagerness most men evince to escape from the former." Another time, Cyrena heard what she at first thought an excellent sermon, until the end, when "the minister closed by pointing his hearers to *Bragg,* and not to Christ."[18]

From the early days of the winter into the spring of 1864, Cyrena's overwhelming concern was *when* the Union army would come and how soon Atlanta would be liberated. Rumors and revised rumors of the movements of both Confederate and Union armies dominated many of her conversations and preyed constantly on her mind. Sorting out fact from fiction proved difficult, and Cyrena as well as the other Unionists had their spirits lifted by reports of Yankee advances. Just as often, however, those spirits would be dashed by Confederate propaganda that glossed over setbacks and inflated advantages. Cyrena learned to read between the lines of reports and to weigh them carefully.

"Sherman defeated, & Johnston pursuing!" read one propaganda-filled report in early May. "I like such defeats & such pursuits as these prove to be," Cyrena wrote, for she had learned that the day before, Union general George Thomas had taken Tunnel Hill and that Dalton had been evacuated by the Confederates, "that place which was so impregnable." The Confederate newspapers had earlier proclaimed "that no power on earth can drive our army from that point" because "Nature had fortified that position so perfectly." Joe Johnston fell back toward Atlanta for strategic advantage, the reports ran, "so that when he *does* make a stand—dead Yankees will be piled higher than Stone Mountain." Cyrena saw through the hyperbole. "The battles are usually reported in this style," she observed. "The vandals were mowed down without number. No loss on our side. One man killed, and three slightly wounded." Retreats became orderly repositionings with no straggling and no loss of armaments. "History will probably show the truthfulness of these so-called—'official reports,'" Cyrena concluded.[19]

Sometimes the thirst for news or for contact with sympathetic souls was overpowering. On Sunday morning, May 15, even though ill, she went to church, not out of "devotion" but rather from "restlessness—a feeling" of not being able to "bear the suspense alone," likely a reference to a desperate desire to know the outcome of the battle at Resaca, forty miles north of Atlanta. She also was curious about what the minister would say concerning the steady Yankee advances and perhaps also about the strategy of withdrawal that Joseph E. Johnston had adopted, though this minister, she noted, had "never preached war" nor *"instructed* God how to deal with 'the vile enemies who are fighting against us.'" At the end of his sermon the minister did pray for victory, but surprisingly added a coda that "if it was God's will that our city should meet the fate that others had recently— we might be resigned!"(Cyrena sardonically observed that she knew several persons who would not be reconciled to such a thought.)

The minister then read a public notice asking all citizens to drive carriages to the railroad depot that afternoon to receive wounded. This order, he added excitedly, meant that "a fearful conflict was going on." With even more excitement he blurted out: "What are the enemy fighting for now— if not to get possession of this city?" The parishioners were to return to the church at four o'clock that afternoon, dispatch the carriages to the depot, and pray for the defeat of the Union army. The minister urged that all of the congregation return for that purpose "and with united hearts present this petition to the Court of Heaven." Cyrena stayed away, but sent Tom Lewis.[20]

The ministerial confession of Atlanta's vulnerability surely confirmed what most of Confederate Atlanta knew to be true despite the chest thumping, the propagandizing, and the unwillingness to admit that the Yankees posed any serious threat to the city. Through the first years of the war, Atlantans had become accustomed to battles fought several hundred miles away. As Margaret Mitchell later speculated, perhaps they had developed a wishful habit of believing that great distance would always separate

Atlanta from the real war. At present, however, the Union army was only eighty-five miles to the north of Atlanta, having marched and fought through the rugged, mountainous north Georgia countryside with great speed during the last weeks. Despite popular sentiment to the contrary, the city stood in imminent peril, and every day the threat increased.

The Unionists wanted to believe in an immediate threat and dreamed of having Yankees in the streets of Atlanta. They talked incessantly about it among themselves, but it would have been foolhardy to suggest the probability, much less the desirability, of such an occurrence in any other quarter. Thus, for Cyrena to hear the clerical confession of what everyone either wanted to be true or feared was true excited her profoundly. "The thought that the conflict to which we had looked forward so long, and fearfully—had actually begun—and the consciousness of what hung upon the issue—stirred my soul as it was never stirred before," she wrote. The minister's declaration made it difficult for her to control her emotions. If the Confederates had developed their capacity for self-delusion over nearly four years of war, Cyrena had carefully kept her grip on reality, and though she had dreamed of the coming of the Yankees, she tried not to be too emotional, a large undertaking for anyone of loyal sentiments caught behind the Confederate lines for more than three years.

Now it was all she could do to maintain composure. The pastor's admission so excited her that she wondered if those in the pew with her would read her thoughts. She bit her lips in order to "keep the color in them." She held her hands "firm together, to keep them from flying up imploringly." She feared that God might hear the Confederate prayers to be offered that afternoon and not the supplications of "those who had prayed for the coming of this 'enemy' as the saviors of their country." As Cyrena left the handsome Presbyterian church across the street from the government square, she felt someone lightly touch her arm. It was "Mrs. M——," perhaps Amanda Markham. "I know how you feel," she told Cyrena, "but have *faith*. God will remember us!" Cyrena was so overcome with emotion that she could not speak, and she exited the church door to return home.[21]

IN THE DAYS THAT FOLLOWED, confusion abounded. Early one morning, Cyrena heard "cheering news" that Sherman had captured Rome and was advancing toward Kingston, news that was wholly revised that afternoon by a passing Confederate who told Cyrena and a friend that the Yankees had been "completely *routed*," were retreating rapidly, and had lost ten thousand prisoners. Moreover, the man added, Grant had suffered huge losses in Virginia. Both reports, he said, were absolutely reliable and had come from "official sources." But that evening the news changed again, and Cyrena heard from a Unionist friend she had gone to visit that the morning's report had been false. "Sherman *is* falling back," the friend told Cyrena, "but he is falling this way." While the two were talking, another Unionist woman, "Miss R," dropped by: "*Have* you heard the good news! God bless the Yankee boys! They have started now in earnest."[22]

Toward the end of May, Cyrena and the other Unionists began to sense significant changes in Atlanta. The owner of the slave Dan, whom the Stones had leased, appeared unannounced early one morning. The slave was frightened that his master had come to take him away. "Every body's running off their black'uns now," Dan told Cyrena. "I just expect he has come to take me away, because the Yankees are so near." Greetings were exchanged, and in conversation Cyrena suddenly grew guarded because the visitor had declared himself to be a "firm Union man—adhearing to the Goverment of the United States with true loyalty." Fearing that he wanted to entrap her, "as has often been done," she began to question him. How had he managed to avoid conscription, Cyrena wanted to know. "He smiled & said he *avoided* it!" and "if he was going to fight—he would fight for the *Right.*"

"Mas' George" revealed that he had not come to reclaim Dan but to say good-bye to him, to urge him not to follow the army when it came through (Which army, Cyrena asked. "Why the Federal army of course," the man replied), and to offer the hope that the two, master and slave, who had "grown up together," might meet again when the war was over. The two men, black and white, shook hands, and Cyrena thought the master's voice "a little *unsteady.*" After the man had gone, Dan came into the house "half laughing, and half crying. 'He didn't take me off with him did he! but I felt mighty bad to part for good with Mas' George, for him & me was raised together. I always knowed he was for the Yankees—though he didn't say much: but I never heard him say any thing for the *Southern Confederacy.*'"

The closer the Yankee army drew to Atlanta, the more changes Cyrena and the other Unionists began to see in the behavior and attitudes of Confederate Atlantans. Hot fear cooled Confederate loyalties, and cold reality warmed attachments to the Union. It became apparent that loyalties, even to the Confederate States of America, could be fragile things. One Unionist man commented to Cyrena that "it was getting to be a fine thing to be a Union man. 'Hats are lifted when I meet some who would not speak to me a year ago. It is now 'Why how do you do Mr. Roberts?—very glad to see you.'" Cyrena also reported a conversation between two Atlanta "ladies" and another Union friend. The two women had come to the Unionist for protection. "I know you can protect me when the Yankees come," one woman said. "You have friends among them & I am coming right to your house to stay, & I shall be all right."

"I thought you said they never would get here," the Unionist woman replied.

"Well I don't believe *now* that they are coming—but if they *should* happen to come—I shall look to you for protection."

Cyrena herself received a call from an "old acquaintance," a man who had broken off relations with the Stones. He told Cyrena that since Amherst's departure, he had often thought about her living alone and that he had become "ashamed that he had not called before!" As he prepared to leave, the man made a little speech: "I regret exceedingly, any thing has occured to interupt our sociabilities; but I'm going to do away with all this— and we are coming to see you soon. It's all foolishness to have these old friendships broken up because there is a war." These sorts of reconciliations, one-sided as they were, occurred frequently, Cyrena noted, as those who had "abused & persecuted" the Unionists "untiringly" tried to ingratiate themselves, betraying their belief that the Union armies would come to Atlanta and that it might be possible to win protection from those they had abandoned or persecuted.[23]

By the last week of May, Atlanta had completely thrown off the bravado of the early spring, and as the summer approached, the city seemed to fly into a heated frenzy brought on by the awful news that William T. Sherman and his lieutenants, through skillful maneuvering and seemingly limitless supplies of fresh troops, had now pierced their way to nearby Dallas, only thirty miles to the northwest of Atlanta, preparing for what would be the Battle of New Hope Church, which began on May 25.

On May 24, Cyrena recorded the transformation of the city. "This has been a wild day of excitement," she wrote. "From early morning until now—engines have screamed—trains thundered along; wagons laden with goverment stores, refugees, negroes and household stuff have rattled out of town. Every possible conveyance is bought, borrowed, begged or stolen." She exulted at the sudden transformation of the most ardent Confederate citizens into refugees from the city, noting with unrestrained pleasure the "packing up & leaving" of those who had boasted about the impregnability of Atlanta and the ability of Joseph E. Johnston to keep the Yankees out of Georgia. It was, she said, "perfectly marvellous to behold."

Some Atlantans, she noted with considerable cynicism, would remain with their property but had decided to "send away their *daughters.*" This was a good idea, she thought, for "the dear susceptible creatures soon become devoted to the *Union* cause after the arrival of the blue coats." She cited instances of Confederate girls (one in Nashville, one in New Orleans) who had wed the "'vile' creatures." One marriage grew out of love; the other was arranged by a mother who thought, "In these times, a Quartermaster was a good thing to have in the family." Still, Cyrena showed great sympathy for the destitute, some of whom were refugees from as far away as Nashville. These "poor families—who can barely live where they are—frightened at the reported doings of the terrible foe—fleeing with the rest—sometimes only taking half of their little all, in their fright. No home to go to—no money to procure one—but the *Yankees* are coming, & they must go somewhere!"[24]

A "delirium of fear and excitement" seized the city. There was a "wild up-heaving" as military camps and fortifications multiplied. At night, she could see campfires in the nearby woods. During the day she could hear the sound of bugles and see large groups of soldiers moving about the city and in the open country near her house. For a few days, the slaves had claimed to hear the sound of cannon at night and in the early morning. Cyrena was dubious; they had imagined the sounds, she told them. But on the morning of May 27, they coaxed her outside to hear for herself what had been audible since early morning. Once in the yard, Cyrena caught "the faintest echo of booming guns," coming, she thought, from the direction of Kennesaw Mountain. The sound "awakened the wildest joy I have ever known," she wrote. For Cyrena, the muffled cannon thunder was grand and wonderful music, "the first notes of our redemption anthem." The cannon could not yet be heard in the city, and when Cyrena told a friend who lived inside Atlanta that the guns could be heard from her house, the woman hurried out to hear for herself. "Mrs. M—— a Southern lady . . . clapped her hands for joy and beckoned. . . . 'Come boys!—come on!—we're waiting for you!'"[25]

Of course, many Southern women had quite a different view of the prospective coming of the Yankees. Cyrena encountered one woman who said that she wished for "a sea of blood between North & South—so broad and deep, it could never be crossed!" Another, who was refugeeing through Atlanta, declared that she would rather see all four of her children dead ("laid out on the *cooling board*") "than to have the Yankees get my niggers." Some of her Confederate neighbors told Cyrena that they would not leave Atlanta in the face of the Yankee advance, all the while making secret preparations to leave. Cyrena had absolute contempt for a newspaper editor who told a Union man that the time had arrived for great sacrifice. "Come! now is the time to die for our country," the editor said. "Let us go out in the trenches and *die.*"

"No—I don't want to die yet. I'll go & carry away the dead," replied the Unionist.

"I tell you Sir—we ought to show our manhood & *die!*" The next morning the editor's newspaper printed an "eloquent" article exhorting Atlantans to fight and "Stand Firm" until the end. "But while his readers were being inspired by so much patriotism," Cyrena wrote, "the brave Editor was on the train refugeeing from death & the trenches as fast as steam could carry him."[26]

If Cyrena had contempt for the editor, she had pity for the militiamen who had been called from reserve to replace regular Confederate soldiers in a last-ditch attempt to stop Sherman. Militiamen set up camps close by the Stone house, cutting down trees to make way for their tents. For a few days, they stood guard in the trenches that had been dug around the city. Cyrena judged many of the men to be well past forty-five, the maximum age for conscription, and perhaps understandably, she sensed in those with whom she conversed a strong opposition to the war. Many of the militiamen, she believed, had been against the war from the start and would have refused to serve but feared retribution against their families and property. She saw "only sad & dejected faces." Even the officers seemed to oppose the war and spoke of "this rebellion." One heaped contempt upon General Howell Cobb, who had recently made what was meant to be an inspirational speech to the militiamen. Cobb, the officer said, would "keep out of danger himself, and has safe places for his sons—but he must drag us from *our* homes to fight for his treason."[27]

On June 2, still more militia companies arrived and crowded into the area around the Stone residence. Those who had mounts came on "worn horses," and because they had no feed for the animals, they helped themselves to the ripened oats in the field on Cyrena's property. "It makes no difference," she wrote, "the fences are fast disappearing—let it *all* go." Four days later, on June 6, the militia vacated the woods and departed for the front. Many of the men were "in tears," protesting that they had no interest in fighting the Yankees and affirming that they would "much rather fight the people who brought this war upon our country, and forced us to leave our homes to murder & be murdered."[28]

In addition to calling up the militia to defend Atlanta, the Confederates impressed large numbers of slaves to shore up the city's defenses, principally on the northern side of the city. Some slaves resisted the impressment and the backbreaking, forced labor involved. Four such resisters escaped and made their way to the Stone house, where they pleaded with Cyrena to hide them, protesting that they had no interest in building fortifications to prevent the coming of the Union army. Cyrena took them in, hiding them in the cotton house between the stored bales, where the summer heat was magnified beyond merely oppressive into intolerable. There they were fed and hidden for several days until, presumably, they made their escape.[29]

Fleeing the city, of course, was not confined to Confederate citizens, blacks, and deserters. Some Unionists also tried desperately to get out of Atlanta, adding to the stream of escaping loyalists who had left the city since the beginning of the war. Thomas G. Healey, the forty-six-year-old contractor and Connecticut native, decided in late June to try and escape the conscript officers by going northwest from Atlanta to his farm in Paulding County, near the Union lines. From there, Healey hoped to make his way back to his native state. Leaving his wife and children in the city, Healey made his way to the Chattahoochee in company with a trusted slave and crossed the river while the slave stood guard. Healey then went overland to his farm, where he hid out for a few days before safely traversing the nearby Union lines. He then traveled to Nashville and ultimately to Springfield, Connecticut, where he received a security clearance and worked in a munitions plant as a mason until the close of the war.[30]

Days later, sometime around July 4, Martha Huntington, a close friend of Cyrena's, decided to try to leave the Confederacy. Cyrena carefully recorded details of the attempt in her diary, giving Mrs. Huntington the pseudonym "Mrs. I." With Sherman bearing down upon the city, "Mrs. I" decided to leave, and she managed to get a passport, permitting her to travel west to Meridian, Mississippi, and from there to the Mississippi River and points north. With her two small children, she went to the railroad depot for a late night departure on "the cars," but before she could board, a detective intercepted her and ordered her to return to her home. According to Cyrena, Mrs. Huntington's friends advised her to remain in the city until the liberation.[31]

Cyrena's account was accurate, but Martha Huntington's own account was fuller. She related how her husband, Henry, then forty-five years old, had left Atlanta in early May. An outspoken man, he had kept to himself as much as possible during the war years, knowing that his Union sentiments could not be paraded. Protected by his age and his occupation as a dentist, the Vermonter avoided conscription successfully, but as Sherman's army drew nearer and bitterness toward Yankees increased, men such as Huntington could no longer evade the army. In early May, a friend warned him that he would be conscripted within two days. To Huntington and to others like him, this was a virtual death sentence—given the extent of the fighting, the bleak outlook for Atlanta, and the fact that inexperienced, middle-aged soldiers would be no match for Sherman's veterans. Huntington was "in despair," "sorely troubled," and faced with the terrible prospect of saving himself while leaving his wife and children vulnerable in the threatened city.[32]

Martha Huntington decided that her husband should leave as soon as someone could take him out of Georgia. A guide was found who would lead Huntington to the north Georgia mountains, where he would be handed over to another guide who would take him out of the state to safety. Once Huntington was safe, the first guide was to return to Atlanta with the Huntington horse and buggy and, after a few weeks had passed, bring the rest of the family out by the same route.[33]

The trip was successful but so dangerous that the guide refused to make another, and Mrs. Huntington and the children were forced to remain in the city. About a month later, they moved in with "Mr. F" and his family, planning to escape the city as soon as possible. After disposing of household goods and property (no mean feat in a city full of surplus property), Mrs. Huntington decided to try escaping by a northern route, moved not only by the desire to join her husband but also by the growing apprehension that Atlanta would become another Vicksburg, besieged and slowly starved into submission. Marietta, fifteen miles to the north, would be a jumping-off point. Through a friend, Mrs. Huntington sought a pass from Confederate authorities but was refused. She then decided to try a southern route by taking a train across Alabama and Mississippi to the Mississippi River, where she would seek transportation to Iowa, where her husband had gone. She planned to take the night train with her children, the eldest of whom was thirteen, the youngest only slightly more than two months old.[34]

The kindly Mr. F took the family to the depot at night. They encountered no difficulty at first, gaining admittance to the cars and luckily finding seats on the crowded train. As the train prepared to leave the station, Mr. F said good-bye and walked away from the cars. In a few moments, however, he returned, bearing the dreaded news that a squad of men had descended upon the depot with the intention of preventing the Huntingtons from departing. Mr. F quietly disappeared and took the Huntington luggage back to his home, fearing that it might be searched for evidence of treason. Forced by the men to leave the train, the Huntingtons returned to their temporary home. The officer in charge escorted them and demanded that the luggage be produced for a search. Mrs. Huntington had carefully destroyed personal papers that could incriminate, but she had saved and hidden "the last words" of her husband in the lining of a fan box. The officer opened the box but did not see the letter. Mrs. Huntington asked him what he expected to find. It was known, the officer replied, that she had been corresponding with her husband and was suspected of sending intelligence out for use by the federals. The officer and his detail left, but the Huntingtons were forced, for the moment at least, to remain in Atlanta.[35]

ON JULY 5, the sounds of distant guns suddenly diminished, and an eerie calm settled on Atlanta. Cyrena feared that the latest rumors of a great defeat of the Yankees could be true, although she knew the Confederates would continue to paint a false picture of military successes in order to boost what little remained of civilian and military morale. The position of the main Union armies was unknown. Reports circulated that a portion of the army had moved toward Fairburn in an effort to cut the LaGrange Road. Confederate general Johnston, it was said, had retreated to the Chattahoochee during the night. He was, Cyrena remarked, "something of a nocturnal traveller." The uncertainty stretched nerves to the snapping point.[36]

With the tension nearly unbearable by the middle of July, waiting for liberation became excruciatingly difficult. Every tidbit of news, every sound of battle, yielded multiple, often conflicting interpretations. The roar of the cannon resumed and sounded much closer, but the accuracy and significance of that too could be debated. Then on the night of July 18, the noise of the guns seemed so close that it made Cyrena believe that surely the Union Army would march into Atlanta by morning. They must move quickly, she thought impatiently, because there were "comparatively few obstructions." Confederate soldiers assured her that taking a stand in Atlanta would be "impossible if Sherman pushes them as he has been doing," but a visceral dread told her that the federals might wait too long, "as they always have done," until the Confederates had time to strengthen the breastworks.

For two weeks since the Fourth of July, Chester Stone, then attached to the Confederate conscript department, had stayed with Cyrena during a furlough. His unit had been camped nearby, and this had relieved some of Cyrena's growing sense of isolation; but the camp was to be moved a hundred miles south, out of the way of the battle, so Chester must leave. Cyrena had hoped that the Yankees would move against Atlanta while he was home. The two said a brief, emotional good-bye with only a "few words spoken, for each felt the seperation & the new dangers surrounding each." Cyrena "hinted" that if Chester stayed a little longer "he might be safe." Chester said that he would feel safe only when he knew that she was all right. "I must trust in God," Cyrena thought. "There was no one else to look to for protection." Chester "hurried away."

In the nearly sixteen months since Amherst had left, Cyrena was far lonelier than she had ever been. The slaves remained and so did the Lewises, but Cyrena justifiably felt isolated. The exodus of refugees since mid-May had gradually emptied the neighborhood. "All of my neighbors have gone—am alone on the hill," Cyrena wrote on the morning of July 19, 1864. All were gone, both those who had remained cordial and those who had piled opprobrium on Cyrena and the other Unionists. It would have been comforting to have someone nearby—no matter the loyalties. A friend, probably the staunch Unionist Mrs. Frank, pleaded that she come into the city and stay with her. Cyrena decided to remain in the house that she and Amherst had built. "This is my home, & I wish to protect it if possible," she wrote that morning. "There may be no battle here—if not I am safe; if there is one, where is any safety?"[37]

By the morning of July 19, Joseph E. Johnston had been removed from the Confederate command and replaced with John Bell Hood. The evening before, Union forces had pulled to within two miles of Peachtree Creek, approximately three miles northwest of the Stones' house. On the morning of July 20, the fighting at Peachtree Creek began, and after a day of bitter, bloody battle, the Confederate forces were defeated. But they remained in city entrenchments.

The next day, July 21, was stupefyingly hot, as Union and Confederate forces maneuvered for another engagement that might decide the contest for Atlanta. Federal troops sought control of Bald (or Leggett's) Hill, which stood about two miles east of the center of the city and approximately one and three-fourths miles southeast of Cyrena's house. A bitter struggle for the hill continued throughout the day.[38]

Cyrena remained at home in the midst of frantic Confederate activity. Her home was just inside the fortified ring of Confederate defenses of the city, with the troops of General Benjamin Cheatham's corps encircling her house, between it and the defenses, and between it and the city. Early in the morning, her yard "swarmed" with hungry Confederate troops, who gathered around the little house that served as a kitchen. Troops climbed onto the porch around the "yard kitchen" with dozens of requests for biscuits, milk, and utensils. "Yes—yes—yes—to every one," was Cyrena's reply, "thinking their wants would come to an end sometime, but they only increased."[39]

An injured Confederate colonel came to the house and asked if he could have a room. She said that he might. Would he protect them? Cyrena asked. "Certainly madam, as long as we remain here," he replied. The colonel sat down to rest beneath a tree before going into the room that Cyrena had prepared for him. A kindly man, he spoke tearfully of his own family and told Cyrena that her decision not to flee had been wise. Then suddenly, "a horrid whizzing screaming thing, came flying through the air and burst with a loud explosion" above the house. Cyrena was shaken. Although she had become accustomed to the "roaring of cannon & rattle of musketry," this was her first exposure to artillery. She ran to the colonel. He told her that it was an artillery shell; the Yankees were "trying the range of their guns." He again insisted that she was safer at home than in town. Another shell soon fell but without exploding. Cyrena had been reassured by the colonel's presence, but orders soon came for his unit to move out. She understood the reasons for the departure. "I can see there is no feeling of security in the positions held by these forces," she wrote. "They are on the move continually."[40]

In the midst of the artillery shelling, the musket firing, and the cannonading, Cyrena had another visitor. Dan had brought Mrs. Frank out from the city. Cyrena's friend had "sent word that she must see me once more in my home; she could not rest in thinking of me here so alone." The two women had barely begun to talk when successive flights of artillery shells passed "so fearfully" over the house and "seemed to be falling into the city." Amazingly, a courier on General Hood's staff quickly took Mrs. Frank back to the city and to her four small children.[41]

In the midst of the havoc, still another visitor came, this one a "poor woman" who pleaded with Cyrena to forge her husband's furlough papers, which had expired at the end of June, so that they appeared to expire at the end of July. "It almost kills William to think of going off & leaving me and the children now, with nothing to eat, & the soldiers all round us stealing what little we have," the woman said. "Fortunately," Cyrena wrote, "I found a bit of indigo, and the expired June unfolded in the fairest July—which caused a whole summer of joy to glow in the poor woman's heart."[42]

Within the previous few days, other visitors had become temporary members of Cyrena's household. Robert Webster, the black barber who had aided and assisted the Union prisoners, and his wife, Bess, had taken refuge there. The Websters also lived on Houston Street, about a half-mile from the Stones, where they had a pleasant, four-room house, well furnished and appointed. A few nights before, Confederate soldiers had suddenly burst into their home, "pretending to search for runaway Negroes," and while holding guns against the couple's throats had stolen all of their valuables: "silk dresses—jewellry watches & spoons were carried off." The two were now hiding in Cyrena's barn and were being protected by a "kind officer," who was also staying there.[43]

Throughout the day, the sounds of battle increased, "becoming fiercer each hour." The Confederate soldiers who passed in and around Cyrena's house offered the assurance that the Union army was being repulsed—an assurance, of course, that gave no comfort. By the end of the afternoon, a "horrible pall of battle-smoke" hung over the entire area, darkening the sky, erasing the twilight. In the dusk, Tom Lewis breathlessly ran into the house. "I tell you," he said, "We've got to git away from here now, for the men are falling back to the breastworks, & they're going to fight *right away*." Tom had no more than spoken

> when an *army* of black mouthed cannons came pouring into the grove & yard. An officer came up quickly & said—"They are falling back & will soon fight at the breastworks. It will not be safe for you to remain here madam." A dark night fell suddenly upon the earth, and how dark the night that shut down upon my heart! Not a star illumined it; hope, courage all gone—no husband or brother near, and an army of men around our home;—cannons belching forth a murderous fire not far away, & these silent ones in the yard, look so black & vengeful, as if impatient of a moment's quiet.

Nearly distraught, Cyrena went quickly from room to room—"not knowing what to do, or where to go; what to save—if any thing could be saved, or what to leave." The soldiers who accompanied the officer took charge, rolled up the carpets, and quickly packed many of the Stones' household items. The troops belonged to the Washington Artillery from New Orleans; they were members of a brigade under Brigadier General Randall L. Gibson. A young lieutenant told Cyrena that they were gentlemen. "My heart thanked them for their sympathy," Cyrena wrote that night in her diary, "but I thought they little knew upon what a 'traitor' they were bestowing it."[44]

Just as suddenly as the soldiers, "Mr. Y——" (possibly Robert Webster, who was also known as Robert Yancey) appeared. He had come to see if Cyrena was safe. Mr. Y and the Louisiana lieutenant then went to Hood's headquarters, where they learned that there would be no significant fighting that night. A Confederate major told Mr. Y that there was a chance that Cyrena might not have to leave her home after all. The soldiers momentarily anticipated orders to fall back toward Atlanta and thought that the city would likely be abandoned by the Confederate army. Cyrena took heart from this speculation, but nothing came of it. And so Cyrena's first trip as a refugee was put off until morning.[45]

At midnight, seated in the parlor of her "dismantled home," with the carpets rolled and standing in the corners, she had the presence of mind to write of the day's events and remembered the pleasant times spent in the parlor on "sabbath twilights," singing the old hymns with friends and family. Outside, she saw "lurid light from the fires dotting the yard & grove." It shone "fitfully in the darkness, revealing groups of soldiers here & there—some asleep on the earth, & some leaning against the trees in a listless way—as if life had no longer any gladness for them." Now she felt completely alone and nearly despondent "as the red waves of War rush madly by—sweeping away our pleasant Home."

Early in the morning, probably before six o'clock, Cyrena prepared for the long-resisted retreat away from the center of the struggle for the city, into Atlanta itself and the home of her friend Mrs. Frank. She said a heartfelt thank-you and good-bye to the members of the Washington Artillery, who had been ordered to move on. They regretted that they could not help her move. She thanked them, promising always to "remember their kindness and sympathy." Before leaving, she packed away most of her books in a large closet, abandoned the piano because there was "no earthly way of removing it," and left gallons upon gallons of preserved pickles and "nice blackberry wine." She also had to leave behind most of her menagerie—pet chickens, pet pigs, and cats. Later that day, almost unbelievably, the kindly Mr. Y went back to the house and with the aid of "some army negroes who were not afraid of shells" brought the piano and a favorite cat to Cyrena at Mrs. Frank's house.

By nine o'clock on the morning of July 22, 1864, Cyrena left the home she loved:

A strong feeling came over me as I passed down the shaded walk, where I had so often sauntered the peaceful summer evenings; but

I looked not back, for I felt as if leaving those pleasant scenes forever. If such upheavings—such sunderings & losses, were to be the entrance gate into the large life of liberty for which I had sighed— if this dark narrow way full of thorns & briers that so pierce & lacerate,—led out into the broad shining land of my Country—I would go fearless, casting back no look of regret & longing for what I left behind.

Cyrena walked the mile to Mrs. Frank's house, in the company of little Poppy and Mr. Y, who brought several small wagonloads of her possessions. After the migration, in the midst of the fury of the battle for Atlanta, and shortly after her arrival at Mrs. Frank's home, her diary abruptly ceases in midsentence.[46]

CHAPTER NINE

"Like the Frozen Snake"

Unionists during Battle and Occupation

Not long after Cyrena's arrival at Mrs. Frank's house—perhaps no more than an hour later—William Tecumseh Sherman, major general, U.S. Army, rode his horse up a lane toward the abandoned house of Augustus F. Hurt, about one and one-half miles northeast of Cyrena's home. The house was only a short carriage ride from the Stones' house, across Clear Creek and up the Cross Keys Road. Hurt and his family had been among the early refugees from Atlanta, leaving the hilltop plantation in the fall of 1862 for the safety of the family's other plantation in Alabama. According to his brother-in-law, the Macon lawyer and judge O. A. Lochrane, Hurt opposed secession "bitterly." The Hurt house, with its two hundred acres of crop and woodlands, stood near the present site of the Carter Presidential Library and afforded the arriving Union general a splendid view of Atlanta, looking southwest toward Cyrena's house, and a reasonably good perspective on the battlefield, looking toward Bald Hill, approximately one and one-half miles to the south (see map 3).[1]

Sherman took possession of a two-story white frame house, which had most recently been occupied by Thomas Howard, a bootlegging neighbor of the Stones. With eight principal rooms, it was a little more than fifty-five

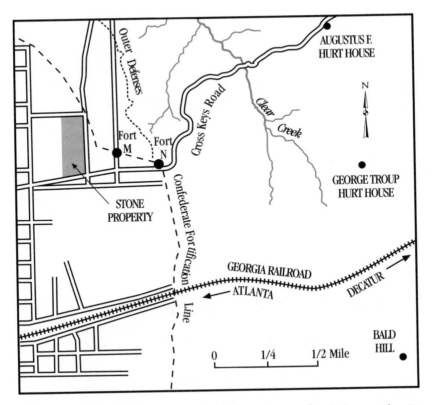

Map 3. Eastern outskirts of Atlanta on July 22, 1864, showing approximate locations of Confederate defenses and the property of Cyrena and Amherst Stone. Based on maps by Lemuel Grant.

feet wide and had a broad front veranda that ran the entire width of the house. On one side, the house had a pleasant bay window. In the rear, there was another veranda, slightly smaller than the one in front and built to enclose some small rooms used as pantries and for storage. The general stepped inside into a twelve-foot-wide hallway that ran the length of the house. The parlor and sitting rooms, located at the front on opposite sides of the hall, were each about twenty feet square. It was into one of these rooms that the body of Sherman's close friend, Major General James B. McPherson, would be carried later that afternoon and placed on an eight-and-one-half-foot long, white pine door taken from its hinges for the purpose. The rooms were barren of furniture; it had all disappeared during the tenure of the residents who had succeeded Augustus Hurt as master of the house. The present master's military steps would have echoed throughout the house as he had entered—if he entered alone—but the house, the yard, and the outbuildings swarmed with Union officers and men. This was command central. From here the orders would come and the directives flow that guided the Union army in its battlefield operations that day.[2]

Sometime during the morning, Sherman looked out toward Atlanta and confirmed what Cyrena had known the evening before: the Confederate troops had abandoned the outer defense ring and withdrawn into the fortifications built by Lemuel Grant in 1863. Cyrena's house stood near two of the promontories in this line of trenches and forts. Grant had denominated them Confederate forts *M* and *N*. His defense line was squarely in Sherman's line of sight, and even without a telescope the Union general could have seen the gun emplacements in the forts as well as hundreds of Confederate troops cutting timber for abatis to shore up the defenses.[3] Pulling back the Confederate troops into the city defenses was part of John Bell Hood's strategy to free enough soldiers to slip out of Atlanta during the night so that they could destroy federal supply trains at Decatur, five miles to the east, and attack the army of General James McPherson from the rear and on its flank. For a variety of reasons, but in large measure because of fatigue and communication failures among the Confederates, the maneuver did not succeed, and the timing of the Confederate offensive planned for July 22 was badly off. As a consequence, most of the conflict came in the afternoon.[4]

ALTHOUGH MUCH OF THE FIERCEST part of the Battle of Atlanta occurred in the area around Bald Hill, approximately one and three-fourths miles southeast of the Stones' home, there was near constant shelling and fighting around the abandoned house throughout the day. The house evidently did not survive the battle because of its closeness to the forts in the defensive line, its nearness to the fighting in the northern sector of the battleground, and its proximity to the artillery from near the Hurt house, the emplacement of which Sherman personally oversaw that afternoon. The exact fate of Cyrena and Amherst's home will likely never be known. It may have been torn down by the Confederate troops in their haste to reinforce the defenses or, like the similarly situated house of Ephraim Ponder on the northwestern defenses, it may have been intentionally shelled because it harbored Confederate sharpshooters on its second floor.[5] Although the Stone house did not survive, other structures on the property did—most notably the house that belonged to Richard Mayes and his wife. Whether the Mayes family remained in the house as long as Cyrena stayed in hers is unknown, but the house escaped the total destruction that befell the Stone house.[6]

The intense fighting, which commenced in earnest about noon, continued throughout the afternoon of July 22 and into the evening, producing great losses on both sides. The awful heat made matters even worse, compounding the horrible suffering of all, but especially the wounded. When night came, the battle slowed to a halt, with Confederate troops pushed back into the city's defenses, having suffered about fifty-five hundred casualties. Union casualties amounted to approximately thirty-seven hundred.[7]

The sterile statistics of war mask the horrific destruction and carnage that accompany battles like the one at Atlanta on July 22, 1864. First, there was the alteration of the physical landscape. Partially wooded and partially open, the suburban areas of the city where the battle occurred were pleasant and in places even beautiful. Cyrena Stone loved to go on outings in the pine woods and luxuriated in the cool calm of the forest, reminded perhaps of the majestic woodlands of northern Vermont with their mixtures of stately hardwoods and conifers. Even before the battle, the war had changed the landscape, as Lemuel P. Grant employed the forced labor of slaves to cut the trenches and build the fortifications that ran in an irregular circumference of earthworks and breastworks around the city. Military axes advanced the desolation as Confederate troops erected new breastworks and shored up old ones on the eve of the battle. Shell and shot did the rest, and by the end of the day on July 22, the mixture of forest and field looked as though a series of tornadoes had passed over the scene, snapping off trees, vacuuming the ground as they went along, then strewing debris across the freshly denuded landscape.[8] The stench of the battlefield in the days that followed was overwhelming—the odors produced by decomposing animal and human flesh so bad, it was said, that all birds but vultures flew away from Atlanta and did not return for weeks.

Oddly, there are few vivid accounts of the aftermath of the bloodletting. Most narratives of the battle concentrate on tales of heroism and courage or provide businesslike recitations of the details of battle as seen, in the main, by the generals, but A. W. Reese, a Missouri surgeon serving in the Union army, recorded an especially vivid and chilling account of the results of the wholesale butchering. On the morning of July 23, just before sunrise, Dr. Reese went onto the battlefield so that he could see it "just as the close of battle left it." The debris impressed him: bloody blankets, shattered weapons, "crushed and battered canteens," all of which lay in thick profusion over the expanse of the field.

But the ghastly morning-after scenes of death, described with a medical man's eye, convey most sharply the devilish outcome of the battle of Atlanta.[9] Immediately in front of the Union lines, "the ground was, literally, piled with the dead bodies of rebel soldiers—They laid, actually, in *windrows* and *piles,*" their bodies "mangled, torn, and battered by balls in every conceivable manner and shape." Most striking "were the *horrible* faces of the *dead,*" who were "laid in ghastly, sickening, repulsive heaps."

> Many of them were shot through the head and laid in a ghastly puddle of their own brains which had oozed from their shattered skulls. Some had fallen forward and laid flat upon their faces, with their white hands clutched full of dust—some seemed to have sunk down dead at once, and remained in a sort of 'doubled up' posture—others lay stretched out upon their sides with faces turned to the ground—but the major part had fallen on their backs, or had perhaps, struggled, in the last death agony, into that position—and so still laid, their white and bloodless hands, with fingers spread apart, thrown wildly up into the air above them, and their glassy, open eyes staring with their *expressionless* balls, straight up towards the pitiless sky.

Most of the dead, Reese observed, "were mere boys" poorly outfitted in "coarse, gray jeans," sockless, and wearing shoes that were "coarse and broken made out of untanned leather." No one who had not witnessed the results of such warfare, Reese concluded, could possibly have any idea "of the actual *repulsiveness* and *horrors* of scenes like those I have just described."[10]

It was a Union victory, although much more limited than Sherman and his generals would have liked. The Confederates failed to dislodge the Union armies from their lines around Atlanta and force them to retreat. Although the Union forces now held a great advantage, the Yankees had not routed the Confederate forces and taken the city. The stage was set for a protracted siege.

The whereabouts and activities of the Unionists during the battle of July 22 are difficult to trace. Alfred Austell remained in the city during the battle. Julius Hayden and his family had retreated to their Stewart County farm in southwestern Georgia. William and Emily Farnsworth remained in the city, and although no evidence exists to document it, the Farnsworths likely continued their practice of aiding wounded and sick Union soldiers.

Among the immigrants, Luther Faught, the foundry superintendent; Charles Bohnefeld, the coffin maker; Christian Kontz, the shoemaker; Peter Huge, the grocer; George Edwards, the pattern maker; and the Lynch brothers all remained in Atlanta. John Silvey, Lewis Scofield, James Dunning, William Markham, and their families also stayed. So did the black Unionists Robert Webster, Richard Mayes, Austin Wright, and Prince Ponder.[11]

Martha Huntington and her three children continued in refuge with the kindly "Mr. F" and his family of four children and three servants, who lived near the square upon which the city hall was located. Like most Atlantans, she was thoroughly terrorized by the cacophony of shelling and bombardment that went on during the battle. First came the booming cannon and the ensuing explosions. Then, Mrs. Huntington reported, "We could hear that queer hissing sound, once heard never forgotten, followed often by explosions." The artillery shells passing overhead had a particularly unnerving effect. "I have heard military men say," she went on, "that nothing was more completely demoralizing to an army than continued shelling. I believe it." The nearby courthouse served as a hospital during the battle. So many soldiers were brought there during and after the fighting and so close were the Huntingtons to the square that they constantly heard the terrible screams and groans of the wounded. Mrs. Huntington felt enormous pity. "If we could have done something for them! But we were powerless and could only sit and shudder, and mourn for misery we could not alleviate."[12]

In the immediate aftermath of the battle, the Unionists reappeared. Robert Webster, the mulatto barber who had hidden in Cyrena's barn, left the Stone property sometime during the battle and went back down Houston Street to his own house, which had escaped serious damage during the shelling. A few days after the battle, Webster undertook a mission of mercy that earned him the lasting admiration of the white Unionists of Atlanta. On July 25 or 26, James Dunning was passing through the city park when he "found" a group of wounded Union soldiers who had been deposited there during the battle and had gone untreated for nearly three days. The exact number of Union prisoners is unknown; certainly there were several dozen, perhaps more. What Dunning saw was wrenching. The soldiers were in unimaginable conditions of heat and filth, racked by pain and tortured by putrid, maggot-covered wounds. They seemed to have been without food and water since the battle. Their "sufferings," Dunning said, "were intolerable."[13]

Dunning first sought the help of some women but was unsuccessful. He then encountered William Markham, Robert Webster, and some other persons whose names he could not recall. Webster's assistance to the soldiers was particularly valuable, Dunning recalled. Not only did he dress their wounds, he also recruited other black men to aid in the task and to take the soldiers to one of the hospitals where they might get treatment. Webster's job required fortitude. James Dunning had always been the most critical of the Atlanta Unionists in judging who should be counted as members of their band. He had no doubts about Robert Webster and conferred upon him what Dunning would have considered the highest honor: "Mr. Robert Webster was one of the 35 or 36 loyal men of the city during the war."[14]

Other Unionists agreed. Webster stayed with the prisoners all afternoon and all night until he was able to arrange for them to be taken to the Roy Hospital in the city, where they might receive treatment. "Webster took charge of the whole matter himself," John Silvey said, "hired other colored people to help him and paid them for their services. . . . His conduct was noticed by the Union men here, and met with their hearty approbation and cooperation." William Markham concurred. Webster was "heart and soul a Union man," who had constantly nursed wounded Union soldiers since the Battle of Chickamauga. He was, Markham said, "entitled to great credit for his conduct." Yet another observer, William Lewis, noted that until Webster began his relief effort, "white and black people" had been afraid to attend to the wounded soldiers, fearing "to go in among them," because of the high level of agitation among the Confederates in the city. Lewis also claimed that Webster somehow managed to take two Union prisoners to his own house and hide them in his attic throughout the remainder of the siege.[15]

Webster was joined in the park by several others of the Unionist group, including the black tinner, Austin Wright. Prince Ponder was also among those who helped the federal prisoners at the old city park that day. Years later, the memory of the terrible condition of the soldiers who had been kept unattended was still powerful. "Some had maggots in their wounds," Ponder recalled. "Some [were] almost rotting with gangrene." Tom Crussell also left his family and came to the park to minister to the Union wounded.[16]

How many more of the Unionists may have participated in this risky humanitarian effort is unknown. E. T. Hunnicutt, deputy provost marshal, passed through a corner of the tree-shaded park and noticed the Unionists ministering to several hundred federal captives. He saw William

Markham, James Dunning, Volney Dunning (James Dunning's son), Tom Crussell, and two or three black men helping the prisoners as best they could. Hunnicutt noticed one prisoner whose amputated arm was "filled with worms." The man's misery was unbelievable. He cried out for someone to kill him.[17]

For the white men who came to the square, the risk of retribution from Confederates was outweighed by the attachment to the Union that motivated them. For the blacks, the prospect of early liberation and deliverance from a slave society would be enough. A cynic might object that these men were hedging their bets that huge numbers of Union troops would soon be in the city and that they would then be hailed for the aid given the wounded. This argument loses its force, however, when it is recalled that all of the men had, for the better part of three years, run considerable risks to advance the Unionist cause. Interpreted in that light, the scenes in the city park after the battle were but a logical extension of their wartime experience as Unionists.

The movements of the Unionists are equally difficult to trace during the six-week siege that followed the inconclusive battle. The heavy rain of Union artillery shells that fell on the city during that time did not discriminate, of course, between Confederate and Unionist households. Virtually all of the residents soon learned to deal with the terror, taking refuge during the bombardments in cellars and in dugout bombproofs reinforced with heavy timber and bales of cotton.

The fictional Cyrena Stone fervently hoped that the Confederates would soon evacuate the city, but they remained, and in the month of August the scream and crash of artillery shells continued almost unabated. In one day, more than a thousand hit the city. On the night of August 11, the house in which she was living took direct hits from five thirty-pound shells. The family with whom she was staying had fled to the cellar, but not before an adult and a child had been badly wounded by flying metal fragments. On August 15, the household awoke at midnight to the familiar whine of a shell that tore through a corner of the house. By then Cyrena and her hosts had become almost blasé about the shelling. Although "they thought that the house was coming down over their heads, . . . no one screamed; each arose and questioned in the calmness of petrified fear, 'What is that? It is a shell!'" which had fallen, unexploded into the yard.[18]

Like Cyrena Stone, others forced to leave their destroyed homes were taken in by fellow Unionists. Holmes Sells and his family moved in with the Christian Kontz family during the siege. During the ordeal, Mrs. Sells had three narrow escapes during a single day. Shortly after arising, a shell dropped into her bed. Then another fell "at her feet at the top of the stairs." When she ran toward the bombproof in the backyard, a third shell narrowly missed her.[19] William and Amy Dyer stayed in their own home throughout the battle. During the siege, Dyer made plans to leave Atlanta for the Union lines, but at the last moment he decided to stay in the city, convinced that the Yankees would soon come in. He fatally miscalculated, for on August 20, during one of the frequent bombardments of the city, Dyer was killed by a Yankee shell while standing in the yard of his property, leaving his wife and three small boys to fend for themselves.[20]

Others also died, including the superintendent of the Atlanta Gas Works, Charles Warner, and his six-year-old daughter, whose deaths were reported to a traveling reporter by William Markham. The fictional Cyrena Stone took note of the same tragedy, adding that the man "had been anxiously waiting for the Northern army to come, all that kept him in Atlanta being his daughter, whom he could not take, and would not leave." When the black barber Sol Luckie was struck by a shell near the center of Atlanta, the seemingly ubiquitous Tom Crussell stood nearby and helped carry the mortally wounded man into a store.[21]

William Markham's house was also struck by shells, an event recorded by his niece, ten-year-old Carrie Berry, who kept a diary during the siege. Carrie's family occasionally took refuge in the Markhams' large cellar on Alabama Street. Carrie also visited other Unionist relatives from time to time. During a lull in the bombing, she went to check on her aunt, Olive Healey, whose husband had left the city in late June. Mrs. Healey was fine (she had her own bombproof), and she and Carrie spent the afternoon together.[22]

The same day, General Sherman halted the bombing of the city, adopting a new strategy designed to force the Confederates out by striking the railroad south of the city. After a Union victory at the Battle of Jonesboro on August 31 and receipt of the news that Union generals were about to sever the last tracks leading to Atlanta from the south, John Bell Hood decided to evacuate the city. Hood made no public announcement, and yet another series of rumors rushed through the city as citizens noticed the unusual troop movements and the mournful behavior of the defeated, battle-weary Confederate troops. By evening, it had become obvious that the soldiers were leaving. The nearly always ebullient Confederate officer and journalist Henry Watterson, who had written letters full of reports on the frivolity in Atlanta earlier in the year, was somber on September 1 when he wrote his fianceé that "we shall certainly evacuate the city tonight." He was "well-mounted," and would leave with General Hood. "I am well," he wrote her. "I am constant. And I do not despair."[23]

On the way out, the Confederates destroyed huge amounts of ammunition loaded on railroad cars that were parked near the car shed, causing an extraordinary series of earsplitting, earth-shaking explosions that literally shook the city throughout and terrified the Confederate population, who wrongly ascribed the cause of the explosions to Sherman's armies. From the standpoint of the young journalist Wallace Reed, the shaken city "lay panting between two flags, under the protection of neither, abandoned by one, and with no hope of mercy from the other." Reed also took careful note of the transformed standing of the Unionists, under way since early in the year. From Reed's perspective, the loyal people "suddenly loomed up into importance, and not a few of their Confederate neighbors hunted them up, and requested them to use their influence" on their behalf. Reed thought the Unionists unusually generous in this regard and noted how they "felt as uneasy as anybody, and showed a disposition to keep on the best possible terms with their fellow-townsmen."[24]

BY DAWN ON SEPTEMBER 2, citizens were peering out of their houses, and a few began to move cautiously about, wondering if the Confederates had gone and if a Yankee occupation had begun. Henry Ivy, a neighbor of the Stones who had lived in Atlanta since 1843 and had known the place since 1830 when "There was nary house here," rose between dawn and sunup and immediately went out. The town was nearly deserted as Ivy picked his way through the rubble-strewn streets toward the corner of Peachtree and Marietta Streets, where he met a friend, Thomas Kile. Kile had the key to a vacated house on the south side of Marietta, and he invited Ivy to go inside with him. There the two men fortified themselves with breakfast whiskey before further exploration of the war-wrecked central portion of the city. Ivy and Kile stayed together most of the morning, finding some solid breakfast between seven and eight o'clock; but for the most part, they simply wandered around.

They soon encountered Unionist John Silvey, who had come from his home to the business section to check on his store. Silvey found it largely as he had left it, with no significant damage and no evidence of looting. The Yankees were on their way in, he told Ivy and Kile. Other than Silvey, Ivy and Kile encountered relatively few Atlantans and witnessed little disruption in the city. They did hear some noise coming from the area of the Confederate commissary near Norcross's corner. When they got there, they saw Confederate soldiers helping themselves to provisions and dividing them with perhaps fifty women and children, hungry and poor, obviously near destitution. At about the same time, a group of Confederate cavalry, left behind after the general evacuation of the night before, gathered on the public square and formed a line across the street. Seventy-five to a hundred strong, they were orderly and commanded by an officer. Perhaps the cavalry formed in response to a crowd of citizens—men, women, and children, black and white—who had begun to gather on the square, or perhaps the crowd had assembled in response to the sight of a Confederate cavalry unit still present in a city that was, for all practical purposes, devoid of Southern troops for the first time in more than three years.[25]

The character of this group of citizens, whether apprehensive assembly or marauding mob, would be a matter of dispute in years to come. Some chroniclers of Civil War Atlanta appear to accept the notion that widespread looting and lawlessness marked the hours between the Confederate evacuation and Union entry into the city. Numerous witnesses, several of whom were Unionists, downplayed the amount of wanton behavior, describing instead a city in numb shock from the battle and siege, greatly diminished in population, and exceedingly and understandably cautious about the immediate future. John Ficken, a cigar and tobacco merchant with ties to the Unionists, saw no such mobs, although he did witness one or two disruptions. Ficken's store itself was broken into by someone who heaved a "big rock" through a pane in his front door. So was another nearby store, which dealt in the same valuable and highly prized commodity. But widespread looting seems not to have occurred.[26]

Unionist Bridget Doyle ate breakfast at her house on Ellis Street and then walked to her store a few blocks away on Decatur Street. For several days, she had slept at the store, gradually moving her most valuable goods—whiskey and tobacco—to her house, fearful of looting by Confederate soldiers and fretting about what might happen when the city finally fell. Doyle stayed close by her store that morning. She saw a group of women and children seeking supplies from the commissary located next door in the Masonic Hall and a few groups of men, drinking and apparently looking for plunder, but evidently finding little. There were also a few stragglers from Wheeler's cavalry and some drunk, abusive soldiers and trailing prostitutes. The feisty old Irish woman remonstrated with the cavalry men: "I told them they were no gentlemen," she later recalled. They answered her by firing a shot into the air, which sent Doyle scooting back into her store. Like the other Unionists in the city, she saw no threatening mobs that morning, but she was most concerned about the Confederate stragglers "who wanted to injure all the Union people who staid here." At about noon, Doyle left her store on Decatur Street and went downtown to greet the incoming Yankees. She longed to find her brother, who was a soldier in the federal army.[27]

Not every Confederate commander had left the area. Brigadier General Samuel Ferguson and some of his cavalry forces remained in Atlanta when the sun came up on September 2. Mayor James M. Calhoun rose early, took his breakfast by 7:30, and then set out for Ferguson's headquarters. Calhoun wanted to consult with the general about surrendering the city. When he reached Ferguson's command post, he quickly discovered that the general wanted no part of any surrender. He opposed it flatly, Calhoun declared. Uncertain of what to do next and worried about the safety of the city, the mayor returned to his home near the courthouse. Only a little time passed, however, before a messenger arrived and declared that the general had changed his mind and wanted the mayor to return to his headquarters. "I done so," Calhoun reported. When Calhoun arrived, the general conceded that "on mature reflection, he thought it best to surrender the City and he would retire with his Command." "When his last man [had] filed past me," Calhoun went on, "then I could go out & surrender the City & if I saw any of his scouts [I was] to tell them to follow him."[28]

Calhoun then gathered a number of citizens to accompany him out of the city to find a Union commander, perhaps hoping to locate William T. Sherman himself; but Sherman was nearly twenty miles away, near Jonesboro. Calhoun and the surrender party met near the center of Atlanta and, after discussing how they should proceed, they began the horseback ride out of the city in search of General Sherman. This part of the story is well and frequently told. The men mounted horses and rode out Marietta Street through the destruction and rubble of battle and bombardment, sometimes having considerable difficulty making their way through the litter and filth of war. It was only a brief ride to the breastworks on the north side of the city. Near there, the group encountered Union troops led by Colonel John Coburn, of the Twentieth Army Corps. Coburn advised Mayor Calhoun to surrender the city in writing to the nearest general, William T. Ward. Calhoun wrote a terse message: "The fortune of war has placed Atlanta in your hands. As mayor of the city I ask protection to non-combatants and private property." By 11:00 A.M., the affair was over, and the surrender party followed the Union contingent back to Atlanta to take possession of the conquered city.[29]

So well known and so often rehearsed are these details that Civil War experts have never paused to inquire more than superficially into the membership of the party that surrendered Atlanta. Such an inquiry might seem to be an excursion into historical minutiae, except that Mayor Calhoun chose carefully in assembling the members of the surrender party. Survival logic suggested to Calhoun and others that it would not do for the city to be surrendered by rebels; it made much more sense to have the surrender party include a healthy number of Unionists. And so it did. James M. Calhoun was not himself a staunch wartime Unionist, but he had had great doubts about the war, had voted against secession, and after the war would swear that he had been a Union man. "Those of us who were Union men were very unpleasantly situated," Calhoun recalled, implying that he had maintained his Union sentiments throughout the war. In addition to the moderate mayor, the surrender party included Julius Hayden, William Markham, Alfred Austell, and Thomas G. W. Crussell, as well as Vermont-born E. E. Rawson, J. E. Williams, and Thomas Kile. Most surprisingly, and notably absent from previous lists, the surrender party also included the black Unionist Robert Webster, who rode along with the white men to present the city to General Sherman.[30]

By noon, Atlanta had begun to fill up with Union soldiers. Fear of Yankees was great among the Confederate populace. Four years of propaganda about Yankee devils contributed to the perfectly normal apprehension that any sane citizen would feel with the arrival of a conquering army. Men and women feared not only for themselves and their children, but also for their fortunes and their futures. Generally speaking, conquering armies during the Civil War had not meted out deliberate violence on large civilian populaces—at least not until the bombardments of Vicksburg and Atlanta.

Union soldiers entering Atlanta reacted to the city and its people in different ways. Many praised Atlanta's handsome buildings and houses but also commented upon the serious destruction wrought by the battle and the siege. One Indiana officer, Robert F. Bence, wrote to his wife that half of the structures had been destroyed in what had been a beautiful city, with "public buildings on a grand scale." Not many people were in evidence, he went on. Most of the citizens, mainly women and children, were glad that the struggle was over and "all pretend to be loyal now." Bence declared, however, that he had "no faith in the Unionism of one fourth of them." The Confederate population that remained was at best disconsolate. William

Le Duc, General Sherman's chief quartermaster, reported that "the secesh think that the fall of Atlanta decided the question of the rebellion. They are despondent if not hopeless." Some were also exceedingly bitter. Le Duc told of talking to one disaffected woman whose fourteen-year-old son had been drugged and conscripted. She hoped that "Davis, Toombs, Yancy, and Cobb" would be thrust into a "bottomless pit of hell."[31]

Women and "half naked children beg on the streets for something to eat," wrote Angus Brucker, a German-speaking medical officer, in a city that had only recently bespoken widespread "wealth and abundance." Brucker laid the blame for "all this" on a "few ambitious slaveholders." Loyalty to the Union had suddenly been regenerated, Brucker asserted. "Hundreds of rebels come daily to our lines and declare that they were forced to fight against their old Union, in which they lived happily and had no complaints." Now, he wrote sardonically, "they are all cured of their deceit and recognize their wrong."[32]

Henry Hurter, a Minnesota artilleryman, thought Atlanta "like all other southern cities." The Gate City of the South, he wrote, was "Rather filthy and badly demoralized." A. W. Reese visited the scene of the destruction of the eighty carloads of ammunition and also the Atlanta Iron Works and Arsenal. More than ten days later, the ruins of the arsenal still smoldered. Through the smoky haze, Reese saw terrific mounds of unprocessed iron ore, "a mass of blackened chimneys" and "a heap of ruined and dismantled machinery." Nearby he saw the destructive results of Hood's order to destroy his ammunition—the "truck wheels of a long line of cars," as well as five "ruined and dismantled locomotives." Numerous artillery pieces had also been left behind, purposefully damaged by the retreating Confederates but not irretrievably so; many were rescued and rehabilitated for use by the Yankees. "What a scene of destruction was here," Reese wrote. "Immense piles of musket-barrels, bayonets, twisted—scorched, and curled up by the fierce and fiery blast—great pools of melted lead—gunlocks—iron-ram-rods—fragments of shell—showers of grape, and other ruins of the conflagration lay around me."[33]

There were, of course, signs all around of the horror of the battle and siege visible not only in the eyes of the hungry women and children but also on the now-still battlefields just outside the city. Hugh D. Gallagher, an Indiana soldier, walked over the battleground that A. W. Reese had visited six weeks before and which had been the site of the Union-Confederate struggle for the city. It had rained hard several times early in September and would continue to do so for much of the rest of the month and into

October, turning the trenched clay battlefields into hilly, stump-ridden gulfs of red mud. Gradually, the rain rinsed away the layers of dirt that covered the hastily dug mass graves into which hundreds of bodies had been piled in the days after the battle. Arms and feet of the dead as well as "headless trunks and mangled remains" jutted grotesquely from the muck in rigid profusion, macabre reminders of the slaughter of six weeks before. At one point a simple sign had been erected: "24 Rebs," it said, showing where "our boys buried that number."[34]

Sherman himself did not arrive in Atlanta for several days, but members of his staff came up from Jonesboro into the city late in the day on September 2. Captain David P. Conyngham was among the first. A journalist, Conyngham was a careful observer of both the city and its people. As he entered Atlanta, he took note of the terrific destruction that had occurred and pronounced the suburbs (where Cyrena Stone had lived) in "ruins." The city itself had also "suffered much from our projectiles," Conyngham reported, with some houses destroyed and others collapsed as a result of the shelling. Getting about was hard; the refuse of war totally blocked some streets. Once-tidy gardens and yards had succumbed to defensive necessity. Where flowers and grass had grown, there were now cone-shaped mounds of dirt piled on top of lumber to protect dugout caves, or "bombproofs," some as deep as fifteen feet into the earth. In Atlanta, Conyngham found "strong proofs of the military despotism of the Confederacy." Everything, he said, had been "made subservient to the army." Old men and young boys had been pressed into service. The military had "swallowed up the blood and wealth of the land, leaving its poor deluded dupes stripped of everything."[35]

FOR THE MOMENT, the Unionists seemed to put aside fear and caution, giving vent to four years' worth of unspent emotion. Forty-seven-year-old James Dunning climbed a pole and attached an American flag to its top. The first American flag to go up in the city was on the Franklin Building on Alabama Street. When William Markham saw the banner flying over the city, "his happiness knew no bounds." The fictional Cyrena Stone also displayed her long-hidden flag as a sign of welcome to the Union troops. "When I unfurled my flag so long imprisoned and received the wild cheers in response, I felt simply blest" she declared. After the war, Aldis O. Brainerd, the St. Albans merchant who claimed a role in Amherst's arrests, described the real-life Cyrena as the troops were marching in. She stood on a busy street corner in Atlanta for perhaps two hours, he said, waving a silk flag as the troops filed by. "She was a splendid looking woman about thirty years old," his account continued, "and the whole army cheered her and her flag as they went past."[36]

Joy and relief could also be seen in reunions between loyal friends and families separated by the war. Richard Henry Hopkins, an officer in a Vermont regiment, sought out his cousin Cyrena Bailey Stone as he entered the city. He wrote to his mother in Vermont that Cyrena "was the noblest woman he ever saw" and "had remained true to the flag all this time and amid scoffs and jeers had ministered to the wants of the Union prisoners there most of the time for two years." She had been, he reported, "shunned and excluded from society but had 'endured all for righteousness sake.'" Back in Vermont, other family members, including half sister Louisa, were overjoyed to learn that Cyrena was alive.[37]

Some Union soldiers seemed surprised to find Unionists and loyal sentiments in Atlanta. "We found more Union sentiment in Atlanta than anywhere else in the South," wrote Julian Hinkley of the 3rd Wisconsin Infantry. "As our Brigade entered the city, at about nine o'clock at night, many of the women brought out buckets of water for us to drink." These women, Hinkley reported, "were very bitter against Hood's army, which they said had robbed them of everything that could be carried off." Other soldiers commented upon the delight that some Atlanta citizens, particularly the women and children, showed in seeing Union troops in the city. Arriving Yankees such as John A. Wilkens, an Indiana soldier, commented upon the groups of citizens who were glad to see the bluecoats, noting that they were "mostly foreigners" who had not wanted anything to do with the war. "Of course," he added, with a touch of Northern nativism, "we could not consider them as union men."[38]

Illinois soldiers encountered Luther Faught, foreman of the Winship and Company Machine Shop. Faught's house had been seriously damaged during the siege, but he and his family had escaped injury. Faught told the soldiers how he had been instrumental in bringing Union men into the machine shops in order to save them from conscription. Faught also told them how he had crated the valuable machinery from the shop, persuading Confederate authorities that he intended to ship it south. But the Maine native delayed shipping the apparatus "until it was too late" and thus saved it for the Union forces. The machine shop, one of the Illinois soldiers commented, was the only one left in Atlanta with machinery, "and it is now running for the Yankees."[39]

Rufus Mead, a Connecticut trooper, quickly made contact with Unionist families in Atlanta. On September 4, two days after the Union army marched in, Mead found one such family living in a tent in the southeastern section of the city. They were, he wrote, "as cheerful as any family I have seen . . . quite a contrast to the generality of the citizens we have met hitherto." Even the family dog was loyal. The canine "lies in one corner of the tent as contented as can be; in fact he is a thoroughgoing Union dog." While in the city, Mead lived "in the dooryard" of three families, "all strong union or northern descent quite intelligent." One of the women told Mead about the "ladies union meetings which they have held in secret all the while yet." She claimed to have "seen 17 union men hung at one time for bridgeburning, after only a mock trial with no positive proof at all." The woman obviously referred to the hanging of Andrews's raiders in 1862.[40]

Union chaplain Myron White, a New Yorker, encountered the pharmacist-minister David Young on September 4. For two weeks White visited with the Young family. Young, whose relationships with the black population were becoming well known, introduced White to a black minister and his congregation, probably the group to whom Young had preached on occasion. White himself also ministered to the group and later was instrumental in establishing a school for their benefit.[41]

The federal command initiated contacts with the Unionists in order to determine the identities of loyal citizens. Intelligence had been gathered for some time concerning the identities of Unionists. Amherst Stone believed that his name was on such a list compiled by officers of General Rosecrans's staff in 1863. By September 3, William G. Le Duc had met William Markham and learned that Markham was wealthy and a strong Unionist. The two first met when Le Duc was trying to find a coffin in which to bury the widow of a high official of the Masonic order in Georgia. Le Duc, who had the same powerful loyalty to the Masonic brotherhood as did many nineteenth-century American men, found a willing assistant in Markham, who was also a Mason. The two soon became fast friends. "I found him to be a loyal man, and one of the few reliable men to be met with in the South," Le Duc testified in 1866. "In relation to his loyalty, I have been informed and I believe that he was at all times under surveillance of the rebel vigilance committee of Atlanta, and at one time he was about to be hung . . . and was only saved by a friend of his on the committee." Markham sometimes came to Le Duc's headquarters with bits of information useful to the federals. On October 3, he confirmed a rumor that Jefferson Davis had visited Macon. In Davis's speech there, according to Markham, the Confederate president "arraigned [Joseph E.] Brown before the people as a traitor and called Joe Johnson a 'thief, liar and traitor.'"[42]

Markham wanted to remain in Atlanta as long as possible, but he was eager that his daughter, Emma, who was married to Robert J. Lowry, be safely removed from the Confederacy. He approached Le Duc about the matter, and the Union colonel, who was scheduled for a thirty-day furlough, agreed to take the Lowrys with him on the journey northward. By the end of September, when Le Duc and the Lowrys left Atlanta, there were no passenger cars available, so Le Duc commandeered a freight car, loaded food onto it, and prepared for a journey that could last up to two weeks. Le Duc shared his car with the Lowrys and made it as comfortable as possible, putting straw on the floor and installing a privacy curtain. Lowry was well fixed financially for the trip; he brought along $30,000 in gold, which he evidently intended to invest when the couple reached New York City, their final destination.[43]

Mary Summerlin, the young widow who had harbored a Union spy in 1863, also made contact with Le Duc and told her story to the Union quartermaster, who took it down word for word. Mary's house had been repeatedly struck during the bombardment, and she had been seriously wounded in the shoulder. She had no means to support herself, she told Le Duc, and "could not go North, except as a beggar." She asked to remain in Atlanta and soon received permission from General Sherman to do so. Le Duc reported that he had sent her story regarding the Union spy to Sherman, who, Le Duc was informed, "made good the loss of her house by our shells, and helped her in other ways."[44]

Another Union officer, William C. Armor, combed the neighborhood near his headquarters trying to "learn who were Union & who were not." Ultimately, the federals came to depend particularly upon Markham, James Dunning, and Thomas Crussell to confirm the loyalty of Atlanta citizens. Such identification could be valuable in determining whether Confederate citizens would be able to travel as they wished, and each of the three men was called upon to determine loyalty before the federals would issue passports to Atlanta citizens who wished to travel to the North.[45]

In fact, it appears that a formally constituted committee reviewed such requests. Samuel P. Richards had heard that "only those who could get vouchers for their loyalty from some one of a committee of several *Union* citizens who had been appointed by the authorities," would be allowed to travel. "So this morning [September 21], I went and presented my letter."

Richards had taken along a voucher from Henry Holcombe "to the effect that I had repeatedly spoken to him against Secession and had voted against it." In the end, however, Richards believed that he would have gotten the pass without Holcombe's letter.[46]

The Unionists themselves contacted the federal forces early to establish loyalty and protect property. Lewis Scofield wrote to the provost marshal general of the Army of the Cumberland in mid-September asking protection for his property. Scofield offered it for government use but asked that he and his family be allowed to remain in their residence. He would, he said, "render the Government any assistance in his power." William Markham lost no time in sending federal authorities a list of his extensive property holdings in Atlanta, offering the structures for use by the army and asking that they be protected. Markham's lengthy list of holdings included a block of five stores, sixteen offices, and two basement rooms on Whitehall Street, the Empire Hotel (then in use as a hospital), Washington Hall (another hotel), and various other commercial and residential properties.[47]

Soon after the occupation of the city, guards fanned out to some of the Unionists' homes, probably to protect them from the grim efficiency of Sherman's quartermaster and commissary officers, men charged with keeping the tens of thousands of federal troops supplied and housed. Within ten days after the fall of the city, groups of soldiers began their orderly dismantlement of buildings and their requisitioning of goods to supply the army. It became evident that Unionist property would not be immune from the voracious needs of the army. Olive Healey, left alone with her children when her husband Thomas fled, watched helplessly as Union soldiers efficiently stripped the Healeys' three-acre lot on Mangum Street of virtually anything of value to the army. Blue army wagons, each drawn by four mules, arrived in the Healey neighborhood, a signal that the pillaging was to begin. First the soldiers tore down the Healeys' one-and-one-half story, well-constructed carriage house. Then they pulled down the stable and barn and took away the lumber from all three structures to be sawed and reassembled into the small, tentlike structures that provided shelter for the troops during the occupation of the city. Next the liberators ripped apart the tall privacy fence that enclosed the three acres that had served to protect the Healeys' orchard and keep "the neighbors from looking in the yard." The animals were next: a cow, a calf, and two fine mules left with soldier escorts. The blue wagons then hauled off four sets of harnesses, Healey's construction tools, twelve hundred pounds of flour, twenty cords of wood, ten thousand board feet of lumber belonging to the contractor, a load of corn and fodder, two wagons, and some tobacco. Finally, soldiers armed with heavy pitchforks set to work digging all the potatoes from the patches that Olive Healey had carefully tended throughout the summer. When they left the neighborhood, the soldiers took with them property estimated to be worth $5,000.[48]

The army made little accommodation for blacks. Polly Beedles was a free black woman married to Henry Beedles, a slave owned by the Georgia Railroad Bank. Polly hired out for twelve dollars a month, and Henry worked on his own until midnight most nights. The two saved nearly everything they made and were able to buy a lot in Atlanta and build a house and stable on it. The couple took great pride in their achievement and put aside money to buy Henry from the bank. They appear to have done well financially during the war. Henry observed that there was plenty of work, and when the Yankees arrived, the newly freed slave went to work for the Union army.

Soon after the Yankee occupation, the blue wagons of the federals appeared at the Beedles' house near the fairgrounds. About 150 men were in the group of soldiers that confiscated the house and provisions. They methodically pulled down the plank fence around the property, and they tore down the house and the stable. Polly Beedles was at a neighbor's house when the wagons arrived; Henry was downtown. She ran toward their home and pleaded with the soldiers to stop. Henry soon arrived, and they both tried to halt the destruction. "Old man," the Union officer said to Beedles, "we must have your house and fence. My boys and myself have no tents and we must [have your?] house to build some tents." Uncle Sam would pay the couple for their loss, the officer promised. Beedles begged him to stop, but the Yankee refused. "They took down all my house, my dwelling, stable, well house, fence and posts. They did not leave a stick of anything on the place." Dejected and disconsolate, Polly and Henry could only watch as their dismantled home was hauled away in the blue wagons.[49]

Union officers did provide some aid to Unionists who had difficulty with the federal authorities. One of the Lynch brothers had been threatened with arrest or imprisonment by the Union provost marshal. Major T. C. Fitzgibbon, a Michigan officer, interceded on behalf of Lynch, declaring that he was "a loyal adopted citizen and friend of his," and Fitzgibbon was apparently successful in staving off the arrest.[50]

The Unionists were pleased with the recognition of their loyalty by the federal troops, but Confederate Atlantans showed thorough disgust at the prospect of the hated loyalists occupying positions of influence within the city. Loyalists such as James Dunning and William Markham did exercise significant influence over the fates of Confederates who, for one reason or another, needed their endorsement and who, like S. P. Richards, were willing to deny or at least minimize their own loyalty to the Confederacy. For the first time in four years, all of the Unionists could now avow publicly their own loyalty and perhaps even benefit from it. The willingness of some Confederates to ingratiate themselves with the Unionists, the tendency Cyrena Stone had recorded in the spring of 1864, accelerated in the autumn. The ranks of Unionists swelled. It was clear now who was influential, and it was also clear that Unionists had been placed in positions to make judgments about the futures of Confederates.

For some Confederate Atlantans, this was galling in the extreme. Thomas H. Bomar, a native of the city and on duty with the Confederate army in Virginia, wrote bitterly to his sister in Atlanta about the new state of affairs. From Bomar's point of view, Atlanta was dead. It was now a Yankee city: "the vile invader has polluted [it] with his vandel hordes." He was happy that "since it has fallen there went with it, many a traitor whom the South nursed in her prosperity." The traitors, of course, were the Unionists and included men such as "Wilson, Norcross, Hall, and Angier, originally Yankee adventurers they have sapped the South until they have become fat on our blood and have . . . returned to their bretheren." Now, "like the frozen snake . . . [and] like the miserable viper they have turned against our country."[51]

The *Intelligencer,* having fled to Macon, joined in the chorus of anti-Unionism and published a letter which, in crude satire, presented a spurious account of a dance at the Trout House on Monday, September 5. The ball had allegedly been attended by Unionists, blacks, and Yankee soldiers (including, it was said, General Sherman). The author of the letter painted an intensely racist picture of recently freed slave women being "feted" by soldiers and Unionists. "Billy Markham brought two nigger women to the ball," the author wrote, "and looked on the scene with grinning admiration. He nobbed with the blue bellies until he had to be retired to a carriage." Mayor Calhoun was also allegedly in attendance, thoroughly drunk, and toasting the Yankee conquerors. Enraged at the slander, Calhoun demanded the name of the author from the newspaper "for the purpose of claiming personal satisfaction." The *Intelligencer* refused to comply.[52]

Although the newspaper account was clearly false, some mingling did go on between Union officers and Unionists, and William Markham was at the center of it. Markham's son-in-law, Robert Lowry, later recalled how General Sherman's "headquarters band" performed in the front yard of the Markham residence on Marietta Street and how Markham gave "the best he had at his house . . . freely to the Union officers and soldiers." General Sherman himself, Generals George Thomas and Henry B. Slocum, and Quartermaster Le Duc, all socialized with Markham, who served cloying "drinks of peach brandy and honey" to his guests.[53]

Over the next few months, Markham became the object of much anti-Unionist rhetoric in the *Intelligencer*. According to the newspaper, Markham engineered an order from Sherman calling for the arrest of Alexander M. Wallace, George W. Lee, and E. T. Hunnicutt for maltreatment of "loyal persons" and prisoners of war in Atlanta. If arrested, the order declared, the three Confederates should be "denied all privileges of captured soldiers and treated and punished as traitors and outlaws." Whether the order was genuine is uncertain, but the *Intelligencer*, as well as Wallace and Lee, pronounced it authentic and used the occasion for splenetic commentary on Markham and the other Unionists.

Within a column labeled "Outlawry," the newspaper demanded retaliation from Confederate authorities, implying that Markham should be murdered. A "mean, vindictive man," he "was well known in Atlanta to be traitorous to the cause of the South," the newspaper declared, but he had been generously permitted (along with Lewis Scofield) to amass a fortune from the operations of the rolling mill. Now, he was "rioting" in his wealth, "free to persecute those whose only offence is they were loyal sons of the South." Wallace attributed the arrest order's origin to Markham's influence on Sherman. He also blamed Markham for persuading Sherman not to complete a prisoner exchange for his son, young George Wallace, who apparently languished in an Atlanta prison. Wallace claimed to have acted properly during the war, never dishonorably or illegally. He did confess, however, to a certain zealousness toward the Unionists: "The head and front of my offending can be found in an ardent devotion to my country and a fearless advocacy of her rights." "My zeal," he wrote, "doubtless gave great offense to the traitors and spies who infested Atlanta, of whom William Markham was the chief, and who was frequently denounced publicly and privately by me as a dangerous man to our cause even before the war for independence was begun." The order implied the freedom to assassinate Markham, Wallace concluded. All Confederate provost marshals and scouts should feel free to do so.[54]

Although Wallace remained fixated on the enemy Unionists, nearly four years of war had taken the heat out of his fierce devotion to the Confederate cause. Among the most inflamed of the secessionists in 1860 to 1861, his ardor had cooled considerably as the war dragged on. Like many Atlantans, his devotion to the Confederacy could, in private, be less resolute than in public. Wallace was devoted to his family and, when away from Atlanta on duty, he worried constantly about his wife and children, who suffered from ill health and perhaps poverty. Apparently, a daughter died while Wallace served the Confederacy, and his son, George, was caught up in the maelstrom that surrounded the demise of the city. "I cannot come home *now,*" Wallace had written to his wife in late 1863, "if you and all I love were dying of starvation." Without someone to replace him, Wallace said, General Bragg would not even approve two days' leave for him. "This may seem stupid or savage or both but it is true," Wallace told her. Obviously war-weary and prepared, at least in late 1863, to face defeat, Wallace was ready to leave the army, move away from Atlanta, and "escape for a time the Yankee invasion and approaching poverty." He sought (apparently without success) a medical discharge. Despite his desperation, he remained in the army until his return to Atlanta in December 1864 and apparently until the end of the war.[55]

Wallace had received his copy of the order from George Lee, who, since he had left the provost marshal's position in Atlanta, had continued in various noncombat roles for the Confederate army. Most recently, the checkered career of Colonel Lee included a court-martial for allegedly having sold exemptions from service. Lee had been acquitted.[56] Lee said that he had received his copy of the order from E. T. Hunnicutt, who had been questioned by a federal officer ("the officer of course not knowing that he was questioning one of the very persons whom he was seeking"). Lee also castigated Markham and implicated Anderson L. Scott in persuading Sherman to issue the order. Lee still took umbrage at being ordered to release Scott from prison in Atlanta. He noted that Scott had gone north, but contended that he had returned to the city immediately after Sherman had taken possession. Lee blamed the "traitors" of the "secretly organized . . . Union Circle" for his having been removed by the Confederate government from command of the Atlanta post. He had instituted a system for dealing with the Unionists, Lee declared, and the government should have stayed out of the way. "The very men whom I arrested and warned the Government of are the identical ones who remained in the city and have resorted to every hellish design imaginable in securing the destruction of loyal Southern citizens' property," Lee said. Markham was "low and pusillanimous," a man with "no small quantity of the *canine* in his composition." He and his colleagues Scott and Scofield were guilty of such egregious acts "as to be unworthy the notice of the most degraded votary Lincoln has."[57]

MEANWHILE, THE FEDERAL military occupation had taken a shocking turn. General Sherman had decided soon after taking the city that he would treat it as a military post and that all citizens would be forced to evacuate. Confederates would go south; those who wanted to travel into Union territory could go north. Sherman issued the order on September 7. The order to evacuate Atlanta profoundly shocked the Unionists. "They thought now the Union army had come," William Le Duc observed, that they could "talk, live and think freely as of old only with more freedom and now the order to remove fills them with dismay and grief." Many if not most, would become "homeless and penniless." Atlanta was about the size of the city in Ohio where Le Duc's wife lived during the war, and he tried to convey the impact of the decision by comparing Atlanta to her Ohio home. "Suppose all men [were] required to leave Mt. Vernon within ten or twenty days and you can imagine the consternation it would produce. When will we go. What will we do for a home. How shall we live, Can we take our property with us."[58]

Unionists had longed for the coming of the Yankees, but now that the Yankees had appeared and Atlanta had become a Yankee city, they found, according to David Conyngham, "our friendship as destructive as the rebels' enmity." Conyngham encountered one old man who professed strong Unionist sentiments and bitterly complained about being forced to leave his home. "I had neither hand nor voice in bringing on this war," he said. "I wanted to live under the old flag." He reported how he had done everything he could to relieve Union prisoners and claimed that his only son had been shot while helping a Yankee prisoner escape. He went on to say that the rebels had stripped him of his property, called him a damned Yank, and would have hung him had it not been for his age. From this Unionist's point of view (and Conyngham agreed), he had given ample evidence of his loyalty. Then he had been ordered to leave the city. "And now what's my reward?" he concluded. "You hunt me from house and place in my old age. . . . I have the alternative of going north and starve, or going into the rebel lines and being hung."[59]

Initially, there were to be no exceptions to the order, but some of the Unionists petitioned to remain in the city. With William Farnsworth taking the lead, the Unionists contacted three of the U.S. surgeons who had been assigned to care for wounded Union prisoners during the war. On September 10, the three wrote eloquently to Sherman on behalf of the Unionists who had consistently aided the wounded prisoners in Atlanta.

The surgeons wrote that the Union wounded had barely survived on the food provided by the Confederates:

> we received almost daily the personal attention of several Union sympathizers who kindly furnished us out of their scanty supply nourishing food such as chickens, potatoes, various kinds of soup and gruel, milk, coffee, tea, soft bread, fruit and underclothing so much needed for these badly wounded cases. The individuals [who] were personally known to have engaged with Mr. Farnsworth in these acts of mercy are
>
> Mrs. A. Stone and family
>   "   H. Stansel and family
>   "   E. Paine
>   "   Bridgett Doile
> Miss A. Packard supplied by her brother-in-law Louis Scofield
> Miss Josephine Woodbury
> Mr. Wm. Markham
>   "   James Dunning
>   "   B. E. Dunning
>   "   Schinck (old gent)
>   "   T. G. Healy
>   "   L. R. Faught
>   "   Ransford (only one of this name in town)

The surgeons thus provided Sherman with a partial list of the Unionists in Atlanta. These were "respectable and industrious people," the surgeons stated, "and perfectly able to support themselves. They anxiously pray and we hopefully request that they be allowed to remain in their homes in this city."[60]

Sherman replied that he recognized "in the very highest degree the service" of the Unionists and was "ready not only to compensate them by reciprocal favors but in any manner." Thus, he gave permission for this small group of loyalists to remain in the city after evacuation, but he added a word of warning: Atlanta would become a fortress, and the Unionists should realize that even *their* homes might be leveled in the erection of fortifications. "I put it to them," Sherman wrote, "if it would not be more comfortable for them to go to some more peaceful home. Think of this, and do not judge from appearances at this instant of time, but rather with a knowledge that the future will make Atlanta an important battlefield."[61]

In the end, about fifty families received permission from the Union army to remain in the city. No definitive list can be found, but most of those permitted to remain were Unionists. Scattered evidence also indicates that non-Unionists who had critical occupations could qualify to remain. Some innkeepers, for example, appear to have been exempted. Robert McCroskey, who supplied Union espionage agents with valuable information, qualified both as Unionist and innkeeper and sought permission through the manager of the Trout House to remain. Army authorities wanted to be clear about the loyalty of persons requesting permission to remain, and applications to stay in Atlanta were closely scrutinized.[62]

The order to leave the city had a profoundly disruptive and emotional effect upon those Atlantans, Union and Confederate, who had weathered the battles and the siege and were now forced to leave their homes and property. Ten-year-old Carrie Berry captured the essence of the adult trauma: "The citizens all think that it is the most cruel thing to drive us from our homes." Her father, Madison Berry, was nearly distraught. "Papa says he don't know where on earth to go," Carrie wrote, while her mother "seems so troubled she can't do anything." The family spirits lifted when Madison Berry "heard that if he could get into business he might stay in Atlanta." The contractor succeeded and won federal permission to remain. Carrie's judgment that her father's occupation accounted for their remaining may have been correct, but it also seems likely that links to the Unionist group and family ties with the Markhams and Healeys contributed to the Berry family's obtaining the much desired approval.[63]

Joshua Hill, Georgia's most prominent Unionist, a resident of Madison, and the defeated candidate for governor in 1863, came to Atlanta in late October to see the devastation and to visit friends, including the remaining Unionists. Hill found "no wanton destruction of property to any extent beyond fencing and outbuildings." Conditions in the city were bad, however, and he told a friend that Sherman had been correct in his "arbitrary order" that Atlanta be evacuated. Hill found those who remained in the city "generally in a pitiable condition with small available means and no market." They were "faring badly," he reported. While in the city, Hill saw Henry Holcombe, Alfred Austell, William Markham, and other Unionists. He judged them to be like most Atlantans, "much troubled." William Markham "had sold his furniture preparatory to leaving." Austell "was preparing to go to LaGrange." Larkin Davis, an Atlantan on the fringe of the Union Circle, "had suffered the loss of all his houses and was living with Austell." The countryside around Atlanta, Hill reported, "as far as the eye can reach is one prolonged scene of desolation. . . . The silence that reigns is only broken by the sound of moving masses of men, trains of wagons, squadrons of cavalry & occasionally a railway train. I wish it could be seen by every war man in Georgia. But I doubt if it would do any good, so visionary & fanatical have they grown."[64]

In the end, the vast majority of those who weathered the battle and siege had to leave. The mythology that surrounds the story of Sherman's occupation of the city insists that the evacuation affected only Confederate citizens. Even recently published books perpetuate this baseless notion. Sherman gave Atlanta citizens a choice: go south or go north. Part of the process leading up to the evacuation of the citizens was managed by William Le Duc, who was charged with interviewing citizens before they were sent out. Although there is no accurate way to know exactly how many citizens in total left the city, apparently about seventeen hundred citizens chose to go south. A detailed listing, widely accepted in Confederate hagiography, has it that 446 families went south. We have no precise number for the number of people going north, but one source indicates that a like number of families went north, and one scholar estimates that a total of approximately thirty-five hundred persons left the city. Thus, it is distinctly possible that as many or more Atlantans chose to go north as were expelled to the south. Virtually all of the Unionists who did not remain in the city went north. Only a few chose the more uncertain path that led deeper into the Confederacy. Julius Hayden and his family had left Atlanta during the battle and refugeed to their farm in remote southwest Georgia. There, the Haydens stayed largely to themselves, venturing out only infrequently because knowledge of Hayden's loyalties preceded him to that part of the state. The only person closely identified with the Unionists who was reported to have traveled South in the forced exodus was E. W. Munday. In actuality, however, Munday remained in the city.[65]

Alfred Austell also went south but not until mid-November. Austell sent his wife and children out of the city before the battle, but the banker-planter stayed in the city to protect his considerable property as best he could. He remained throughout the Union occupation, but when Sherman departed in November, he also left and fled to LaGrange, Georgia, and then went into hiding in Alabama, surreptitiously passing back and forth into Georgia. On one such trip, Confederate officials in West Point, Georgia, arrested and charged him with disloyalty for failing to report for military duty. Austell later said that the Confederates ordered him to report to General Howell Cobb in Macon, but that when he arrived there, confusion reigned because of the approach of Sherman's troops, and he simply ignored the order.[66]

Others remembered differently. According to Jared Whitaker, Austell was brought to Macon by Confederate military authorities. Whitaker, whose office was in the same building as Howell Cobb's, received a message one morning from Austell, who was housed in a nearby hotel. Austell told Whitaker that he had been arrested for remaining in Atlanta after the Confederates had left and for being a Union sympathizer and traitor. It was all false, he said. Although he had opposed the war, he did so because he was convinced the South would be defeated and slave owners would then lose their chattels. He had pretended to be a Union man, Austell went on, in order to save life and property. Austell asked Whitaker to intercede on his behalf with General Cobb. Whitaker called on Cobb and his adjutant and told them Austell's story, adding his opinion that Austell was likely capable of being loyal to either the North or South, given appropriate circumstances. Austell then met with Cobb and managed to secure his release. Whitaker was unable to say why Cobb decided to release him.[67]

Evidently, Austell had also tried secretly to send a large sum of cash southward out of Atlanta. William Le Duc reported to General Sherman that some Atlanta Unionists, including Mrs. Holmes Sells, had been approached in Chattanooga by a man named Dick Turpin, who claimed to be a spy for Sherman. Turpin, "A man with intensely black whiskers," dressed completely in black velvet, and with "the appearance of a sensual, cunning scoundrel," claimed that he and a female agent (a Mrs. Clements) "had fixed Gen. Austelle." According to Turpin, the unlucky Austell enlisted Mrs. Clements to take the money south through the Yankee lines. Turpin, who was in league with the woman, took the money and bragged that he had caused Austell's arrest.[68]

Some Unionists who went north left soon after Sherman arrived in the city; others waited until the Union army was nearly ready to depart. Most went first to Nashville and proceeded from there to various places, including Iowa, Ohio, Washington, D.C., New Jersey, Pennsylvania, and Connecticut. Perhaps the largest number went to New York, where numerous exiled Georgians already resided. The exact dates of departure for each of the Unionists remaining in Atlanta are impossible to ascertain. Of those who got permission from Sherman to remain, nearly all decided to leave after it became known that the Union forces would themselves leave the city, raising the frightening certitude that Confederates would soon be in charge again.

It was during the interim between Sherman's decision to leave and the actual departure of the Union forces that most of the remaining Unionists decided to go. Word of their decision quickly reached the *Atlanta Intelligencer* in exile, which gloated over the reported departure of "Dunning, Scofield, Markham, Stone and all the rest of the mongrel curs." All loyal citizens should be "devoutly thankful," the newspaper opined, that the "curse of their traitorous presence will no more disgrace Atlanta."[69] Flawed as the information was in its particulars, most of the Unionists had indeed departed by late October or early November.

William Markham and his family went to New York City, where the resourceful Markham quickly made contact with Daniel Chaffee, who had left Atlanta in the early days of the war and was now employed as a special agent for General John A. Dix, commander of the Department of the East of the U.S. Army, headquartered in New York City. Chaffee arranged for Markham to meet Dix, who had issued an order requiring that all Southern Unionists report to his office to take an oath of allegiance. Later Markham would meet again with Dix in an effort to organize loyal Southerners who were living in the city. James Dunning and his family left Atlanta on November 6, traveling first to New York City and then to Jersey City, New Jersey. Olive Healey joined her husband in Connecticut. Mrs. Holmes Sells went north in late September, possibly to Pennsylvania. Christian Kontz took up residence in Washington, D.C., where he opened a shoe repair shop. Robert McCroskey went back to east Tennessee. David Young, A. N. Wilson, and Lewis Scofield went to New York.[70]

Sometime during the autumn, Cyrena Stone decided to leave the city. She traveled to Nashville and there reunited with Amherst before proceeding to New York City, where Stone had opened a law practice. Soon, and with great happiness, Cyrena would return to the familiar confines of East Berkshire for a long, pleasant reunion with family and friends in northern Vermont.[71]

Most of the Unionists took General Sherman at his word that Atlanta was no longer to be a city, that it would become a military post and a hazardous place to remain, and the majority of them left. Neither the coterie of Unionists who remained nor those who departed could have suspected that the Union forces contemplated further destruction of Atlanta and that, in the end, much additional Unionist property would be destroyed or consumed by fire. Neither could they have suspected that the destruction would be planned with exquisite care, nor that General Sherman would, by his intervention in the planning, inject moderation into a design for wholesale destruction.

THE BURNING OF ATLANTA has a hold on the American psyche of the strength of the Battle of Gettysburg and the surrender at Appomattox. The film *Gone with the Wind* may be largely responsible, its visual images of a great municipal conflagration telling a story incomplete as to both time and manner of destruction. Margaret Mitchell and the historians who have written about this event have had it more nearly correct. Until recent documentary discoveries, however, we have not known key details regarding the military preparations leading up to the destruction of the city and the shift in plans that occurred just before the destruction began.

Detailed planning for the immolation of Atlanta began with the senior officers of three regiments that had served as provost marshal guards in Atlanta since early September and who had become familiar to, even friendly with, the Unionists. Amiable ties notwithstanding, it was evident that the 2d Massachusetts, the 33d Massachusetts, and the 111th Pennsylvania Regiments would discriminate little if any on the basis of loyalty when it came to military exigency. With an eye clearly on the future, Colonel William Cogswell, who commanded the combined units, carefully saved the essential papers that contained the most detailed thinking about what to destroy and how to destroy it before the Union forces abandoned the city on November 14. Until recently, these documents have lain undiscovered and unread in an archive in Cogswell's home state of Massachusetts.[72] Although the actual destruction of the city was carried out under the command of Colonel Orlando Poe and although features of Poe's work differed from the plans Cogswell and his men designed, these documents present a clear view of how a nineteenth-century army approached the systematic devastation of an American city.

In late October, Cogswell ordered each of his three regimental commanders to prepare a "Plan of Destruction" for specific parts of the city assigned to each unit. Each was to tell the colonel what would be destroyed, who would destroy it, and how it was to be destroyed. It was a clearly conceived, simple plan made easily understandable by neatly drawn maps with numbers carefully keyed to structures marked for destruction.

Charles Fessenden Morse responded for the 2d Massachusetts. "I have the honor," he wrote to Cogswell, "to submit the following plan for the destruction of buildings assigned to me, and the names of the officers detailed for the execution of it." Like the other officers involved, Morse intended to use both fire and explosives to implement the plan. "I propose to mine the large brick passenger depot at the four corners and to complete its destruction by fire," he wrote. The adjacent wood sheds and stables would also be burned. The Georgia Railroad roundhouse and freight depot would need to be mined, but fire would easily destroy the buildings adjacent to it. The "large chimney nearby" would also require mines. The Georgia Railroad freight depot and platforms would be burned as would the workshops and materials in the yard. Morse's regiment also had the responsibility for destroying the Atlanta Machine Shop and its adjacent sheds. A combination of explosives and fire would do the trick here. Morse also relayed plans for the destruction of the freight house "out on Geo. R. R., water tank and flouring mill nearby to be destroyed by fire—Chimney of flouring mill will be mined."

The efficient Massachusetts officer also included a detailed description of the method he would use to mine buildings that could not be destroyed by fire, complete with a carefully drawn sketch showing how a chamber would be excavated at an angle from inside the building and reaching under the wall. Inside the chamber was a wooden box holding a sack of powder. A wooden tube poked through to the surface and contained a fuse that ran a safe distance outside the building. The space around the box would be "filled with earth and stone and rammed hard." Altogether, Morse estimated, he would need five hundred pounds of powder, one thousand feet of fuse, "axes, spades, and picks," and only one day to prepare.[73]

The other two officers gave Cogswell similarly crisp reports. William Walker of the 111th Pennsylvania would take charge of the destruction of the "Stone Freight Depot." This sturdy building required mining "in a number of places, for which purpose the stone flags of the floor will be raised and mines placed inside." Only the roof of this structure could be destroyed by fire. By contrast, the Western and Atlantic freight depot could be burned. The W & A roundhouse, however, would require mining and the "pulling down [of] the iron pillars" of the inside wall. "The Roof," Walker observed "is easily burned." The turntable could also be fired; the troops would collect fuel and force it under the table and then ignite the combustibles. The railroad's machine shops would have to be mined "together with the arches and Boiler beds." Surrounding buildings, including the car sheds, could be burned.

Walker also bore responsibility for destroying the bridge that crossed the railroad tracks in the center of town (it would be fired in the center and at both ends). Walker also planned to destroy the "Gas house" belonging to the Atlanta Gas Light Company, of which the Unionist Julius Hayden was president, as well as the large carpenter shop and foundry on the opposite side of the road. In addition, Walker and his men would destroy the Winship Foundry and Machine Shop, along with its nearby sheds and buildings.[74]

The 33d Massachusetts provided an unsigned "plan of Destruction" and a keyed map of central Atlanta detailing the Regiment's targets. Massachusetts's succinctness and thoroughness left little room for interpretation.

PLAN OF DESTRUCTION

No. 1. The stable on Mitchell Street with brick walls, burn the inside out. Half round Engine house mine under the four corners and blow up. Turn table belonging to the same—burn.

No. 2. Two brick blacksmith shops on Hunter Street burn the inside out. Large wooden building (store house) on the Corner of Mitchell & Forsyth St. burn, one blacksmith and carriage maker shop between Forsyth St. & Whitehall street burn.

No. 3. Burn each side of Whitehall Street from Mitchell St. to the railroad crossing.

No. 4. Burn Peachtree St. each side except the N.E. corner as per plan.

No. 5. Burn Rebel Barracks.

No. 6. Burn Trout House, Washington Hotel & Barracks in vicinity.

No. 7. Burn College (*marked* "Dome Building" on plan).[75]

Before the plans could be carried out, however, General Sherman intervened and ordered that Captain Orlando M. Poe take charge. Sherman determined that fire should not be used in the destruction, as called for in Cogswell's plans and that instead those buildings designated for destruction would be brought down by demolition engineers who would use battering rams and other heavy equipment, ruining the designated portions of the city by "breaking up furnace arches, knocking steam machinery to pieces, and punching all boilers full of holes." Fire and explosives used in the manner called for in Cogswell's plan would have doubtlessly produced much wider destruction. Fire, almost impossible to control, would spread from block to block, and given the wide geographic area covered in the Cogswell plan, fire might destroy the entire city. Poe determined that only after the engineers had applied their nonpyrotechnic skills would fire be used and then only to burn any leftover rubbish. The overall destruction was to begin on November 12.[76]

Sherman's orders were followed: the only time that fire was used by the engineers inside the city was in burning railroad ties on November 15 as a part of the general destruction of the railroad network that Cogswell and his group had also planned. Nevertheless, as early as November 11, an extramural burning of Atlanta had begun, almost sporadically it would seem, as groups of Union soldiers, determined to leave Atlanta in ashes, started fires. Perhaps, as David Conyngham noted, some "rebel incenderaries" may have been involved. In his diary, Captain Poe attributed the burning of private property in Atlanta to "unauthorized persons," an allusion to soldiers acting without orders. Later, he would say that "many buildings in the business part of the city were destroyed by lawless persons, who, by sneaking around in blind alleys, succeeded in firing many houses which it was not intended to touch."[77]

Some public buildings did escape the conflagration, including churches and the city hall. History has traditionally given full credit to Father Thomas O'Reilly, pastor of the Church of the Immaculate Conception, for saving the churches. O'Reilly, it is said, pleaded with General Slocum to spare them. But there were others who, during the fiery holocaust, helped to stave off attempts to destroy the churches, and they were Unionists. Both Mrs. Henry Holcombe and Michael Lynch were present near the city hall during that awful night and added their pleas to those of O'Reilly for sparing the churches and the nearby city hall. Mrs. Holcombe later said that it was she who personally prevented the torching of the houses of worship.[78]

It is not possible, of course, to determine how much Unionist-owned property was destroyed by unauthorized burning or as a result of Sherman's orders, because no detailed plans such as those developed by Cogswell have survived. Cogswell's plan, however, called for numerous structures owned by loyal persons to be blown up, burned, or both. In the Cogswell plan, an entire block of stores belonging to William Markham, as well as two hotels, including the Empire Hotel and the massive, 150-room Washington Hall, were to be destroyed—as well as other property owned by the wealthy Markham throughout the business section of the city. In addition, the Atlanta Gas Light Company, of which Julius Hayden was president, was also to be destroyed.

SHERMAN'S MOTIVATION in issuing orders intended to minimize the amount of destruction in Atlanta cannot be determined. There is no evidence to suggest that he may have had the property of loyal people in mind when he altered the Cogswell plan, but the Union general had shown concern for the Unionists, as had many of his officers. And reducing destruction of Unionist property would have been in keeping with the army's earlier practices of sparing, whenever possible, the property of loyal persons from destruction.[79] After Sherman, little remained of Atlanta, and few citizens remained in it. But those who did stay were Unionists. They had stayed in the city from the beginning of the madness to its culmination in the destruction of the city. For a few days, Atlanta was theirs and theirs alone.

CHAPTER TEN

The Loyalty of Reconstruction, the Reconstruction of Loyalty, 1865

Battle, siege, and Shermanesque destruction created an apocalyptic panorama in the exhausted city. Overspread with pungent smoke, pocked by pools of fetid water, menaced by packs of hungry dogs, and assaulted by the rotted remains of thousands of dead animals, Atlanta belonged in one of the lower rings of Dante's hell. The withering heat of summer and the drenching rains of autumn gave way to a winter of sleet storms and cold temperatures. Ice followed fire.

For a few days in mid-November, the Unionists presided over the desolation, living uneasily in a depopulated city that only months before had bustled with the wartime energy of more than twenty thousand people. Very soon, they were joined by groups of vagrants and the dispossessed, who scuttled in and about destroyed Atlanta, pilfering and scavenging their way through the detritus left by evacuees and armies, gathering whatever plunder they could. On November 19, the male citizens of the city assembled at the city hall and tried to make sense of things amidst anarchy, hunger, and the prospective return of vengeance-seeking Confederates.[1]

Although survival was the all-consuming concern, it would only be a short while before the calculus of loyalty would once again enter their lives.

Throughout the South, Unionists lived in fear of the abandonment of garrisoned towns by Union armies. Although the forced exodus of Atlantans had greatly reduced the numbers of those who would be affected, the fifty families who remained in Atlanta, whether Unionist or not, were subject to the reprisals of returning Confederates, who charged that in staying they had willfully consorted with the enemy.[2]

By the first week in December, with Sherman's army closing in on Savannah, Confederate troops once again occupied Atlanta. Within a few days, the *Intelligencer* returned from Macon, announced that "The city is fast filling up," and predicted that business would soon resume. Among those in the first wave of returnees was a surely exhausted Mayor Calhoun, but hard core Confederates also filtered back into the city, including former city marshal Oliver H. Jones and former provost marshal George W. Lee.[3]

Barely a week passed before the *Intelligencer* revived the issue of loyalty. Atlanta would soon "rise from the ashes," the newspaper proclaimed, as a result of the "devoted loyalty and enterprise" of the citizens. "We write of *loyalty*," the unchastened editors emphasized, "for the reason that ever since the day Georgia seceded from the old and rotten Union, Atlanta has been cursed with the presence of men and women who were as spies in its midst, and did all in their power secretly to promote its downfall." In the past, large numbers of Atlantans had "gone over to the enemy . . . proof strong as holy writ of their disloyal proclivities. In the future, Atlanta *must* not contain, *must* not heed, and *must* not . . . tolerate the presence of such as citizens, much less place them in high positions."[4]

Despite the overwhelming tasks of restoring life to the city the returning Confederates eagerly sought retribution from the small group who had stayed, and they engineered yet one more wave of terror against the Unionists, conveniently broadening the definition of disloyalty to include anyone who had made the unpatriotic decision to remain in Atlanta while the Union forces were there. Although the record provides scant insight into the events that transpired in Atlanta during the late winter and early spring of 1865, the effort to punish Unionists represented the last significant attempt to enforce loyalty to the Confederacy in Atlanta. In the early months of 1865 few Atlantans, the *Intelligencer* notwithstanding, could have been unaware that the Southern nation was moribund.

Madison Berry, with ties to the Unionist group but with no obvious record of disloyalty to the Confederacy, drew the ire of Confederate authorities for wanting to keep his family in its still-intact home. He was arrested and taken to Macon to be tried for disloyalty. Berry had served as a clerk in the Union quartermaster's office during the occupation, and this, together with his close family ties to the Unionists, made him a likely target. Berry's family was terrified at what might happen to him, and the family especially feared that he might be forced into service during an increasingly desperate time for the waning Confederacy. Held for three weeks in Macon, Berry somehow managed to secure his release and returned to Atlanta in early January 1865.[5]

Early in December, twelve armed rebel soldiers and an officer quickly surrounded John Silvey's house, and arrested him for disloyalty, particularly because of his remaining "in Atlanta while the Yankees were in possession of the city." The Confederates took Silvey to their headquarters, the officer in charge telling Silvey that he was accused of several unspecified acts of disloyalty. Silvey was held for nearly a week and then, like Berry, taken to Macon under guard. In Macon, security was lax. Silvey went to see Robert J. Cowart, who seems to have been an Atlanta acquaintance and attorney, and asked what it would cost to gain a release from rebel authorities. Cowart set the price at 4,000 Confederate dollars. Silvey paid. Cowart then called upon Governor Joseph E. Brown, who was in Macon at the time, and returned with a document ordering Silvey to Atlanta, there to await further orders from Brown—instructions that never came. It is not clear who got the money.[6]

E. W. Munday also incurred retribution from the Confederates, likely because he was Silvey's brother-in-law. Munday also remained in Atlanta during the occupation, working as a wagon painter for the Union army. He was arrested on December 9, 1864, a few days after the Confederates returned. Munday's young son had just died, and he and his family were on their way to the cemetery to bury the child. It was a cold day and a winter storm was in progress, sleet stinging the faces of the funeral processioners, when Confederate soldiers arrested him on grounds of disloyalty. A Catholic priest, likely Father O'Reilly, intervened and persuaded the soldiers to let the family continue to the cemetery. After the burial, when the grief-stricken Munday and his family returned home, the soldiers broke into the Munday home. They called him a traitor and placed him under arrest. Munday's wife, overcome with grief at the death of her son and terrified by the break-in, became extremely emotional and begged the soldiers to promise her that they would not kill her husband. They refused to answer until the woman had asked three times. Finally, one of the men relented and told her that she would see her husband again. Like Silvey and Berry, Munday was taken to Macon. What happened to him there is uncertain, but he survived the war and ultimately returned to Atlanta.[7]

The Confederates tried to arrest the bookseller Michael Lynch, who also stayed in Atlanta during the occupation, but they failed. The wily Lynch evaded the arresting officers by hiding in various places, finally taking refuge in a tiny garret in his own house, where he remained for nearly three months before he thought it safe to come out. Lynch, who had worked six weeks for Sherman's army after the fall of Atlanta, believed that the Confederates intended to arrest everyone who had remained in the city during the occupation, but if the cases of Berry, Silvey, Munday, and Lynch himself are any indication, the rebel authorities were either lax in enforcement of that intent or gradually so preoccupied with survival and with the rapidly worsening Confederate military situation that the punishment of the few remaining Unionists seemed less and less important. Nevertheless, that eventual outcome did nothing to temper the fear felt by the hunted Unionists. While the terrified Lynch hid in his garret, he could hear the Confederate searchers below declaring that they would take him "dead or alive."[8]

Meanwhile, the Atlanta Unionists in exile fared better than their colleagues at home. The plans William Markham had discussed with General Dix for a meeting of exiled Unionists in New York bore fruit in February 1865, and a call went out to all "loyal Georgians" to attend a meeting at the Cooper Institute, a venue Dix had secured through a personal request to Peter Cooper. An item in the *New York Times* said that the meeting would result in a "public expression of opinion" by "loyal refugees in regard to the duty of Georgians at home to take the necessary steps to secure peace by 'laying down their arms and submitting to national authority.'" For good measure, the organizers also invited loyal citizens of the other rebellious states, as well as "citizens generally" to attend. The notice was signed by Markham, James Dunning, Amherst Stone, Lewis Scofield, A. N. Wilson, David Young, and six other Georgia Unionists (non-Atlantans) then residing in New York.[9]

What a Savannah, Georgia, newspaper would later call the "great loyal meeting" (the *Times* noted that it was lightly attended) took place on February 16, 1865. The group unanimously elected Amherst Stone chairman, and he "was received with much applause." The meeting's purpose, chairman Stone announced, was to express solidarity with the loyal people of Georgia and to convince all Georgians to lay down their arms. According to the newspaper account, Stone then read "an eloquent and feeling address, which was frequently interrupted by applause." After Stone's speech, the assemblage passed a set of resolutions, which the *Times* reprinted in full. The resolutions explained secession as a conspiracy of the radical leaders of the South, condemned slavery, endorsed the Thirteenth Amendment, praised the brave (though misguided) soldiers who served the South, called for the unconditional surrender of the Confederacy, and thanked the people of New York for their hospitality to the loyal refugees. A speech by a Macon Unionist followed the reading of the resolutions. Then James Dunning ("a working mechanic of Atlanta, Ga.") made some unreported remarks. The meeting concluded with yet another "lengthy address" by the slave-owning Stone, who "declared himself an abolitionist."[10]

Stone thus began to redefine the bounds of his own loyalty, transforming himself into an abolitionist, perhaps seeking recognition as a radical Republican. He also sought to repair his reputation in Vermont. Sometime after the end of the war, he and Cyrena renewed their acquaintance with Aldis O. Brainerd, the St. Albans merchant who claimed a role in Stone's arrests. Stone coldly greeted his old friend and quickly proclaimed that he had always been loyal to the Union. "I am just as true to the government as any man could be," he declared, "I have been true blue all through." Given the events that followed his return to Georgia a few months later, the value of a clarified or, in Stone's case, reinforced loyalty would be evident. Many Confederates had easily put aside the four years of attachment to the Confederacy, voluntarily taking the oath of allegiance upon reaching the North. One surviving list of oath takers in New York during 1864 and 1865 includes numerous Atlantans, Confederate and Unionist, who swore allegiance to the United States. Whether enhancements of loyalty by Unionists or reversals of loyalty by Confederates, different versions of past loyalties were harbingers of the loyalty of Reconstruction.[11]

During the winter and into the early spring, Stone busied himself with other activities in addition to the practice of law, principally trying to lay the foundation for a postwar political career. His connections with Henry Raymond and his visibility among Southern exiles in New York seem to have brought introductions to other prominent New Yorkers. Stone began to court the powerful, and ultimately he found connections to such politically influential men as Henry W. Bellows, president of the U.S. Sanitary Commission; George Opdyke, a former mayor of New York City; Samuel Osgood, a prominent churchman; and Peter Cooper, all of whom would ultimately endorse him for a federal appointment.[12]

In early 1865, Stone's New York legal practice received a little free publicity in the Atlanta newspapers. One of his business cards had fallen into the hands of Jared I. Whitaker, his former neighbor, the restored proprietor of the Atlanta *Intelligencer* and, for years to come, a thoroughly unreconstructed Confederate. Before seeing Stone's card, Whitaker clearly believed that Stone remained in a Northern prison, that he had gone to the North "in good faith and with the avowed design of trying to promote his interests." To learn that he had "regularly gone into business in the land of the enemies of that country which received him generously and treated him kindly as an adopted son" was too much for Whitaker and the *Intelligencer.* Time, the newspaper warned, would ultimately set "all things even."[13]

Throughout the early spring, Atlanta remained in Confederate hands. Only days after the April 9 surrender at Appomattox, however, the Unionists began returning to Georgia, ready to resume life, do business, and take power. Although survival was still the primary concern, loyalty was not forgotten by either those Unionists remaining or those who had left. Throughout the war, the Unionists had held tenaciously to the hope that when liberation came, they would be rewarded. Loyalty would be recognized by the federal government, and those who had been loyal would be critical, perhaps even dominant, in the shaping of a new South based upon faithfulness to the principles of Unionism. For the Atlanta Unionists, there had been a series of confirming signs that ultimately such a future would be realized. The selection of Andrew Johnson, the embodiment of unconditional Southern Unionism, as the vice president of the United States, implied that a victorious North would acknowledge the value and importance of Southern Unionism. Abraham Lincoln, soon to be martyred, had consistently emphasized that Reconstruction would be predicated upon the existence of a strong class of Southern Unionists. The coming of Sherman's armies and the influential role accorded to the Unionists provided another confirmation. It was difficult not to conclude that after the war was finished, there would be a political vacuum that the most prepared and powerful of the Unionists would fill. Atlanta Unionists could easily surmise that they would, in a postwar world, benefit politically from persistent loyalty.

The chaos of the immediate postwar era frightened and confused many former Confederates. Who would be punished for the rebellion? How severe would requitals be? Would Unionists come to power? Would they visit vengeance on the vanquished? Virtually all white Georgians were uncertain and apprehensive about the course of Reconstruction under Andrew Johnson, an intense enemy of the planter aristocracy, who, while wartime governor of Tennessee and vice president of the United States, promised punishment for Southern treason. Only eleven days before Lincoln's assassination, Johnson declared that though he favored leniency for some Southerners, including the poor and what one historian has characterized as "honestly deluded southern soldiers," he harbored no doubts about how the wealthy and powerful secessionists of the South should be treated: "I would arrest them—I would try them—I would convict them and I would hang them."[14]

Throughout this period, Southerners constructed revisionist accounts of their own prewar and wartime activities, a reconstruction of loyalty that continued throughout 1865 and 1866. Unionism, once considered the mark of treason, was redefined as it had existed in the antebellum context. Southerners who had ultimately embraced secession but had argued for going slow on disunion now claimed the mantle of Unionist. Others who more enthusiastically embraced secession but professed to have supported a peaceful resolution of the conflict at one point or another during the war, now presented themselves as Unionists. It was hard to find an ardent secessionist. The same cold fear that Cyrena Stone had witnessed among firebrands who had briskly converted to loyalty as Sherman approached the gates of Atlanta reasserted itself in a cool political logic that produced thousands of latter-day Unionists. After the war, Confederate Atlantans such as bookseller Samuel P. Richards embraced Andrew Johnson's "Dam' nasty oath" eagerly and cynically, becoming "once more good loyal citizens of the U.S." The wealthy just as eagerly sought pardons, explaining how they resisted secession and deplored war, yet had no choice but to "go with the State." This logic enabled all but a few to claim that they had been Unionists, loyal adherents to the United States either before the war or at some point during the war. It also hinted that unconditional Unionists would have a hard time achieving political power, because huge numbers of former Confederates had recovered their voting rights under the Amnesty Proclamation. Oaths, so long revered within the code of Southern honor, became nothing more than expedients to the recovery of citizenship and a seat at the national hearth.[15]

Amherst Stone was among the first to come home, arriving in mid-April 1865, and embracing a logic of postwar politics suggesting that unconditional Unionists would govern in Georgia and throughout the defeated Confederacy. Stone returned to Georgia with an attractive political portmanteau. A prewar Unionist who resisted secession and refused to "go with the state," he had emerged as a leader of the Georgia Unionists-in-exile and pursued political power between and after imprisonments in the North.

He had also become a Republican and gained the attention of prominent members of the party, who endorsed him for federal office. Because of his political connections and because he had secured the support of influential national Republicans and Georgia Unionists, Stone clearly believed that he would be appointed U.S. attorney for Georgia in the early days of Reconstruction.[16]

Stone returned to Georgia—but not to Atlanta. He still owned property in Atlanta and retained a network of clients and friends there, but he also had plenty of enemies in the city, including his onetime business associate, Jared I. Whitaker, and some angry former partners in the blockade-running scheme, who likely wanted restitution, retribution, or both. Thus, in mid-April 1865, Stone went to Savannah, perhaps believing that his presence would be required there because the U.S. District Court would reopen in Savannah in the summer of 1865. Savannah had other attractions as well. It had largely escaped damage during the war and remained an important port city that might recover more quickly than Atlanta, affording plenty of on-the-side private practice for an ambitious, energetic U.S. attorney. The city's population also contained some Unionists, perhaps more than Atlanta, and this promised some ideological comfort for Stone, as did the presence of a militantly Republican newspaper, the *Savannah Daily Herald,* an army newssheet that had become a civilian daily in January 1865.

Thousands of U.S. troops were stationed in and around Savannah, guaranteeing that early Reconstruction might not be an uncomfortable time for Savannah Unionists, who, while relatively numerous, still constituted only a small minority of the white population. They had received, however, some extremely strong guarantees of safety from William T. Sherman, who issued a decree early in January 1865 that they would be protected and that revenge would be exacted against Confederates who sought to punish them. If Unionists were "molested by the enemy," summary punishment would be inflicted on the perpetrator "or his family made to suffer for the outrage." If a Unionist were murdered, then "a rebel selected by lot" would be shot. In "aggravated cases," retaliation would be "extended as high as five for one."[17]

So Amherst Stone crested into Savannah in mid-April 1865 to begin Reconstruction. Probably arriving by steamer from New York, he opened a law office, took up residence, and plunged into postwar politics. We do not know whether Cyrena was with him. In fact, we cannot say much at all about Cyrena Stone in the postwar era—where she was, what she was doing, what she thought about Reconstruction, what her relationship was with her husband. Clearly, she was in Vermont a few months later, in the autumn of 1865, when she wrote an essay that was later published in a Savannah newspaper, but no evidence suggests whether she had come to Savannah with her husband in the spring. Perhaps she had gone to Vermont for one of the long visits that had been her prewar custom. Cyrena Stone may have leaned quietly back toward anonymity, living in the shadow of Amherst, who had now returned from his wartime absences to reassert himself in the postwar South. Or, perhaps Cyrena was not entirely comfortable with the conventions of gender relations that demanded such subservience. When Amherst fled Atlanta in early 1863, she independently faced the dangers of being a Unionist and the uncertainty of survival in a city in the path of destructive war. Postwar visits to Vermont may have preserved some of the independence that she exercised during the war, but in the end we cannot say, for neither diary, novel, nor other documents survive to tell where she was or what she was doing.[18]

On April 22, 1865, eight days after the assassination of Abraham Lincoln and very soon after Amherst Stone disembarked in Savannah, residents of the city joined in a public ceremony to mourn the fallen president. Few native-white Savannahians would have openly mourned Lincoln's death. But local Unionists, transplanted Northerners, thousands of freed slaves, and many companies of Union troops and sailors stationed nearby came together in an impressive display of grief. Members of the occupying forces organized the memorial with the help of the Unionists and Northerners. Held out of doors beneath the giant, moss-draped, live oak trees on Johnson Square, the conclave drew enough people, black and white, to fill the spacious square; the surrounding streets; the "door steps, windows, balconies, and even the roofs of the adjacent houses." Detachments of Union soldiers accounted for much of the crowd (they had marched, unarmed, to the square), but, according to the *Daily Herald,* "a great number of negroes" and "a fair proportion of citizens" also attended.

A speakers' platform, carpeted and furnished with chairs for fifty dignitaries, stood east of the Nathanael Greene monument, clad in flags and draped in black, which presides over the square. A large U.S. flag, red stripes covered by black cloth, stood behind the flower-bedecked platform, which was itself festooned in black and white drapery. Black-banded regimental colors decorated the corners. Black banners ("sable tokens of grief") stretched from massive branch to massive branch of the trees overhead, bearing white-lettered slogans of remembrance: "How are the Mighty Fallen"; "He died, but his work still lives"; "The memory of the past is blessed"; "Lincoln—lover of his country, lover of his race." The piebald crowd sang a hymn composed for the occasion: "Almighty God! we bow the head, And bring to Thee our ruler dead; Oh! help us to accept Thy will, And let thy power shield us still." Two army bands played patriotic music.

In nineteenth-century custom, speakers presented appropriate resolutions (crafted well beforehand), and those in attendance passed them by acclamation. The resolutions mourned Lincoln and depicted his assassination as the inevitable product of the South's treason. Similar leitmotifs ran through the speeches of the first three orators: Brigadier General Milton S. Littlefield; Colonel Stewart L. Woodford, chief of staff to Major General Quincy Adams Gillmore; and Brigadier General Cadwallader C. Washburn. When General Washburn finished, the band played "The Star-Spangled Banner." As the strains of the national anthem faded away, the next speaker went to the podium. He was Amherst W. Stone.[19]

How or why Stone became one of the speakers at the memorial service cannot be explained except by reference to his powers of self-promotion. Perhaps he persuaded the managers of the affair that he was soon to become a federal official, or perhaps he had connections within the U.S. Army, which had organized the observance. The *Daily Herald* identified Stone in the briefest of terms, saying nothing of his background in the original newspaper account of the affair, but recording in the next day's edition that he was a longtime resident of Atlanta who had presided over the "great loyal meeting" at the Cooper Institute in New York the previous February. Stone likely contributed to the reconstruction of his own reputation. Some months later, the local reporter for the R.G. Dun & Company, busily noting the credit reputations of Savannahians, routinely recorded that Stone was a recently arrived lawyer with a good practice *and* that he had served as colonel of a Massachusetts regiment during the war. Unionist, self-described abolitionist, and putative Massachusetts colonel, Amherst Stone strode to the speaker's podium in Savannah with the confidence of a man who professes a distinguished past and hopes for a promising future.[20]

"An unexpected and terrible calamity has fallen upon the nation," he declaimed. "Our rejoicing is turned into mourning, and the whole nation is 'contracted in one brow of woe.'" Stone earnestly and passionately praised the assassinated Lincoln but warmed most fully to his oratorical task when he condemned treason, excoriated Southern elites ("sires of ruin who inaugurated rebellion in seeking the destruction of those whose only offense was a love for the Stars and Stripes"), and blamed Confederate leaders directly for Lincoln's murder. "I know that their rebellious hearts could conceive and their heads plan hellish deeds of darkness," Stone declared, "but did not think the instrument could be found for so vile and cowardly an act as was perpetrated in Washington the night of the 14th." "Hell itself," he thundered, "would blush at its own purity in comparison with such an act and the devil resign his sceptre in disgust before the authors of such treason."

Stone's words resonated with outrage (perhaps heartfelt, perhaps calculated) at such treachery, but he predicted that a "humane, generous Christian government" would be magnanimous towards "the masses of a people who are our brothers, who have been misled by a few wicked and designing men." Magnanimity would have to be earned, however, and former Confederates would have to display a genuine loyalty to the United States in order to rejoin the national fold. "No indefinite negative love of the government will do," Stone asserted. "It must be earnest and sincere; and if there are those who hate the Government, I would advise them to seek some other country more congenial to their own feelings."[21]

STONE'S SPRINGTIME ORATION went to a central issue of early Reconstruction, raising the issue of loyalty and asking whether defeated Confederates should be restored to citizenship without demonstrating an "earnest and sincere" devotion to the government. The requirements, vague as they were, bore more than passing resemblance to Confederate demands for Unionists to choose between loyalty and exile during the secession crisis and wartime. Those in power had defined political loyalty during the war, and Amherst Stone believed that those in power should prescribe the standards by which loyalty was measured after the war. Stone's speech anticipated Andrew Johnson's broad amnesty policy and its generous provisions for the bulk of the Confederate population, but the oration's harsh tone also mirrored the new president's powerful animus toward the Confederate leadership. From the perspective of Amherst Stone, whose loyalties were hardly pure, the Confederate elite amounted to nothing more than a pack of traitors, "sires of ruin" as he called them, who deserved condign punishment.[22]

While Stone settled in at Savannah, others of the Unionist group were returning to Atlanta. By mid-May, James Dunning was back in the city, and within a short time, Jonathan Norcross, William Markham, Julius Hayden, David Young, Thomas Healey, Martin Hinton, Lewis Scofield, and most of the prominent loyalists had returned. The establishment of the

Bureau of Freedmen, Refugees, and Abandoned Lands in 1865 had particular relevance for some who wanted to return but had no money. A group of Unionists who had migrated to Cincinnati, Ohio, after the fall of Atlanta found conditions there none too good. Tom Crussell, C. P. Cassin, Richard Parson, and their families together with several other Atlantans who claimed to have been Unionists sought travel aid from President Johnson.

The Georgians described themselves to the new president as "heavy, though uncomplaining sufferers," victimized by the destruction of their city. They could never have anticipated that they would have been compelled to leave Atlanta, they told the president, and had virtually no means of providing for their families in Cincinnati, where they were unwelcome strangers. They wanted to go home. They implored the president to provide for their return by rail, fearing to go on foot, for they would have to pass through the treacherous mountains of east Tennessee. They acknowledged that Johnson knew none of them personally, so they invoked the name of their mutual friend, Alexander N. Wilson, who was in Washington at the time. Johnson granted the request, and the Freedmen's Bureau provided transportation to Atlanta for the refugees and their possessions. Christian Kontz, the Unionist brewer-turned-cobbler, also succeeded in getting bureau help for his return to Atlanta from Washington, D.C. Besides Amherst Stone, other Unionists who did not return to Atlanta included Henry and Martha Huntington, safely ensconced on an Iowa farm, and C. T. C. Deake, who remained in East Tennessee. James A. Stewart, who left Atlanta in early 1864 to take up residence in Rome, Georgia, spent time in Atlanta but continued to reside in Rome.[23]

On May 4, 1865, Union soldiers once again took control of Atlanta, accepting the second surrender of the city, this time from Confederate lieutenant colonel and former mayor Luther J. Glenn. The federal officer in command, Colonel Beroth B. Eggleston, an Ohioan, began the reconstruction of Atlanta immediately, distributing food, banning the sale of intoxicating beverages, and, within ten days, ordering the arrest of all blacks without passes from their former owners or employers in an attempt to restrict the movement of the freed people. The *Intelligencer* warmly endorsed Eggleston's conduct and especially his generosity to hungry troops of the Confederate army. Some days later, the federals ceremonially raised the U.S. flag over city hall, where Eggleston had his headquarters. The 5th Iowa band played "The Star-Spangled Banner" as soldiers pulled the flag up to half-staff height in memory of President Lincoln. Some Atlanta ladies, it was reported, had sewn the banner. Thus, in Atlanta as in Savannah, the traditional ceremonies of patriotism and loyalty to the republic were officially restored as the hastily cobbled, four-year-old rites of loyalty to the Confederacy disappeared, at least temporarily, from public pageantry.[24]

Well before the May breeze had begun to ripple the flag flying over city hall, Atlanta Unionists were trying to shape the reconstruction of Georgia by influencing the president in his selection of federal officials for the state. Two of the Unionists, Alexander Wilson and James A. Stewart, were east Tennesseans with direct ties to President Johnson. Wilson hailed from Johnson's hometown of Greeneville. Both sent the president regular observations about the politics of Reconstruction in Georgia. The Unionists also had significant political ambitions, and before the end of 1865, their hopes for prominent federal appointments in Georgia would be in large measure fulfilled. Amherst Stone was lobbying for appointment as U.S. attorney for Georgia, and John Erskine sought the federal judgeship for the state. In addition, Alexander Wilson, James A. Stewart, Nedom Angier, Alfred Austell, Henry Holcombe, and James Dunning were interested in federal positions.[25]

Alfred Austell had already begun a campaign to win an appointment from Johnson. Austell left Georgia sometime during early 1865 and went to New York, where he took up residence at the St. Nicholas Hotel. He had suffered heavy financial losses during the war and lost much of his property, including, of course, the fifty or so slaves he kept on his plantation. Austell now sought to capitalize upon his wartime Unionism, shaky though it may have been, to win political appointment and to rebuild his wealth. After a visit to the White House, he wrote a letter to Johnson in which he recalled his own east Tennessee roots; identified himself as a "Duglas Democrat"; gave Erskine, Wilson, Joshua Hill, and Isaac Scott as references; and prevailed upon the president to make him U.S. marshal for Georgia. The once wealthy Austell was desperate. Unable to secure a position that would provide him with income, he also wrote in confidence to Joshua Hill, pleading for Hill's help and asking that he intercede with John Erskine to recommend him for the marshal's position. "I must do something for a living," Austell plaintively wrote.[26]

Interest ran very high, of course, about the loyalties of persons Johnson would choose for the four most important posts in the state: provisional governor, U.S. district judge, U.S. attorney, and U.S. marshal. These four officers, plus collectors and assessors of revenue for each of four districts in the state, constituted the primary federal appointments to be made in Georgia during the first days of Reconstruction. Unionists throughout the state, including the Atlanta group, looked to Johnson to reward the loyal and put Reconstruction in their hands. Georgians and Southerners of all political stripes anxiously awaited any news concerning President Johnson's views on Reconstruction. Vindicated Unionists wanted to hear that they would be at the center of influence in a reconstructed Georgia. Moderate Georgians who had resisted disunion but had "gone with the State" at the time of secession worried that there would be a harsh, retributive reconstruction. Members of the secessionist elite, embittered and defeated, feared the most and the worst—treason trials, confiscated property, black suffrage. For the moment, key questions from the government's point of view were whether Southerners would behave loyally toward the United States and on what terms they might resume citizenship.[27]

On May 19, three Atlanta Unionists, Alexander Wilson, James Dunning, and William Markham, met with the new president in Washington. The three were among the most militant of the Atlanta loyalists, and although each retained numerous ties with Atlantans who had forsaken the United States, their loyalty had been twice vetted in the Union occupations of the city. They intended to probe Johnson's views on Reconstruction, and they put forward John Erskine for appointment as U.S. judge. The federal judge would hold the key to other federal appointments, including U.S. commissioner, and thus the appointment of a strong Unionist was vital to the loyalist camp. Next to appointing a provisional governor for Georgia, the judgeship was the most important appointment that President Johnson would make. After the meeting, James Dunning acted as spokesman. He brought from the White House a not entirely clear message about the course of Reconstruction. President Johnson, he said, looked kindly on the masses of people in Georgia who he believed were at heart loyal but had been "overreached by the cunning of artful and unscrupulous leaders." Good relations could be reestablished between Georgia and the federal government, Dunning reported, if it were quickly acknowledged that slavery "was dead forever and ever." Once this occurred, other problems could be easily dealt with. Johnson was not inclined to leave the military in charge of the state, Dunning said, "beyond the period when the civil administration might be safely resumed." All governmental offices in Georgia, however, were considered vacant, and every action taken by previous occupants since the beginning of the war was considered "null and void." If the people of Georgia "really desired a loyal civil Government organized in Georgia," Johnson reportedly said, "then there would be some spontaneous movement in their primary assemblies." Dunning concluded from Johnson's remarks that the course of Reconstruction depended heavily on how the people of the state comported themselves. He had no doubt, however, that "men who were prominent in the late rebellion . . . [would] not be allowed to assume control of the matter of reorganization."[28]

While the three Atlanta men sought information and favor from Andrew Johnson in Washington, Amherst Stone was busily constructing a political base in Savannah by organizing the pro-Union elements of the city. In late May, about a month after his speech at the Lincoln memorial observance, Stone emerged as a leader of the Georgia Union Club, which held its initial public meeting in a second-story hall above the local express office. He was the principal speaker on this occasion and delivered a long, politically passionate address that the *Daily Herald* printed in its entirety.

Stone's second Savannah speech sang the praises of the Union and celebrated the war sacrifices made by the North and the Unionists. He made a slight bow to the idea of sectional reconciliation, but his principal emphasis was upon the treason of the South's leaders and the great damage done to the nation as a result of secession. Stone traced the doctrine of secession to John C. Calhoun, who would be "remembered only in sorrow that he ever lived." He repudiated the notion that Lincoln's election gave the South just cause for secession, noting that the aristocracy intended then and still intended to preserve itself and its privileges whatever the cost. The great mass of the Southern people could be persuaded to join in the rebuilding of the nation, Stone believed, but he called for retribution against the leaders of the revolt.

Stone condemned Southern clergymen with equal zeal, castigating them for promoting and perpetuating the ideas of secession and rebellion, observing that only a few Catholic priests might be exculpated of those crimes. Protestant ministers had made it a special errand, Stone went on, to "seduce" the women of the South from their love of the Union by equating secession with doctrines of religious correctness. "Pretending not to be politicians, they preach[ed] treason with double effect, availing themselves of the confidence placed in them by the women they first seduced from their love of the Union . . . [and] by inflammatory remarks, disloyal conduct, appeals to their honor, pride and courage, [they] succeeded in deceiving the young men of the land into the whirlpool of treason."

No one in the crowd in Savannah could have known of the massive intellectual inconsistencies that afflicted the speech's author. Stone, of course, had managed to conceal from public view the great bulk of his activities that might cast doubt on his own loyalty. No matter. It was in many ways a splendid speech for its time and place. It showed the power and emotion many loyal Americans felt about the great sacrifices of the Civil War and their fears that the rebellion's leaders would go unpunished. It had fire and clever construction, containing just the right amount of rhetoric predicting the future greatness of the nation. Soon, of course, such rhetoric would become the property of radical Republicans and later generations of Northern politicians, who would dredge up the Union sacrifices of the Civil War for political purposes. And that was just what Amherst Stone did. Though undoubtedly convinced in his own mind of the correctness of what he said, his speech was given strictly for the purpose of advancing his own political career. He was among the first politicians to "wave the bloody shirt."

Those in attendance at the meeting adopted a resolution that reflected many of Stone's sentiments, calling for the president to appoint a *military* governor for Georgia. It was necessary to have a military governor, the group resolved, "until the power of the enemies of the United States Government shall have been so crippled as to cease to be dangerous and the ballot box so guarded as shall ever prevent a recurrence of the terrible scenes from which we have been delivered by the United States Government." The next night, in another meeting, the group voted to send a delegation to visit Andrew Johnson and convey the political sentiments of Savannah and Chatham County to him. A delegation of eleven men, including Amherst Stone, were chosen to go. Stone was elected chairman.[29]

Another Georgia delegation (and perhaps a third) arrived in Washington at about the same time as the Savannah group. The two decided to merge, and they chose representatives to make the visit to the White House. Stone and three of the Savannah delegation joined six other Georgians, including James Johnson (who would soon be named provisional governor); O. A. Lochrane, the Macon judge; Richard Peters, the Atlanta businessman; and John W. Duncan, an Atlanta banker. At some point in the discussion between the two groups, the Savannah delegation put aside the idea of pressing for a military governor. The *Washington National Intelligencer* declared the men of the United Delegations to be "all staunch Unionists," but Alexander Wilson had already written to President Johnson with a more critical appraisal of the members of the various delegations.[30]

John W. Duncan, Wilson wrote, "was an old Democrat and a good Union man, and has the propensity to find out evry thing and make himself usefull to the persons in authority." Richard Peters was "a rich man, who, though no politician gave freely of his money to fight against Secession, while it did good, but [who] seemingly, went over to the enemy, after Georgia seceded, and blowed for Jeff's crowd." Wilson reported, however, that Peters was now "humble penitent, and a worthy & sensible man." O. A. Lochrane had been a worthy jurist during the war and had been asked by Union men to remain in office to provide them with as much protection as possible. William F. Herring of Atlanta was, according to Wilson, "an ass, a lick-spittle, an infernal secessionist [who] never adhered to any thing that required manliness." Wilson had kinder words for Isaac Scott of Macon, whom he suggested to Johnson as a good candidate for provisional governor. Unfortunately, he noted, he had recently learned from Scott that the war had ruined his health and that he would not take the job. Wilson also used the occasion to praise his old friend, Amherst Stone, "a genuine Union man" who was now an applicant for the position of U.S. attorney from Georgia. A good lawyer, Stone would be "faithfull to the interests of the Government." Wilson commended Stone to Johnson for "your most favorable consideration."[31]

The United Delegations delivered to the president a slate of nominees for federal office in Georgia. For three of the principal appointments, they recommended James Johnson of Columbus for provisional governor, John Erskine of Atlanta for U.S. judge, and Amherst Stone of Savannah for U.S. attorney. They also suggested appointees for U.S. marshal and for the positions of collectors of revenue and assessors in each of four districts in the state. Alfred Austell did not win their nomination for marshal, but Alexander Wilson was put forward as collector of revenue in the third district, and Henry C. Holcombe of Atlanta was nominated for assessor in the same district.[32]

The president partially followed the group's recommendations in his initial appointments for Georgia. The press quickly reported the selection of James Johnson as provisional governor, John Erskine as U.S. judge, Amherst Stone as U.S. attorney, and James Dunning as U.S. marshal. The *Savannah Daily Herald* enthused over Stone's appointment, noting that he was "a gentleman of excellent address and pleasing manners; and will doubtless discharge the duties of his office to the satisfaction of the Court and the country." The *Daily Herald* also reported a New York newspaper's account of Stone's appointment. It was a publicist's dream come true. "This [the appointment] is a just recognition of the unswerving loyalty which cost Mr. Stone his home and all earthly possessions. Exiled from Atlanta, he took refuge in the hospitable North, and has since resided chiefly in this city." Stone, the paper concluded, "has never failed, on the proper occasions, in the expressions of the most radical Union sentiments. In the selection of such men to sustain the offices of our Government, the President acts wisely."[33]

It must have been a satisfying, perhaps exhilarating, moment for Stone. Part of an important delegation from his adopted state, he was convinced that his assiduous efforts to win political office had paid off. Amherst Stone, who scarcely one year earlier had been imprisoned in Fort Lafayette as a Confederate agent, occupied the powerful position of U.S. attorney for Georgia. In that office, perhaps he would play an important role in bringing the traitorous ex-Confederates of Georgia before the bar of justice.

BUT AMHERST STONE never took office as U.S. attorney. The press reports had been wrong. Other Atlanta Unionists had received appointments— including Erskine as judge, Wilson as collector of revenue for the Savannah district, and Nedom L. Angier as collector of revenue for the Augusta district—but no supporting records exist in the appointment registers of the federal government to indicate that Stone ever was appointed, and no records indicate that he ever acted as federal attorney in the U.S. District Court for Georgia. What transpired between the press reports and the appointment of another man, Henry S. Fitch of Indiana, to the post six months later is unknown. It may have been nothing more than spoils politics. The successful appointee was a Union army veteran and the son of a politician with ties to President Johnson. Or it is possible that someone inside the president's circle, knowing of Stone's mottled past, blocked the appointment. For the ambitious Stone, who had successfully maneuvered his way through the Civil War, ingratiated himself with Northern politicians, relocated to Savannah, and acquired influence in Reconstruction Georgia, it was an exceedingly bitter disappointment. Stone returned to Georgia likely full of pride in his evanescent appointment. When it became apparent that he would not be appointed, he nonetheless decided to remain in Savannah, practicing law and Republican politics while pursuing other federal appointments.[34]

Atlanta's other loyalists had done well in the federal appointments. In addition to Erskine, Wilson, and Angier, Henry Holcombe, James Dunning, and James A. Stewart eventually reaped federal posts, as did Amherst Stone, who would become a Freedmen's Court judge in 1866 and later U.S. commissioner. In the wake of the appointments, a general spirit of optimism suffused the politically active Unionists. Alexander Wilson sent hopeful commentary to Andrew Johnson concerning the mood of the state in mid-June

1865. He was pleasantly surprised at what he found. Georgians, he wrote, "are as tame as sick kittens. The cry is, 'What shall we do to be saved.'" They acknowledged defeat, he said, and had a "wholesome fear" of the government in Washington. Wilson saw "no disposition to be turbulent," even on the part of the "original ranters."[35]

Reconciliation was also in the air when a large public forum took place in Atlanta on June 25. Clearly intended to be broadly representative of the white population, the meeting had been called by a politically diverse group of Atlantans, including Mayor Calhoun, militant Unionists James Dunning and John Silvey, and three other men who had been Confederates. Mayor Calhoun occupied the chair, and B. D. Smith, who in 1861 had been characterized as a violent secessionist, was chosen secretary. Calhoun gave a conciliatory, strongly pro-Union speech. A committee composed of Dunning, Alfred Austell, George W. Adair (an antisecessionist delegate to the 1861 convention who later "went with the state"), Jared I. Whitaker, and John M. Clarke (about whom nothing is known) drew up resolutions that expressed full confidence in the Johnson administration, called for a healing of national wounds, and declared the assassination of Lincoln to have been "horrible and horrifying," a tragedy worthy of "universal execration." Speeches followed, delivered by Adair, Dunning, and Lucius J. Gartrell, a former U.S. congressman and Confederate general. All told, the meeting exuded a general tone of reunion and reconciliation.[36]

James A. Stewart concurred in Alexander Wilson's assessment of political conditions in Georgia and joined the rhetoric of reconciliation. Because Johnson had set a positive tone during his brief administration, Stewart predicted that readmission of the Southern states and reabsorption of the masses of Southern citizens into the Union would go smoothly. "There is no record in history," he wrote, "of an erring people manifesting so earnestly a willingness to retrace their steps and help to repair the wrongs they have committed." Stewart also called for the release from prison of his old friend Alexander H. Stephens. "Every body asks," Stewart wrote to Johnson, "Why is Stephens held in prison, whilst Howell Cobb, R. Toombs, Gov. Brown, B. H. Hill, and others, are permitted to go at large?"[37]

On July 4, 1865, standing in the courthouse square in Atlanta, Stewart led observances of the first Independence Day celebrated in the city after the war, reading aloud the Declaration of Independence and portions of Washington's Farewell Address to the assembled crowd. It was a fitting task for a militant Unionist, a duty to be relished. The *Atlanta Intelligencer,* war weary at last and apparently ready to join the chorus of reconciliation, praised its old nemesis, noting that Stewart gave "some most excellent advice as to the future—counseling forbearance among those whom past differences and past trials had estranged." Thus, the newspaper seemed ready at last to lay aside the remnants of Confederate patriotism, declaring the new object of loyalty to be the United States, not the Confederate states.[38]

The newspaper hinted, however, at a disruption during the celebration and issued a general call for support of "the work of reconstruction and peace" by "every good and patriotic man." The disturbance probably resulted from an oration on the same day by David Young, who returned to Atlanta in late June after exile in Bergen, New Jersey. Young, who preached to and worshiped with blacks during the war, arrived in Atlanta ready to commit himself to beginning a school for freedmen. In his July 4 speech, Young declared that "other things being equal, I consider a negro as good as a white man." Such rhetoric was bound to incite white Atlantans, and apparently it did. Young provided a fuller explanation of the effects of his remarks than did the newspaper's oblique reference to a disturbance: "This has arrayed prejudice against me," he wrote, "and vengeance is sought, but Federal bayonets protect me. I am fully committed and expect to work for the poor despised negro."[39]

Stewart's and Young's differing views on the rights of black citizens foreshadowed a division among Unionists over whether the freedmen should become full citizens. James A. Stewart thought white Southerners would persist in the spirit of reconciliation if federal policies restricted "negro suffrage, negro equality, or whatever tends to the rekindling of sectional animosities." He asked that Johnson "shield us, if possible" against these things. White Southerners, he wrote, "are willing to give up slavery; but they are not yet willing to place themselves on terms of political and social equality with the African race." The freethinking, slaveholding Stewart, who could raise fundamental questions concerning church and state and who had been among the stoutest prewar defenders of the Union, would not admit the possibility of equal rights for blacks. Young, also a slaveholder, but with long experience as a Methodist clergyman, repented his involvement with slavery and embraced a radical position in his call for equal rights and equal education for blacks. In time, and insofar as it is possible to determine, a few of the leading Atlanta Unionists—Stone, Wilson, Dunning, and William Markham—came close to Young's position. Stone and Wilson both embraced biracial politics, and Dunning proved to be a persistent advocate for black education and black rights. William Markham, later president of the Union League in Georgia, presumably worked to advance the cause of the freedmen through that biracial organization.[40]

The optimism of early Reconstruction did not endure. In midsummer, James Dunning sketched a less sanguine picture of postwar politics than did Wilson or Stewart. It was true, he wrote to President Johnson, that the masses of people were sick of war and wanted to conform to "the new order of things." The elite, however, were a different matter. "There is," Dunning wrote, "Among us the *Old* Leaders a Large Portion of which are Among your Excepted Classes Named In Your Proclamations."

> It is this Class who Clamor on the Streets About their *Disablities* under which they Labor and who Talk constantly About the Oath of Allegiance, Amnesty, and *Special Pardons* which they Desire to obtain *at once* In order that they may vote at our coming Elections. Their Zeal about this is wonderful and before long a Shower of Petitions will Rain on your Head at Washington.[41]

By late October, Alexander Wilson had embraced James Dunning's political pessimism. Ensconced in Savannah as U.S. collector of revenue, Wilson wrote to Andrew Johnson that the "Secessionists in lower Geo. are still full of venom and hang together like a pack of thieves." Although none was so foolish as to advocate resistance to the federal government, there was a general inclination to "play Possum" until Southerners were permitted to return to Congress. The delegates elected to the state constitutional convention from the up-country were generally good men, Wilson wrote; those from the Southern half of the state were "Gasbags or toads," interested in promoting leniency toward ex-Confederates. Both groups generally sang Johnson's praises, Wilson reported, but he warned the president that "the hard headed Union men who suffered persecutions are a little *Soured.*" Militant Unionists were angered at some of the pardons issued to militant Confederates such as Benjamin C. Yancey and said that if men such as Yancey could be pardoned, then treason was no longer a crime. "I think this is more from a desire to see such men punished through pride rather than patriotism," Wilson wrote, "but it is a fact in Geo. that those who have been the best Union men during the war are taking a position against the Administration."[42]

Another general meeting of the Atlanta citizenry on September 30 made it abundantly clear that with suffrage restored to the vast majority of white male Southerners, federal appointments were the only politically influential posts Georgia Unionists would occupy during presidential Reconstruction.

At the meeting, Atlanta's citizens elected delegates to the September state-wide convention that would consider the terms of Reconstruction Andrew Johnson had set for readmission of the Confederate states. They chose two die-hard Confederates—Jared Whitaker and N. J. Hammond—and the more moderate George W. Adair. William Markham stood for election as a delegate but received only about half the number of votes that went to each of the three Confederate victors. Another Unionist candidate, C. P. Cassin, claimed only a handful of votes.[43]

The autumn elections confirmed that political power, at state and local levels, would reside with the old Confederates and not with the Unionists. The congressional race for Georgia's seventh district, which included Atlanta, drew three candidates of diverse loyalties. William T. Wofford was a prewar Unionist, a Confederate general, and the favorite. James P. Hambleton, the physician-publisher whose loyalties were decidedly malleable but publicly pro-Confederate, also ran, as did Henry G. Cole, the militant Marietta Unionist. Wofford captured 347 votes in Atlanta, Hambleton took 269, and Cole garnered 19. Wofford won the district vote and the seat. William Markham sought a seat in the state legislature but ran third in a field of eight candidates contending for two seats.[44]

After the elections, Alexander Wilson became even more alarmed at the increasingly conservative cast of Reconstruction. Only one of the state's new congressmen (Wofford), he wrote to Andrew Johnson, had been a prewar Unionist, and he had also been a Confederate general. "Open hostility" Wilson said, existed toward the federal government in all parts of the state on the part of those who had taken the amnesty oath and even by some men whom Johnson had pardoned. So dire was the situation that Wilson believed that if the military left Georgia, "not one emphatic Union man" could stay "in the State and live." Wilson had become thoroughly radicalized. He believed that the atmosphere in Georgia was even more poisonous than it had been before the war, and he called for the sternest measures. "I now think the immediate trial, conviction, and execution of Jeff Davis, followed by the trials, convictions and executions of Lee, Johnston, Bragg and that concentration of all lies and bragadocio [P.] G. T. Beauregard would have the effect of restoring a hearty respect for the Government," he wrote to the president.[45]

James A. Stewart had also changed his views. Stewart had declared for Congress from northwestern Georgia, but withdrew from the contest when Johnson appointed him postmaster of Rome. Stewart's candidacy would likely not have fared well (despite some support that appeared in the newspapers) if his reading of the political situation in the state was correct. That assessment coincided with Alexander Wilson's. Union men, Stewart wrote, were still "the objects of bitter persecution by Secessionists who have purjured themselves in taking the amnesty oath." He feared that former secessionists might soon return to power, and he reported that some were "boasting" that Unionists would be "driven out of the South."[46]

Stewart was right. During a "dry, windy night," just before Christmas 1865, arsonists tried but failed to set fire to his house in Rome using what the Rome newspaper described as an ingenious powder fuse. A few months later, terrorists attempted to burn down Stewart's newly constructed flour mill in Rome. This attempt was also thwarted, but with no thanks to city officials, whom Stewart accused of being uninterested in apprehending the guilty parties. A nervous Stewart began to stand watch every night. Although he received sympathy from some local residents, it did little to relieve him of the "wearing effects of suspense and dread." Until the resurgent "spirit of rebellion" was stamped out, he told President Johnson, Unionists would never be able to live in "peace and security."[47]

FEAR, FRUSTRATION, and a creeping sense of betrayal characterized Unionist commentaries about the political situation in Georgia as 1865 ended. Dispersed and no longer bound by the exigencies of war, the Atlanta Unionists had ceased to exist as a group. Insofar as we can tell from the fragmentary surviving records, the women played almost no role in postwar politics. The immigrants and artisans who made up an important part of the wartime group slipped back into political anonymity. The black Unionists, Robert Webster and Prince Ponder, were far less visible than they had been during the war, although we do have a tantalizing glimpse or two of Webster during this era—on one occasion, hosting a grand party to celebrate the moving of the state capital from Milledgeville to Atlanta in 1868.[48] Some of the most prominent loyalists had left the city or never returned. Amherst Stone, Alexander Wilson, and James A. Stewart, among others, lived elsewhere. Because no significant body of papers exists to give insight into the dynamics of the Unionists in the postwar period, we can never be sure of how much communication they had with each other or how tightly they were bound to each other politically or personally.

From hindsight, the Unionists' expectation that they would exercise significant power in postwar Georgia had little grounding in political reality. Once Andrew Johnson decided upon a generous approach to Reconstruction—one that emphasized the reestablishment of basic civil rights for former Confederates—the political weight of the Unionists' newly enfranchised opponents doomed their aspirations. The politics of loyalty became concomitantly less relevant. To be sure, the continued prominence of a few Unionists in city politics offered living reminders of the loyalism of the Civil War era, but as Reconstruction drew to a close, and the Democratic "redemption" of the state loomed, they became less numerous and less relevant.

CHAPTER ELEVEN

Claims of Loyalty

Political expectations had economic parallels. After years of living under constant pressure and peril, Atlanta Unionists had been severely affected by the coming of the Union armies. Union shells destroyed Unionist houses. Union soldiers burned Unionist businesses. And the Union army confiscated loyalist property, including commodities such as cotton and tobacco, as well as corn, beef, horses, and virtually anything else of importance to the war effort. To be sure, many of the transfers of property were voluntary, although some of what the Unionists provided was taken under conditions of compulsion or near compulsion. Still, receipts were issued and promises of compensation made when Unionists surrendered property to the officers of Sherman's army.

After the war, however, conflicting ideas appeared over what constituted loyalty to the United States. These ideas arose at the same time as a number of related legal and political questions of extraordinary complexity. Together, they cast fundamental doubts on whether Southern Unionists had actually been loyal and if they, like persons who lived in the Northern states, should be compensated for the loss of property supplied to or confiscated by Union forces.[1]

Less than two months after the Union evacuation of Atlanta, refugee-ing Atlanta Unionists had started the process of seeking compensation from the federal government for confiscated property. In the immediate post-war period, they would pursue compensation through a Minoan maze of federal bureaucracy and in the U.S. Court of Claims. Beginning in 1871, they would take their cases to the congressionally created Southern Claims Commission and thereafter into the federal court system on appeals from the commission. Incredible as it seems, it was a process that would stretch over a period of nearly fifty years for some of the Unionists and their descendants. Those Unionists who sought compensation for lost property saw loyalty at least partially in terms of financial self-interest. Attachments to the Union thus had more than intangible patriotic value. At the same time, federal agencies and the courts made judgments about which persons had actually been loyal and what loyalty meant, judgments made on legal grounds and in legal terms crafted by lawyers and bureaucrats. As surely as definitions of loyalty before and during the war turned on ideology, politics, and morality, the claims era defined loyalty almost entirely in financial and legal terms.

In January 1865 Alexander N. Wilson, living in Nashville, acted as agent for Unionists who hoped to recover funds for cotton taken by the Union army. Thomas Scrutchin, who worked for the Atlanta mercantile firm of McNaught and Ormond, wrote that Wilson was "prosecuting some cotton claims against the Gov. with some prospect of success." Wilson, Scrutchin went on, "seems to think upon proof of loyalty he will have no difficulty in getting the money." No record exists of Wilson's having filed such a claim, and thus it seems likely that he was acting on behalf of others who were beginning to explore ways in which they might be compensated for lost cotton.[2] In the same month, David Young was preparing to file a claim with the government, seeking compensation for tobacco taken by Sherman's forces. During January 1865, Young gathered testimony in New York City from Union army officers and prominent Unionists, including William Markham and James Dunning, documenting his loyalty and shoring up facts concerning the loss of his tobacco. Four other Unionists—Alfred Austell, Amans Delphey, Michael Kreis, and Michael Lynch—soon would join Young in the effort and likely began preparing their cases at the same time.[3]

THE SUBSEQUENT EXPERIENCES of David Young and the other four illustrate the tedious, frustrating procedure as it pertains to claims for compensation from the government in the postwar era. The five first hired a

Washington, D.C., law firm, North and Primrose, to undertake the claim. The claimants had no difficulty establishing their loyalty. J. M. Blair, who had served as one of Sherman's commissary officers and was in charge of requisitioning tobacco, declared that he believed all five of the men to have been loyal and that they had turned over their tobacco to him "as soon as they were made aware of the requirement to do so and were entitled to compensation." Various sworn statements regarding loyalty, along with detailed statements concerning the amounts of tobacco taken, were sent first to the office of the commissary general for subsistence in June 1866. They were disallowed on September 30, 1866.[4]

Young and his cohorts then appealed to President Johnson, whose secretary referred the claims to the Special Claims Commission of the War Department for disposal. The commission reviewed the claims and rejected them in late December 1866. The five men next turned to the Department of the Treasury, submitting the claim and a supporting legal argument directly to Secretary Hugh McCulloch. They argued that the tobacco constituted captured or abandoned property and under the law governing such matters, their claim would fall within the jurisdiction of Treasury. The secretary wrote back saying that he disagreed with their "elaborate" argument, rejecting the idea that the tobacco was captured or abandoned property and noting, for good measure, that the property in question had never been in the possession of Treasury. Furthermore, McCulloch added, no statutes covered the matter and it was thus a matter for Congress.[5] In early 1868, for reasons that are unclear, the five Unionists then sent their claims to the third auditor of the Department of the Treasury, who transmitted it "for examination and report" to the Commissary General for Subsistence, where it had been rejected two years earlier. Once more the commissary general declined to honor the claim.[6]

Meanwhile, Young and his colleagues dispensed with Primrose and North and hired a new lawyer, Henry Sherman. Sherman specialized in such claims and took the case on a contingency basis, the five men agreeing to give him one-third of any amount collected. Sherman argued that recent decisions of the Supreme Court were liberalizing and had made it possible for departments and bureaus that "ordinarily" had jurisdiction over such claims to honor them more easily. On this basis, he appealed to the Third Auditor in March 1870 to review the claims. A month later the Third Auditor sent the matter once more to the commissary general for subsistence for "further consideration." Two months after that, the commissary general concluded that the tobacco was taken by the army, the claim just, and the loyalty of the claimants probable. Nevertheless, the official concluded, he rejected Sherman's well-reasoned, complex brief and declared the claim unpayable because the pertinent law applied only to states not in rebellion. Further legislation would be required, he concluded, before the claim could be paid. That legislation would appear within a year, making it possible for Young and his colleagues to seek compensation under the rules of the Southern Claims Commission, which was established in 1871.[7]

While Young and the other four Unionists sought relief from the various federal agencies for the loss of tobacco, other Unionists tried to get compensation for cotton they had lost to the federal government during the war. These Unionists sought relief under the provisions of the Captured and Abandoned Property Acts, and they took their cases to the U.S. Court of Claims, which had responsibility for settling cases arising from the so-called cotton claims. Congressional legislation in early 1863 had placed claims for confiscated cotton under the newly created court's jurisdiction and at the same time provided that persons who filed claims would have to demonstrate that they had been loyal to the United States.

In the postwar era, Congress increasingly acted in ways that tended to restrict definitions of loyalty and repudiated claims of loyal Southerners as a part of a more stringent policy of Reconstruction toward the South. On the other hand, the decisions of the Court of Claims were more liberal, both in the definition of loyalty and in compensating claimants for confiscated cotton. And in turn, those decisions of the U.S. Supreme Court that grew out of Court of Claims appeals tended to be supportive of awards and determinations of loyalty. Thus, Unionists from throughout the South, who despaired of congressional policy that lumped all Southerners together (taking little or no cognizance of those who had remained loyal), were heartened by the actions of the Court of Claims.

In administering claims that stemmed from the seizure of loyal persons' property in the South, the Court of Claims had to decide whether the claimant actually owned the property that was seized and sold, whether he or she was entitled to the proceeds, and whether he or she had given "any aid or comfort to the recent rebellion." The court defined the latter terms to include any "assistance or encouragement" to the rebellion and said that the claimant must show that he or she *"never"* provided any aid or comfort to the rebellion. It softened this language, however, with the observation that "mere residence" in a rebellious territory "and an unwilling submission to the usurping government" would not bar a recovery: "Where the great body of the inhabitants of a section or district rebel against the constituted authorities, individuals are not required to resist where such resistance would be futile and unavailing. It would be merely to invoke destruction upon themselves, without any corresponding benefit to their country."

It would be a "cruel injustice," the court concluded, to exclude the loyal Union people of the seceded states from the benefits of the law. The judges believed that they were fulfilling the terms of a "beneficent statute" by restoring "to men of undoubted and unquestioned loyalty to the country the proceeds of the property which was wrested from them through the mistakes or inadvertence of the public agents."[8]

The law provided that claims would have to be filed within two years after the rebellion's suppression. Atlanta Unionists who had cotton seized during the occupation of the city filed claims with alacrity and in most instances succeeded in winning awards, some of which were very large. Among the first cases considered by the court were those of William Markham, John Silvey, Julius Hayden, R. H. McCroskey, Thomas Crussell, Alfred Austell, John Lynch, and James Lynch. In fact, Markham, McCroskey, and Silvey were listed among the first half-dozen claimants from across the South to receive awards from the court. Fundamentally, the claims of each of these Unionists were similar. Each had invested in cotton during the war, and each had made that cotton available to the Union army officers soon after the federal army entered Atlanta in September 1864. In all cases, the officers involved were either Colonel William Le Duc, chief quartermaster of the 20th Corps, or Captain E. E. Hade, an assistant quartermaster. Le Duc had come to know several of the claimants well and testified on their behalf. In most instances, there appears to be little doubt that the Unionists actually owned the cotton for which they claimed reimbursement. Similarly, their loyalty to the Union was not subjected to in-depth, searching inquiries of the sort that would characterize claims filed in later years with the Southern Claims Commission. Each of the cases, however, was different from the others, both in the determination of facts relating to the cotton in question and in the establishment of the claimants' loyalty.

Like all Atlantans who owned cotton, William Markham was interested in preserving it from depredation or seizure and with avoiding the treasonous taint that General Sherman had assigned to possession of the white fiber. Soon after Sherman's army had entered Atlanta, Markham asked William Le Duc for advice. Le Duc told him that if he delivered his cotton to the quartermaster corps, the army would take possession, sell it, and transfer the proceeds to the U.S. Treasury. The army would provide him with a receipt. Markham would then be entitled to claim the proceeds. Le Duc, fully convinced of Markham's loyalty, assured him that he would most likely be compensated.

Markham had stored the cotton on the farm of his son-in-law, Robert J. Lowry, four miles southeast of Atlanta. According to Lowry, Le Duc sent troops out to the farm; the troops brought the cotton in and delivered it to Markham, who then turned it over to Hade. Hade gave Markham a recipt for ten bales of cotton, which were in good condition, but he refused to give a receipt for the other four, which were "imperfectly baled." All the bales became part of a huge shipment of cotton that the army sent from Atlanta to Cincinnati during the fall of 1864. Markham also claimed reimbursement for an additional thirteen bales, which he said had been seized in Florida. In all, he asked the government for reimbursement in the amount of $11,040.

As would become the practice in the Court of Claims and in the Southern Claims Commission, the U.S. attorneys composed standing interrogatories so that testimony could be gathered without witnesses having to travel to Washington, D.C., where the court was located. Arguments before the court were conducted by Washington-based attorneys for the claimants and by the government attorneys assigned to the case. The standing questions about the cotton mainly focused on the factual basis for the claim, although in the instance of Markham, the government attorneys wanted to know if Markham intended to ship his Florida cotton out through the blockade, thus voiding any claim that he might have had and perhaps raising questions about his loyalty as well. The questions posed by the government attorneys concerning Markham's loyalty looked to whether Markham had supported the Confederacy by holding civil or military office, taking an oath of allegiance, or supporting the Confederate Constitution.

Markham, like virtually all the Unionists who would file claims, tried to establish his loyalty through the testimony of other Unionists and of Union military personnel (usually officers) who had contact with the Unionist group in Atlanta. Of course, most of the witnesses summoned by those who prosecuted claims against the government testified favorably as to the claimant's loyalty but sometimes—particularly under the later, more rigorous scrutiny of the Southern Claims Commission—some witnesses would damn their fellow Unionists with faint praise. In a few cases, they forthrightly accused claimants of disloyalty to the United States and characterized claims as fraudulent.

In Markham's case, there was no such difficulty. Witnesses for his loyalty included James Dunning, Lewis Scofield, and Markham's son-in-law, Robert J. Lowry. For many years thereafter James Dunning would be called upon both by claimants and by the government to testify on the loyalty of Atlantan claimants. Almost inevitably, Dunning offered blunt estimates of loyalty and never shrank from negatively characterizing marginal or doubtful Unionists. James Dunning and William Markham as well had been relied upon by the government for determinations of loyalty since Sherman entered Atlanta, and the two men would continue to be utilized in that way for the better part of two decades. In depositions, Dunning inevitably described his own experiences as a Unionist, alluding to his imprisonment, describing his refusal to do business with the Confederate government, and setting a standard of loyalty by reference to his own outspoken, unequivocal Unionism.

Dunning had no doubts about William Markham, whom he characterized as "decidedly" loyal. Markham had not served as a Confederate official or taken any oath. With regard to giving "aid or comfort" to the Confederate government, Dunning provided a forthright response: Markham had done so "indirectly, but never voluntarily," an answer that could have alluded to a number of elements of Markham's behavior during the war. Dunning likely was thinking of Markham's commercial activities, but he could also have given the same response about any Unionist resident in the Confederacy who continued to pay taxes or who, even under duress, made contributions for the relief of the Confederate wounded. The court had few doubts about the loyalty of William Markham as well, for it decided without equivocation that he was loyal and entitled to compensation for a portion of his confiscated cotton. Markham received an award of $3,602.70.[9]

Robert H. McCroskey's claim resembled Markham's. McCroskey had purchased fifteen bales of cotton from an Atlanta cotton merchant, who had bought it from various farmers. McCroskey and his lawyers could show conclusively that the cotton had been appropriated without McCroskey's permission; the irascible merchant likely could not bring himself willingly to give up any of his property. His petition to the court was strong, however, and included testimony from Dunning and C. P. Cassin as to his unequivocal, sometimes foolhardy professions of loyalty. The solicitors for the Court of Claims raised virtually no serious questions about McCroskey's loyalty or the credibility of his claim, and he received an award of $5,404 for his lost cotton.[10]

John Silvey received the largest award of the three, proving that he had surrendered thirty-nine bales of cotton. The court awarded Silvey slightly more than $14,000, a substantial amount of money in the immediate postwar South. Silvey, like Markham and McCroskey, called on James Dunning to prove his loyalty. Silvey also called his brother-in-law, E. W. Munday, and George W. Lee's former deputy E. T. Hunnicutt, who was also Silvey's brother-in-law. In years to come, Hunnicutt would become a fixture of sorts in claims litigation, giving depositions and witnessing for claimants who wanted to establish that Confederate officials had labeled them as Union men and had watched them closely. In support of Silvey's claim to loyalty, Hunnicutt recalled how the two had differed strongly over secession, he being an ardent "secessionist" and Silvey a militant opponent. Hunnicutt was evidently a persuasive witness as he recalled how a sergeant in the provost guard had called upon Silvey early in the war to contribute to the outfitting of the guard. According to Hunnicutt, the wealthy Silvey had said that he would rather see the Confederacy "sunk into hell than to give a dollar."

Silvey sought additional compensation from the Court of Claims in subsequent litigation that extended over nearly four years. In addition to the cotton for which he had already been compensated, the wealthy Silvey claimed that seventy-seven more bales had been taken from him and no receipt given. The facts of the case were complex. Silvey had purchased the cotton in question during 1862 and 1863 and stored it on a lot that he owned in Atlanta near the Western and Atlantic Railroad in full view of persons passing by on the railroad. There was no doubt that he owned such an amount of cotton. As Union forces neared Atlanta, Silvey worried that rebel soldiers would burn the cotton, so he quietly moved it to three different locations in the rural areas around Atlanta. After the Union forces captured the city and orders had been issued concerning cotton, Silvey informed Captain Hade in writing of its existence but said that it was not in condition to be shipped. He then sought passes from the military to go into the country, repair the bagging, and bring the cotton back to the city. Soon, Union soldiers brought it in and placed it at the railroad depot, where it remained for a brief period before being shipped northward to Nashville. No receipt was issued, because by that time Captain Hade had already left the city. Nevertheless, the court was persuaded that the cotton had been delivered into the custody of the federal authorities at the Atlanta depot.

The U.S. Treasury Department objected, saying that no distinct record existed that the cotton had passed through the hands of the appropriate

Treasury official in Nashville. This became the key issue in Silvey's case: whether the government had performed its duty properly and whether the burden of proof to show that the cotton had passed through Nashville rested with Silvey or the government. The Court of Claims held that the government was at fault, and it awarded an additional $27,715 to Silvey. The five-member court split, however, and the government appealed to the U.S. Supreme Court, which divided "equally on the facts found by the Court of Claims" and thus delivered no opinion.[11] The government then moved for a new trial in the Court of Claims. Three years after the original decision and after lengthy, complicated arguments concerning the government's duty in such cases, the court found in Silvey's favor and let the judgment stand.[12]

OTHER UNIONISTS' CLAIMS with the court also led to extended litigation. Thomas Crussell sought compensation for seventy-five bales of cotton that Union forces had taken without providing a receipt. The court inquired closely into Crussell's loyalty and in doing so disclosed some of the primary benchmarks used in the late 1860s to determine loyalty. All the witnesses called had testified to Crussell's loyalty. He had opposed secession and remained opposed to it throughout the war. No witness had reported that Crussell had ever provided support for a Confederate soldier or a soldier's family or that he had contributed money or other goods to the Confederate cause "directly or indirectly." Neither had he aided in the raising of Confederate troops; nor had he "expressed sympathy" for the Confederate cause. Moreover, Crussell's loyalty had not been "merely passive"; he had demonstrated "his faith by his works on every suitable occasion." Crussell satisfactorily proved ownership of the cotton and showed that it had been received by the army, but he, like Silvey, ran into difficulty on the question of whether he could prove, in the absence of documentation, that the cotton had actually been disposed of by the federal authorities and the proceeds paid into the Treasury. The government was unable to prove that it had not disposed of or destroyed the cotton, and thus Crussell won a judgment of $26,275. The government then gave notice of appeal to the U.S. Supreme Court. When, after two years, the case was placed on the Court's docket, the government sought a delay, declaring that a new trial would be sought in the Court of Claims on the basis of newly discovered evidence. Eventually, the government dropped the motion for a new trial, and the appeal was heard by the Supreme Court, which found in Crussell's favor.[13]

Julius Hayden's claim brought out additional standards by which the Court of Claims would make judgments concerning loyalty. Hayden sought compensation for nearly two hundred bales of cotton. The government argued that the amount of cotton Hayden claimed as lost was "very vague and indefinite." Government attorneys also questioned his loyalty. Hayden, they said, had the burden of proving that he did not give aid and comfort to the enemy. His flight to south Georgia, they argued, was enough to "falsify" the profession of loyalty. In their view, Hayden could have as easily taken his family to the Union lines, which at the time of his departure from his farm near Atlanta were only three miles away. The court pointed to the consistency of Hayden's loyalty throughout the war and rejected the argument, noting that his family was made up entirely of "females" and that fighting was occurring all around Hayden's house. The Southern route appeared to be the safer route. "It was impossible," the court concluded, "for him to carry his family through the military lines so as to seek the protection of the United States." In reaching this decision, the court thus established the principle that "A loyal person surrounded by contending armies is not bound to abandon his family; and removing it to a retired place of safety, though within the Confederate lines, is not aid and comfort to the enemy." Hayden's judgment amounted to the huge sum of $50,581.[14]

The court stretched its loyalty determinations yet farther with the claim of John and James Lynch, who together sought reimbursement for 108 bales of cotton. The Lynches had purchased the cotton nearly two years before the war ended and had moved it around in order to keep it from being captured by the Confederate government, finally securing it in a shed built especially for the purpose on a lot owned by James Lynch. The Lynch brothers had no difficulty in establishing ownership of the cotton and could also clearly show that the federal authorities had taken possession of the cotton. As with the claims of Crussell and Silvey, the government's records were imperfect, but the court concluded that the Lynches' cotton had been sold by the government and the proceeds deposited in the Treasury.

The judges did raise questions, however, concerning the loyalty of the Lynches as defined by the Captured and Abandoned Property Acts and by their provision that loyalty rested only on persons who had never given aid and comfort to the enemy. Three issues arose in the Lynch case that cast some doubt upon their claims of loyalty under the law. First, the court learned (likely through the standing interrogatories) that John Lynch had purchased stock in Amherst Stone's ill-fated blockading scheme. Stone himself testified and emphasized that the scheme was to be carried out only if the approval of the federal government could be gained, and he also pointed to the intention of the organizers to bring back medical supplies into the Confederacy for humanitarian purposes. Although other witnesses raised questions about Stone's intentions (suggesting, for example, that he kept the money the company raised), the court decided that the Lynches could not be found to have given aid and comfort to the enemy as a result of taking part in a scheme that was not intended actually to run the blockade, because Union permission was to be sought, as Stone testified. Despite the arguments of the deputy solicitor general, the judges also accepted the Lynches' claim that the medicines were to be used to alleviate the sufferings of many Union people. The government's lawyers also argued that the Lynches' membership in the home guard should prevent them from winning their case. The judges disagreed on this point as well, declaring that membership in the home guard was a way to avoid conscription and service in the Confederate army and that the Lynches had actually never been called to active service and had thus had not aided in the rebellion.

Finally, testimony revealed that the Lynches had made at least one ten-dollar contribution toward the support of a Confederate company raised out of the Irish community in Atlanta. The court carefully weighed the context of this and similar donations made by other Unionists, in the end giving weight to the enormous pressures put on loyalists, especially in the early days of the war. "These claimants, as well as every other person residing in the community suspected of loyalty to the United States, was in great peril," the judges wrote, and their apprehensions of danger were well founded.

> Many were compelled to flee to the mountains and hide themselves in dens and Caves of the earth to escape the frenzy and barbarity of those who were bent upon destroying the government and all who adhered to it. The conduct of men and the motives that influenced them under such circumstances are not to be explained and interpreted in the light of peace, and the presence of the protecting power of the Government, but as they stand exposed and affected by the power and presence of a usurping government, backed by the excited passions and lawless conduct of the frenzied populace.

Thus, the Court of Claims decided in favor of the Lynches' claim and awarded them $38,909.[15]

Alfred Austell, who was seeking compensation in connection with his tobacco claim, turned his attention to the Court of Claims as well and filed a cotton claim. Austell could prove ownership of fifty-two bales of confiscated cotton and could show receipts. Like the cotton of most of the Atlanta claimants, Austell's was commingled with a large amount of the fiber that had been captured in Atlanta and transported through Nashville to Cincinnati. However, Austell had some difficulty proving loyalty. The government charged that he had been engaged in blockade running, but the court decided that in his efforts Austell, like the Lynches, had contemplated seeking the approval of the U.S. government to bring back "articles suited to the wants of the people." The agent for the venture, the court noted, had been captured on the way to Washington, and nothing came of the project; thus, there had been no blockade running and no giving of aid and comfort to the enemy. Austell was awarded $12,385.[16]

For Atlanta Unionists with the means to invest in cotton during wartime and the guile or temerity to prevent that cotton from falling into Confederate hands, the Court of Claims proved to be a godsend by providing substantial cash awards for cotton and loyalty. Almost all the Unionists who sought reimbursement from the court had been businessmen of means before the war and maintained or even improved upon their economic standing during the conflict. The economic devastation that came with the destruction of the city, and the confiscation of property, destroyed well-off men such as Alfred Austell and shook even the very wealthy, such as William Markham, Julius Hayden, and the Lynch brothers. For some of these men, the Court of Claims provided financial boosts of great magnitude in a relatively brief period of time.

THE COURT ALSO CONFIRMED that loyalty to the Union had worth. At a time when congressional attitudes toward Southerners in general were taking a punitive turn, the Unionists were bitterly chagrined at being lumped together with masses of the disloyal. For those Unionists with valid claims, the avenue to compensation also led toward confirmation of loyalty, an intangible result, to be sure, but one of great intrinsic value to those who believed that they had for four years, as the Court of Claims noted, withstood the "excited passions and lawless conduct of the frenzied populace."

From hindsight, the court displayed a remarkable flexibility in adjudicating the "cotton claims" of the Atlanta Unionists. Its definitions of disloyalty under the Captured and Abandoned Property Acts were humane, taking into account as they did the context of daily testing by hostile authority and retributive neighbors, as well as the constant psychological stress of such testing. Mere membership in a home guard, coerced contribution of minor sums to Confederate military units, even implementation of blockading schemes of dubious intent, did not defeat the Unionist claims of loyalty and their claims upon the U.S. Treasury.

Legislation in 1871 establishing the Southern Claims Commission stemmed in part from the dissatisfaction of Southern Unionists with the federal government's inaction on the great bulk of claims from loyal citizens and from a loosening attitude toward loyalists among members of Congress. The commission relied greatly upon the methods employed by the Court of Claims in dealing with the cotton claims, using many of the same procedures, dealing with the validity of property claims, and most important, delving into the loyalty of claimants. The commission's approach to the terms of loyalty, however, had more rigor and system than the Court of Claims and involved special agents in the field who often assiduously investigated claimants to determine loyalty and whether property claims were factual.

Standing interrogatories became part of the commission's procedures, and on the question of loyalty they were greatly detailed, probing virtually any connection claimants might have had with the Confederate cause or government. All claimants and witnesses, as well as any person who testified in hearings, would be expected to respond to searching queries concerning residency during the war period (six months before and after), where their sympathies lay, how consistent they had been with respect to loyalty to the Union, what they had done for the Union, whether they were prepared to do more or less, whether they had relatives in the Confederate or Union service, whether they had been employed by either government, whether they contributed property to the Union cause, where they had stood on secession, their "feelings" regarding key Union victories, who the leading Unionists in their section were, whether they had been victimized by Confederate authorities, how they had responded to Confederate pressures, whether they had business connections with the Confederacy or with state governments, whether they had contributed to the raising of troops for the Confederacy, whether they had taken oaths to the Confederacy or received amnesty from the Union, whether they had belonged to a vigilance committee or a home guard, whether they would have done anything to prevent the establishment of loyalty to the Confederacy, and several dozen other considerations. By close questioning of claimants and witnesses, the commission thus intended to determine the character and persistence of the person's relationship to Unionism and his or her resistance to the Confederate cause.

It was easier and less expensive to file claims with the Southern Claims Commission than it had been with the Court of Claims, and the commission reviewed a greater variety of property losses than had the court. Thus, larger numbers of claimants appeared who wanted to establish both their right to compensation and their Unionism. Greater accessibility was aided by the appearance of a number of lawyers both in Washington and elsewhere who were willing to prosecute claims on a contingency basis. By requiring that the names of all claimants be posted in public places, however, the commission hoped to minimize the number of fraudulent applications from citizens with a proclivity for profit and a record of disloyalty.[17]

In Atlanta, the men who had filed cotton claims were, with the exception of Robert McCroskey, well off and willing to risk the costs associated with litigation before the Court of Claims. The much larger cross section of Atlanta citizens who sought compensation through the Claims Commission included immigrants, blacks, and a few women. Some of these persons had no clear connection with the Unionist group in Atlanta but had good foundations from which to plead loyalty. Others who had been closely connected with the Unionists would find it difficult to qualify for compensation because their loyalty would be questionable under the rigorous standards erected by the Southern Claims Commission. Still other claims came from Atlantans who had been partisan Confederates, and as foolish as it seems from hindsight, they apparently gambled that they could either conceal their pasts or fool the commission.

At least ten of the staunchest Unionists filed no claims of any sort to recover property lost at the hands of the federal armies. Among those who filed no claims was James A. Stewart, who disposed of his property and left Atlanta for Rome, Georgia, in early 1864. William Farnsworth—frequently cited along with his wife, Emily, as the Unionists most committed to easing the miserable existence of Union prisoners—and Alexander N. Wilson— the Atlanta Unionist who wielded the greatest political influence during the immediate postwar years—also filed no claims. Neither did Anderson Scott, the physician who aided Andrews's raiders; Henry Huntington, the dentist; Luther Faught, the foundryman; or William Manning, who, like Dunning and Scott, had been imprisoned for his Unionist sentiments. Bridget Doyle gave some thought to filing a claim and contacted a lawyer, but put off completing the paperwork and finally let the matter drop.[18]

Notably, James Dunning, the most vociferous of Atlanta loyalists, never sought recompense for losses. It is hard to imagine that Dunning lost nothing for which he might have received reparation. It is easier to conjecture that the crusty engineer, citing principle and sacrifice, refused to seek compensation, as his loyalty would never have been disputed by Atlanta Unionists or by federal army officers, who quickly recognized Dunning and William Markham as the most prominent of Atlanta's tories. By the standards of the Court of Claims, Dunning would easily have qualified, but the Southern Claims Commission had erected much higher barriers to the establishment of loyalty and offered far fewer opportunities for excusing even the most minor smudge that could blemish a reputation for loyalty. The commission and its agents were exceedingly thorough in investigating claimants, and they had the cooperation of efficient employees in the government departments where surviving records of the Confederate government came to rest after the war. These clerks provided the commission with background investigations of claimants that then became a part of the record and thus subject to public disclosure. Had such an investigation been undertaken with James Dunning as its subject, inquiring clerks would have discovered that even this most ardent Unionist had inconsequentially profited from a business dealing with the Confederate government. It was a piddling amount, and for whatever reasons he had accepted it.[19] Whether it would have defeated any claim the loyal Dunning might have filed is unlikely even given the stringent standards of the Southern Claims Commission, especially in view of his militant Unionism and his imprisonment. It is intriguing to speculate, however, that Dunning may have known that if he filed a claim he would have to answer questions under oath about whether he had done business with the Confederacy. A brutally honest man, Dunning would have answered affirmatively and then would have had to explain deviation from the high standards of loyalty he set for himself and for others.

Those who did file claims and proved their loyalty to the commission's satisfaction represented about one-third of the members of the Union Circle in Atlanta. Each had to negotiate the stiff commission standards for the measurement of loyalty and each had to supply precise documentation of confiscated property.

Not surprisingly, Amherst Stone saw opportunity in the establishment of the Claims Commission and decided to pursue compensation for an iron safe and a bale of cotton that Cyrena had turned over to federal authorities in September 1864. Stone also sought compensation for additional cotton valued at more that $30,000. Stone had no receipts for any of the cotton except the one bale for which Cyrena had received a receipt, but he provided detailed descriptions of the other forty-one bales complete with identifying labels. To prove his loyalty Stone planned to call on witnesses A. N. Wilson, John Lynch, Lewis Scofield, James Dunning, William Markham, and his brother, Chester. To prove the facts pertaining to the seizure of the forty-one bales of cotton for which he had no receipts, he planned to summon his brother, A. N. Wilson, and another man whose name was Thomas M. Jones.

Stone was among the first of those who filed claims with the Southern Claims Commission, but the commissioners never rendered a decision either on Stone's loyalty or on the validity of his property claim. Stone's claim ultimately joined the more than five thousand other claims that were barred from consideration by the commission because the files were never completed. It is likely that Stone dropped the matter because he learned that the commission's investigators had uncovered evidence that illuminated the weaknesses of Stone's claim to have been consistently loyal to the Union. Government clerks performing a routine investigation of Stone quickly turned up evidence in the Confederate archive on his blockade-running scheme and statements questioning Stone's loyalty.[20]

Perhaps Amherst Stone simply decided that he stood little chance of winning his claim or perhaps he knew that a further and more thorough investigation would inevitably yield plentiful evidence concerning his arrest and imprisonment in the North. Since the war, he had been quick to capitalize politically upon his reputation as a Union man. Even in an era when news traveled slowly and public attention to the character of minor governmental figures such as Stone was not intense, Stone could easily have believed that pursuing a claim that raised questions about his wartime loyalty would damage his position and jeopardize his political future.

Nedom Angier had no difficulty persuading the commission of his loyalty or the justness of his claim. Witnesses to Angier's Unionism came from the group of elite businessmen who saw themselves standing at the center of Atlanta loyalists. William Markham, Thomas Crussell, Julius Hayden, John Silvey, and Alfred Austell all confirmed Angier's steadfastness in the Union cause. Angier had no difficulty either in documenting his claim that a schooner he owned, and which he operated as a trading vessel after he had fled to the North, had been seized by Union forces in 1865, just before war's end. The commission awarded Angier about two-thirds of the $3,200 he claimed, a relatively generous judgment by a group of men who were usually very conservative in determining the value of Unionist property.[21]

John Silvey, one of those who testified to Angier's loyalty, claimed only a modest amount of $500 for mules requisitioned by the army, compared to the nearly $41,000 he had already received from the Court of Claims. Normally penurious and skeptical, the commissioners awarded Silvey $400, and in recounting the elements of Silvey's Unionism, they revealed the high standards they used to measure claims of loyalty.

> Mr. Silvey was a resident of the city of Atlanta throughout the war. He was a Union man and remained loyal to the Union cause. He voted against secession "voted openly on a ticket written on a big piece of foolscap paper." He was often threatened and cursed by the rebels. His family was cursed and abused. He had three nephews in the Confederate army, two were killed and one John Silvey in pursuance of claimant's advice deserted and entered the Federal army and served through the war. He told these nephews that he did not want anybody of his name to fight against the United States. He remained in Atlanta during the Federal occupation, was conscripted and arrested because as they alleged [he was] disloyal to the confederacy and especially because he remained in Atlanta [during Union occupation] was taken to head quarters and was told they expected to prove several acts of disloyalty to the confederacy . . . was kept under arrest in Atlanta several days—taken to Macon under guard where he employed a lawyer and paid $4,000 in Confederate money to get released—was released by Governor Brown and returned to his home. He did nothing to aid the Confederacy.[22]

Martin Hinton also won the approbation of the commission. The commissioners plainly admired Hinton and his family for enduring "persecutions on account of their Unionism, such as we rarely meet with"; they recalled Hinton's imprisonment as a spy and the constant threat in 1862 that "he would be hung, if not by the authorities, by the mob." Hinton's settlement included compensation for houses that had been taken apart by federal troops and for a confiscated cow and calf. Union soldiers had dismantled four houses belonging to Hinton—one of six rooms and three smaller dwellings. In addition, they had continued the "de-fencing" of Atlanta, tearing down enclosures belonging to Hinton which contained nearly ten thousand board feet of lumber. Hinton also won reimbursement for cash he had given to Union surgeon Samuel B. Houts to use for the benefit of prisoners.[23]

William Dyer's widow (who had been married and widowed again) filed a claim asking for compensation for the Dyers' house and storehouse (which had been dismantled by Union troops) and for livestock, lumber, wood, and a buggy, all of which had been confiscated by the federals. The commissioners had no doubt about the Dyers' loyalty, but they allowed only about one-seventh of the $1,430 claimed.[24]

Prince Ponder filed a claim for more than $4,000 in provisions and livestock that he maintained had been taken by the federals. The largest single item was for about two thousand bushels of corn, the harvest from seventy acres on Julius Hayden's farm. Hayden had given the crop to Ponder when he left for southwest Georgia, and Ponder moved to the Hayden farm. The commission refused to allow this portion of the claim, but they did award Ponder $675 for other items he had lost. The commissioners confirmed Ponder's loyalty, however, and his ability to make money. He was, they judged, "energetic, industrious and money making and owned as much if not more property than any colored person in Atlanta." Henry and Polly Beedles, who had lost everything to the Union occupation in 1864, recovered $272 of the $1,120 they claimed.[25]

Robert Webster easily persuaded the commissioners of his loyalty. The testimony of the other Unionists was simply overwhelming in its praise of Webster for his ministrations to Yankee prisoners throughout the war and especially during the bloody aftermath to the battle of Atlanta. Webster filed a sizable claim—slightly more than $10,000—nearly all of it for tobacco he said was taken from him during the occupation. The commission heard extensive testimony in Webster's case and rejected his claim primarily because the prominent mulatto barber-businessman could produce no receipt for the tobacco. Moreover, the commissioners accused Webster of attempting to produce false testimony to support his claim.

A key part of the case rested on the allegation that Webster had taken large amounts of tobacco from the ransacked store of John Silvey on the morning after the Confederate evacuation of Atlanta, later claiming it as his own and seeking compensation for it from the government. Despite testimony from several of the key Unionists (including John Silvey) rejecting the allegation that extensive looting had actually occurred and testimony from Silvey himself that his store had not been pillaged, the commissioners relied upon the testimony of several ex-slaves that Webster had participated in the looting and thus acquired the tobacco. In the end, however, the commissioners rejected the claim because Webster could produce no receipt from the U.S. Army for the tobacco, despite testimony from John

Silvey that he had accompanied Webster to get a receipt that Webster later claimed to have lost. More than thirty years after the rejection of his claim, Webster's heirs sought to reopen the matter before the Court of Claims, but they had no more success persuading the judges in 1908 than Robert Webster had with the commissioners of claims in the 1870s.[26]

David Young, who had filed a claim for tobacco along with four other Unionists in 1865 and had unsuccessfully sought compensation from several government agencies, turned to the Southern Claims Commission in 1872. Young added more items to his claim than he could have been compensated for by the other agencies, including a horse, some fodder, and the entire contents of his drugstore on Whitehall Street. The commission had no difficulty agreeing that Young was loyal; his record of Unionism, and particularly his reputation for treating blacks as equals, weighed heavily in his favor. The commissioners also readily agreed to pay Young nearly $4,000 for the tobacco the federal forces had confiscated, but they adamantly refused to pay the minister-pharmacist any of the $8,000 he claimed for the contents of his drugstore, declaring that Young's evidence for the seizure of the drugs and furnishings of his store was "got up in a gross and loose way to make foundation for a claim."[27]

The commissioners confirmed the loyalty of Michael Lynch, George Edwards, Christian Kontz, Amans Delphy, and Peter Huge. All these men were immigrants, some with stronger claims to loyalty than others. Michael Lynch had been constant and active in his Unionism throughout the war, from the time in which he sold "treasonous sheets" until the weeks during which he hid from the Confederate soldiers when they reoccupied Atlanta. George Edwards also seemed to have a solid claim, having been a strong Unionist, but Kontz, Delphy, and Huge gained the imprimatur of the commission as quiet Unionists—men who tried as best they could to remain loyal to the Union without calling undue attention to themselves.[28]

THE COMMISSIONERS MADE their judgments about the Atlanta Unionists usually in consistent fashion, thoroughly investigating loyalty, requiring ironclad documentation of property seized or taken, and applying what would appear to have been very conservative estimates of the value of Unionist property during the war, often going to great lengths to determine what prices of goods and property had been at that time. Some of the Unionists undoubtedly made overly generous estimates of the value of their property, perhaps taking into consideration the conservative approach of the commission or the income lost on property during the war.

Unionists vouched for each others' loyalty, but analysis of the claims in the context of many other sources does not reveal collusion by the Atlantans to defraud the commission through inflation of loyalty or distortion of facts concerning property. The commission and its investigators relied upon universally acknowledged members of the Union Circle for testimony concerning the loyalty of many claimants and for background information as well. In particular, they sought the opinions of James Dunning, Thomas Healey, Henry Holcombe, William Markham, and John Silvey regarding claims. The Unionists took pride in their loyalty and were quick to point out fraudulent claims. "Came here since the war. What can he claim?" Thomas Healey said of Edward L. Jones when he filed a claim. Healey pronounced L. P. Peacock, another claimant, a "worthless rebel." James Dunning acidly commented that claimant Thomas Hornsby was "reported loyal since the war. Not known to be previously," and when Henry Banks entered a claim, Dunning replied that "he was for Union, slavery, cotton, or anything else to make money." Some claimants, such as Pliney R. Oliver, showed amazing audacity, but received short shrift from Unionist John Silvey. "Reckless fellow," Silvey said. "In rebel army."[29]

Rarely did the Atlanta Unionists differ about who had and who had not been loyal. The most significant disagreement occurred when Alfred Austell sought in 1864 compensation for seven thousand pounds of tobacco worth an estimated $15,000. Austell had successfully pursued a "cotton claim" in the late 1860s and had been declared officially loyal by the U.S. Court of Claims when it awarded him more than $12,000. Some Atlanta Unionists concurred in the court's assessment. Thomas Crussell endorsed Austell's claim of loyalty, as did Robert Webster and Austin Wright. Thomas Jordan said that Austell was "considered" a Union man, and William Farnsworth concluded that Austell could be classified as a Unionist. On the other hand, Thomas Healey strongly condemned Austell, who, in Healey's view, "went with the current. Would do anything for money." Henry Holcombe agreed: Austell was "a policy man [who] talked and acted both sides."[30]

James Dunning offered stinging criticism of Austell. "Mr. Austell was not classed among the Union men here during the war," Dunning said. "He was what might be termed a neutral man." Austell would sometimes declare that the Confederacy was "a doubtful enterprise," but Dunning claimed that the wealthy banker-planter would never say that "the rebellion was wrong"; nor would he "ever advocate the cause of the Federal Government at any time." On one occasion, Dunning recalled, "I heard him say he was a conditional Union man; that is he was Union providing slav-

ery and all its rights could be preserved and not without." Moreover, Dunning concluded, Austell "kept company with and was in constant communication with the leading rebels."[31]

In presenting his claim, Austell sought the endorsements of two prominent Georgia politicians: Joshua Hill and Benjamin H. Hill. At the time of
his testimony, Joshua Hill was a U.S. senator. Undoubtedly Georgia's most
prominent wartime Unionist, Hill had run for governor in 1863 and had
polled about one-third of the vote in his contest with Joseph E. Brown. Hill
lived sixty miles from Atlanta, in Madison, but traveled to Atlanta frequently
during wartime. He recalled Austell's opposition to the war, observed that
Austell agreed with his own political views, and noted that Austell had support from Unionists and others for governor of the state, a reference to
rumors that Andrew Johnson might appoint Austell as provisional governor in 1865.[32]

By calling Benjamin H. Hill as a witness to his loyalty, Austell appeared
to gamble that Hill, as a member of the U.S. Congress, would be listened to
attentively by the three members of the Southern Claims Commission. But
all three commissioners were stout Republicans and stern patriots who knew
that Hill, although a prewar Unionist, had joined the secessionist ranks and
served as a Confederate senator. Ben Hill testified that from a Confederate
point of view, Austell was unquestionably a Unionist. He and Austell had
known each other well before the war, and when Hill embraced secession,
Austell continued to oppose it. "He never concealed his views from me," Hill
recalled. From Hill's perspective, Austell belonged to "a class of native sons
of the South, who were always called Union men—they were opposed to secession and to the war and willing at any time to make terms with the United
States and come back." Loyal Confederates, Hill went on, allowed these men
"to entertain such sentiments because everybody knew from their character that they would not be treacherous, that is, they would not subject themselves to criminal persecution for infidelity to the Confederate Government.
At the same time they were, in heart, outspoken Union men, ready always
to settle." Austell, Ben Hill concluded, "was a Union man just like Joshua
Hill. . . . What ever services he rendered the Confederate government was
forced, or was done in the ordinary business transactions of life to make a
living." There was a distinction, Hill insisted, in being a "true Southron" and
being a "true [or "willing"] Confederate." A "true Southron" loved the
South but might oppose disunion. Ben Hill argued that Austell held on to
his convictions concerning the Union while remaining a true "Southron."
The commissioners thought these distinctions casuistic.[33]

In the end, the commissioners agreed with James Dunning and other critics of Alfred Austell that he could not have been loyal by the standards of the Southern Claims Commission. They cited Austell's involvement in the unsuccessful blockade-running scheme; his financial dealings with the Confederate government; and his own testimony, which was "not altogether frank, ingenuous and free from dissimulation." In short, the commissioners concluded, Alfred Austell may have been loyal to the United States by the standards of the Court of Claims, or, for that matter, by those of former Confederates such as Ben Hill, but he could not be considered loyal by the standards of the Southern Claims Commission: "According to their [Joshua and Benjamin Hill's] signification of the term, he [Austell] may have been, and undoubtedly was a 'Union Man.' But he falls far short of having remained 'a loyal adherent to the cause and the government of the U.S. during the war.' It is only this latter class of persons who are entitled to relief through this Comm[ission]."[34]

Like Alfred Austell, Thomas Crussell could not establish his loyalty to the satisfaction of the commissioners of claims, although he had had no difficulty whatever in satisfying his Atlanta colleagues or the Court of Claims. Investigators for the commission found a witness who claimed that Crussell had "rejoiced" over the Confederate victory at Bull Run, and after reviewing Crussell's attempt to escape the South in 1862, the commissioners decided that the desire for escape had been concocted only as an afterthought; the men had actually been willing servants of the Confederacy. The commissioners also accused Crussell of having sought to serve the Confederacy when he applied to become a commissioner of public works during the war. E. T. Hunnicutt, George W. Lee's deputy and a friend of Crussell, disagreed and swore that Crussell hoped to get the job and to use the position as a cover in order to escape from Georgia.[35]

The commissioners had little confidence in Hunnicutt's testimony (or for that matter, in that of Prince Ponder, who also supported Crussell) and dismissed it, but Hunnicutt's testimony jibed with other accounts of Crussell's loyalty. Hunnicutt's claim that Crussell wanted the public works position in order to get out of the Confederacy seemed unbelievable to the commissioners, and when they queried Hunnicutt about it their disbelief grew. Hunnicutt swore that Crussell had discussed the scheme with him and that he advised him that it was very dangerous. Why, the commissioners asked, would a Unionist discuss with an officer of the provost guard his plans to seek a public position in the Confederacy in order to escape from the Confederacy? Had Hunnicutt informed his superior officers of Crussell's intent? No, Hunnicutt replied, and he had a powerful reason for not informing them. "We were both brother Masons," Hunnicutt testified, "and I would not report him, and would not do so again. If a man belonging to the federal army were to show me the evidence that he was a Mason I would not report him. I have protected a great many Union officers and soldiers on the same ground, and would do so again." When asked by one of the commissioners whether it was "a usual thing to do," Hunnicutt replied that "it is so with me. I only answer for my own conscience." Hunnicutt effectively contended that proof of Masonic affiliation by a Unionist or a Union soldier would be sufficient cause for him to commit treason against the Confederacy.[36]

More than 120 years later, Hunnicutt's testimony has a ring of truth. The power of the Masonic bond has been remarked upon by scholars, and there were a few times in Civil War Atlanta when it was cited in connection with breaches of correct Confederate conduct. If Hunnicutt told the truth, the fraternal and religious bonds of Masonry took precedence over the civil religion of Confederate patriotism and the law itself. Fraternal bonds, powerful and respected by white male Atlantans, thus added another layer to the complex matrix of loyalties in Civil War Atlanta.

William Markham had also received a substantial settlement in the Court of Claims for cotton that had been seized as well as concomitant certification of loyalty by the court. Markham enjoyed the complete respect of Atlanta Unionists, and all agreed that he had been tenaciously pro-Union throughout the war. As thoroughly reviled by militant Confederates as he was highly regarded by Unionists, Markham was clearly Atlanta's most prominent Unionist as well as one of its wealthiest men.

In 1873, Markham filed a claim with the Southern Claims Commission for nearly $5,000 in rents of buildings he owned that were occupied by the Union forces. Curiously, he submitted no evidence, and his claim received no attention because of the lack of documentation. In 1878, federal legislation decreed that such claims would be forever barred from consideration unless claimants filed supporting evidence by March 1879. Markham apparently presented no evidence to the commission, and his file joined approximately five thousand others that were "barred forever there after."[37]

In 1903, twelve years after William Markham's death, his son and daughter tried to recover the rents Markham claimed the federal government owed him as a result of the occupation of his property by General Sherman's forces. Marcellus Markham and Emma Lowry received assistance from the

U.S. Senate, which referred a bill for their relief to the Court of Claims. Markham's heirs raised the stakes, claiming that their father had actually been owed about $10,000. In support of their claim and in order to establish their father's loyalty, they submitted extensive testimony from his cotton claims of 1866 and took new and detailed testimony from many of the old men living in Atlanta in 1903 who remembered Markham and his wartime Unionism. Both those who were Confederate and those who were Union testified that Markham had been a staunch Unionist, always loyal to the United States.

Attorneys for the U.S. government, likely too young to remember the war, aggressively investigated Markham's background and the validity of the claims. As they pointed out to the court, they had the advantage of access to the captured records of the Confederate government, which had not yet been organized when Markham filed his claim for cotton in 1866, forty years earlier. The archive had been accessible to the Southern Claims Commission, but there is no evidence that the commission ever investigated Markham's relationship with the Confederate government.

The attorneys discovered that Markham and Lewis Scofield had done business with the Confederate navy in the production of iron plate for ships. They also found that Markham had rented several of his buildings to the Confederate government for use as hospitals, as offices for Provost Marshal George W. Lee, and as a harness shop. The attorneys also uncovered a voucher showing that Markham had sold $35,574 worth of cotton to the Nitre and Mining Bureau of the Confederate government. In addition, they alleged that Markham had been a member of a local militia group and thus had supported the Confederate cause. Witnesses testified that Markham and Scofield acted under compulsion in rolling iron for the Confederate navy. Others testified that the Confederate government typically seized property that was needed for the war effort and paid property owners whatever suited the government's convenience. The commanding officer of the Fulton County militia swore that Markham and others like him were compelled to serve and that Markham "would not conform to the rules and regulations, when he could possibly avoid it."

The case dragged on for six years, and not until 1909 did the court decide the issue. When it did, it relied almost totally on the documentary evidence of the Confederate archive and not at all on the testimony concerning Markham's loyalty, interpreting the evidence in the most conservative manner possible. Forty-four years after the conclusion of the war and fifteen years after Markham's death, the court declared that "William

Markham was not loyal to the government of the United States throughout the late Civil War."[38]

FOR UNIONISTS AND CONFEDERATES who lived through the war in
Atlanta, the court's declaration would have seemed bizarre in the extreme.
In wartime Atlanta, Markham personified Unionism and was regarded as
the leader of the Union Circle. The government officials who intensively
investigated his case, however, could not see the shades of blue that characterized Unionism in Atlanta. Unlike the Court of Claims in the 1860s
or the more conservative Southern Claims Commission in the 1870s, they
took no account of the context in which Markham, and other Unionists
like him, tried to maintain their loyalty. Whether through professional ded-
ication to the law or a baleful adherence to bureaucratic process, the
government lawyers of 1909 gave no indication that they understood the
complexities of loyalty in Civil War Atlanta. In Markham's case, they determined loyalty through a legal exercise devoid of the human drama that
surrounded questions of allegiance and patriotism on the Confederate homefront. There was irony in Markham's having been universally regarded as
disloyal by Confederate Atlantans and universally regarded as loyal by Atlanta
Unionists, only to be posthumously declared by government lawyers not
to have been loyal to the United States.

Postscript

Interstate 89 flows south into Vermont from the Canadian border, and for much of the fifteen-mile stretch between Canada and St. Albans it follows the path of the Confederate raiders, led by Lieutenant Bennett Young, who robbed the banks in that prosperous Vermont town of more than $200,000 on October 19, 1864 (see map 2). The traveler who takes exit 20 and drives northeast on Vermont 105 follows the approximate route the St. Albans raiders took as they fled. To the east, past the point where the raiders turned toward Canada, Vermont 105 parallels the Missisquoi River as it meanders past Sheldon, Sheldon Springs, Sheldon Junction, North Sheldon, and Enosburg Falls before leading into East Berkshire, Cyrena Stone's birthplace. In East Berkshire, now a quiet village that has lost nearly all its antebellum prosperity, the traveler who turns right at the service station crosses a bridge over the Missisquoi onto Highway 118. On the left, several hundred yards down the road, stands the Congregational Church of East Berkshire, where Phinehas Bailey pastored and where Cyrena and Amherst Stone were likely married. The visitor who goes into the carefully maintained cemetery behind the church and walks toward the huge old maple tree that stands in the northeast corner soon discovers the headstone of the reverend Phinehas Bailey and his wives. To the left of Bailey's grave is the four-foot-high obelisk erected in memory of Jennie Arthur Stone, Cyrena and Amherst's daughter. Between the two markers, nearly invisible when the summertime grass in the cemetery is three or four inches high, is another marker, no more than eighteen inches long, which bears only the letters *ENA*. Almost certainly this small headstone marks the grave of Cyrena Stone.

Because there are only scattered bits of evidence, we know very little about Cyrena's life after the war. She seems never to have settled into Savannah. The loss of her much cherished home in Atlanta and separation from friends and acquaintances with whom she had survived the war must have been difficult. As the wife of a prominent Republican politician in Reconstruction Savannah, she would have been reviled by the established families of the old Georgia city—if they chose to notice her at all. Conservative, intolerant Savannah did not easily welcome outsiders, particularly those identified with the North and the victorious Yankees.

If there was the likelihood of conflict and ostracism in Savannah among strangers, there was always the certainty of repose and acceptance in Vermont among old friends and family. And it was to Vermont that she went, frequently it seems and at various seasons of the year. Cyrena had a powerful attachment to the state, with its graceful meadows and valleys, sparkling rivers and lakes, and majestic green mountains. Family members still lived there, her kin as well as Amherst's. One of her sisters lived in Sheldon, fewer than five miles from East Berkshire, close by the Missisquoi. Amherst and Cyrena owned property in Sheldon; it seems likely that they had a house there.

There is no record of Cyrena Stone's precise activities or her whereabouts from late 1865 until late 1868, but it seems probable that she spent a good portion of her time in Vermont. We know that Cyrena was not well. Before the war, she had sought medical treatment in New York for an unspecified illness, and after the war, her health problems seem to have become more severe. Perhaps her stays in Vermont and the purchase of property in Sheldon were related to the presence at nearby Sheldon Springs of waters with therapeutic properties—even the power to cure cancer, it was said.

In late 1868 while Amherst remained in Savannah, Cyrena was desperately ill, in Sheldon near her sister. By mid-December, she was in excruciating pain and for a full week only occasional spells of unconsciousness afforded her any relief. On a Saturday afternoon, as the darkness and cold of the Vermont winter set in, she lay dying five miles from her childhood home, a thousand miles from Savannah and her husband. She finally succumbed late in the afternoon on December 18. She was thirty-eight years old.[1]

"Poor Amherst," Cyrena's sister wrote in the family's peculiar shorthand, soon after Cyrena had died, "We did not send soon enough."[2] Stone apparently left Savannah on December 17 and presumably attended services for Cyrena before she was buried in the cemetery in East Berkshire. On January 9, 1869, three weeks after Cyrena's death, he was in Washington, D.C., testifying at congressional hearings dealing with the Ku Klux Klan and the state of Reconstruction in the Southern states. In 1870, by the time the U.S. census taker visited Stone at his residence on South Broad Street in Savannah, he had remarried, this time to a woman twenty years his junior. For a few years, Stone maintained his prominence in Republican politics in Georgia, holding a succession of minor political appointments before becoming U.S. commissioner in 1871. He served as an elector in the election of 1872, but the following year Georgia Republicanism was slowly dying while conservative Democrats "redeemed" the state.[3]

In September 1873 Stone left Georgia to accept an appointment from President Ulysses S. Grant as U.S. judge in the territory of Colorado, where his two brothers, one a Confederate, one a Union veteran, had relocated. Judge Stone traveled a circuit in Colorado for some years and caught public attention from time to time: once when he was kidnapped by outlaws enraged by one of his decisions; another time when he was publicly attacked by a young woman angry that he had broken off an affair with her. Amherst Stone ultimately left the federal bench and during the last years of his life lived in Leadville, Colorado, where he practiced law and served as a judge until his death in 1900 at the age of seventy-four.[4]

AFTER THE WAR, most of the other Atlanta Unionists slipped away into quiet anonymity. Atlanta grew prodigiously during the decades after 1865; by 1900 the population of 100,000 was one hundred times the size the city had been when some of the Unionists had settled there. Population growth and the increasingly cosmopolitan character of the city with its New South, profit-hungry orientation made anonymity easier and also contributed to a gradual loss of identity for the Unionists as a group. Never more than one hundred families strong, they had constituted a significant, troublesome minority in Civil War Atlanta, but as each postwar decade slid by, their presence became more diminished and less easily remembered. By the turn of the century, many were dead. Those who were memorialized in either obituary or biography seldom had anything of a political nature attached to their lives.

Many simply disappeared without trace after the claims era had passed. Prince Ponder vanished, and so did Austin Wright, Richard Mayes, and Henry and Polly Beedles. Robert Webster appeared at least once more on the public stage in Atlanta, briefly calling attention in the pages of an Atlanta newspaper to his sense of racial identity and to his dual identity as black man and white man, as the slave of Benjamin C. Yancey and the putative son of Daniel Webster.[5]

Virtually all the female Unionists except Cyrena Stone disappeared into the shadows of their male-dominated families or, like most of the men, simply faded from sight.

A few of the men, however, achieved political or financial prominence. William Markham rebuilt his fortune after the war and was active in Radical Republican politics. He was president of the Union League in Georgia and ran unsuccessfully for mayor and for U.S. Congress on the Republican ticket.[6]

James A. Stewart spent the remainder of his life discussing popular sovereignty, abolitionists, and Radical Republicans. He maintained his correspondence with old friends Andrew Johnson and Alexander Stephens, and he wrote political tracts excoriating conservative democratic politics. He also evidently wrote a six-hundred- to seven-hundred-page manuscript history of the politics of the Civil War era. It has disappeared and was apparently never published.[7]

Nedom Angier enjoyed political success after the war. He served as a delegate to the Constitutional Convention of 1867–68 and was elected state treasurer in 1868. Angier achieved considerable fame in Georgia when he tussled with Governor Rufus Bullock, a fellow Republican, over the disbursement of public funds. Angier prevailed and, according to a biographer, "his name has been a household word throughout the State." After his term as treasurer, Angier served as mayor of Atlanta, winning the office in 1876.[8]

Alexander N. Wilson had a long political career after the war and was a powerful force in Republican politics in Georgia. As collector of internal revenue and as U.S. commissioner, Wilson allied himself with prominent black politicians in coastal Georgia and became a favorite target of conservative Savannah newspapers. In time, he went into business in Savannah, and toward the end of his life he returned to Atlanta as a high school principal.[9]

Thomas Healey returned to Atlanta from Massachusetts soon after the war and became a successful and wealthy builder. John Silvey and Julius Hayden also became wealthy men after the war, building their wealth in part on the sizable settlements of claims they and other Unionists received from the Court of Claims.

Martin Hinton, whose Unionist exploits made him a marked man in Georgia and Alabama, lived for a time in Topeka, Kansas, after the war and was last heard from in New Mexico in the 1870s. Anderson Scott returned to Massachusetts and the practice of medicine. Lewis Scofield continued in the foundry business in Atlanta, as did William Farnsworth. Holmes Sells practiced dentistry until he returned to his native Pennsylvania a few years before his death. Henry Holcombe held a series of local political posts and tried his hand at the grocery business. David Young moved to Columbus, Georgia.[10]

Alfred Austell made another fortune and became one of Atlanta's most powerful businessmen and a conservative politician remembered for opposing publicly funded secondary education. After his death, he would be remembered both as loyal Confederate and as Unionist. And, in one of those odd errors committed by historians, he would be incorrectly recorded in scholarship as Confederate General Alfred Austell, his old prewar militia title posthumously winning him the stars of a rebel commander.[11]

The Lynch brothers continued to live in Atlanta, and they also prospered after the war. Michael Lynch was highly successful in the book and stationery business and left an estate valued at between $150,000 and $200,000. At Lynch's death, an Atlanta newspaper gave him a "Lost Cause" send-off that would certainly have amused the old Unionist, who sold "treasonous" newspapers during the war and hid out in his garret for weeks evading vengeful Confederates after Sherman left. "All through the war Mr. Lynch was one of the most devoted of those who loved the South and its cause," the *Atlanta Constitution* patriotically declared."[12]

James Dunning continued his outspoken ways until he died. An agent of the Freedmen's Bureau and a long-time postmaster of Atlanta, he also served as provisional chairman of the Constitutional Convention of 1867. A strong supporter of education for blacks in Atlanta, he championed a variety of similarly unpopular causes. He led a notably unsuccessful campaign to erect a statue of Abraham Lincoln in central Atlanta.[13]

Over a period of decades, the Unionists also gradually faded from Atlanta's *memory* of the Civil War. Some never returned to the city and were quickly forgotten. For generations those persons black or female were invisible to history. In the events surrounding the battle and siege of 1864—cataclysms that produced giants who dominate the scholarly and popular chronicles—Unionists were only minor characters. And gradually the cult of the Lost Cause took such a powerful hold on the white Southern imagination that it drove from popular historical memory those who were out of conformity with the ideological purity of Confederate nationalism as it was remembered or who did not easily fit into the stereotypes and mythology of *Gone with the Wind*. In the popular mind, the presence of Unionists in Atlanta could only tarnish the sanctity of Confederate memory.

IN THE END, of course, the historical picture is more complex and the continuum of loyalty more extended than fictional and historical accounts of Civil War Atlanta reveal. For Atlanta Unionists (and for many Confederates as well), loyalty was frequently imperfect, rarely unconditional, and often influenced by circumstance. Confederate pressures forced Unionists to make minor concessions to loyalty that postwar purists might regard as betrayal but which the Court of Claims and the Southern Claims Commission saw as unavoidable. Competing loyalties also produced concessions, but in some instances competing loyalties could be reconciled. Cyrena Stone's loyalty to her country persisted despite the conflicts generated by the Confederate service of her brother-in-law and her husband's chameleon-like behavior. We have only a slight indication of the emotional strains that these conflicts of loyalties produced for Cyrena, but we have powerful evidence of the passion and durability of her loyalty to country. Cyrena Stone came as close to unconditional loyalty to the Union as was possible in that portion of the Confederate South remote from significant populations of loyalists. We can only surmise what might have occurred if she, like Antigone, had been forced to make a final choice between government and family.

Amherst Stone's Unionism, seemingly staunch in the prewar period, could obviously be adjusted to circumstance. That Amherst Stone was almost universally regarded by Atlanta Unionists as a "loyal man" both during and after the conflict shows that the Unionists themselves understood that perhaps no home front loyalty, Union or Confederate, could be simon-pure given the circumstances in Civil War Atlanta. In the Stone family, the loyalty of one brother to the Confederacy and the loyalty of another to the Union complete the illustration and indicate how complex the experiences of a single family could be in the vortex of war. For the Atlanta Unionists and indeed for their Confederate cousins, the terms and dimensions of loyalty were intricate and illuminate the complex nature of human allegiances in times of grave stress.

One of the most remarkable aspects of the relationships between Confederate Atlantans and their Unionist fellow citizens is that personal loyalties sometimes triumphed over political loyalties. The ties of class reflected in the meliorative actions of Mayor Calhoun and others toward the Unionists likely stemmed from long-standing social and economic bonds that bound upper-class Unionists with their Confederate peers. Perhaps the most significant aspect of the "reign of terror" was in its limitations, partly resulting from the ties between Unionists and Confederates but also from the inefficiencies of the military authorities in Atlanta. A more effective provost marshal might simply have hanged the Unionists.

Discussions of loyalty invite questions about the nature of disloyalty. Loyalty can be passive, but disloyalty requires overt or covert acts against the object of loyalty. There can be no doubt that Atlanta's Unionists, in acting out their loyalty to the Union, were thoroughly disloyal to the Confederacy. The steady, repeated acts of disloyalty performed by the Unionists frequently crossed over into treason. Espionage occurred; aid and comfort to the enemy were routine. The comparatively mild response of the authorities to these acts of treason may reveal ineptitude, but it also hints at a steady growth of disaffection among Confederate Atlantans and an increasingly flimsy loyalty to the Confederacy as the war wore on.[14]

The language Unionists used to describe the objects of their "national" loyalties is instructive and helps us understand the nature of those loyalties. Unlike Confederates, Unionists placed little or no value upon loyalty to states. They never spoke of being loyal to "Old Georgia" or to any of the other states. Most strikingly, in the sources examined for this study, Unionists never referred to their own actions and attitudes as constituting loyalty to the nation. They referred most frequently to having been "loyal to the government of the United States," "loyal to the United States," "loyal to the Union," "loyal to the Union cause," "loyal to the country," or "loyal to the Old Flag." Thus, if we take this small group of Unionists literally on their own terms, they did not have, strictly speaking, a concept of loyalty to the *nation*. "Nation" was a term of ambiguity in the mid-nineteenth century, narrow enough to encompass an ethnic group, broad enough to encompass a collection of states, but seldom, if ever, referred to by itself as the object of loyalty. Atlanta's Unionists clearly saw their loyalties as focusing primarily upon the "United States" and, more particularly, "the government of the United States."

In the strictest sense, then, patriotism, not nationalism, motivated Unionists to remain loyal.[15] Although many were long-time residents of the South and some were natives, most had been brought up outside the Deep South and were steeped from childhood in the catechism of American patriotism. After secession, Confederate Atlantans, like other Southerners, participated in the erection of a completely new set of rituals and symbols that formed the basis of a revised patriotism. Hastily invented practices became revered traditions overnight. Old loyalties had to be purged, devalued, and discredited. New ones had to be fabricated. An ersatz patriotism developed, complete with frequent, publicly displayed contempt for the symbols of the United States. Atlanta Unionists desperately wanted to hold onto the beliefs and practices that made up American patriotism. They ridiculed the instant and, from their point of view, false patriotism of the Confederates. They were motivated, like many Northern soldiers, by the sanctity of the idea of Union and the other elements that collectively constituted an American patriotism passionate enough to survive four years of war.[16]

Religion motivated others. Patriotism fused with religion in Civil War America, with patriotic practice an important adjunct to Christian ritual. Secessionists were convinced that God walked with their cause, and Unionists were equally confident that God stood on their side. Christian loyalty was a frequently invoked concept. Ministers in both North and South confidently claimed God's benediction, and religion became a tool in the invocation of "folk loyalty."[17] Dissidents such as Cyrena Stone were repulsed by the expropriation of God's favor to the South and the blasphemy of Southern clerics who justified, then blessed, and finally sanctified *the Cause*. For Cyrena Stone, and likely for others of the Union Circle, religion and loyalty were inseparable. Loyalty was morally correct. To have been disloyal would have been to sin.

Self-interest accounted for the behavior of some Unionists. Although liberally dosed with humanitarian motives, the actions of the black Unionists showed clear self-interest. They had no interest in the Confederate cause and a vital stake in advancing the day when the Union armies would arrive. Freedom was the issue. Some of the white male Unionists also acted from self-interest and were motivated by a deep desire to avoid service in the Confederate forces. Loyalty to the Union was cited as the reason for their refusal to serve the Confederacy, but they were also clearly intent on preserving their families, their lives, and their fortunes. Interestingly, few if any took up arms for the Union once they had escaped the Confederacy or once the Union armies appeared in Atlanta. Some Unionists profited economically during the war, making money directly or indirectly from the Confederate war effort while others refused to do so. Here the lines between loyalty and self-interest are not always clear; nor is it always clear which value predominated. After the war, some Unionists decided to seek large sums of money in compensation for loyalty, while others did not—perhaps from a sense that such compensation would sully loyalty. It is hardly likely, however, that during the war Unionists were prescient enough to identify Unionism with postwar economic survival.

Personal characteristics and temperament undeniably account in some measure for the behavior of Atlanta's Unionists. Some were iconoclastic. Some were antiauthoritarian. Some were highly individualistic. Some were reckless. Some were idealistic. Others were simply stubborn. In the end, the motivations for loyalty, as well as the terms of loyalty, varied greatly among the individual persons who formed the Union Circle in Atlanta.

In studying the Unionists of Atlanta and their treatment in the Civil War city, we learn that loyalty was at once enduring and fragile. We also learn that loyalty blinds persons to flaws in the objects of loyalty. And we see how revolutionary groups engender loyalty through coercion, threat, rewards, fear, propagandizing, and intimidation. Old loyalties have to be discredited; new ones fabricated. Eventually, loyalty is reconstructed. The compromises of loyalty from both Confederate and Union perspectives illustrate the difficulty of building and maintaining loyalty, and thereby unity, in a revolutionary setting. If, as David Potter has written, "in psychological terms, a nation exists only subjectively as a convergence of men's loyalties," then the Confederate task of constructing a new nation was a daunting task of extraordinary difficulty.[18]

No easy answers can be given when asked if this or that person was "loyal." Loyalty in Civil War Atlanta was contingent, circumstantial, and subject to a plenitude of definitions shifting over time. Legend, fiction, and cults cannot easily accommodate these complexities and deny us a thorough rendering of the Atlanta experience during this period of our greatest national trauma. Cyrena Stone's determination to make a record of loyal life in the South expands our understanding of the trauma and leads us to a richer vision of the mosaic of life in Civil War Atlanta, one fully as riveting and dramatic as any fictional creation.

In Search of Miss Abby

In 1976, a manuscript dealer sold to the University of Georgia library an eighty-page document written in longhand on legal-sized sheets. The content of the document indicated that it was a diary, although the form and character of the entries suggested that it was a transcription and not the original. The diary spanned the period of January 1 through July 22, 1864, and was written by an unidentified woman of strong Union sympathies who lived in Atlanta, Georgia, during the period leading up to the cataclysmic battle and siege of Atlanta during the late summer of that year. Possibly unique among diaries pertaining to the American Civil War, the document reflected the experience of a Union woman who recorded the frightful, violent tumult that marked the beginning of the death agony of the Confederate States of America.

Keeping such diaries in the Confederacy could be a dangerous exercise. If authorities discovered a disloyal diarist, the outcome could be deadly, as was the case with a Montgomery, Alabama, man who was hanged for recording thoughts summarily judged to be unfriendly to the Confederacy.[1] Perhaps aware of these dangers, the author of the Atlanta diary protected her identity (referring to herself only as "Miss Abby"), obscured the identities of others who also belonged to a small community of Unionists living hundreds of miles behind the Confederate lines in the rebel city of Atlanta, and concealed information that might lead Confederate authorities (or twentieth-century historians) to her or her allies.

Before the diary could be authenticated and made useful as a historical document, its author had to be identified from among the twenty thousand or more persons who inhabited Atlanta during 1864, when the city's population was swollen with refugees, military personnel, and other transients. From hindsight, the process used to identify the author seems simple, and perhaps it would have been for a scholar more skilled in the Civil War era and more familiar with some of the important record groups and manuscript collections that undergird Civil War history. But it turned out to be a complicated process for me, eventually involving more than the identification of "Miss Abby," for at nearly every turn, it seems, there were new questions to answer and confusions to clarify.

Common sense and an anxious concern that the diary might be a portion of an already well-known, perhaps even published, document led to the usual examination of bibliographies dealing with Atlanta during the Civil War and associated topics, and to substantial relief that the project might have a future, because there was no mention of either the diary or a character called Miss Abby. Close scrutiny of guides to major manuscript collections including the National Union Catalog Guide to Manuscript Collections, as well as the National Union Catalog itself, divulged no leads. I also consulted a specialized guide listing American diaries in manuscript, as well as a listing of published American diaries. The search circled closer to home, with inquiries made to archivists of major collections in the Southeast, including Georgia, seeking information about newly acquired manuscripts and collections not listed in the major guides.

No results issued from these efforts, but along the way several candidates for authorship had presented themselves, including an Atlanta school teacher, whose first name was Abbie and who kept a diary during that period. But Abbie M. Brooks and Miss Abby were not the same, as was evident from a perusal of Abbie Brooks's diary at the Atlanta History Center. Brooks was of decidedly Southern orientation and with few, if any, of the characteristics of the Miss Abby revealed in the diary.

It required several close readings of "Miss Abby's Diary" to recognize clues that could lead to her identity. The most obvious perhaps were references to various landmarks and locations around Atlanta, including some tantalizing references to the first initials of neighbors' last names.

Perhaps if these neighbors could be identified, then that might lead to Miss Abby. So I began mapping exercises, with careful attention to geographic clues in the manuscript. There were several references to visits to hospitals and a specific reference to a hospital on the hill. The military hospitals in Atlanta were mapped, using a map taken from an 1870 city directory, a map of sufficient detail, it would seem, to enable the location of key points despite the fact that it was produced five years after the war's conclusion. In addition, maps were procured that showed the general location of the various Confederate defenses built around Atlanta, because Miss Abby's house clearly lay very near some of the breastworks built to defend the city. The general location of conscript camps around the city were also entered when they could be determined, because the manuscript made specific reference to a nearby conscript camp where "Arthur," a character in the diary attached to the "Conscript Department," was assigned.

The author of the diary was clearly a member of an Atlanta church, so churches were also mapped. Instinct as well as some hints concerning the character of the church services suggested to me that Miss Abby might have been a Presbyterian—or at least a Calvinist of some variety; the tone of her writing seemed to indicate that she did not belong to the more evangelical denominations then present in Atlanta: the Methodists and Baptists. And she was clearly not Roman Catholic or Episcopalian. Also, it seemed that she went rather easily back and forth to church; perhaps she lived near one of the two Presbyterian churches in the city.

Next, the matter of the persons living nearby was attacked. Miss Abby referred to a Mr. Newman whose home was near hers. There were no Newmans listed in the 1859 city directory, but four appeared in the 1870 city directory. Miss Abby also referred to a friend, Mrs. I, and although it was not clear where she lived, persons whose names began with I were located and mapped, as were the four Mr. Newmans who appeared in the 1870 directory. (Later, I learned that the reference to Mrs. I was, in fact, a false clue, because Mrs. I proved to be a pseudonym for Martha Huntington.) Miss Abby also frequently referred to her close friend Mrs. Frank, so the few persons whose name was Frank or Franklin were also included on the maps, because Mrs. Frank evidently lived about one mile from Miss Abby.

General histories of Atlanta as well as a few wartime studies make fleeting reference to the presence of a few Unionists in the city, providing usually no more than a few names. An initial (and somewhat hurried) pass through these scholarly and popular works yielded a list of six or eight Unionists whose identities were known and who had gained general recognition for being Unionists. The locations of their homes were also mapped.

When all these factors were mapped and studied, two areas of the city seemed to provide the most logical location for Miss Abby's residence. Both areas were near Confederate fortifications. The first was an area near the northwestern city limits where two men whose names began with the letter *I* lived. The second was much more likely. Located in an area roughly bisected by Houston Street, it contained the residences of Henry Ivy, Nicholas R. Ivy, and Thomas Newman. A conscript camp was located approximately one mile to the northeast. In addition, two of the city's military hospitals fell within the zone: the so-called Institute Hospital (at the location of the Atlanta Female Institute) and the Atlanta Medical College Hospital. Moreover, the area also contained the residence of Thomas G. Healey, prominent Unionist and husband of Olive M. Healey. Of course! Olive Healey was clearly Miss Abby.

Mrs. Healey's identification as the elusive Miss Abby was not long lived. A quick trip to the 1860 manuscript census for Fulton County, Georgia, and to the slave census for the same year provided me with some details about her that did not square with the Miss Abby of the diary. Mrs. Healey had children and no slaves. Miss Abby seemed to be childless and clearly had several slaves living within her household.

More census work followed. The only place-name mentioned in the diary that could be linked to Miss Abby's past was Ticonderoga, mentioned in apparent connection with a childhood romp through the old Revolutionary battlefield there, although it is not entirely clear that the reference was to the diary's author. Assuming that Miss Abby had lived in Atlanta since 1860, I combed the Fulton County manuscript census for women whose native state was New York. At the same time, a thorough search was conducted for all women named Abby or Abigail. And I always kept an eye open for someone who lived on enough acreage to have a field of oats, a cotton house, and other outbuildings, as well as for one who had approximately five slaves living in the household, both men and women. This excursion revealed more than a dozen candidates, but for one reason or another none fit the preceding characteristics of Miss Abby or her broader profile.

What was that profile? Miss Abby seemed to be a number of things, some based on mere guesses. Obviously a vigorous woman, she seemed to be relatively young, perhaps at most middle aged. She also seemed to be a person of some means; references to her home and its contents, the presence of slaves in the household, and the general tone of her writing all suggested a person who belonged at least to the middle class. It also could be inferred from an analysis of the dialogue in the diary that there may have been white servants in the household as well as slaves. Based on the quality of her written expression, Miss Abby seemed to have been a person of intelligence, with perhaps more than an average education. Her marital status was somewhat in doubt. Only a few references were made in the diary that could be connected to a possible husband, and some were ambiguous; but the mention of the imprisoned "H——" in the March 12, 1864, entry and the reference to "no husband or brother near" on July 21 could both be interpreted as references to an absent husband, as could the allusions on March 12 and May 15 to husbands who had departed the wartime city. The language of the diary clearly showed that Miss Abby was not a Southerner. Intuition and scattered references to various topics throughout the diary pointed toward the Middle Atlantic states or New England as her home region.

A return trip to the map brought a sudden inspiration (and one that should have come much earlier). Miss Abby was not a New Yorker; could she have been a Vermonter? After all, Ticonderoga sits upon the shore of Lake Champlain. Scarcely three miles across the water is the Green Mountain State. This brought me back to the census and hours of laborious searching for Vermonters in Atlanta, searching that could have been more easily done the first time through. This time there were several apparently viable candidates, including the wives of E. E. Rawson, Sidney Root, and Amherst W. Stone, all prominent Atlantans and all native Vermonters.

Neither the Rawsons nor the Roots lived in the area previously identified as being the likely location of Miss Abby's residence, so the search focused on Mr. and Mrs. Stone. Most important, the Stones lived on Houston Street, squarely within the area identified as Miss Abby's neighborhood. Amherst Stone's name was clearly legible on the manuscript census form and so was his occupation (lawyer), but Mrs. Stone's, like that of many persons on the census rolls, was indecipherable and appeared to be "Czanna" or something close to that. Despite various attempts at reading it sideways, upside down, and backward (even tracing over the name), it still did not resemble any given name known to me.

There was much more information in the census tracts that gave me hope that Mrs. Stone might be Miss Abby. The Stone household included a married white couple, Thomas and Mary Lewis, and their year-old son, Homer, as well as another white male, C. A. Stone, no doubt a relative of Amherst Stone. Thomas could obviously have been the Tom mentioned in several parts of the diary. And perhaps C. A. Stone was the Arthur who spent time in the Stone household and who was assigned to the Confederate Conscript Department. In addition, the slave census for Fulton County revealed that the Stones owned six slaves: one man, two women, and three children. Moreover, examination of the membership rolls of various Atlanta churches disclosed that the Stones had been founding members of Central Presbyterian Church, a confirmation of the earlier hunch that Miss Abby was a Calvinist.

Although the case for Mrs. Stone seemed ever more solid circumstantially, there was still nothing to connect her with Unionist activity in Atlanta until a close reading of James M. Russell's dissertation on Atlanta during the period of 1847 to 1890 disclosed a brief mention of Unionist activity in the city together with a listing of nine Unionists, including "A. S. Stone," who was described as a merchant.[2] Could A. S. Stone the merchant be Amherst W. Stone the lawyer?

A letter to Professor Russell yielded a gracious introduction to the papers of the Southern Claims Commission (see chapter 11), information concerning the guides to the papers, and the loan of a microfilm copy of some of the allowed claims of Fulton County, Georgia. Had Amherst Stone of Fulton County, Georgia, filed a claim with the Southern Claims Commission? Unfortunately, no. But when the microfilm copy of the allowed claims arrived, the pieces of the Unionist community in Atlanta began to come together for the first time. Most important, buried within the various documents that made up the claim of Thomas G. Healey was a letter from three U.S. Army surgeons who had tended the Union wounded in Atlanta during the war. These surgeons cited a dozen Atlantans who had given aid to the wounded Yankees. The second entry on the list was "Mrs. A. Stone and family."[3]

Still, precious little was known about Mrs. A. Stone or her family. Standard secondary sources, including Franklin Garrett's three-volume history of Atlanta had half a dozen references to Amherst W. Stone, such as when he had arrived in Atlanta and his association with various entrepreneurial undertakings. Most important was the information (later proved erroneous) that A. W. Stone had been appointed U.S. district attorney for Georgia in the immediate aftermath of the Civil War, a solid indication that the transplanted Vermonter had Unionist credentials sufficient to merit this appointment in the tumultuous postwar era. Armed with this knowledge, I then moved to the multivolume index of Savannah, Georgia, newspapers compiled in the 1930s by the WPA. The index led to numerous articles in various Savannah newspapers detailing the Reconstruction-era political involvements of A. W. Stone. Most significant, however, was a terse notice in the December 30, 1868, edition of the *Savannah Morning News:*

DIED

STONE—At Sheldon, Vermont, on December 18th, Mrs. Cyrena A. Stone, wife of Col. A. W. Stone, of Savannah, Ga.

Locating Amherst Stone in earlier Vermont censuses had proved fruitless. He was not listed in the 1850 census. The 1840 census, which would have been taken when he was about ten years old, did not list the names of children. Vermont was full of Stones in the mid-nineteenth century, however, and a large portion of them seemed to be concentrated in the northern one-third of the state.

"Miss Abby" was seemingly Mrs. A. Stone, who was now Cyrena A. Stone, and she had died in Sheldon, Vermont. The search for Miss Abby's Vermont roots began. Taking into account the strength of Miss Abby's religiosity and her apparently Calvinist upbringing, I adopted the hypothesis that she might have been the daughter of a Presbyterian or Congregationalist minister. With the aid of two Vermont-based researchers who pointed out key secondary works, I shifted the focus to Franklin County, Vermont, where Sheldon is located, in an attempt to locate ministers who held pastorates there in the 1830s, around the time when Cyrena Stone would have been born. Two candidates appeared, the Reverend Phineas Kingsley and Reverend Phinehas Bailey, who had been the minister at the East Berkshire Congregationalist Church at the time Cyrena Stone was born.

A research trip to Vermont in search of wild geese at first yielded nothing. Preliminary letters to various archives offered few leads, although the Vermont Historical Society in Montpelier did report that it held a few documents pertaining to Phinehas Bailey. Neither the vital records at Montpelier nor records in Town Clerk offices in various villages in Franklin County divulged any information concerning the birth of Cyrena Bailey. The records of the town clerk in Sheldon, however, confirmed the date of her death and her father's name. Cyrena A. Stone's maiden name was Cyrena A. Bailey. She was the daughter of Phinehas Bailey.

Serendipity had struck. The Vermont Historical Society archives contained a copy of Phinehas Bailey's manuscript autobiography. The author had focused largely on his principal subject, but there was enough family information included to add a few details. Cyrena A. Bailey's middle name was Ann, not Abigail, as I had hoped, although her paternal grandmother's name was Abigail. And the date of her marriage to Amherst Stone was also provided, along with some bits and pieces concerning her brothers and sisters. In addition, Phinehas Bailey occasionally commented on his daughter's emigration to Georgia and her relatively frequent trips back to Vermont.

More serendipity followed. A preliminary telephone inquiry to the Special Collections Division of the Bailey-Howe Library at the University of Vermont had not struck a chord with archivist Kevin Graffagnino, but he later connected my somewhat vague inquiry with Phinehas Bailey. While I was in Vermont, a letter arrived at my home in Athens, Georgia. The contents, read to me by telephone, reported the existence of a manuscript collection at the university that contained papers pertaining to the Bailey family.

The Francis L. Hopkins Collection does contain a wealth of correspondence regarding the Bailey family, much of it dealing with the life of Cyrena Stone's half sister, Louisa Bailey Whitney. Although there was considerable information concerning Cyrena, there were no letters to or from her and, unfortunately, no original diary as I had hoped. Moreover, much of the correspondence in the collection had been written in the obscure shorthand that Phinehas Bailey invented and which he taught to his children. Fortunately, much of the contents of the manuscript collection had been transcribed by an indefatigable researcher, Jeffrey D. Marshall, who had also published two articles dealing with the Bailey family, one focusing on Phinehas himself, one on daughter Louisa. Another collection of Bailey documents, I learned from Graffagnino, was at the Bennington Museum in Bennington, Vermont. On a later trip to the state, I discovered that this collection (kept in a magnificent old camelback trunk) consisted in the main of hundreds of Bailey's sermons written in the shorthand. A careful sorting of the contents of the trunk brought two more diaries to light—one kept by Cyrena's stepmother, Betsey Fisk Stone, and another kept in the shorthand by her half sister, Louisa Bailey Whitney. There were, however, no documents produced by or sent to Cyrena Bailey Stone.

Back in Georgia, I telephoned Marshall, at that time employed at the Massachusetts Historical Society, and the conversation proved immensely helpful. Marshall mentioned that while he was doing research on the Baileys, he had encountered a reference to a novel written by Louisa Bailey Whitney that related, he thought, to the siege of Atlanta. Before the telephone had reached its cradle, I had reached the rare books section of the University of Georgia Library. In the catalogue, under the name of Louisa Bailey Whitney, was an entry for *Goldie's Inheritance: A Story of the Siege of Atlanta,* published in 1903 in Burlington, Vermont. The three pristine copies looked as though they had never been examined. When I began to leaf through the pages, I quickly realized that the story was based on the life of Cyrena Bailey Stone and was written from the perspective of a Unionist woman living in Atlanta during the Civil War. The novel hovers between history and fiction as it tells the story of a young Vermont woman who leaves the state to take a teaching position in Atlanta a few years before the opening of the Civil War. She remains in Georgia after the outbreak of the war, firmly maintains her loyalty to the Union, and secretly gives aid and comfort to Union prisoners held in Atlanta. Embedded in the novel are large, unexpurgated chunks of "Miss Abby's Diary" and other substantial sections, covering the years from 1861 through 1863, which I believe to be drawn from missing portions of the original diary. It quickly became evident that Louisa Whitney had based her book in part on the same document the University of Georgia had bought in 1976.

Several literary clues pointed to this conclusion. First, there are telltale similarities in language between the fragment the University of Georgia acquired (and which is embedded in the novel) and earlier portions of the book. Commonalities in phrasing, word choice, and construction are clearly evident. Second, the two women's literary styles are quite different. Cyrena wrote in a smoothly flowing narrative style full of observations on people and events. Louisa tended to the romantic and even the grandiose, writing in a stilted, less sophisticated way than her half sister. Unfortunately, the two styles collided in the narrative and produced a book that is often disjointed. Fortunately (for me, at least) Louisa Whitney seems largely to have stitched together substantial portions of Cyrena's earlier diary, adding insertions here, making modest alterations there, and relying often on dialogue to carry the plot she imposed on Cyrena's account.

Third, Whitney faithfully includes dates in the narrative that follow the chronology of the diary in 1864 and the author's style of writing dates as headings for diary entries. Moreover, the dates in the pre-1864 portion of the narrative accurately reflect actual occurrences in the city that would have been impossible for Whitney to know about without a document in her possession such as the complete Civil War diary of Cyrena Stone.

The circumstances surrounding the "reign of terror" in 1862 and the appearance of a spy in the Stone household in September 1863 are but two examples. I am also convinced that Louisa Whitney incorporated a few letters to or from Cyrena into the narrative. The complete diary has disappeared. I have used those portions of the novel that seem to incorporate the missing diary (carefully and sparingly) to reconstruct the story of Cyrena and the other Atlanta Unionists. By careful analysis of the texts of both novel and diary and the use of many other documentary sources, the reader can judge where fiction ceases, fact ensues, and a heretofore invisible segment of life in Civil War Atlanta, greatly in contrast with Margaret Mitchell's vastly more popular account, comes to light.

Meanwhile, my research had been proceeding on another front. The discovery of the Bailey material in Vermont and of *Goldie's Inheritance* confirmed the authorship of "Miss Abby's Diary," but a number of questions remained unanswered, particularly about Amherst Stone and his whereabouts during the war. The diary refers to a missing "H——" and implies that he was imprisoned. Assuming that *H* stood for husband, I incorrectly concluded that the Unionist Stone was likely confined in a Confederate prison for disloyalty. In fact, he was incarcerated in the federal prison at Fort Lafayette in New York.

Visits to the National Archives in Washington, D.C., where I concentrated on the papers of the Southern Claims Commission, revealed only shards of evidence about Stone, but when I sought the advice of archivist Michael Musick, I was directed to several major record groups: the Confederate Citizens Papers, the records of the Union provost marshal general, the incoming correspondence of the U.S. secretary of war, the Turner-Baker Papers, and the papers of Record Group 109, which contains many of the captured papers of the Confederate government. In each of these massive record groups, but especially in the provost marshal general records and the Turner-Baker Papers, I found substantial material dealing with Amherst Stone, including almost all the material relating to his arrests and imprisonments and the moving account of Cyrena's presence with him on the mail stage from East Berkshire to Burlington after the first battle of Bull Run. In time, other record groups in the National Archives would complete the picture of Amherst Stone as a blockade-running, opportunistic lawyer with a marvelously well-developed capacity for survival.

In addition to the records of the Southern Claims Commission, the records of the Court of Claims, rarely used by historians, provided many details of the history of Civil War Atlanta unknown until now. Not only do they yield details about Cyrena and Amherst Stone, they also contain much material that pertains to lesser-known persons in the city and are especially fruitful for those who study black life in Atlanta. Virtually all of the material concerning Robert Webster, Prince Ponder, and Richard Mayes comes from this unexplored record group. The relationship of the slave Richard Mayes to the Stones would have been completely lost had not a thorough review of the records of that court been undertaken.

The search for Miss Abby ultimately became a hunt for literally dozens of figures important to the story and for others, such as the spies mentioned in chapter 7, whose stories come mainly from an underused source in the National Archives containing less than a dozen archival boxes. The Scouts, Guides, Spies and Detectives collection not only provides confirmation of the fears of Confederate Atlantans that spies regularly penetrated the wartime city, it also contains totally unexpected material, such as the escape adventures of Marcellus Markham also described in chapter 7.

In the end, the most elusive of the Unionists was Cyrena Stone's friend Mrs. Frank. Despite every attempt to find this woman, her identity remains a complete mystery. Although several persons seemed to be likely candidates (including the wives of Alexander N. Wilson and Nedom Angier as well as a Miss Frank Whitney who attended church with Cyrena), none could be conclusively shown to have been the Mrs. Frank of the diary and novel.

I have speculated that the "Miss Abby's Diary" that the University of Georgia owns is only a partial transcription of an original diary, probably kept in the Bailey shorthand, which covers the entire war years. This transcription, it seems likely, was made by Cyrena. The writing style differs markedly from that of her sister, Louisa Bailey Whitney, and thus appears not to have been altered. Despite a persistent effort, I have not been able to locate either the missing portions of the diary or any of Cyrena Bailey Stone's letters. The family cherished "Aunt Cyrena's" diary, and, in the early part of the twentieth century, a cousin sought to borrow it from Louisa Whitney so that her young daughter could read and profit from it. Mrs. Virginia Burnham, a half grandniece of Cyrena Stone, whom I located through letters to the editors of village newspapers in northern Vermont, believed that the diary was intact when the Bailey Papers were transferred to the University of Vermont and the Bennington Museum Library. However, the trail of these documents and their coming to rest in those repositories is complicated. They passed through the hands of several antique and manuscript dealers, including the one who sold "Miss Abby's Diary" to the University of Georgia. He has consistently declined to provide any information on the provenance of the diary either to me or to the director of the Rare Books and Manuscripts Division of the University of Georgia Libraries. Perhaps the publication of this study will lead to the discovery of the complete diary.

Thus, this book about the Unionists of Atlanta rests upon the identification of the author of its central document, the diary that follows. The pursuit of her identity is something of a historical detective story, the twists and turns of which may be commonplace to historians, perhaps not so familiar to those who do not study history. Without knowing her identity, we could never be sure of the authenticity of the document and would be completely unaware of the rich story of Cyrena Stone, Amherst Stone, and the Unionists of Civil War Atlanta.

Miss Abby's Diary

New Year's morning—1864. [January 1, 1864]

The sun breaks through the clouds so goldenly, after these many days of darkness and storms—I half believe it is a bright omen of good things in store for us this year—which perhaps will be a New Year indeed, in the history of our Nation. But Hope is so weary sending out its dove, which flits over the desolate wastes, finding only Strife & Pain & Death; it comes back to the heart with tired wing—but no olive leaf of Peace.

Ye friends so far away—the loved, the true! I send you a New Year's greeting. Fain would I reach out my hands across the dark gulf that severs us, & clasp yours once more—but no! I can only fold to my heart with *spiritual* arms, those with whom I have had sweet communings & *lived*. But the chilling thought comes—perhaps I am forgotten by those whom I remember in that far-away land. O, it seems so far-away now, & still receding! The clouds & the Night settle down heavier and closer around us. The way grows narrower, and the day-star for which we have watched—breaks not yet through the thickening darkness. Still I am blest, for now and then words of cheer & loving remembrance are borne to me, as if by spirit hands. I know not how they come, or care—so I may but rejoice in their coming.

Then I am made glad by so often meeting those whose hearts are full of a lofty patriotism, that shrinks not at giving up houses & land, men servants & maid servants—if they may but have a Country once more.

Ye who dwell in the old North-land, can never know as it is known *here*—how little life and earthly possessions are worth, without a *Goverment* to cling to;—how *dark* it seems to look up, and see no star illumined banner waving above you! But we nerve ourselves against despair, and believe yet, that this Strife between Truth & Treason must soon end—triumphantly for Truth. Trampled Freedom will arise from the dust, with her starry robes unspotted,—& Columbia's land be so lifted up—purified & peerless, that we shall be proud to call it ours.

"The pale, pale face, my Country, yet shall flush with ripening bloom."

Jan 20th [January 20, 1864]

Farmer T—called this morning—wanted me to buy his load of "fodder." "You'd better take it—I reckon it[']s the last fodder or any thing else I shall ever bring you." "Why so?" I asked. "Well, I'm ordered off to Virginy. They've got me in this war at last. I didn't want to have any thing to do with it any how. *I* didn't vote for Secession—but them are the ones who have to go & fight now—and those who were so fast for war, stay out. I thought I was old enough, and had worked hard enough to stay at home the balance of my life." Drawing a deep sigh—"but they've got me now, and I spose there's no getting away from them. I don't want to fight the Northern folks, they've always treated me well enough. Where shall I put this fodder?"

Mr. T—— lives out ten miles in the country, and has brought us good things for man & beast, year after year. His honesty, industry and contentment command the respect of all who know him. We grow to liking such characters; we love to see them happy and prosperous. So I am conscious of a pleasurable emotion, whenever I see that kind honest cheerful face coming towards the house; then the nice fresh butter, eggs &c that come when the face does,—makes the arrival of Farmer T——, a pleasant episode in this quiet life of mine. But the face looked sad this morning—though meek & resigned. After Mr. T—— bid me good bye, he turned back to say—"I reckon my old woman will be coming to town sometimes, and she'll bring you butter & eggs when I am gone."

I felt really sad when I saw him going away—driving his old horses which he seemed to have a fresh admiration for—sitting up in that great lumbering wagon—looking so martyr-like, as if he clung to life and *his* loves, but it was his duty to go & get killed, and try to kill somebody—though he didn't know what for.

Long I sat and thought and wondered as many others do no doubt—why such things are permitted;—why the innocent and loyal must so suffer, while the guilty & rebellious can stay at home in quiet & safety. But it should be enough for us to know what He wills it—the great Father, whose compassion is so infinite.

I went today to the hospital on the hill; it has been some weeks since I was there. The Union Soldier is improving rapidly. How glad he seemed, when he saw me coming near him! I looked over to the window where the Tennessee boy was lying, when I saw him last, but the little bed was vacant; the pillow clean, & comfort folded back as if waiting for another occupant. I asked an attendant where that sick one was who used to lie thus. "O he died yesterday, and was buried." Gone home at last—thought I—and his yearning heart is at rest.

This has been an uneventful day, but I am sitting on the veranda at the Sun-down hour, to tell how it passed. It is winter now—winter in name, though the air is soft as an evening in May. But no flowers are blooming around me—only withered leaves; they drop now & then in a quiet way, as the aged lie down to die. Ah—this leaf of Southern life is not *withered,* but it falls back so cold upon my heart!

We wait still for the mighty to come and roll away the stone from the tomb into which Secession has consigned us—without any embalming. We hope to step forth free men & women, and live as we have never lived in this land before. It is terrible to dwarf the Soul, that the body may exist.

There are three classes who are looking anxiously for the coming of the victors. Those who love their Country and their Goverment with true loyalty of Soul—the poor who are suffering for the commonest comforts of life, and this nation of negroes who have patiently waited through long years for their deliverance to come. They stretch forth their hands in wild yearning, for what every human heart craves—its birthright of freedom. In the commencement of the war, the fear was universal, that there would be "risings" & "insurrections" without number. But nothing of the kind. The negroes go along with the same submission that characterizes the race. As almost every available white man is ordered to the field—ladies are often left alone on large plantations, with hundreds of slaves to care for. One soldier told me his mother's plantation was surrounded by six others—and there was not a white man on one of them. There are isolated cases of insubordination & murders, but they are no more frequent than in times of peace.

After Mr. Lincoln's proclamation, great apprehension was felt as to the result among the negroes; for not the most ignorant one could be found, but what knew of it, and understood its import. Yet no change was visible; though who can tell of the wild joy that thrilled their hearts, when they felt that their chains were at last broken! Who can tell how many "Praise de Lord!—Praise de Lords!" went up from cabin homes, where dusky forms were gathered around the lightwood blaze—or were winged to heaven silently, because they *dared* not be spoken—& were accepted by Him who hears not words alone.

Very strict regulations are enforced, all of which are submitted to quietly. If negroes are found out after nine o'clock in the evening, even with passes from their owners, they are carried off to the "Caliboose." They can have no social "pleasuring"—and long before their church was taken for a hospital, no meetings were held without a force of policemen being present, with their clubs in readiness.[1] These measures seem impolitic, for there is no surer way to convince them that the whole thing is wrong, and a consciousness of power is thus forced upon them—should they choose to use it.

I remarked to a Southern lady, that it was surprising that those from whom so much trouble had been anticipated, had given the least. She thought it was because a grand faith in their final freedom had given them patience, and they were determined to wait & see what this war would do for them. She said it would be the worst culamity that could befall the South, if such a thing was possible, that they should gain their independence; for the slaves then having all hope cut off, and no North to look to would not any longer submit to their masters, and we should witness scenes never dreamed of before. Mrs. —— said if there were no other reasons for hoping the Southern Confederacy would be a failure—this would be enough. Arming the negroes has been under consideration sometimes—and it amuses them exceedingly. This lady's waiting man, a faithful and intelligent servant, said to her one day—"Missus, they better keep them guns out of our folks hands—cause they dun 'no *which way we going to shoot!*"

A woman came to see me to day, and bursting into tears said—"My husband can't get detailed any longer. He has already been published as a deserter, and how *am* I to get bread for my children, when meal is twenty dollars a bushel, and I have such poor health!" Then she cried out again—"O, I wish these Yankees would ever get here, before we are all murdered and starve to death!" This woman has five children; the eldest, a daughter about sixteen, has a bad cough—but walks two miles to town to obtain Goverment sewing—pants, coats &c. She stops here frequently to rest, for the material is of the heaviest kind. She gets one dollar for pants, a dollar & a half for coats, and fifty cents for shirts. She has been sewing for months to get a pair of shoes, and came yesterday to show them to me— she was so delighted. She is now saving her tickets, and not drawing the money for her sewing, fearing she would have to spend it—until she has enough to buy her a calico dress. Calico is ten and twelve dollars a yard. Is it any marvel that crime and prostitution are so common? This girl is intelligent and refined in her feelings, and she often cries when she tells me of the insults she receives from the men who deal out the work.

Many a woman walks eight or ten miles to town to get sewing; they often have no shoes, or only those made of cloth "pitched within & without"—and rarely ever wear stockings—for the simple reason they have none. The dresses of these countrywomen are sometimes made of flour sacks dyed with bark; gingham "sunbonnets" were long ago dispensed with,—and those made of straw or the long leaved pine take their place.

Feb 14th 1864 [February 14, 1864]

Sabbath. What *rest* there is in this word Sabbath! Like a hushing lullaby, it falls upon the weary spirit that has battled with the world through six toilsome days. It is a "Peace be still" to the wild waves of ambition, of care and unrest—to which if we listen, they "obey," and sleep until the stormy voices of a Monday-morning world awaken them again.

I remained at home this morning—substituting the children's miniature Sabbath school for church services; for if I attend the latter, I am like the woman who spent her all upon physicians, and was "nothing bettered, but rather grew worse." I become only more & more embittered, by hearing from the pulpit such vile aspersions continually cast upon the Goverment—such prayers for its destruction—such assertions that "our cause is just, and a just God *will* crown it with success."

After dinner, a gentleman and his wife called; they apologized for calling to day, but Mr. B—— said he was in trouble, and wanted sympathy. He is past "45"—the present conscript mark, and says he has considered himself a free man, if such are to be found within the limits of the Confederacy. But on going to Savannah, he was arrested and in spite of his exemption papers, and his statements as to age, they enrolled him on the conscript list. He is a Southron, but says he will die before he will ever fight for this cause. He obtained a week's furlough, which he will improve by leaving this sunny land. One would think it was Pandemonium instead of the fair South, to which longing eyes were once turned, as if it were an Eden of blessedness and beauty. Now, to escape is the question—as well with rebels as Unionists. The former rush to Europe from the pleasant land their folly has turned into a Sodom;—they hasten from the flames their own hands have kindled.

This friend asked to see a little starred treasure he knew I had, and when it was spread before him, he did not speak, for a minute or two. His wife rallied him, for his eyes brimed up full; but he spoke at last—"O God! when shall we see this dear old flag waving in triumph over this wretched land! I wish every act of wickedness & oppression perpetrated here, might be published to the whole world; but it can never be told. The powers of darkness reign, and every thing that can degrade, oppress, and crush out the last remaining spark of freedom and manhood, is resorted to. I lost my own self respect, by bribing the officers as I did, in order to obtain my leave of absence." He bid me good bye with a "God bless you." He goes tomorrow & his wife and children will follow, as soon as he has had time to cross the lines.

Have just read an article from the New York News—"What is this war for?" Can it be that there are any in the North, who are trying to discourage patriots who would lay down life to save their country—any who seek to cripple the Goverment as it battles with its would-be destroyers? Southern Papers have boasted of these things—but we could not believe them possible. Let all such home-traitors come and taste the tender mercies of those whose favor they seek, and a speedy cure would be effected. The briefest sojourn at Andersonville would be sufficient.

March 1st 1864 [March 1, 1864]

Mrs. B—— spent the day with me. She was very sad, for she has been unsuccessful in trying to make her exit from this country. Says she will never ask her friends to be so untruthful as to commend her as loyal to the Davis goverment, in order to obtain a passport, for she will be *free* when she leaves this land, and will not place herself under any restraint, which she would feel that she did, by receiving a passport, one of the conditions being "not to communicate any thing that may prove detrimental to the Confederate States." Her husband has not been heard from since he left. She knows nothing of his fate—whether he waits to welcome her on the other side, or has been suddenly dispatched by some murderous guerrilla.

Mrs. B—— loves and hates, with all the ardor of her Southern nature. She loves her country and hates its enemies. "O" said she to day—"Mr. Lincoln is too good—too lenient. I wish he could be removed, and a perfect *tiger* be put in his place; for every one who ever voted for secession is guilty of murder, and should be treated accordingly."

A gentleman of opposite sentiments from this lady, said to me not long ago—"We must not give up now, dark as our prospects seem. Every man must volunteer (he had his exemption paper secured) for if this thing fails, there are some men who will certainly have to hang. Jeff Davis, Howell Cobb, Bob Toombs and others. If the U.S. Goverment don't hang them, our own people will, for bringing upon us so much misery and destruction."

March 12th 1864 [March 12, 1864]

Rare sport is now to go shopping. No purse is large enough to hold all the "needful" that is *needed* to make more than one purchase. From my account book, which I propose to keep for the amusement of future generations—I copy this entry.

1 pd pepper	$ 10.
1 qur beef	73.
1 bottle bay rum	20.
2 ounces ginger	4.
1 broom	6.
1 ham	54.
1 bushel "cow peas"	18.
1 sack of flour	120.
4 pds butter	40.
3 gallons syrup	60.
1 whip	20.
1 buggy & harness	1500.
50 pds coffee	500.
Merino dress	400.
Calico dress	140.
Gaiters	110.

A green silk "love of a bonnet," with pansies & plums $150.

When I was out this morning, a Harper's magazine was given me. It is long since you and I have met old friend—but no signs of age or change are visible on your familiar face. The same bright cheerful look, as when you made your monthly visits to my pleasant home. Willie who is now contemplating the pictures on the cover, says—"Why Miss Abby—that little girl with a basket of chips on her head, *haint spilt them all out yit!*" He remembers the picture, and his fancy, that the basket was full of *chips* instead of flowers;—owing no doubt to "early associations."

After dieting on "pure Southern literature" so long, these words from the breathing thinking world, seem doubly welcome. Here are Iceland travellers telling of the realm of frost & snow—where grandeur and beauty dwell.[2] Who imagined any body was enjoying any thing save *feeding* & *fighting!* Upon the Editor's Table, the feast of reason is still spread in largeness and benevolence of thought. And that old Easy Chair I rejoice to know is not upon its "last legs" yet, but goes trundling around, picking up [gems?] and scattering them again. The Drawer too, is filled as in the peaceful joyous days. From the battle field, and camping ground, come sounds of mirth occasionally, and it is well—better, than to forever strain the heart, to hear only the wail of anguish.

But O Mr. Harper—if you had only harped more upon the fashions! for the fair ones in Secessiondom are longing to know of the latest styles for their "homespun" frocks. Though you could have no assurance that this particular number was destined to float down to Dixie by way of Havana Nassau and various other ports. This Magazine is rather of an ancient date—but just as good for us benighted heathen. My dear Harper—your more favored readers who live in a breathing atmosphere, cannot know what it is to pant in a huge tomb, shut out from all true life;—pant for the strong deep respiration which the air of freedom gives. They cannot know what it is, to only catch the far off murmurs of the great active living world, with no full, clear notes falling upon the soul.

We are glad to see you are battling for the right. No vacillations—no hidden disloyalty—but outspoken devotion to truth. Oh bid them hasten, who have promised to come! With one hand outstretched to beckon them on—with the other we point to those who weary in their long waiting, have died,[3] and are dying;—we point to these vermin-haunted prisons, where the brave are fearfully perishing—while looking for deliverance or exchange. Alas, the "exchange" for which they wait is only to give up a wretched existence called Life, and be tumbled into the trenches, which the inhuman keepers are ambitious to have filled with a hundred a day.

Saturday evening [March 12(?), 1864]

—and alone. Sounds of distant music from the band float hither. The Band! but it discourses not those grand old anthems of our Nation—where remembered strains still echo in the soul, though Memory is almost dead. Well, if Hope must die—let memory perish too. We tire of hearing forever—"Bonnie blue flag" and Dixie—and think it would be delightful to be awakened some of these bright spring mornings, by Hail Columbia!

My friend Frank called to day—perfectly cast down. She is heart broken, because her husband has left her with her four little ones to battle with this terrible life alone. He was obliged to leave, for he had continually to act falsehoods, in order to live at all; and even falsehood could not any longer keep him from the Front. Ladies whose husbands go North, are the subjects of bitter animadversions now—but they care very little for them. It is amusing to hear of the wondrous things that are to be done "after we gain our independence." Some propose to have "Every Yankee that remains here, chained with a negro, and compelled to work by his side." Nearly every paper advocates the propriety of never allowing a man of Northern birth, to vote in the South again!

Welcome letter again from H——.[4] He tells me to leave this land, and not stay a moment for any pecuniary consideration—hinting that it may be long before our anticipations are realized. But he leaves the decision with me, as he can know nothing of the difficulties attending an exit from these boundaries. The few of whom I have taken counsel—say remain where I am by all means. It is easy always to follow advice which accords with our own inclinations. So long have these great hopes been linked with life, that a life *without* them—or without seeing their realization—would seem zestless & void. It would not be enough, to sit in a quiet room, a thousand miles away, and read in some morning paper—"On the 1st of ——, long lines of blue swept through the streets of Atlanta—

"And banners waved like blessing hands." Bands of music spoke out the wild joy which loyal hearts could not utter for very gladness. They came as conquerors this time, and not as captives."

Oh no! this is not enough. I must see the triumphant army as it marches proudly into the city, where it had been so often said—"The Hessians shall never come!"—must hear the notes of victory—must clasp the hands of those who have waited together for the day of rejoicing. How would it grieve the heart of the traveller who had wandered far, and climbed footsore & weary the Alps' highest summit, to watch from thence the rising Sun,—and just as his glad eye caught the first golden gleamings in the eastern sky—if he *then* must turn from what his soul had fainted to behold—descend to the monotonous scenes below, and loose the joy of a life time!

[The following paragraph has been marked over.]

When with friends—when alone as now, or if I wake in the dark—grim prison-walls loom up before me; but no good can come of my going there. They tell me, by remaining here, I can better aid in obtaining H——'s release—*by & by.* So I shall wait for the close of the drama—wait where is my home, and where are my hopes.

Ridged up earth encircles our city, and the "workbreasts" as little Willie calls them, are very near my home. When I first saw the ditches deepening, and the red clay heaping up—a feeling of suffocation came over me. It seemed as if the earth was opening her mouth to swallow us up.

Years ago, I went wandering round among the old ruins of Ticonderoga—spell bound. Every broken down wall whispered a wonderful story, and every little hillock was some heroe's grave to me. On those old embankments, grass was growing, and wild flowers blooming: the little rusty cannonball which I found partly unearthed, seemed a priceless treasure. O with what a wild charm, was every foot of the battle-ground invested! But no wierd old woman in the little cabin where the romping girl sat down to rest—ever looked into her hand so wisely, and told her she would sometime go way off to a beautiful land—but dark years would come. Her home would be surrounded by forts and fortifications—and perhaps cannons would thunder about her, and men fall thick as autumn leaves. Yet the soldiers assure me it will not be so. They say these ditches are no protection—a cat could jump across them. "A battle here? No madam. Give yourself no uneasiness. In case it was possible for the enemy to come down into Georgia so far, and Johnston falls back here—the boys all say they will fall back *home,* for we'll know then there's no use in fighting any longer. As to that, they say it would be a heap better to give up now, before we're all killed off. They are deserting every day any way."

Johnston is much beloved by his men; he cares for their comfort, and treats them kindly. Bragg was an object of hatred; he was unmerciful and cruel. His soldiers were often shot down by his orders, for the slightest offense. One was put to death for stealing a chicken. Another obtained leave of absence to go home and attend to a sick wife. She died, and he remained two or three days over his time to care for the motherless children, and started back to his command. He was met by a guard who came to arrest him as a deserter, and as such was taken to the camp: he related the circumstance which detained him—but it was of no avail—he was ordered to be shot at once. They began to bandage his eyes; he would [not] allow it—saying it was not necessary—he was a man, and had met death too often on the battle field to shrink from it now. So he folded his arms across his breast & was shot down by his comrades. The man related this, said he never fainted before, but he could not witness this scene unmoved—for the soldier had been with him all through the war, and always faithful and brave. Many similar instances are reported, which show the cruelty, of the former Commander. His soldiers used often to declare they would aim their bullets at him first—were they ever engaged in battle.

There is a Battery erected near by, manned by soldiers who are any thing but "protectors." They are engaged in extensive robberies every night; nothing is considered safe which can be carried away. Being no respecters of persons, they call upon all alike;—one night taking four thousand dollars worth of provisions from my neighbor's store room—the next entering a poor woman's house and robbing her of every article of clothing of which she had disrobed herself upon going to bed—and all of her children's garments also. Last night they called at "our house";—broke into the kitchen—carried off two tubs of linen—took every implement lying about the yard—and more than all, they stole my beautiful George—my Turkey gentleman the last of his tribe, I had permitted to live. Four years ago, he was dedicated for a feast day. He went to his slumber away up in a lofty oak, and we thought him safe, but alas he is gone. He will never grace my table on feast days, or fast days;—will no more strut about with *swelling* pride, the lord of these premises. O, George McClellan—to think your life should be given at last to rober-rebels! It is to be hoped that the man whose name you bear, will never follow your "illustrious example."

Sabbath [March 13, 1864]

—after church. A good sermon this morning, but it was spoiled by the last word, which was Confederacy, instead of Heaven; once they were thought to be synonomous by some—but one would judge it was not so now, for the eagerness most men evince to escape from the former. Not long ago, I listened to a really eloquent sermon, but the minister closed by pointing his hearers to *Bragg,* and not to Christ.

Cannot read or think to day. All begin to feel that we are on the eve of stirring events. These immense preparations which we hear are being made by "the enemy"—show that something will be done sometime. Strange rumors come to us. The voices of Spring whisper solemn things. There is a hush and quiet which portends a storm. Let it come!

I feel restless to day. Am tired of this monotonous life and scenery. Wish I could see those lofty mountains sweeping against the sky, that used to look so grand and holy when the Sabbath sunbeams fell upon them. We need something more than soft air and sweet flowers, to *thrill* the soul; we can *float* on these—but can be lifted up only in the presence of Mont Blancs and Niagaras.

March 20th 1864 *[March 20, 1864]*

Various have been my experiences to day. Long I lay upon my pillow this morning, listening to the howling of a cold March wind, which mingled with a few bird songs only, made not a very joyous matin. I arose depressed in spirit—turned from the morning repast, and shut myself away from all intruders. Ashamed to own it—but I had fainted by the way—had not endured to the end. So I took up my mother's Bible, which fell open—and my eye caught this;—"And the Lord shall guide thee continually, and satisfy thy soul in drought, & make fat thy bones: and thou shalt be like a watered garden, and like a spring of water, whose waters fail no." Had a voice from the blue skies above called my name, & addressed to me these beautiful words—they would not seem any more spoken *to* me—than when I read them on those leaves yellowed by time—in my mother's Bible. They were cooling streams in the desert, and my heart was already like a "watered garden," and I *felt* the little joy-flowers blossoming there.

After dinner came a poor woman—a soldier's wife to obtain sewing. In tears as usual—her husband gone—she sick—and the same cry—"How *can* I get bread for my children!" Soon after she left, two more came on the same errand. The husband of one killed in battle long ago, the other sick & wounded. They said their rich neighbors persuaded their husbands to volunteer in the first war, promising that their families should never suffer. But the promise was forgotten, & the little sewing they could get, hardly kept them alive. This class of women know nothing about work, save of the coarsest kind; they could make a flour sack, sweep a cabin, & bake a "hoecake," and this is about all—so it is less trouble to give to them, than to employ them. It always excites the ire of negroes to see charities bestowed upon "Ole poah white folks"—no matter how sick or helpless they may be. "Why don't they go to work?" "They are sick and cannot work." "What they been doing all the time fore they got sick? They're lazy and no-count. That's the reason they haven't got nothing to live on when they gets sick."

The next comer was a young girl who came to beg assistance in writing a letter to her Lieutenant lover at the Front, who had proved faithless, or was killed—she didn't know which. But she wanted a letter written that would reach his heart, and remind him of broken vows—if he was alive—

if not, it would do him no harm! So between us a most *affecting* letter was written which will of course bring the young man to his knees. Wandering lovers are so easily won back! But all the true ones will not come back now for—

> "Ah me! how many a maiden
>   Will Wake o' nights, to find
> Her tree of life, love-laden
>   Swept bare in this wild wind"!

The last "call" was "Ma says please send her some blackberry wine—the baby's got the cramps." The Night and the Storm have Come now, and both are welcome—for quiet & solitude will come with them.

My "Home Guards"—David & Dan, are sleeping in an adjoining room—my old shaggy protector has stretched himself by the door, with head reposing on his paws—and Poppy is dreaming too.[5] Before the mirror, where he stands for hours during the day, to admire himself—is perched no horrid black raven—but my dove Rosy, poised on one foot, with head folded beneath a white wing. How many whiter wings, and watching eyes that these mortal eyes see not, are hovering about me—I cannot know; but somehow a sense of security fills my heart, and this solitude and stillness seem not oppressive. Stillness within—which is unbroken even by cricket's chirp, or "Old Clock on the Stairs" ticking out—

> "Forever—never!
> Never—forever!"[6]

O Muffee, jump down. You have lain curled up in my lap like a great black catapillar long enough. I must brighten the fire;—don't like these fitful flashes. There! now the flames are dancing. A dark mysterious furnace sending out its warmth from some unknown place—you don't know where, is nothing compared to the old primitive fireplace, where you can throw on the "lightwood" and watch the sparks & the flames, which seem kindly & pleasant like sympathetic friends. With a cat & a dog—a child—a book—pencil and paper, and bright cheerfull fire—who can be lonely? An yet—the cat & child fall to sleep for want of petting—the book is dropped—pencil lies on the paper unused—the fire dies down, because thought leads me out away from the present;—bidding me peer now into the future—then compelling me to wander far backward. There are dreams we keep on dreaming;—there are remembered looks—there are happy and sorrowful memories folded away in the heart's deep places,—and sometimes we go softly there, as we would glide silently into the darkened room where our holy dead are lying. We gently lift the white veil that covers them—take away the withered flowers, and strew fresh ones there—give another and another look—let the lifted veil fall back again, & go away.

March 22d 1864 [March 22, 1864]

To day, I received a letter from my friend Mrs. B——. She had succeeded in getting as far as Gadsen Ala. Her adventures are amusing; she paid eight hundred dollars for a conveyance to take her forty miles, and was perfectly jubilant with the expectation of soon crossing the lines. By dots and mysterious sentences, she tried to convey to me some news which she dared not write in full—but I could not comprehend their import.

The orchards that were aglow with peach blossoms a few days since, are blackened and blighted now. The frost has cut off the sweet prophecies of delicious fruit which were hung out—a thousand of them—on every twig. A dreary prospect—is a long Southern summer without a single rosy-cheeked peach to cheer us. So it has been every year since the war began—and yet we are told "God is on our side."

Mrs. F——h spent the morning with me.[7] she says the prisoners have been dying rapidly, since the U.S. Surgeons have left. The Confederate M.D. who has the care of them now, remarked to a person, who understood what he meant, & reported to a friend of the prisoners—that he "managed to get rid of the ——— Yankees mighty fast, since he began to attend them." One of the prisoners told a lady that he had not been taking any medicine of their own surgeons—was not sick—but as soon as they left, the rebel Dr. brought him medicine and compelled him to take it two or three times a day—and he was sick now in earnest, and was growing worse. They all believe that slow poison is being administered to them—but say they would as soon die, as go to Andersonville.

Why they are not exchanged, seems incomprehensible to these poor suffering men—who feel that they are forgotten by a Government they risked their lives to save—and are now left to die a thousand deaths in these wretched Southern prisons.

The following announcement is made in one of the morning papers. "We have been permitted to examine a February number of Godey's Lady Book. It appears from the fashion plates, that the Yankee women still dress as gaudily as ever. We observed no new styles of mourning dress for the many thousand of their Yankee brothers who are *manuring Southern soil with their rotting carcasses.* They wear hoops, very small collars and pretty high hats. As large numbers of their men have been killed, we 'guess' the Yankee girls are preparing the way to dress as nearly like men as possible, just to keep up the idea that *men are about!*" Then advice is given to the Dixie girls to make their own fashions for all time to come—to show their independence—and manufacture their hoops out of grapevine if nothing better can be had, &c.

Another article on Gen Butler—who is certainly blessed with titles—which are Beast, Brute and Ghoul.

A rare bit of history was published in one of our city papers not long ago—relating to Mr. Lincoln's earlier life. The Editor in announcing it says—"We publish to day, the pedigree of the vile monster Lincoln. Its truthfulness may be relied upon. None will fail to read it."

"An object of so much abhorrence, as the man or animal now disgracing the Presidency of the North, must excite some curiosity as to his history—which when given, will convince us that he is a most fit and appropriate instrument for the administration of the besotted, vulgar & fiendish views of the Yankee bigots, whose suffrage made him their chief magistrate." Then follows a long account of the early & later life of the subject of calumny—whose true name is stated to be Abraham *Hanks*. "He has not one redeeming trait of character. His corruption seems to be radical, his faults inbred, his meanness and duplicity organic. His proclamation is a stupendous crime, a curse to his name, to which the infamy of a Nero or a Caligula will be light & harmless. To the North he bequeaths a load of crime that will weigh down its reputation in the eyes of the civilized world. Hereafter the name of Lincoln will sound every depth of degradation and infamy."[8]

April 9th [April 9, 1864]

We have been to the barracks to day. When we arrived at our place of rendezvous—Mrs. F——h's Poppy looked into Nelly's basket, which was filled with good things, and whispered to her—"O, Nelly—don't give them nice cakes to the Southern *Condeffassy* Soldiers—give them to the poor Yankees!" They made some kind of a compromise between them;—the *Condeffassy* boys were to have a few of the nice cakes—but the greater part were destined for the Soldiers who were not of the "Condeffassy" order. All but eight of the prisoners have been sent to Andersonville; six of them are very low, and not expected to live. The other two—Joe & Frank are nurses.

There are sixty deserters in the Confederate prison hospital, and Mrs. F——h carries them milk soup biscuits &c, at least every week, and sometimes oftener. She has a sincere compassion for them—then too, she can thus gain access to the few remaining prisoners, who seem dependent upon her for almost life itself. No fitful impulsive charity is hers—gushing forth at first sight of suffering, then subsiding—but earnest continuing in well doing—consulting never, self interest or ease. It is no holiday freak with her, as with the rest of us, who occasionally get our courage up enough to challenge watching eyes and bitter threats.[9]

We first went to the Confederate hospital. Here pale shriveled hands reached out to welcome one they had learned to look for! "It appears like it's a mighty long time since you've been here—but it aint but a few days." They each one had a doleful tale to tell to their patient listener—of all their aches & pains—of what they had, or hadn't had to eat. When the distributions were completed, and our baskets *apparently* almost emptied—Mrs. F——h looked into hers, and carelessly said to the adjutant standing near—"We have a few biscuits left—guess we'll give them to the Yankees." He replied as *carelessly*—"You going in there? Well I'll go with you." Then Mollie had an attendant too—for wicked girl! she had allowed herself to be so fascinating, and such a good secessionist in order to get access to the prisoners—that a not very youthful—but simple good-hearted widower had lost his heart, and watched for her coming as eagerly as the rest of the *captives*. O these prison-romances! This is one, then Joe loves Jennie, a bright-eyed noble girl—who goes with Nellie to comfort the imprisoned—but she loves another one who has been exchanged long ago; proving it true that the "course of true love," is somewhat rough at least. In other prisons, I have heard of strange beautiful stories—of captives now & then catching glimpses of some sweet pitying face—of vows being exchanged in mysterious ways, and promises given of returns and welcomes after the war. After the war! no pen of mortal can write out the sorrowful changes—the heart-aches and heart-breaks—the bitterness and disappointments that will come then. But it will be recorded somewhere, and by One in whose sight, no human grief seems a little thing.

Mrs. F——h whispered as we stepped into the door—You & Nelly go on—Mollie & I will take care of our *guard*." So she talked pleasantly with the adjutant about our bright prospects—recent defeats of the Federals, and Mollie interested the widower in her own peculiar way—while Nellie was slyly hiding things under pillows besides the "few biscuits"—and pockets were emptied of more contraband articles. Joe expected to be soon exchanged, and said he would take as many letters over the lines, as his friends wished to send. We need have no fears—they would be sewed up in his clothes, and would be safe.[10]

While the watchful adjutant was being entertained by one as *watchful* as himself—Joe was making his revelations to me. "Frank there—went all round this city last night. One of the Confederate soldiers that was guarding—got him a rebel uniform—and took him round. He saw every ditch, every fortification and preperation which has been made to meet our army; he says there is nothing to prevent our men from walking right in here—and I think they will do so soon too. If we are exchanged as we expect to be—they will find out some things they don't know now—for if they had any idea how matters stand down here—I'm sure they wouldn't stay round Dalton much longer."

But we could make no excuse for remaining longer, so hurried away. As we were going out the door, I looked back—and those weary wistful faces were turned towards us *so clingingly;*—the pleased happy looks were dying out, and the old sadness coming back. How selfish it seems, to leave people to bear their sorrows alone! And we half feel that it is selfish to be happy in the brightness and cheer of our own homes—when sometimes we remember these faces, so full of pain and loneliness and starvation.

March 24th 1864 [March 24, 1864][11]

The days go by with a strange quiet at home & the Front. Spring seems loth to adorn the land with sweet flowers when they are so soon perhaps, to be bathed in blood—to be trampled in the dust by the tread of fierce warriors rushing on to victory or defeat. Miniature leaves are just unfolding on the trees—which should long ago have hung out their green banners.

Now and then we are startled out of our stupor, by rumors that the long expected battle has begun, and wild hopes ray out from every such rumor—for the fearful contest which we have watched from afar, has come so near us now. So near—that we almost put our ears to the Earth, and with finger upon the lips—listen breathlessly, that we may catch if possible—the sound of coming footsteps—footsteps of an "army with banners"—which when unfurled above us, will proclaim Liberty indeed.

Reading is mostly laid aside now, for if I take up a book—nothing of its contents are remembered when it is laid down. So my time is taken up in watching the up-shooting of seeds in the garden—the bursting of rose buds, and in sometimes obeying the voice of my "Beloved"—who bids me come away!—for the winter is past, the flowers appear on the Earth—the time of the singing of birds has come, and the voice of the turtle is heard in the land.

Oh this wild unrest that fills the heart in Springtime! What is it?—from whence doth it come? It sometimes seems as if a thousand birds were caged within, with choked voices, and *could* not sing;—a thousand flowers prisoned in rough calyces, & *could* not blossom outward. In this glorious time when all Nature is flowering & winged & voiceful—one longs for wings and voices too.

Am sitting by the window which I opened wide, and the sunshine flooded all my heart, as it did my room. Beautiful thoughts are whispered to me—but they are not mine, no more than are the bird songs which I hear, or the breath of flowers that is borne past on the sweet morning air. I cannot utter them—so they flutter and float about like foam upon the stream, which whirls in eddies awhile, then glides away—away.

Farmer T's wife just now drove up to the door. With a subdued voice, she asked if I wanted any butter and eggs this morning—then burst into tears. "I've lost my baby, and next oldest child since I was here, and my husband is sick way off in Virginy—and now they're going to take this boy away from me,"—turning to a young lad sitting by her. What will become of me? I can't work my farm myself." Pointing to a large house, not far way—"Why don't Mr. Newman go to the war?[12] He was mighty fierce for it, and a great secessioner. I reckon you're powerful glad your husband aint here to be dragged off and killed up all for nothing. But good bye! I don't know as I can ever bring you any thing more. I shall be all alone with my letter girls after Jeems here, goes off to war." Poor woman! my heart ached for her—but I could only extend my hand, and give her as tearful a good bye as she gave me.

So there is never a little moment of sunshine and beauty—but this cruel war is forced upon our thoughts.

Arthur has been home for a few days assisting in the garden management—enlarging strawberry beds, and planting with "great expectations."[13] Tom & Dan are turfing the yard, and seem ambitious to have a green carpet spread out suddenly over it. Dan just looked up very wisely & said—"Maybe we're fixing all this for nothing, for perhaps they'll fight right here. What would you do then Miss Abby?—Whar'd you say at?" Tom did the answering—"Oh hush such talk! I spect to wake up any of these mornins, and see this yer town just filled with Yankees. Jerry told me last night, that a black man told him, that he heered two white men talking the other day—and they said all them that didn't want to stay here after the Yankees come, had better be gittin out o' *this* place mighty peart.[14] One on 'em said he just had saw a man that come through. He had been a *spy-in* like, and he told them, there was no end to them Yankees! The whole country round Chattanooga was just *blue*—and it was no use in trying to keep 'em back—for they'd got started, and would go whar they was a moun' to. Our folks has a heep of *insurance* any how—to say they're driving them back—they always whips 'em—when they're coming this way all the time."

May 6th 1864 [May 6, 1864]

We have been raiding through the woods to day—a pleasant little party of the fair, the young, the brave—and some that were not fair nor young nor brave; some too were of Union and some disunion proclivities. But May sunshine and May airs harmonized all these conflicting elements—and we "made believe" we were happy.

It seems strange—this persistent attempt to forget the strife and sorrow of War—& now when it is so near us—stranger still. This same spirit of determination to eke out pleasure whenever, and wherever it can be found was exhibited in the tragi-comic scene at the depot the other day. Wounded soldiers were lying about on the hard floor, and rough boxes with somebody's loved in them—were scattered around. A merry negro came along, and seating himself upon one of these coffins—began to tune up his rather delapidated "fiddle";—the *live* soldiers hearing it—begged for a "good lively chune"—and pushed their dead comrades here & there, to make room for their shuffling feet. The "light fantastic toe" was *tipped,* until the cars came along, which was to take them to the front—& death.

The woods are so beautiful now—in Nature's coronation time. Honeysuckles are flaming among the rich leafage of the forests—some bright scarlet—some just blushing with pink—and others of deepest orange. The dogwoods in the denser woods look so white—as if covered with snow that had forgotten to melt. Woodbines climbed up so provokingly high with their red & yellow blossoms—we could not reach them, and the gorgeous trumpet flowers are more ambitious still. And *such* a profusion of yellow jessamines!—they are by far the sweetest flowers that adorn these Southern woods. They climb too—and hang high their golden bells which sing out hyms of perfumed praise. But Oh the Serpent-haunted marshes where these flowers live their beautiful life! So should our Souls blossom out in beauty and goodness—be our surroundings never so dark and unlovely.

Some of our party danced—some rowed on the pond—some wandered off to talk of their bright dreams—and a few others sat down on the soft carpet made by the dead foliage of the long leaved pine. They sat there and wreathed wild haw blossoms around their hats—though they talked not of love or flowers but of the battle which has begun. One had just told the news—"They are fighting terribly to day, & Johnston has taken ten thousand prisoners. He has driven Sherman beyond Chattanooga, & there is great rejoicing in town over the news—for they say the Yankees will not dare to make another advance after such a defeat."

M—— turned her face to me with a most despairing look and said—"What *is* the use of hoping any longer? It is always so—*defeated! driven back!* I wish I could die! I do not want to live if our *Goverment* cannot. Think how England would triumph over us! think of the rejoicing here!"—and the fair girl threw from her tear-bedewed flowers she was twining together—as if they innocent things—breathed with hate and treason instead of sweetest perfumes.

Seeing the rest of the party coming towards us—we wandered off still farther—lest Mollie's tears might betray her. We went into the thicker forest, where green bay trees "spread themselves";—the holly with its coral berries gleamed in the Sunshine—and there were oaks that

—"Stream with mosses
And sprout with mistletoe."

The mocking birds mocked—with their wild gushing songs—our heart's anguish—and this splendor of Spring in a Southern Clime was all unheeded—for there be grander emotions now to stir the soul—than these things can awaken.

But we were ordered to return—"going home!" And Mollie joined the company as smiling as if she had never done any thing but laugh all her life. We have learned our lessons well,—can cry when we would laugh—and laugh when we would cry.

9th [May 9, 1864]

Sherman defeated, & Johnston pursuing! But I like such defeats & such *pursuits* as these prove to be. Yesterday Gen. Thomas took Tunnel Hill under his care, and Dalton is evacuated by the Confederates—that place which was so impregnable, "Nature had fortified that position so perfectly, that no power on earth can drive our army from that point." Now—"Johnston is only falling back to get a better position; and when he *does* make a stand—

dead Yankees will be piled up higher than Stone Mountain. Gen. Johnston knows what he is about; he is following out a plan he had long ago—to draw Sherman down into Georgia—cut off his supplies, and bag the whole Vandal tribe." And many rejoice over this *bagging* which is to be.

The battles are usually reported in this style. "The vandals were mowed down without number. No loss on our side. One man killed, and three slightly wounded. Retreats invariably—We fell back in good order. No straggling, and no loss of artillery." History will probably show the truthfulness of these so-called—"official reports."

15th [May 15, 1864]

A solemn Sabbath this has been. Though sick in soul & body—I went to church. Devotion was not the impetus that sent me there—but a restlessness—a feeling that I could not bear this suspense alone. I must mingle with the multitude—and perhaps some friendly hand would clasp mine—some voice whisper—"Courage!" "Faith!"

I wondered too—what would be said in the pulpit to day; and if there would be thanksgivings for *victories.* Though our present pastor has never preached war—but the gospel; and has not as many ministers have done—*instructed* God how to deal with the "vile enemies who are fighting against us." Victory was prayed for as usual, but a petition was added that if it was God's will that our city should meet the fate that others had recently—we might be resigned! I thought of several who would not be very *unreconciled.*

At the close of the sermon, a notice was read—requesting the people to send their carriages to the depot at four in the afternoon, to take the wounded which would arrive to the hospital. The minister then remarked, they could know by this, that a fearful conflict was going on. And with much excitement added—"What are the enemy fighting for now—if not to get possession of this city?" He appointed a meeting at the church at four o'clock when the carriages would come to the depot—for the purpose of praying that our enemies might be defeated, and we gain the victory. All was urged to be present, and with united hearts present this petition to the Court of Heaven.

The thought that the conflict to which we had looked forward so long, and fearfully—had actually begun—and the consciousness of what hung upon its issue—stirred my soul as it was never stirred before. Words have no power to describe my emotions. I bit my lips to keep color in them, and was afraid my next pew neighbors would hear my thoughts. I actually held my hands firm together, to keep them from flying up imploringly—for I trembled with fear, lest God would hear these prayers which were to be offered, and those who had prayed for the coming of this "enemy" as the saviors of their country—must again sink in despair. Oh how I longed to clasp the hand of the merciful One, and tell him *why* we asked that our Government might triumph. It was for this;—that Truth & Right & Liberty had long been in chains—bound by this soul-crushing despotism, beneath which so many were languishing.

When passing out of the church door—some one touched my arm. I turned & saw Mrs. M——, who was waiting for me. She pressed my hand and whispered—looking at me so earnestly—"I know how you feel—but have *faith.* God will remember us!" Her large eyes glowed with a light which warmed my heart—but I could not speak, and we parted.

A black pall, like the curtain of death, hangs over the sky—as if the Sun refused to look upon these terrific scenes. Birds flit silently from tree to tree, and the leaves hang listless, as though the very zephyrs held their breath to catch the tidings from the battle field.

A friend has just left me. She said although it was the Sabbath—she was compelled to come—for her heart was so full of hopes and fears, she must see some one to whom she could speak as she felt. She thought if we were so alone—we had reason to thank God that our husbands were far removed from these scenes of war, and were not to be brought home mangled and dead, as she had seen some brought home to day.

Tom has returned from the depot;—said there were a great number of carriages there—but only a few wounded came down on the train. The reason of it was because the Federals had possession of the battle ground—& all the wounded were in their hands. Hope is again in the ascendant, but always, *always* mingled with pain—is the thought of triumph, when the *price* is remembered.

"Blood is flowing—men are dying; God have mercy on their Souls!"

18th [May 18, 1864]

The news this morning is of an indefinite character. "Banks' surrender confirmed" in flaming capitals, heads the telegraphic column as usual. The defeat seems to be used as a *sweetener* for any unfavorable dispatches which have to be recorded. "Glorious news from Virginia! Grant's loss twenty seven thousand, including ten General officers. Yankees repulsed at Drury's Bluff, one thousand left dead on the field." "The Front" is coming this way rapidly; it being not quite as stationary as formerly: still the enemy are repulsed always. One correspondent says May 16th—Heavy fighting along our right to day. Johnston has fallen back to Calhoun. Our army is in splendid spirits, and all it wants to insure victory, is the word "Forward!" Unfortunately—the *word* seems to be "Backward!" "We have *repulsed the enemy at every point* & the evacuation of the position held by us yesterday, was not compulsory. Our troops are perfectly confident of success, having every assurance that the great Cheiftain will yet drive the enemy from the field just left.

"Several of the Missouri troops in the Yankee army deserted their ranks & came into our lines, declaring their determination to fight no longer with the Miscegenators.

"Since the opening of the Battle of Resaca, it is believed that the Enemy's loss in killed & wounded, will exceed 8000. The Yankees had a jollification over their supposed triumph on Monday night. There was playing of brass bands & cheering to a romantic degree—which will be changed to a more doleful measure before General Johnston has disposed of them."

Sometime ago, a great deal was said about the reinlisting of soldiers, & reports were published every day, that all of this company & that regiment had reinlisted, and there was great enthusiasm among the troops. Private Soldiers say there was very little *voluntary* reinlisting; sometimes only one in a whole regiment—when the roll was called—gave their names as volunteers. But at the point of the bayonet, or with conscription before them—they were compelled to "go in for the war." Desertions were far more frequent than reinlistments.

19th 1864 [May 19, 1864]

Most cheering news came this morning, of the advance of Sherman's army towards Kingston, the capture of Rome. But at noon our gladness was changed to mourning. I had been spending the morning with a friend; we were secretly rejoicing at the prospect of soon greeting the conquerors, & of being permitted perhaps to welcome back those whom the war had made exiles. We had been wandering in the garden—and my arms were literally filled with May roses. As we stood by the gate saying a few more *last* words—a gentleman passed by, & we asked if there was any news since morning. "Oh such *good* news ladies!" and his hands were up lifted for joy. "The Yankees are completely *routed*. They are retreating as fast as they can, & Johnston is chasing them; we has taken ten thousand prisoners. Then there has been a fight in Virginia, and Grant has lost sixty thousand men. This is all perfectly reliable; it came from official sources." The face must keep its color—white or red—though the heart stops beating, or flames up in scorching pain. A faintness came over me, and pressing the hand of my friend—I hurried home through the grove. The roses were thrown away; I didn't love them;—didn't love any thing I fear. Dan saw me coming & opened the gate. "Why Miss Abby—what's the matter? You don't look so peart as you did this morning. Been hearing something bad I reckon. But never you mind! I'll put old Zephyr into the rockaway after dinner & take you to town to some of your friends, and you'll hear something different maybe." Accepting this proposal, I called on a lady. She met me smiling & joyful; "Have you heard the news?" Yes, I had heard—but there was nothing to be glad about. "Nothing? Why there is every thing? The Union boys are marching on as fast as they can. Sherman *is* falling back—but he is falling this way. Cheer up! God will not suffer us to be disappointed after all our prayers & tears & hopes."[15] Just as I was leaving—Miss R—called in—her face aglow with joy. "*Have* you heard the good news! God bless the Yankee boys! They have started now in earnest."

While riding home, Dan said "Well I reckon you heard something better'n what you heard in the morning, by the way *you alls* talked & laughed. I knowed it would be so—I just knowed it. It stands to reason that our folks aint whipping as they say they be, when they're coming this way all the time."

Sweet May showers have fallen, and the blended fragrance of roses & honeysuckles—young leaves and the moist earth—is enchanting; it floats into the very soul, & gives an inner joy indescribably—but only for a moment: for we know to night, pale cold faces lie still and upturned, while this soft moonlight falls upon them. Mothers, and wives who know not their widowhood—were not near to lift the dear head from the hard earth, or kiss the icy lips which could not speak their last good bye. Eyes look upward which are not yet glazed with death—look upward, and the prayer of faith is whispered to a Savior not unloved in the strength of manhood. Others perhaps look upward too, with prayer—who never prayed before; but our Father is so full of compassion & tender mercy—he hears even at the eleventh hour.

21st [May 21, 1864]

Dan came in this morning quite agitated. "There's Mas' George coming yonder—& I just expect he has come to take me away, because the Yankees are so near. Every body's running off their black'uns now." After the salutations of the day I asked the gentleman if he was going to take Dan away.

"Not if he wishes to remain, & you wish to keep him. He has always been a good boy, & I shall allow him to do as he pleases. My only fear is, that he will be enticed away to follow the army when it comes here, as it most assuredly will, and I should never know what became of him." I asked which army he alluded to. "Why the Federal army of course." To my surprise, I found him to be a firm Union man—adhearing to the Goverment of the United States with true loyalty. I asked how he had avoided conscription. He smiled & said he *avoided* it! If he was going to fight—he would fight for the *Right*. Once or twice I felt alarmed at what I had said—thinking what if all this was premeditated, and a "strategic move" to make me commit myself as has often been done. But I banished the suspicion, believing it better to trust & be deceived—than to doubt those who are true. We had a pleasant talk, and Mr. —— left me expressing an earnest wish that I might not have to wait much longer for my hopes to be realized. As he stood talking to Dan, I could not congratulate myself upon seeing another man who could be put on the list of Southern Worthies. I heard him say—"Well Dan—you & I have played together when little boys, & have grown up together. But I'm going to leave you now; perhaps we may meet again when the war is over, and perhaps not. I hope you will be honest and industrious as you always have been. Do not wander off with the army, but stay where you can have a home." He shook hands with him & bid him good bye—& I thought his voice was a little *unsteady*. Dan came in half laughing, and half crying. "He didn't take me off with him did he! but I felt mighty bad to part for good with Mas' George, for him & me was raised together. I always knowed he was for the Yankees-though he didn't say much; but I never heard him say any thing for the *Southern Confederacy*."

Strange changes are taking place, and it is beautiful to note the contrast between things *now* & *then*. A gentleman was saying to me the other day, it was getting to be a fine thing to be a Union man. "Hats are lifted when I meet some who would not speak to me a year ago. It is now "Why how do you do Mr. Roberts?—very glad to see you." Two ladies went to an acquaintance of mine, & asked her protection. One said, "I know you can protect me when the Yankees come; you have friends among them & I am coming right to your house to stay, & I shall be all right." The lady replied—"I thought you said they never would get here." Well I don't believe *now* they are coming—but if they *should* happen to come—I shall look to you for protection." Others have attempted to make friends with those they have abused & persecuted untiringly for being suspected of Union sentiments, & showing kindness to prisoners.

An old acquaintance called yesterday, to see how I was "getting along." He had often thought of me staying here alone, and was ashamed he had not called before! When leaving he said—"I regret exceedingly, any thing has occured to interupt our sociabilities; but I'm going to do away with all this—and we are coming to see you soon. It's all foolishness to have these old friendships broken up because there is a war." I acquiesced of course; but friendships renewed, which have been broken up by bitter ungenerous words—seem never satisfying—never any more real heart-friendships.

This afternoon Mrs. M—— came to sit awhile with me; said she did not know when she could come again, as soldiers were encamping round every where, and it was not pleasant for ladies to go out unattended. Said she still missed her hope & faith in secret. "Every little while I take out that wee picture of a flag you sent me, & pray that it may not be long before a *real* one may wave above us. But you must show me yours—I have never seen it." So I held up before her, the forbidden thing, and she exclaimed— "O, do let me take it in my own hands!" And never shall I forget that look, as she bowed her head, and kissed its beautiful folds—reverently, as if it were some precious friend lying dead before her. But a *resurection* hope flowed in her tearful eyes as she folded it again and gave it back to me say-ing—I beg of you hide this and keep it *so* safe. I tremble for you when I think you have this in your possession, for I have heard such bitter threats. But you will not *always* have to hide it. I *know* you will not. Now sing me the old Star Spangled Banner, & I will go. I told her Bob was so near the house, he could hear—& while watching his horses, his ears would watch too. "You needn't be afraid of Bob; he is my telegraph. I get all my news from him. I do not wish my husband to know the interest I feel in the advance of the Federals—so Bob keeps me informed of the latest news from the front. Now sing away, and I'll sit by the window, where I can look down the walk & see if any one is coming." So I sang the dear old song, with my watcher at the window. She hardly waited for the last words, when she came quickly & folded me in her arms—her heart too full to speak. She hurried away, and I was alone. I wonder if these are little things to record; but they are my life. What other interests for us now? What else could absorb our thoughts, while waiting for *life* or *death?* How these mem-ories—tragic & sweet—will come back to me, in the years that come!— for in all my girlhood gladness, there was no such deep fearful joy as now swells my heart.

Standing alone—peering into the near future, knowing not what lies in the darkness beyond—yet with these hopes & experiences, I can always say—

"I have a heart for any fate."[16]

24th 1864 [May 24, 1864]

This has been a wild day of excitement. From early morning until now—engines have screamed—trains thundered along; wagons laden with goverment stores, refugees, negroes and household stuff, have rattled out of town. Every possible conveyance is bought, borrowed, begged or stolen. Such packing up & leaving of those, who but a short time ago said with great boasting & assurance, that Johnston would never fall back here, & allow the Yankees to step a foot on Georgia's soil—is perfectly marvellous to behold. One is amazed in witnessing these wonderful changes. Now there are fears & tremblings—& some who leave their pleasant homes—know not where to go: many who have been refugeeing all the way from Nashville—sojourning first at one place, then at another—are preparing for another flight. While some say they have "run from the Yankees long enough, and are going to stay here & abide their fate." It is painful to see poor families—who can barely live where they are—frightened at the reported doings of the terrible foe—fleeing with the rest—sometimes only taking half of their little all, in their fright. No home to go to—no money to procure one—but the *Yankees* are coming, & they must go somewhere!

Some very prudent parents say they will remain to take care of their property, but shall send away their *daughters*. It is well no doubt, for the dear susceptible creatures soon become devoted to the *Union* cause, after the arrival of the blue coats. A young lady in Nashville, whose father was compelled to take Federal officers to board—had a servant lay down a piece of carpet wherever they had walked. *She* would not set her foot where a vile Yankee had stepped! But alas, for the mutability of the fair one's heart! In three weeks she was married to one of the same "vile" creatures. In New Orleans, a fond maneuvering mother, who once actually chased a Union lady *with an axe,* because she knew of her sending food to the prisoners—brought round an alliance of her daughter with a Federal Q.M. Evidently thinking in these times, a Quartermaster was a good thing to have in the family.

In passing our church this morning, I noticed a lady coming down the steps with hym book, footstool & sundry other devotional attachments. She saw me passing but turned her head the other way, although we were friends before the war began. She remembered some of her words it is to be presumed. I hope there was no unworthy triumphing in my heart, as they came back to me this morning. "Ask him that fleeth, & her that escapeth, What is done?" Ah! the boys in blue are coming.

I met a gentleman—a Southern Unionist staunch & true; he was walking with a Confederate officer—and bowed very slightly and sedately. After he passed, something, which often impels us to look back, made me turn my head; at that instant, his head turned too, & his face was covered with smiles. I knew then, his heart was as glad as mine—but our intuition, schooled as it has been these years—tells us where to laugh, & when not to.

These are days of strange & thrilling interest, solemn too as death. Such a wild up-heaving as is now going on around us; encampments & fortifications appearing every where. Tent-fires gleaming in the dark forests, near & far—bugles sounding, soldiers coming and going; every thing & every body in a delirium of fear & excitement.

To day, two dear friends and neighbors came to bid me good bye. We have long lived by each other; the first-ripe peaches—the first spring roses were always exchanged, and all these sweet neighborly kindnesses, which make life exceedingly pleasant. True they have differed with me in sentiment since the war—but kindly differed. With them, Secession had not swallowed up Christianity, nor dug a grave for every sweet affection, & tender memory. So it was with real heart-pain that I parted with S—— and L——. They said as they were leaving—"Perhaps we shall never meet again—*here*"—& her lips quivered. No—we probably never shall—& this thought gives added sorrow to such seperations.

27th [May 27, 1864]

For several mornings past, the servants have asked the first thing—"Did you hear them cannons last night and early this morning?" I always answer no, and tell them it is all their imagination. As usual they rushed in this morning greatly excited—"I reckon you heard them last night didn't you?" No—I went to bed for the purpose of sleeping, & it is all your fancy—hearing cannons. "No *maam*! If you will come out doors, you can hear 'em right now." To please them—I went. "There! just listen way yonder! didn't you hear *that*?" No—my obtuse ears could heard nothing. "Why Miss Abby!

where's your *years?* Lordy! you hear *then* didn't you?" Yes—I *heard.* Far northward—over the river—beyond old Kenesaw and the hills of Altoona— I could catch the faintest echo of booming guns. When my ear had rec- ognized the sound, it soon became a reality, which awakened the wildest joy I have ever known. O that music!—the first notes of our redemption anthem. Never fell upon my ear any thing half so sweet—so grand; nor on earth, will any sound so thrill my soul again.

28th [May 28, 1864]

Mrs. Frank & I had arranged for a ride this morning. I called and found her in tears. She said there was not a moment of quiet in the streets all night long. Yesterday, the owner of her servants had sent for them, & they were packing up to leave, crying all the while, & begging her to keep them. This one and that one had been in—the door bell had not been quiet a moment since daylight. Each person that came, had a different story to tell. The Yankees were retreating, the Yankees were coming. Johnston had got in their rear again and cut off their supplies—the eternal quietus now—and Johnston was falling back to Atlanta.

In the dead of night, my friend was awakened by some one calling her. She arose instantly & went to the window: standing by the fence which was very near the house, was her next door neighbor in her night robes— making her seem like some weird spirit of sorrow, for she was wringing her hands & crying—"What will become of us all? We are going to leave tomorrow—& you had better go with us. I cannot bear to think of you stay- ing here alone with your four little children. I tell you there will be a battle here, and blood will flow in these streets"—then she could not proceed for weeping. So she talked and cried, while soldiers tramped by, and wagons rumbled along. Mrs. F—— said her nerves were completely unstrung—she felt as if in a burning Sodom. But alas! no delivering angels come to take us by the hand and lead us forth into a land of peace. This lady had made every arrangement to go North—disposed of her wardrobe and furniture, and by paying three hundred dollars in gold to a man in the rebel Congress— has procured a passport to take her over the lines. Just upon the eve of leaving, she was informed by a gentleman, who though a secessionist, was a friend, that she had better abandon the idea—for if she attempted to leave she would be prevented from doing so; for there were detectives waiting to arrest her—when ever she should set out to make her exit from this land. He had means of knowing that there were some twenty or thirty names in the Provost Marshal's hands—of persons subject to arrest—Mrs. F——

& my own being among the honored ones. So with battles and bloodshed at our very doors—a seige—death and every possible horror in prospect— we have now the added one of being arrested for some unknown crime. Pleasant position for ladies whose husbands are far from them, and friends here who would protect us, are powerless to do so.

Since I returned home, a lady, whose name is also among the doomed, called in great trepidation; said she came to tell me I must burn or bury every scrap of writing, that would excite suspicion. "For you know they say you have been corresponding with the enemy ever since they came to Chattanooga and giving them information—& if we are all arrested, your house will certainly be searched. I have burned my little paper flag, and every rag I had with red white & blue in it. I tell you I don't want to be arrested & sent farther off into the Confederacy, just as the Federals are coming. I have waited for them too long for that"—And the tears filled her eyes. It was a new idea—my keeping the enemy informed! What next?

They have not heard the cannonading in town. Mrs. M—— a Southern lady—was delighted, when I told her the firing could be distinctly heard from this point; said she would walk over in the morning, just to convince herself the Yankees had actually started this way.

We have been standing under the trees, listening to the far-off sounds of war. When Mrs. M—heard the first booming, she clapped her hands for joy, and beckoned—as if those warriors, enveloped in the smoke and dust of battle—could see these small white hands inviting them hither, and hear her say—"Come boys!—come on! we're waiting for you!"

30th [May 30, 1864]

To night the thunder is sounding in the heavens, as if God with *his* artillery was calling the nations to battle. The lightnings flash, and the rain is pouring in torrents. I am alone—only as kind servants are my company, & my loving household pets. But they are all asleep long ago. Never did thunder-voices sound so cheering. Each mighty peal that rolls through the skies, speaks like God. O, it is sweet to be reminded *now*—that he lives & reigns. We forget sometimes the Arm that is strong to deliver—in thinking of what many *may* do, and of what he does *not* do.

Before the morning comes, I may be awakened from my lonely slumbers, by booming cannon and fiery shells; but these thunderings and lightnings tell me of a High Tower—a Fortress—a *Rock of defense*. Infinite is the love that gives itself such names, that we may more easily confide in His care. The sublime protection, and *over-shadowing,* suggested by them—never entered my soul before.

What a Niagara of emotion can surge through our being—and yet the eye remain calm—the lips silent. But I must not think to night;—must not call up memories of a peaceful land, where mountains lift up their blue peaks to bluer skies—where the robins used to sing in beechen trees, and brooks laughed & rippled along through lillied meadows. I wonder if the brooks & birds sing now as then;—if the fern spreads its feathery plumes in damp mossy dells, and the blue & white violets are peeping up in the tall grass on the hill. I marvel if the memory of these pleasant scenes and friends— of one ever ready to cheer & sympathize,—is only a dream. Have I been always thus alone? Was there always war & terror & tumult about me? and never any sunshine & brightness and peace? Was there always somebody praying for vengeance?—and ladies saying as one said the other day—"I wish there was a sea of blood between the North & South—so broad and deep, it could never be crossed!" And another who lived not a hundred miles distant, who was making haste to refugee said—"I rather every one of my children (she was the mother of four) should be laid out on the *cool-ing board,* than to have the Yankees get my niggers."[17]

June 1st [June 1, 1864]

One more day of peace; have not been out—only to a neighbors to bid her good bye—as I heard she was to leave town soon. But she says she shall remain where she is. Many tell me so—who are all the while secretly pack-ing & making haste to flee. I am often asked—"Are you going to stay here when the Yankees come?" My answer is invariably—I have no other home to go to & shall stay in this one—if permitted to do so.

One remark is frequently made now—"I believe our own soldiers do as bad as the Yankees, and I had as lief one would be here as the other, as far as stealing & badness goes; but of course we don't want the Yankees to come." Not at all maam!

A little nearer each day, and each day the cannons are heard more distinctly. Sherman flanks and fortifies, and Johnston falls back—still in search of the *right place.* Every day's paper reiterates—"No cause for despondency. We know certain things which we *could* tell—but the time has not yet come. It will soon be seen that our General knows what he is about—and the hireling heathen polluting our soil with their presence— will see it too."

One editor said to a Union man—"Come! now is the time to die for our country. Let us go out in the trenches and *die.*" "No—I don't want to die yet. I'll go & carry away the dead." "I tell you Sir—we ought to show our manhood & *die!*" The next morning an eloquent article appeared—"Stand firm!" But while his readers were being inspired by so much patriotism—the brave Editor was on the train refugeeing from death & the trenches as fast as steam could carry him.

To night, the rain falls gently, unlike the storm of last evening—so to night a calm trust fills my heart, and the wild fears which oppressed me have all departed. Yet I am sad still, for there is sorrow & gloom every where around me. But a short distance from my home—the malitia are stationed; they are composed mostly of men past the conscript age—who had a right to expect exemption from camp life. Many of them too have opposed the war from the beginning—& have passed through the fires of treason unscathed in soul. One man said he could & would escape across the lines—but he had reason to believe his two sons would be hung in revenge—& his house be burned over his defenseless family. So he stands guard in the ditches, through storm and sunshine, with hundreds of men like him—praying for deliverance.

When the malitia are ordered to the front—they are put where Uriah was.[18] A Southern man in a neighboring town, whose loyalty was well known—was ordered off instantly to the Front. He bid his family farewell—& told them he should never see them again—but to be assured he should never fire one shot against the flag of his country, or the men defending it.

He was placed in the foremost ranks & was shot down the first day. His body was sent back to his family—so mangled it could barely be recognized. Noble man! and there be many—many who thus lie down in martyr graves.

There have been hurrying to & fro to day—people leaving town—Johnston's wagons & stores coming in. Rumors of fighting here & retreating there, and the ubiquitous Yankees every where;—just crossing some river on a new flank movement—and now way down on the Macon road—going to release the prisoners at Andersonville.

2d [June 2, 1864]

There has been great mourning and lamentation in our family to day—for good faithful Zephyr is dead. He was only a horse—but I should be comforted could I believe there was a heaven for horses—where they might wander in green fields forever.

Dan came to my window at midnight, & called out in a solemn voice—
"Zephyr's dead Miss Abby." I bounded up—& Poppy hearing the wailing—
arose too. Some crayon ought to have been near to sketch the group as
they stood in the morning moonlight, weeping over that noble beast. A
famous horse he was; some called him Old Union—because of his strange
propensity to turn up to some of the good people's houses. But O Zephyr!
I have somewhat against you, for your last labor was for the Confederate
goverment: yet it was not voluntary, and this "pressing into service"—caused
your death. All your wonderful goodness and affection, and that marvellous intelligence—even though exhibited in perverseness sometimes—comes
before me now, and tears flow again.

Evening

Our old friend is buried down there under the oak: beneath a rose bush
close by, are the *smaller* graves of my Bobolinks and Canary family. So they
go—my loves.

Across the way—camp-fires are gleaming, and the lights flickering
through the trees, have a cheerful look. But the hearts of the soldiers are
not cheerful. They have just left their homes, and as one after another comes
to the well for water—I see only sad & dejected faces.

It surprises me to hear the officers speak of "this rebellion"—& tell
of this and that one, who helped bring it on—& now would not fight for
it. Howell Cobb made a speech to them the other day, and an officer referring to it said—"*Such* a man calling down God's blessing upon us, was nothing less than blasphemy. He is very lavish of his *blessings*, but he is sure
to keep out of danger himself, and has safe places for his sons—but he must
drag *us* from our homes to fight for his treason."

On every side, I am surrounded by "protectors." New companies
arrived late this afternoon. They hitched their worn horses here & there
among the trees; as they had no forage for them—our field of oats was very
soon appropriated. It makes no difference—the fences are fast disappearing—let it *all* go.

6th. [June 6, 1864]

It is quiet to night in the grove over the way. No bugle notes are heard—
no fires gleaming among the trees, giving a feint of cheerfulness. Orders
came this morning—"To the front!" and tents are rolled up—banners
furled—and off the soldiers go with sick—sick hearts. Many of them actually in tears; some said—"I don't want to go and fight the Yankees—I'd much

rather fight the people who have brought this war upon our country, and forced us to leave our homes to murder & be murdered."

7th [June 7, 1864]

The malitia—"Joe Brown's Pets"—"The New Issue"—were ordered away to day.[19] Lt. W—— called this morning. His only brother is fighting on the other side; he gave me his name and command—saying perhaps I might meet him when the Federals came—& *he* might never see him again. He begged me to assure him his position was not voluntary—there was no choice in the matter. He looked sorrowful enough when he said good bye.

So all is quiet on this side & that—where a few days since, soldiers were cutting down trees, and pitching their tents. But "The Front!" was sounded in their ears, and the camp-grounds are silent to night.

Sabbath [date uncertain][20]

This has been a quiet day of beauty & rest. Am sitting under this dear old tree—enjoying the too brief twilights in this pleasant clime—thinking— *thinking*. The sun went down amid rose and purple tinted clouds. Sometimes we have beautiful sunsets here. Oh, what a weight of care, doubt and fear rests upon my heart! yet I have tried to forget every possible ill, and *trust*.

It is comforting to know that all this sabbath-beauty of to day, is only a promise of what unfolds in sweetest—grandest fruition in that Peaceful Land—where there has never been but one rebellion—& there will never be another.

I have had no company to day—only Aunt Cherry who "called by to see how I was coming on." "Here you is—all alone—you & your cats and dog; but *them* cats seem like folks any how. They've got so much sense like. I never seed cats that knowed so much, and they're always setting close by you. I 'specs you're mighty lonesome here all by yourself. Miss—does you reckon the Yankees'll ever git here?" "O, I don't know. Do you wish them to come?" "Of course I does; though I don't 'spect to leave my folks. I wouldn't be so *niggerfied* as that—after they've done raised me and took care my little children. But we black folks is going to be free—the Bible says so—and I think the time is mighty near. Why my old father and mother told us when they was about to die—'Chilen's remember what I tell you. You will be freed from bondage—when we are in our graves—and we die in this faith.' *We've* had this faith too, and it has kept all the black'uns quiet and peaceful, when every body was so 'fraid the niggers was going to rise.

Rise! what'd we want to rise for when the Good Lord was rising for us? Well good bye! I hope you'll ave a good time to pay for all the bad times you've had."—And she waddled off down the walk—singing a "hime" in a low soft voice.

Some new phase of this war-life appears every day. For two days I have been jailer; the cotton house is the jail, where four negro men are hiding between cotton bales; they say the heat is intolerable. For some days past, a rigorous "pressing" of negroes has been going on: they take all the negro men to be found and send them off to build fortifications on the Chatta-hochee. Those in my care begged me to hide them—saying—"We don't want to make no fortifications to keep away the Yankees *our*selves. Let our folks build their own fortifications. The black'uns they *have* got, are dying up like any thing, for they works 'em so hard, and half starves 'em besides."

It is amusing to see Margy take them their food.[21] She looks up & down the street, and on every side—then goes to the door of their prison & calls softy—"Boys—here's yer vittuls; come and git it quick. There aint arry offi-cer about."

10th [June 10, 1864]

Fast Day again! Stores are closed and all business suspended. The mayor has appointed this as a day of fasting and prayer; the especial cause being the rather too rapid marching this way—of the "ruthless foe." We are to pray that they may be defeated, driven back and our righteous cause pre-vail. Were good old Elijah here, possibly he would say—"Your god is pur-suing, or he is in a journey, or peradventure he sleepeth and must be awaked"![22]

The voices of prayer are heard in every church in the city. From over the hills, the cannons boom—boom, and in the skies above, there are mighty thunderings—the rumbling of God's chariot wheels.

Every morning Dan goes to town for the news, and brings me always a note from my dear F——. To day she writes—"I have just seen a gen-tleman right from the front. He says the Yankees will get the worst whip-ping they ever had. Johnston is just falling back to *give it to them.* Then a neighbor has been in who took great delight in telling me she has *reli-able* information that Johnston had turned upon the Yankees, and they were retreating as fast as they could—& Tennessee would soon be ours. That Beauregard with twenty five thousand men would be here to day, to rein-force Johnston! I am in dispair and nearly crazed. Do come soon and tell me something cheering."

So it is ever; if our hopes begin to revive, some terrible news will come to crush them. It seems as if this suspense and anxiety would take away our reason—if any is left. Still we keep on

"Straining our ears for the tidings of War,
   Holding our hearts like Beacons up higher,
For those who are fighting afar."

July 4th [July 4, 1864]

There are memories of famous Fourths away back—when white dresses and blue ribbons flourished and fluttered;—when gay cavaliers with the most antic of horses, took each their elect lady to some wonderful "celebration": a long address full of *new* thoughts—a dinner in an arbor—a flag waving from a tall pole & the firing of a cannon made a "glorious Fourth."

But *this* Fourth—heralded in by the thunder voices of two mighty armies contending for the mastery, eclipses all weaker memories. Bomb!—bomb! how grand this music! The glad news which came this morning too—makes it a "glorious Fourth" for us. Marietta was given up yesterday, and to day, the Flag of the free proudly floats from the heights of old Kenesaw.

Four years ago, a friend said so sanguinely—"Next summer you can celebrate your independence beneath the Stars & Stripes in every Southern town. He was a more hopeful than truthful prophet. But we thought *to day* would be ours;—yet we can wait a little longer—deliverance is so near.

It was rumored that Gen. Sherman said he should take dinner in Atlanta the fourth of July; so when long before daylight, the most terrific cannonading was heard—apparently just over the river—we thought he was coming to *breakfast* as well as dinner. It was scarcely light when the servants came rushing in greatly excited—"I reckon you hear them cannons *now.* The way they are just roarin!'" Tom said "Miss Abby you'd better let me kill Gen. Grant, (the little fatted pig) for maybe they'll be here to dinner sure enough!"

Evening.

They did not come to dinner. Against my will, I went to a picnic. It was a small party—and any thing but a happy one. Some ladies were present, who had left their homes in northern Georgia—fleeing from the Federals. Their manners were haughty, and words bitter. An officer remarked that Sherman promised to dine in town to day. He would like to get up his bill of fare; the principle dish would be a pint of pounded glass in a quart of whiskey. A Union man said quietly—"*Half* that quantity would be sufficient."

Sometimes there was an attempt at gayety, but the old joyousness was gone. There was thoughtfulness or sadness in every face, and to be on the way home, away from searching looks, was a sweet relief. I fell quite assured this is the last picnic, I shall attend in the *Southern Confederacy.*

5th. *[July 5, 1864]*

Not a sound is heard this bright morning, save the mocking bird's song; booming cannons have long been our sunrise anthem, and lull-a-by at night. But it is strangely quiet now;—so quiet, we fear the latest rumor is true— The enemy is gloriously repulsed, with tremendous loss. Our loss only *one man killed,* & *two slightly wounded.* The truth is kept from us.

Johnston's army fell back to the river last night. "Joe" is something of a nocturnal traveller. His headquarters are now this side of the river. It is reported that a force of the Union army are near Fairburn, endeavoring to cut the LaGrange road; Where the main army is, we have no way of knowing.

A young man was telling me to day of an incident he witnessed in some of the recent engagements. The Federals were charging a battery, and the color bearer was shot; before he fell another soldier rushed up & caught the flag, but soon shared the fate of his comrade. A brave boy snatched the banner so dear to him from the dying man, who yet held it erect—and he too was killed; the Stars & Stripes did not fall, until it fell with the *seventh* brave man, who laid down his life to save it from dishonor. And *these* are the "low hirelings who are only fighting for pay!" No love for contry here? Ah—

"Our old Land leans beauteous above *such* darlings as they die,
And bosomed in her arms of love, her slain ones richly lie."

The young man relating this incident, is an officer in the Confederate army, but his heart & soul is on the other side. "Oh" said he—"when the old flag went down at last by the side of those brave men—I almost forgot where I was. I could not *see*—for the smoke & dust—or *something else.*"

Is not our life twofold? sorrowful and lonely may be the waking hours, but when sleep cometh, blessed communion for which the soul has yearned—is sometimes given us. Who has never awaked in the morning, gladdened by the remembrance of loving words spoken to them in dreams?— by the memory of some dear face which bent over them in the stillness of night?—a face perhaps that was hidden away long ago. We feel the soft kisses, and all through the day, whispered words of tenderness and affection, echo softly in our hearts. Who shall say there are not low whisperings which the soul alone can hear?

Then sometimes we wander in other lands; richest landscapes are spread out before us, and these bright dream-pictures we never forget. Grander mountains & lovelier scenes than ever my earthly eyes looked upon, have risen before in the visions of the night; and I bless God we can *see* & *hear* even when we sleep.

Last night I laid a weary head upon my pillow, and my heart was faint; but sleep came, and with it a dream which I cannot help recording, for it is continually before me, in all its grand and beautiful distinctness.

There was a broad river; one of its banks was low and shaded with trees whose long branches dipped gracefully in the stream. The opposite shore was a high cliff covered with green moss and rarest flowers. I was standing in deep water which *almost* overflowed me—gazing entranced upon a vast army crossing the river two by two, keeping step & time. They were all "mighty men of war," and dressed in blue uniforms; the water rippled and curled in eddying foam about their limbs, as they marched proudly on. Their banners were lifted high, and borne unfurled across the river; but *such* a light as they were bathed in, is impossible to describe, for there is nothing earthly to which I can liken it. They seemed *spiritualized*—glorified, as if they had been dipped in sunset hues; but through this heavenly tinting gleamed the *Stars* & *Stripes,* and I stood with clasped hands exclaiming—"O, how beautiful!—how glorious!"

On the cliff, half reclining among the flowers, and looking with intense interest upon these modern warriors—were the spirits in their immortal bodies, of Washington and many other noble heroes of the first Revolution. They were smiling and waving their hands as if in blessing, upon that mighty host crossing the river.

An ancient sage, whose long white locks fell upon his shoulders—reminding me in my dream of Ossian's hoary forest-kings—floated to me on the waves, and said "Child, do not fear!" then taking me in his arms, just as the waters were swelling in angry billows around—bore me safely to the other shore.[23]

I awoke;—the sharp rattle of musketry, which is now discernable, and the thundering cannons, were still voicing the deadly strife of man. I felt that War—fearful & bloody, was each hour, coming nearer—nearer; but I felt too, that a Hand would lead me—an Arm bear me through the deep waters;—they would not overflow me. And *that* Army marching in triumph, proudly lifting its banners high—shall I not see it?

Nothing new this morning, only "a right smart skirmish" some-where—no one know where. I was just told of Mrs. I's attempted exit from the city.[24] She is a dear friend and my heart pities her. Her husband crossed the lines sometime ago, and the wife disposed of her home—condensed her wardrobe for herself, two children & a servant into one trunk—secured her passport, and went to the depot last night at eleven o'clock to take the cars. She was going North—by way of Meridian Miss. At the depot she was met by a detective, who said he was compelled to detain her until her baggage could be searched—but as it was late—he would escort her home & call the next morning. He did so, and expressed his surprise at finding nothing contraband. "Why madam I have had orders to watch for you at the depot, ever since you obtained your passport—and prevent your leaving town. My duty is to watch, and I have it to do. I can show you three houses from your window, where they are making Union flags this very moment."[25]

The friends of Mrs. I—believing it would not be long before she could go North by a nearer & pleasanter route—advised her to remain where she is, for the present.

19th [July 19, 1864]

For nearly two weeks Arthur has been home; his being in the conscript department has kept him out of active service and his encampment was so near, I have not felt wholly alone.

But the camp has just been removed a hundred miles away, & yesterday was A's last day of furlough. How have I hoped & prayed each night, that the morning would find us free! Last night the clash of arms sounded so near, it seemed as if the Union Army would surely march in before another sun would rise. They might come now, & meet with comparatively few obstructions;—but no, they will no doubt do as they always have done—wait until strong breastworks are erected, over which brave men must march on to death—before victory. The Confederate soldiers do not expect to make a stand here—say it is impossible if Sherman pushes them as he has been doing. So I have hoped each day & night, until the last has come & gone & Arthur has gone too.

There were but few words spoken, for each felt the seperation & the new dangers surrounding each. I hinted that if he should remain a day or two longer, he might be safe. He quietly said he should soon be *safe*, when he heard of my safety. I must trust in God—there was no one else to look to now for protection—and he hurried away.

All of my neighbors have gone—am alone on the hill. A friend has urged me to move to town & reside with her; but this is my home, & I wish to protect it if possible. There may be no battle here—if not I am safe; if there is one, where is any safety? A gentleman who has removed from town—wishing to be somewhere else when the "Hessians" arrived—offered me his fine residence—whether wholly from benevolent motives—I do not know.

21st [July 21, 1864]

Early this morning, the Hospital Division fell back in the grove. In a moment, the yard kitchen & porch swarmed with soldiers asking for this & that. "May I git an inyun out of the garden?" "Have you got arry biscuit you would let me have?" "Could I git a little milk?" "Will you loan me a kittle or pan?" Yes—yes—yes—to every one—thinking their wants would come to an end sometime, but they only increased. The servants were over-whelmed with importuning soldiers, & it was long before breakfast could be served.

The Col. came to the door, & asked if he could procure a room, as he was an invalid. I asked in return—if he would protect us. "Certainly madam, as long as we remain here." So he seated himself under a tree, allow-ing no soldier to enter the house or garden. He was a kind hearted Chris-tian man, & seemed to deprecate the war; spoke of his own family with tears, and said he could pity others left unprotected. He thought I was wise in not "running from the Yankees," & said if all who refugeed had remained in their homes, they would have saved themselves immense losses & suffering.

We were getting accustomed to the continued roaring of cannons & rattle of musketry, surrounding us with the fiery guerdon [?] of War; but at noon, a horrid whizzing screaming thing, came flying through the air, and burst with a loud explosion above us. Rushing into the Col's room where he was reposing, and the servants following perfectly *pale* with affright, I cried out—"O Col! what was *that*?" "It is a *shell* madam. I beg of you to be calm. I think there is no danger here—you are safer than you would be in town. The enemy are only trying the range of their guns." So we left the soldier to his slumbers, which were not disturbed by any thing so slight as a few *shells*. But not long—for here came another & another scream-ing through the air, & the poor Col. was again appealed to. "I beg of you madam, be calm, & put your trust in God. He alone can protect us." I tried to trust—but be *calm*—when these murderous things were flying over our very heads—how *could* I!

A shell fell, unexploded not far from the house, & every servant ran out to analyze it; but they were told they had best let it alone; perhaps they would become sufficiently acquainted with them! I had begun to think it very nice & consoling to have some one to bid me "be calm"—and who was not afraid of shells—when orders suddenly came to the Hospital Division to "fall back!" I can see there is no feeling of security in the positions held by these forces. They are on the move continually. Our kind hearted Col. bid me good bye saying he hoped I would escape unharmed, advised me to remain in my home, & remember *where* to put my trust.

After this Division had left—Dan went for Mrs. Frank. She sent word that she must see me once more in my home; she could not rest in thinking of me here so alone. While we were talking—the shells came flying over the house so fearfully, & seemed to be falling in the city—that she became alarmed for the safety of her children, & said she must leave me. "But how *can* I! your friends are all wondering what you mean by staying where you are surrounded by so much danger." Dan had become so "demoralized" by these few shells, that he could not be induced to venture out in the open air—so a courier on Hood's staff, kindly offered his services as driver—laughing not a little at Dan's fears.

Gen. Johnston is removed from his command, and Hood succeeds him. Johnston would not "stand"—so his successor is expected to do wonderful things. When censured for continually falling back, Johnston replied—"We can rebuild cities when demolished, but if this army is once destroyed, we can never raise another." His men love and honor him, & regret his removal.

Midnight

Words cannot picture the scenes that surround me—scenes & sounds which my soul will hold in remembrance forever. Terrific cannonading on every side—continual firing of musketry—men screaming to each other—wagons rumbling by on every street, or pouring into the yard—for the few remnants of fences—offers no obstructions new to cavalryman or wagoner,—and from the city comes up wild shouting, as if there was a general melee there.

I sit in my dismantled home tonight, feeling that our earthly loves, and all our pleasant things, are ours so slightly. Am in this little parlor where quiet happy hours have glided by, as I thought & dreamed;—where in other sabbath twilights we used to sing the dear old sacred songs; where have been social joys & pleasant communings, and friend clasped the hand of friend in true companionship of soul. And to night? Ah—I stand alone on a now desolate island, where my heart had always a summer, & life seemed one radiant morning! Alone—& reaching out my hands in vain, as the red waves of War rush madly by—sweeping away our pleasant Home.

Every thing is quiet within—but the spirit of confusion reigned here for a while: there is the carpet rolled up in one corner—piano wheeled out & standing askew—sofa in the middle of the room—Dan & Poppy dropped down on a mattress fast asleep, while Rollo & my two cat friends sit watching me as if afraid I should leave them. In another room—books tied up in sacks—dishes in bedquilts—& nobody knows what all scattered around. The barn is the refuge of Bess & Robert; they had a cozy home of their own, which their industry had filled with many comforts; but poor things! they have but little left, & are guarding that little now.[26] Some soldiers entered their house the other night, pretending to search for runaway negroes; but very soon pistols were placed upon their throats, while some of the party searched, Every thing of value they had—silk dresses—jewellry watches & spoons were carried off. Because they were negroes, some cavalrymen near by, were appealed to in vain. A kind officer is now staying with them—& they will be protected.

All day the firing increased—becoming fiercer each hour; still the soldiers said—"there is no danger—we are driving back the enemy." Towards evening, I was standing in the yard, listening to the firing, & expressing my fears of still nearer approach of battle-scenes. One kind soldier-friend replied—"O that is nothing; that firing is a long way off from here. Don't give way to your feelings madam. I can assure you, our army will never allow the Yankees to take Atlanta!" The dubiousness of this consolation almost made me smile, but I answered in a woeful tone, that they had taken many places of late, apparently as secure as this, & sometimes I thought this city would share the fate that others had. Bess & Robert had a relieved look on their tearful faces, as if delighted that I was safely out of that. They are always watching to see how I can extricate myself from any such difficulty and always reporting—"When you said so & so—that man watched you mighty hard"—or "I was afraid you would say something you oughtn't to, but you come out all right."

At dusk, which is not "twilight" now—with this horrible pall of battle-smoke hanging over us—Tom came running in quite out of breath—"I tell you Miss Abby, we've got to git away from here now, for the men are falling back to the breastworks, & they're going to fight *right away!*" He had hardly spoken, when an *army* of black mouthed cannons came pouring into the grove & yard. An officer came up quickly & said—"They are falling back & will soon fight at the breastworks. It will not be safe for you to remain here madam." A dark night fell suddenly upon the earth, and how dark the night that shut down upon my heart! Not a star illumined it; hope, courage all gone—no husband or brother near, and an army of men around our home;—cannons belching forth a murderous fire not far away, & these silent ones in the yard, look so black & vengeful, as if impatient of a moment's quiet.

Shall not say whether I "wept" or *cried;*—whether I stopped to take from my pocket a handkerchief, or snatched up my muslin dress every now & then, as I went from room to room—not knowing what to do, or where to go; what to save—if any thing could be saved, or what to leave. But the soldiers did not wait for my thoughts, for they went into the parlor, and had the carpet rolled up—pictures packed & many other things, before I knew it. They belong to the Washington Artillery from New Orleans.[27] Our little courier—Lt. S—told me as they came into the yard, I would find them kind & gentlemanly,—and so I have. How pleasant to come in contact with refined & cultivated minds, even should we think them on the wrong side!

Some of them were standing in a group, looking on pityingly—as they saw how I felt, when the "situation" was realized, and I heard one to say in a low voice—"I tell you boys, if our army ever sets foot on northern soil, we ought never to leave one house standing, to pay for such suffering as this." My heart thanked them for their sympathy but I thought they little knew upon what a "traitor" they were bestowing it.

Precious is a friend in need. Mr. Y—— came from town to see if we were safe—just after the men fell back.[28] He & Lt. S set off at once to Hood's headquarters, to ascertain if there was a probability of a battle to night. They returned at ten o'clock, & reported no fighting expected until morning.

Amid the dark memories of the day past, there is one pleasant one. A poor woman came to me in great distress, & wished to see me alone; we retired to a quiet room, & she turned the key herself, as if afraid the hangman was after her. "*Have* you got any blue ink? Here is William's furlough which is out to day; but if you could only change this June into a July, he wont have to go back to the army, for I know the Yankees will be here in a week if they are *ever* coming. It almost kills William to think of going off & leaving me & the children now, with nothing to eat, & the soldiers all round us stealing what little we have." Fortunately I found a bit of indigo, and the expired June unfolded in the fairest July—which caused a whole summer of joy to glow in the poor woman's heart. Her William was waiting for her at the door, and when she showed him the glorious transformation—his face was transformed too.

Every now & then I hear an imploring scream from some hapless chicken which wanton soldiers are taking down from its "roof-tree." But dear Betty *you* are safe—you & your children tied up in a basket, waiting with the rest of us, for the morning exodus. "Betty" is an important member of our "interesting family" and to secure her safety, was about the first thought of the servants. She was an orphan chick, snow white with only one black feather which adorned her crest—and so petted, that when she grew up to henhood, she exhibited wonderful propensities,—such as travelling up & down the piano keys, whenever she could steal into the parlor, and sometimes a "golden egg" would be left upon the music box she so much fancied. Of course her progeny are precocious and marvellously musical; they are Baalam & Balok, Huz & Buz his brother, and their manner was, to sit under the tree, by the door & crow in succession the live long day. When next they will crow, it is impossible to predict.

So here we are watching out this fearful night—waiting for a still more fearful morning. The lurid light from the fires dotting the yard & grove— shines fitfully in the darkness, revealing groups of soldiers here & there— some asleep on the earth, & some leaning against the trees in a listless way—as if life had no longer any gladness for them.

Major W. told Mr. Y quietly, that possibly I might not have to leave my home after all—for they were looking for orders every moment to fall back, and that was why they dared not take their wagons to remove us to town. They expected the city would soon be evacuated by the Confederate troops. The prospect for "refugeeing" is not very bright, the only horse power on the premises now, being the skeleton of an old blind animal, which Tom is the proud possessor of; he calls him the euphonious name of *Battonrooch.* Every thing that hath breath in our family, is honored with a name.

22nd [July 22, 1864]

We have found a refuge with kind Mrs. Frank and an earnest welcome. She gathered me in her arms when I arrived this morning, & said "Poor woman! *have* you escaped with your life; but cheer up. I have good news for you. Hood is going to evacuate the city to day; it was sacked last night—and such scenes were never heard of before. The soldiers expected to leave—& they broke open every store, & scattered provisions in the street;

the poor people & negroes are gathering up the spoils." It was expected that Hood would leave to day, but the order has been countermanded—so report says.

Day had hardly dawned, when Robert & all the servants were tumbling things on the dray. The Washington Artillery were soon ordered to another point; the officers came to bid me good bye, & expressed regret at not being able to render me assistance; said if they were to remain here, my home should be protected. I shall always remember their kindness & sympathy.

The moving was a slow process—only a small dray load at a time, & a mile to go; but we hurried off what we could by nine o'clock—when minie balls came whizzing by so fast, & the shells screaming over the house, I told the servants they need stay no longer. Besides old *Battonrooch* looked as if on his "last legs," or rather on his legs for the last time.

Stowing away most of the books in a large closet, & locking the door, I fancied they would be safe until the storm would subside, so I could get them away. The piano was left, as there was no earthly way of removing it; but fortunately Mr. Y. found some army negroes who were not afraid of shells, that brought it over this afternoon. But there were gallons of nice blackberry wine & jars of pickles—destined for *sick soldiers* which were not gotten away; and alas, for Betty and her children! In the rush & hurry, the precious basket was forgotten, as was Gen. Grant & his kin, who shared the fate of all fat pigs I suppose—for when Mr. Y. went back this afternoon, not a live creature was to be seen, excepting Tiger who came up to him purring so imploringly—he put him in a sack & brought him to me. No cat was ever so welcomed.

When we set out this morning, I felt somewhat as if I was "refugeeing" myself. Mr. Y.[,] Poppy & I, each with hands & arms loaded, and Rollo following on in the rear at a rather solemn pace, with his immense tail which he usually kept swinging high, now drooping to the ground. He seemed unable to comprehend the confusion around him. Poppy had insisted upon taking a pair of cologne bottles which were standing on my bureau—but I told her to never mind those, she had enough to carry. "Well let me take the pretty green bonnet then!"—But I hurried her out of the house; so all the way to town, the silence was every now & then broken by—"Now Miss Abby, it's too bad you wouldn't let me take them pretty blue cologne bottles!" This anxiety about *cologne bottles,* when the shells were flying in every direction, & the battle had begun just beyond our home—made me laugh in spite of every thing.

A strong feeling came over me as I passed down the shaded walk, where I had so often sauntered the peaceful summer evenings;—but I looked not back, for I felt as if leaving those pleasant scenes forever. If such upheavings—such sunderings & losses, were to be the entrance gate into the large life of liberty for which I had sighed—if this dark narrow way full of thorns & briers that so pierce & lacerate,—led out into the broad shining land of my Country—I would go fearless, casting back no look of regret & longing for what I left behind.

How fearful are the sounds of battle! We have heard them to day; we could see clouds of smoke ascending—where we knew men were falling— dying. A "glorious victory" is reported to night, and there are great rejoicings. "We have taken thousands of prisoners—any amount of artillery, & captured six flags. Gen. McPherson is killed." The last we do not yet believe, for in every engagement, one or more Union officers are always reported killed. The heart-sickness that comes over us, when we hear *such* tidings—none can know, but those who wait, as

Introduction

1. Numerous sources discuss the concept of multiple loyalties. A frequently cited source is Harold S. Guetzkow, "Multiple Loyalties: Theoretical Approach to a Problem in International Organization" (Princeton, N.J.: Center for Research on World Political Institutions, 1955). In the paragraph that follows, I have drawn particularly on George P. Fletcher, *Loyalty: An Essay on the Morality of Relationships* (New York: Oxford Univ. Press, 1993). Throughout the book, I have relied heavily upon the preceding sources and upon John H. Schaar, "Loyalty," *International Encyclopedia of the Social Sciences* (New York: Macmillan, 1968), 9:484–87; Schaar, *Loyalty in America* (Berkeley: Univ. of California Press, 1957); and R. T. Allen, "When Loyalty No Harm Meant," *Review of Metaphysics* 43 (Dec. 1989): 281–94. Allen is particularly suggestive in separating loyalty from related concepts, such as faithfulness, fealty, and fidelity.

2. "Every Northerner," the *Atlanta Daily Intelligencer* declared on June 11, 1861, "is by the laws of nations, an enemy to every Southerner." Scholars have previously commented upon the service that Northerners provided in helping Southerners to understand who they were. See, especially, Charles Royster, *The Destructive War: William Tecumseh Sherman, Stonewall Jackson, and the Americans* (New York: Knopf, 1991), 182.

3. There is little literature dealing with Unionism in Georgia. Thomas Conn Bryan, *Confederate Georgia* (Athens: Univ. of Georgia Press, 1953) provides a helpful

overview that has not been improved upon substantially by historians in the last forty-five years, although F. N. Boney, *Rebel Georgia* (Macon, Ga.: Mercer Univ. Press, 1997) nicely summarizes the topic and some recent literature. Jonathan Sarris, "The Madden Branch Massacre: Loyalty and Disloyalty in North Georgia's Guerilla War" (master's thesis, Univ. of Georgia, 1994) is suggestive and useful. Older studies include James A. Riley, "Desertion and Disloyalty in Georgia During the Civil War" (master's thesis, Univ. of Georgia, 1951), and Ellen Sumner, "Unionism in Georgia, 1860–61" (master's thesis, University of Georgia, 1960).

I have benefited from studies of Unionism in the South, in particular, the pertinent sections in Carl N. Degler, *The Other South: Southern Dissenters in the Nineteenth Century* (New York: Harper & Row, 1974), and James Marten, *Texas Divided: Loyalty and Dissent in the Lone Star State, 1856–1874* (Lexington: Univ. Press of Kentucky, 1990). Daniel W. Crofts, *Reluctant Confederates: Upper South Unionists in the Secession Crisis* (Chapel Hill: Univ. of North Carolina, 1989) is also helpful. I have also learned from the sections on Unionism in Michael Fellman, *Inside War: The Guerilla Conflict in Missouri during the American Civil War* (New York: Oxford Univ. Press, 1989); in Peter F. Walker, *Vicksburg: A People at War, 1860–1865* (Chapel Hill: Univ. of North Carolina Press, 1960); and in Ernest B. Furgurson, *Ashes of Glory: Richmond at War* (New York: Knopf, 1996). An older study, Georgia Lee Tatum, *Disloyalty in the Confederacy* (Chapel Hill: Univ. of North Carolina Press, 1934), is the only book that seeks to provide a comprehensive view of disloyalty in the Confederacy.

For background on the idea of Union in antebellum America, I have relied heavily upon Paul C. Nagel, *One Nation Indivisible: The Union in American Thought, 1776–1861* (New York: Oxford Univ. Press, 1964).

4. The considerable literature on Southern women during the Civil War largely ignores Unionist women and women born outside the South. See, especially, Drew Gilpin Faust, *Mothers of Invention: Women of the Slaveholding South in the American Civil War* (Chapel Hill: Univ. of North Carolina Press, 1996), and George C. Rable, *Civil Wars, Women and the Crisis of Southern Nationalism* (Urbana: Univ. of Illinois Press, 1989).

5. There are brief references to the Unionists in James Michael Russell, *Atlanta, 1847–1890: City Building in the Old South and the New* (Baton Rouge: Louisiana State Univ. Press, 1988), 94–95; Robert Gibbons, "Life at the Crossroads of the Confederacy: Atlanta, 1861–1865," *Atlanta Historical Journal* 23 (Summer 1979): 31–33; and Wallace P. Reed, *History of Atlanta, Georgia* (Syracuse, N.Y.: D. Mason, 1889), 187–89. See, also, Thomas G. Dyer, "Vermont Yankees in King Cotton's Court: The Case of Cyrena and Amherst Stone," *Vermont History* 60 (Fall 1992): 205–29, and Dyer, "Atlanta's Other Civil War Novel: Fictional Unionists in a Confederate City," *Georgia Historical Quarterly* 79 (1995): 147–68.

Chapter One • The World of Cyrena and Amherst Stone

1. Mrs. L. M. Whitney, "Memoir of Rev. Phinehas Bailey," Vermont Historical Society, Montpelier; hereinafter cited as Whitney, "A Father's Legacy." The memoir bears the inside title "A Father's Legacy." It is cited as such to distinguish it from

Bailey's autobiographical memoir cited in note 2. I have used these documents as well as other sources to reconstruct the Bailey family's movements and composition. See, also, Jeffrey D. Marshall, "The Life and Legacy of the Reverend Phinehas Bailey," Occasional Paper no. 9, Center for Research on Vermont (Burlington: Univ. of Vermont, 1985), and Marshall, "The Straightest Path to Heaven: Louisa Bailey Whitney and the Congregational Foreign Missionary Movement in Nineteenth Century Vermont," *Vermont History* 55 (Summer 1987): 153–66.

2. Whitney, "A Father's Legacy," 31–42; "Memoirs of Rev. Phinehas Bailey, Written by Himself. Transcription from Shorthand Notes now in the possession of his daughter Mrs. Louisa M. (Bailey) Whitney, Royalton, Vermont July 1902," Vermont Historical Society, 43; hereinafter cited as Bailey, "Memoirs." Probably founded by Bailey, the Berean Society was oriented toward careful study of the scriptures, after the example of the members of the church at Berea in Greece during the early days of Christianity. J. Gordon Melton, ed., *Encyclopedia of American Religions* (Detroit: Gale Research, 1993), 551–52.

3. Whitney, "A Father's Legacy," 34–35.

4. A collection of Cyrena Stone's published writings is found in the Bailey-Hopkins Scrapbook, Francis L. Hopkins Collection, Bailey-Howe Library, University of Vermont, Burlington, hereinafter cited as Bailey-Hopkins Scrapbook. Cyrena always used a pseudonym, but each of her writings is identified in the family scrapbook as her work. Her sister Mary A. Bailey as well as her half sister Louisa M. Whitney also published writings that are contained in the scrapbook. I base the speculation concerning Cyrena's having been a teacher on evidence from Louisa M. Whitney, *Goldie's Inheritance: A Story of the Siege of Atlanta* (Burlington, Vt.: Free Press Association, 1903), 68, discussed further in the subsequent text.

5. For an intriguing discussion of the shorthand system, see Marshall, "The Life and Legacy." Some of the surviving family correspondence is written in the shorthand. Much of it has been transcribed by Jeffrey Marshall of the University of Vermont. In her youth, Louisa Whitney kept her own diary in the shorthand. It is contained in the Bailey Collection at the Bennington Museum, Bennington, Vermont. Examples of Bailey's shorthand system can also be found in the shorthand collection of the New York Public Library.

6. Whitney, *Goldie's Inheritance*, 5–38. There is a photograph of Louisa M. Whitney as a young woman in the Hopkins Collection, University of Vermont, Burlington.

7. *Census of the United States*, 1860, Franklin County, Vt., 48.

8. Abby Maria Hemenway, ed., *The Vermont Historical Gazetteer: A Magazine Embracing A History of Each Town, Civil, Ecclesiastical, Biographical and Military* (Burlington, Vt.: A. M. Hemenway, 1871), 2:114, 94.

9. *Leadville (Colo.) Herald-Democrat*, May 1, 1900; Lewis Cass Aldrich, ed., *History of Franklin and Grand Isle Counties, Vermont* (Syracuse, N.Y.: D. Mason, 1891), 228–29.

10. Hemenway, *Vermont Historical Gazetteer*, 2:112.

11. Thomas C. Reeves, *Gentleman Boss: The Life of Chester Alan Arthur* (New York: Knopf, 1975), 33–35.

12. Hemenway, *Vermont Historical Gazetteer*, 2:94; obituary of Lydia Samson Stone, Bailey-Hopkins Scrapbook.

13. *Census of the United States,* 1850, Fayette County, Ga., 21; Carolyn C. Cary, ed. *The History of Fayette County, 1821–1871* (Fayetteville, Ga.: Fayetteville Historical Society, 1977), 21, 38.

14. Bailey, "Memoirs," 53; clipping of death notice of Jennie Arthur Stone, Bailey-Hopkins Scrapbook.

15. Clipping from the *Augusta (Ga.) Chronicle & Sentinel,* Aug. 15, 1854, Bailey-Hopkins Scrapbook.

16. *Atlanta Daily Intelligencer,* Jan. 10, 1862; E. Y. Clarke, *Illustrated History of Atlanta* (1877; reprint, Atlanta: Cherokee Publishing, 1971), 42.

17. James Michael Russell, *Atlanta, 1847–1890: City Building in the Old South and the New* (Baton Rouge: Louisiana State Univ. Press, 1988), 39.

18. Hemenway, *Vermont Historical Gazetteer,* 2:112; Bailey-Hopkins Scrapbook; deposition of Amherst W. Stone, Mar. 20, 1869, in *Markham* v. *United States* (case file no. 11137), Court of Claims, RG 123, Federal Records Center, Suitland, Md.; "Biography; Stone, Hon. A. W.," Colorado Historical Society, Denver.

19. Wallace P. Reed, *History of Atlanta, Georgia* (Syracuse, N.Y.: D. Mason, 1889), 93–94; deposition of Amherst W. Stone, Mar. 20, 1869, in *Markham* v. *U.S.;* Georgia, vol. 13, p. 144, R.G. Dun & Co. Collection, Baker Library, Harvard University Graduate School of Business Administration.

20. Reed, *History of Atlanta,* 93–95; Kenneth Coleman and Charles Stephen Gurr, eds., *Dictionary of Georgia Biography,* 2 vols. (Athens: Univ. of Georgia Press, 1983), 2:684–85.

21. Franklin M. Garrett, *Atlanta and Environs: A Chronicle of Its People and Events,* 2 vols. (Athens: Univ. of Georgia Press, 1954), 1:489.

22. The Atlanta Bank, an earlier financial institution, had been controlled by out-of-state interests and had earned the reputation of a wildcat bank. Thus, the establishment of the Bank of Fulton rested at least in part upon the founders' hopes to build a bank that would have the confidence of the local business community after a time of instability in Atlanta banking. See Russell, *Atlanta, 1847–1890,* 50–51.

23. Garrett, *Atlanta and Environs,* 1:406, 408–9, 456; Reed, *History of Atlanta,* 424.

24. Garrett, *Atlanta and Environs,* 1:447; Russell, *Atlanta, 1847–1890,* 64.

25. *Atlanta Daily Intelligencer,* Feb. 7, 1860; Garrett, *Atlanta and Environs,* 1:456–57.

26. Superior Court Minutes, Sept. term, 1862, Fulton County, Ga., 278, microfilm, Georgia Department of Archives and History, Atlanta; Russell, *Atlanta, 1847–1890,* 45. In 1860, Stone's office was above McNaught and Ormond's Store; *Atlanta Daily Intelligencer,* Jan. 4, 1860.

27. Florence W. Brine, "Central Presbyterian Church," *Atlanta Historical Bulletin* 3 (July 1938): 182.

28. Superior Court, Deed Records & Mortgages, Fulton County, Ga., vol. A, 1854, 272; vol. G, 1863, 304, Georgia Department of Archives and History, Atlanta; "Miss Abby's Diary," Hargrett Rare Book and Manuscript Library, Main Library, Univ. of Georgia, Mar. 12, 1864. Houston Street is today John Wesley Dobbs Avenue, and Harris Street is Highland Avenue. Hilliard and Jackson Streets are still so named. The deed records from the 1860s are often confusing and unclear, but I am reasonably certain that the four streets mentioned in the text formed the bound-

ary of the Stones' home place. It is not clear, however, what the names of these streets were when the Stones constructed their house in the 1850s—if the streets had names. Neither is it clear exactly when the Stones built their house. A visit to the property today confirms the perspective that the Stones had on the city. Numerous sources and maps locate both Hurt houses. I base the description of the area on a photograph contained in Mills B. Lane, *The People of Georgia: An Illustrated Social History* (Savannah: Beehive Press, 1975), 210–13.

29. I have reconstructed the neighborhood by using *Williams' Atlanta Directory, City Guide, and Business Mirror, 1859–1860* (Atlanta: M. Lynch, 1859); *Census of the United States,* 1860, Fulton County, Ga.; and land records for Fulton County, Ga. For the location of Robert Webster's house, see Reed, *History of Atlanta,* 208, and deposition of Robert Webster, May 31, 1872, in *Webster* v. *United States* (case file no. 13502), Court of Claims, RG 123, Federal Records Center, Suitland, Md. For assistance in mapping the Stones' neighborhood, I am indebted to Ted Kalivoda of the University of Georgia.

30. "Miss Abby's Diary," passim. The reference to the fireplace, piano, outbuildings, oat field, and cotton house are in various parts of the diary. The presence of the berry bushes and fruit trees can be deduced from references to the preservation of fruits and the cultivation of strawberries; ibid., Mar. 24, 1864. The "walled garden" reference is found in Superior Court, Deed Records & Mortgages, Fulton County, Ga., vol. G, 1863, 304, Georgia Department of Archives and History, Atlanta. The "turfing" reference is in "Miss Abby's Diary," Mar. 24, 1864. The description of the neighborhood is based upon the photograph in Lane, *The People of Georgia.*

31. *Slave Census,* 1860, Fulton County, Ga.; Whitney, "A Father's Legacy," 53.

32. Whitney, *Goldie's Inheritance,* passim. *Goldie's Inheritance* is listed in Albert J. Menendez, *Civil War Novels: An Annotated Bibliography* (New York: Garland, 1986), but I have found no mention of it elsewhere. Louisa Whitney is incorrectly listed as Louise Whitney (p. 141). Goldie's "inheritance" refers to the legacy of character and religiosity left to the protagonist by her father. There is a vast literature on *Gone with the Wind* and Margaret Mitchell. An insightful work is Darden A. Pyron, *Southern Daughter: The Life of Margaret Mitchell* (New York: Oxford Univ. Press, 1991). Pyron's work contains a brief bibliography but includes other finding aids that will lead the reader to the scholarly literature dealing with Mitchell and her book.

Louisa Bailey Whitney was born in Hebron, New York, in 1844, the daughter of Betsey Fisk Bailey and Phinehas Bailey. Like Cyrena, Louisa had a pious upbringing in her parents' house and steeped herself in the doctrines of Bailey's Calvinism; as a child, she showed a particular interest in the American missionary movement. Educated at the famous People's Academy in Morrisville, Vermont, and later at Mount Holyoke Seminary in Massachusetts, Louisa wrestled with religious doubts, but in 1868, three years after her graduation from Mount Holyoke, she and her new husband began life together as missionaries in remote Micronesia, where they lived and worked for ten years. After encountering difficulties with administrators in the missionary movement, they returned to Vermont and more conventional pastoral appointments for the next twenty-five years. See Marshall, "The Straightest Path to Heaven."

33. For a discussion of the writings of prominent Victorians about the Civil War, see Anne C. Rose, *Victorian America and the Civil War* (New York: Cambridge Univ. Press, 1992).
34. Whitney, *Goldie's Inheritance,* preface, unnumbered page [3].
35. Ibid., 8
36. Ibid., 68.
37. Ibid., 73–130, 42–46.
38. Ibid., 68.
39. Ibid., 41–42.
40. Louisa Bailey to Mary Bailey (transcribed from the shorthand), May 16, 1861, Francis L. Hopkins Collection, Bailey-Howe Library, University of Vermont, Burlington.
41. Tax Digest of Fulton County, 1861, Atlanta History Center.
42. *Slave Census,* 1860, Fulton County, Ga.; *Goldie's Inheritance,* 211–12; "Miss Abby's Diary," Mar. 20, Mar. 24, July 22, 1864.
43. Deposition of Richard Mayes, Mar. 24, 1874 (Southern Claims Commission), in *Mayes* v. *United States* (case file no. 4618), Court of Claims, RG 123, Federal Records Center, Suitland, Md.
44. Deposition of Richard Mayes, Mar. 24, 1874, in *Mayes* v. *U.S.;* deposition of Prince Ponder, Aug. 2, 1889 ibid.; copy of deed from Amherst W. Stone to Richard Mayes, June 19, 1868, ibid.
45. Deposition of Richard Mayes, Mar. 24, 1874, in *Mayes* v. *U.S.;* copy of deed from Amherst W. Stone to Richard Mayes, June 19, 1868, ibid.
46. Ibid.
47. "Miss Abby's Diary," May 21, 1864.
48. *Census of the United States,* 1860, Fulton County, Ga.; Georgia, vol. 13, p. 192, R.G. Dun & Co. Collection, Baker Library, Harvard University Graduate School of Business Administration.

Chapter Two • *Loyalty under Fire*

1. The most comprehensive treatment of the response in Georgia to Brown's raid is found in Clarence L. Mohr, *On the Threshold of Freedom: Masters and Slaves in Civil War Georgia* (Athens: Univ. of Georgia Press: 1986), 3–19.
2. *Atlanta Daily Intelligencer,* Jan. 5, 6, 1860.
3. Quoted in Michael P. Johnson, *Toward a Patriarchal Republic: The Secession of Georgia* (Baton Rouge: Louisiana State Univ. Press, 1977), 11.
4. Steven A. Channing, *Crisis of Fear: Secession in South Carolina* (New York: Simon and Schuster, 1970), 58.
5. Carl N. Degler, *The Other South: Southern Dissenters in the Nineteenth Century* (New York: Harper & Row, 1974), 99–100.
6. *Atlanta Southern Confederacy,* Aug. 11, 1861.
7. The 1860 census counted 7,615 whites, 1,914 slaves, and 25 free blacks. *Population of the United States in 1860; Compiled from the Original Returns of the Eighth Census . . . ,* 2 vols. (Washington, D.C.: Government Printing Office, 1864), 1:74. An estimate of the total population in 1861 placed it at 13,000. See E. Y.

Clarke, *Illustrated History of Atlanta* (1877; reprint, Atlanta: Cherokee Publishing, 1971), 50.

8. Deposition of James Dunning, Jan. 8, 1870, in *Webster* v. *United States* (case file no. 13502), Court of Claims, Federal Records Center, RG 123, Suitland, Md.

9. *Atlanta Daily Intelligencer,* Jan. 16, 1860.

10. *Williams' Atlanta Directory, City Guide, and Business Mirror, 1859–1860* (Atlanta: M. Lynch, 1859); Georgia, vol. 13, p. 79, R.G. Dun & Co. Collection, Baker Library, Harvard University Graduate School of Business Administration; Marta Lockett Avary, ed., *Recollections of Alexander H. Stephens; his diary kept when a prisoner at Fort Warren, Boston Harbour, 1865; . . .* (New York: Doubleday, Page, 1910), 476.

11. J. A. Stewart, "A Lecture on Sectarian Influence in Schools . . ." (Atlanta: C. R. Hanleiter, 1859), 5; no. 11 in Liberal Pamphlets collection, Houghton Library, Harvard Univ.

12. *Atlanta Daily Intelligencer,* Jan. 16, 1860.

13. Ibid., Feb. 6, 1860.

14. *Atlanta Southern Confederacy,* Feb. 7, 1860; quoted in *Atlanta Daily Intelligencer,* July 23, 1860.

15. *Atlanta Daily Intelligencer,* Jan. 27, 1860.

16. Frank Klement, *Dark Lanterns: Secret Political Societies, Conspiracies, and Treason Trials in the Civil War* (Baton Rouge: Louisiana State Univ. Press, 1984), 7–33.

17. *Atlanta Daily Intelligencer,* Mar. 21, 1860.

18. Ibid., Mar. 22, 1860. Wallace evidently was one of the most vocal secessionist leaders. See *Atlanta Tri-Weekly National American,* June 2, 1860, box 24, William G. Le Duc Collection, Minnesota Historical Society, St. Paul.

19. *Atlanta Daily Intelligencer,* Mar. 28, 1860.

20. *Census of the United States,* 1860, Fulton County, Ga.; "Volney A. Dunning," in *Pioneer Citizens' History of Atlanta, 1833–1902* (Atlanta: Pioneer Citizens' Society of Atlanta, 1902), 381; Georgia, vol. 13, p. 123, R.G. Dun & Co. Collection, Baker Library, Harvard University Graduate School of Business Administration; *Cassville (Ga.) Standard,* Feb. 26, 1852; Franklin M. Garrett, *Atlanta and Environs: A Chronicle of Its People and Events,* 2 vols. (Athens: Univ. of Georgia Press, 1954) 1:628–29, 679, 705, 739, 746, 802, 893, 908; 2:435.

21. *Atlanta Daily Intelligencer,* Mar. 21, 1860.

22. Ibid., May 18, July 11, 1860.

23. Ibid., June 7, 1860.

24. Ibid., July 23, 27, 1860.

25. Deposition of Julius Hayden, June 23, 1877, claim of Nedom L. Angier, Records of the Southern Claims Commission (Allowed Claims), Fulton County, Ga., RG 217, National Archives, Washington, D.C.; similar citations appear hereinafter as Records of the Southern Claims Commission, and unless otherwise indicated, the references to approved claims are to those that originated in Fulton County, Ga.

26. *Memoirs of Georgia; containing historical accounts of the state's civil, military, industrial and professional interests, and personal sketches of many of its people,* 2 vols. (Atlanta: Southern Historical Association, 1895), 1:702–3; Alexander St. Clair Abrams, *Manual and Biographical Register of the State of Georgia*

for 1871–72 (Atlanta: Plantation, 1872), 4–6; Garrett, *Atlanta and Environs,* 1:346–47, 363, 476.

27. Deposition of Amherst W. Stone, Mar. 20, 1869, in *Markham v. United States* (case file no. 11137), Court of Claims, RG 123, Federal Records Center, Suitland, Md.

28. *Census of the United States,* 1860, Fulton County, Ga.; Garrett, *Atlanta and Environs,* 1:351, 956.

29. *Williams' Atlanta Directory,* 83; deposition of William Farnsworth, Jan. 13, 1873, claim of Thomas G. Heal[e]y, Records of the Southern Claims Commission (Allowed Claims).

30. Wallace P. Reed, *History of Atlanta, Georgia* (Syracuse, N.Y.: D. Mason, 1889), 28–33; Kenneth Coleman and Charles Stephen Gurr, eds., *Dictionary of Georgia Biography,* 2 vols. (Athens: Univ. of Georgia Press, 1983), 1:39–40; W. S. Northen, ed., *Men of Mark in Georgia,* 7 vols. (Spartanburg: South Carolina Reprint, 1974), 3:357–65; "Claimant's Abstract of Evidence," in *Austell v. United States* (case file no. 13859), Court of Claims, RG 123, Federal Records Center, Suitland, Md.

31. Deposition of William Markham, Jan. 20, 1873, claim of David Young, Records of the Southern Claims Commission (Allowed Claims).

32. Deposition of C. T. C. Deake, Jan. 23, 1873, in *Crussell v. United States* (case file no. 10491), Court of Claims, RG 123, Federal Records Center, Suitland, Md.

33. Deposition of Michael Bloomfield, Nov. 7, 1866, in *Lynch v. United States* (case file no. 2502), Court of Claims, RG 123, Federal Records Center, Suitland, Md.

34. *Atlanta Intelligencer,* Nov. 5, 1860 (for Dunning and Holcombe); for evidence of Stewart's sentiments regarding Douglas, see chapter 2; Alfred Austell to Andrew Johnson, June 16, 1865, in Paul H. Bergeron, ed., *The Papers of Andrew Johnson,* vol. 8: *May–Aug. 1865* (Knoxville: Univ. of Tennessee Press, 1989), 246; deposition of Julius A. Hayden, Mar. 10, 1869, in *Hayden v. United States* (case file no. 2543), Court of Claims, RG 123, Federal Records Center, Suitland, Md.; deposition of Richard M. Wall, Nov. 13, 1866, in *Lynch v. U.S.*

35. "Miss Abby's Diary," Hargrett Rare Book and Manuscript Library, Main Library, Univ. of Georgia, Mar. 1, 22, 1864.

36. *Atlanta Daily Intelligencer,* Oct. 11, 1860.

37. *Census of the United States,* 1860, Fulton County, Ga.; quotations in *Atlanta Daily Intelligencer,* Nov. 4, 1860.

38. *Atlanta Daily Intelligencer,* Mar. 14, 1861; Johnson, *Toward a Patriarchal Republic,* 133.

39. Deposition of Richard M. Wall, Nov. 13, 1866, in *Lynch v. U.S.*

40. *Atlanta Daily Intelligencer,* Aug. 13, 1860.

41. Robert W. Johannsen, *Stephen A. Douglas* (New York: Oxford Univ. Press, 1973), 786–89, 798.

42. *Atlanta Daily Intelligencer,* Oct. 13, 1860; Garrett, *Atlanta and Environs,* 1:472.

43. Johannsen, *Stephen A. Douglas,* 788–89, 799–800.

44. Deposition of Julius A. Hayden, Mar. 10, 1869, in *Hayden v. U.S.;* deposition of James M. Bryant, Jan. 4, 1867, in *Wells v. United States* (case file no. 2494), Court of Claims, RG 123, Federal Records Center, Suitland, Md.

45. Garrett, *Atlanta and Environs,* 1:475.

46. Deposition of H. C. Holcombe, Dec. 29, 1866, in *Wells* v. *U.S.* Henry C. Holcombe, a native of South Carolina, arrived in Atlanta sometime during the mid-1840s. Born in 1820, Holcombe became active politically and was elected to the city council in 1849 and periodically thereafter. He managed a hotel (Washington Hall), dabbled in slave trading, and was chosen city clerk on several occasions, settling into that office for much of the last decade before the war and continuing in that post during wartime despite his well-known Unionist sympathies. Holcombe supported the Constitutional Unionist candidate, John Bell, in the presidential election of 1860. Holcombe owned property assessed at $9,000. *Census of the United States,* 1860, Fulton County, Ga.; Garrett, *Atlanta and Environs,* 1:237–38, 282, 309, 372, 406, 425, 525; Assessor's Book, City of Atlanta, 1861–62, Atlanta History Center.

47. Amherst W. Stone to General John A. Dix, June 28, 1864, in Case Files of Investigations by Levi C. Turner and Lafayette C. Baker, 1861–1866 (microfilm) (case file no. 2441), RG 94, Records of the Adjutant General's Office, 1780s–1917, War Department Division, National Archives, Washington, D.C.

48. Quotation in deposition of Julius A. Hayden, Mar. 10, 1869, in *Hayden* v. *U.S.; Census of the United States,* 1860, Fulton County, Ga.; Georgia, vol. 13, p. 147, R.G. Dun & Co. Collection, Baker Library, Harvard University Graduate School of Business Administration; deposition of Thomas G. Healey, Jan. 23, 1867, in *Hayden* v. *U.S.;* Garrett, *Atlanta and Environs,* 1:282–83, 315, 318, 331, 336, 346, 351, 397, 409, 411, and 438.

49. Deposition of Thomas G. Healey, Jan. 23, 1867, in *Hayden* v. *U.S.*

50. *Atlanta Daily Intelligencer,* Nov. 10, 1860.

51. "Don't Despair of the Republic. Dispatch to Crittenden and Douglas, and Their Reply," Dec. 6, 1860, in J. A. Stewart, *Conservative views. The government of the United States: what is it? Comprising a correspondence with Hon. Alexander H. Stephens, eliciting views touching the nature and character of the government of the United States, the impolicy of secession, the evils of disunion, and the means of restoration* (Atlanta: Franklin Printing House, 1869), 65. A copy of *Conservative views* is in the DeRenne Library, Hargrett Rare Book and Manuscript Library, Univ. of Georgia Libraries. Deposition of John Silvey, June 23, 1877, claim of Nedom L. Angier, Records of the Southern Claims Commission (Allowed Claims); deposition of F. L. Whiton, January 24, 1865, claim of David Young, ibid.

52. Keyes A. Bailey to Louisa Bailey, Aug. 20, 1860, Francis L. Hopkins Collection, Bailey-Howe Library, Univ. of Vermont, Burlington.

53. Ben Kremenak, ed., "Escape from Atlanta: The Huntington Memoir," *Civil War History* 11 (June 1965): 161.

54. Ibid.; deposition of John T. Cunningham, Oct. n.d., 1867, in *Lynch* v. *U.S.;* quotation in deposition of Marcellus O. Markham, Sept. 28, 1903, in *Markham* v. *U.S.*

55. Deposition of Philip McIntire, Apr. 16, 1875, claim of Philip McIntire, Records of the Southern Claims Commission (Allowed Claims); deposition of George Edwards, Jan. 18, 1872, claim of George Edwards, ibid.; deposition of Thomas Jordan, Feb. 12, 1878, claim of Thomas Jordan, ibid.; deposition of Thomas G. Healey, Jan. 11, 1873, claim of Thomas G. Heal[e]y, ibid.; deposition of William L. Hubbard, Apr. 9, 1869, in *Markham* v. *U.S.;* deposition of Thomas G. W. Crussell, May 29, 1872, in *Crussell* v. *U.S.*

56. Deposition of James M. Clay, Sept. 27, 1867, in *Wells* v. *U.S.* Norcross was clearly regarded as a Unionist by some Confederates, but he was rarely identified by the Unionists themselves as being an active member of their group. See Thomas Bomar to My Dear Sister, Sept. 17, 1864, in Bomar Family Papers, Special Collections Division, Woodruff Library, Emory University. On Berry, see chapter 10. Also see *Pioneer Citizens' History of Atlanta,* 275–76, and deposition of Madison R. Berry, June 10, 1873, claim of John Silvey, Records of the Southern Claims Commission (Allowed Claims).

57. Deposition of Julius A. Hayden, Mar. 10, 1869, in *Hayden* v. *U.S.*

58. Reed, *History of Atlanta,* 104–5.

59. *Atlanta Daily Intelligencer,* Mar. 4, 1861.

60. Ibid., Mar. 9, 1861.

61. Ibid., Mar. 11, 20, 1861.

62. J. A. Stewart to Hon. A. H. Stephens, Mar. 16, 1861, in Stewart, *Conservative Views,* 66–67. There are two letters dated Mar. 16, one of which seeks permission from Stephens to publish the other.

63. J. A. Stewart to Hon. A. H. Stephens, Mar. 16, 1861, ibid., 67–73. This is the letter that Stewart sought permission to publish.

64. "Holly" [Cyrena Bailey Stone], "The Spring of 1861," in *Atlanta Commonwealth,* clipping in Bailey-Hopkins Scrapbook, Francis L. Hopkins Collection, Bailey-Howe Library, University of Vermont, Burlington. This essay, like most that Cyrena Stone published, includes the printed phrase "For the Commonwealth," or a similar phrase to indicate the newspaper in which it was published. See n. 4, p. 331.

65. Phinehas Bailey to Louisa Bailey, Jan. 22, 1861, Francis L. Hopkins Collection, Bailey-Howe Library, University of Vermont, Burlington.

Chapter Three • "The Knell of All Our Bright Hopes"

1. Ben Kremenak, ed., "Escape from Atlanta: The Huntington Memoir," *Civil War History* 11 (June 1965): 162. Kremenak identifies the author of the "Huntington Memoir" only as Mrs. Henry Huntington, wife of an Atlanta dentist. Mrs. Huntington was Martha Huntington and, like her husband, was a native of Vermont. In 1861, she was thirty-five years old; her husband was forty-three. *Census of the United States,* 1870, Polk County, Iowa.

2. The original manuscript of the Huntington memoir cited in the previous note is located in the Special Collections Division of the Main Library, the University of Iowa, Iowa City. The quotation used here is drawn from that source and not the edited document. Hereinafter cited as "Huntington Manuscript."

3. Louisa M. Whitney, *Goldie's Inheritance: A Story of the Siege of Atlanta* (Burlington, Vt.: Free Press Association, 1903), 143.

4. First quotation in Kremenak, ed., "Escape from Atlanta," 162; second quotation in "Huntington Manuscript."

5. For an informed evaluation of schooling and the development of patriotic sentiment in the North, see Jean Baker, *Affairs of Party: The Political Culture of Northern Democrats in the Mid-nineteenth Century* (Ithaca, N.Y.: Cornell Univ. Press, 1983), 71–107. Baker shows the pervasive presence of patriotism and the

inculcation of patriotic sentiment in Northern schools. She excludes Southern schools on the grounds that education was "qualitatively different" in the South and attended by only 18 percent of the 1850 school-age population in the South Atlantic and South Central states as opposed to 65 percent in the North Atlantic and 50 percent in the North Central states. William R. Taylor, in "Toward a Definition of Orthodoxy: The Patrician South and the Common Schools," *Harvard Educational Review* 36, no. 4 (1966): 412–26, argues that Southern educational spokesmen believed that the schools should be used to inculcate Southern values and not American patriotism. For a somewhat different view, see John S. Ezell, "A Southern Education for Southrons," *Journal of Southern History* 17 (Aug. 1951): 303–27. Of course, numerous Southern schools were conducted by Northern immigrants. See Thomas Dyer, ed., *"To Raise Myself a Little": The Diaries and Letters of Jennie, a Georgia Teacher, 1858–1883* (Athens: Univ. of Georgia Press, 1982). Also see George C. Rable, *The Confederate Republic: A Revolution against Politics* (Chapel Hill: Univ. of North Carolina Press, 1994), 178–84.

For a recent interpretation of the usages of patriotism in antebellum (mainly Northern) schools, see Cynthia M. Koch, "Teaching Patriotism: Private Virtue for the Public Good in the Early Republic," in John Bodnar, ed., *Bonds of Affection: Americans Define Their Patriotism* (Princeton, N.J.: Princeton Univ. Press, 1996), 19–52. A. V. Huff Jr., in "The Eagle and the Vulture: Changing Attitudes toward Nationalism in Fourth of July Orations Delivered in Charleston, 1778–1860," *South Atlantic Quarterly* 73 (Winter 1974): 10–22, argues that Charleston orators paid less attention to the "glories of the Revolutionary generation" after the Missouri Compromise and gradually "spoke increasingly with one voice against the hostile actions of the federal government."

6. Whitney, *Goldie's Inheritance,* 144–45. The *Atlanta Commonwealth,* May 2, 1861, contains a detailed account of the floral bombing of Fort Sumter that confirms the version in *Goldie's Inheritance.* An underused source, the *Commonwealth* is rarely cited by scholars. An accessible collection of the newspaper is located in the library of the Boston Athenaeum, Boston, Mass. All citations to the *Commonwealth* are to issues owned by the Athenaeum. To my knowledge, the collection has not been microfilmed.

7. *Atlanta Southern Confederacy,* Apr. 24, 1861.

8. Ibid., May 14, 1861.

9. Ibid., May 15, 1861.

10. *Atlanta Daily Intelligencer,* May 15, 1861.

11. *Atlanta Southern Confederacy,* May 17, 1861.

12. *Atlanta Commonwealth,* May 22, 1861. See chapter 7, "Exit and Espionage," for the episode involving Émile Bourlier.

13. *Atlanta Southern Confederacy,* June 21, 1861.

14. *Atlanta Daily Intelligencer,* June 26, 29, 30, 1861; *Atlanta Southern Confederacy,* June 26, 30, July 9, 1861.

15. *Atlanta Daily Intelligencer,* Apr. 23, 1861. Michael Lynch, thirty-seven years old in 1861, emigrated from Ireland to New Jersey in the 1840s, where he worked for a few years as a farm laborer before moving to Savannah. He came to Atlanta, perhaps as early as 1847 or as late as 1853, and went into the book business. By the

time of the secession crisis, he had established his own store and was "doing well for the times," when an R.G. Dun & Co. reporter sent in an evaluation of Lynch's business. *Census of the United States,* 1860, Fulton County, Ga.; Carol Louise Hagglund, "Irish Immigrants in Atlanta, 1850–1896" (master's thesis, Emory University, 1968), 54–72; Bruce Manning to Thomas G. Dyer, Nov. 3, 1991, in possession of Thomas G. Dyer; claim of Michael Lynch, Records of the Southern Claims Commission (Allowed Claims), Fulton County, Ga., RG 217, National Archives, Washington, D.C.; similar citations appear hereinafter as Records of the Southern Claims Commission, and unless otherwise indicated, the references to approved claims are to those that originated in Fulton County, Ga. Georgia, vol. 13, p. 68, R.G. Dun & Co. Collection, Baker Library, Harvard University Graduate School of Business Administration. There are numerous references to the Lynch brothers scattered throughout Franklin M. Garrett, *Atlanta and Environs: A Chronicle of Its People and Events,* 2 vols. (Athens: Univ. of Georgia Press, 1954).

16. *Atlanta Daily Intelligencer,* Apr. 24, 1861.
17. *Atlanta Daily Intelligencer,* May 25, June 4, 1861.
18. "Miss Abby's Diary," Hargrett Rare Book and Manuscript Library, Main Library, Univ. of Georgia, Mar. 12, 1864.
19. "Josiah Seamans Peterson," in *Memoirs of Georgia; containing historical accounts of the state's civil, military, industrial and professional interests, and personal sketches of many of its people,* 2 vols. (Atlanta: Southern Historical Association, 1895), 1:897–99.
20. Wallace P. Reed, *History of Atlanta, Georgia* (Syracuse, N.Y.: D. Mason, 1889), 186.
21. *Atlanta Southern Confederacy,* May 4, 1861.
22. *Atlanta Commonwealth,* May 2, 1861; *Atlanta Daily Intelligencer,* May 4, 1861.
23. Deposition of Josiah Peterson, Apr. 11, 1873, claim of Henry Holcombe, Records of the Southern Claims Commission (Barred and Disallowed Claims), RG 233, National Archives, Washington, D.C.
24. *Atlanta Southern Confederacy,* May 15, 1861.
25. *Atlanta Daily Intelligencer,* June 29, 1861.
26. *Atlanta Commonwealth,* July 31, 1861.
27. *Atlanta Southern Confederacy,* July 30, 1861.
28. James R. Matthews to Andrew Johnson, June 12, 1865, in Paul H. Bergeron, ed., *The Papers of Andrew Johnson,* vol. 8: *May–Aug. 1865* (Knoxville: Univ. of Tennessee Press, 1989), 224–25.
29. *Atlanta Daily Intelligencer,* Apr. 27, July 4, 1861.
30. Ibid., Aug. 4, 1861.
31. *Atlanta Southern Confederacy,* Aug. 11, 1861; *Atlanta Daily Intelligencer,* Aug. 13, 1861.
32. Deposition of John Silvey, June 9, 1873, claim of John Silvey, Records of the Southern Claims Commission (Allowed Claims); deposition of Nedom L. Angier, June 23, 1877, claim of Nedom L. Angier, ibid.; "Volney A. Dunning," in *Pioneer Citizens' History of Atlanta, 1833–1902* (Atlanta: Pioneer Citizens' Society of Atlanta, 1902), 381.

33. *Atlanta Daily Intelligencer,* Apr. 17, 1860; Henry Clay Fairman, *Chronicles of the Old Guard of the Gate City Guard: Atlanta, Georgia, 1858–1915* (Atlanta: Byrd Printing, 1915), 8, 33.

34. Fairman, *Chronicles of the Old Guard,* 18–27; Whitney, *Goldie's Inheritance,* 141; "Miss Abby's Diary," July 19, 1864.

35. Whitney, *Goldie's Inheritance,* 141.

36. Fairman, *Chronicles of the Old Guard,* 18–27; *Atlanta Southern Confederacy,* Apr. 18, 1861.

37. *Atlanta Southern Confederacy,* Apr. 18, 1861.

38. Fairman, *Chronicles of the Old Guard,* 27–32.

39. Ibid., 33; quotation in Whitney, *Goldie's Inheritance,* 145; "Miss Abby's Diary," July 19, 1864. The letter I ascribe to Chester Stone is drawn from *Goldie's Inheritance.* In the novel, it is attributed to Amy Fay's husband, Egbert Fay, who is serving with the Gate City Guard at Laurel Hill.

40. Mrs. L. M. Whitney, "A Father's Legacy" [Memoir of Reverend Phinehas Bailey], 64–65, Vermont Historical Society; "A[.] O[.] Brainerd, Address to the Ladies— Wives of the Veterans in the G.A.R. Room, St. Albans, [April 15, 1895]," typescript, St. Albans Historical Museum, St. Albans, Vt.

41. William Clapp to Major John A. Bolles, Sept. 19, 1864, Union Provost Marshal General's File of One-Name Papers re Citizens (microcopy no. 345), National Archives, Washington, D.C.

42. Ibid.; Vermont, vol. 12, p. 24, R.G. Dun & Co. Collection, Baker Library, Harvard University Graduate School of Business Administration. James C. Stone had serious business difficulties in 1842 and 1843 and was the object of several lawsuits, including one initiated by William Clapp in 1842. Clapp was a frequent visitor to the courts of Franklin County, Vermont, usually on errands to sue for debt or recover merchandise sold. See *William Clapp* v. *James C. Stone,* book Q, 131, County Court of Franklin County, Court House, St. Albans, Vt., Sept. term, 1842.

43. William Clapp to Major John A. Bolles, Sept. 19, 1864, Union Provost Marshal General's File of One-Name Papers re Citizens (microcopy no. 345), National Archives, Washington, D.C.

44. "The Dying Soldier," in Bailey-Hopkins Scrapbook, Francis L. Hopkins Collection, Bailey-Howe Library, University of Vermont, Burlington.

45. *Atlanta Daily Intelligencer,* July 4, Aug. 22, Nov. 12, 1861; *Atlanta Southern Confederacy,* Aug. 27, 1861; Rable, *Confederate Republic,* 44–45, 56, 74. Rable is one of the few historians who addresses the issue of reconstruction in 1861 in any detail.

46. J. A. Stewart to Hon. A. H. Stephens, Nov. 5, 1861, Alexander H. Stephens Papers, vol. 23, Library of Congress.

47. The deportation and sequestration laws are treated in detail in William M. Robinson Jr., *Justice in Grey: A History of the Judicial System of the Confederate States* (Cambridge: Harvard Univ. Press, 1941); see p. 57. Few, if any, studies exist of the impact of these laws upon individual communities.

48. Ibid., 228; deposition of John W. Trimble, Nov. 2, 1866, in *McCroskey* v. *United States* (case file no. 2513), Court of Claims, RG 123, Federal Records Center, Suitland, Md.

49. *Atlanta Southern Confederacy,* Oct. 18, 23, 1861.

50. Garnishment Docket 1861–63, RG 21, Confederate District Court (Atlanta), Federal Records Center, East Point, Ga.; Samuel P. Richards diary (typescript), Nov. 2, 1861, Atlanta History Center.

51. *Confederate States of America v. Amherst W. Stone,* Writ of Garnishment, RG 21, box 3, Confederate Papers, United States District Court (Atlanta), Federal Records Center, East Point, Ga.; *Confederate States of America v. L. O. Wilson,* ibid.; Minutes, Northern District Court, Confederate States of America, 1862, 469, Federal Records Center, East Point, Ga. A. W. Stone to Major Gen'l John A. Dix, June 28, 1864, in Case Files of Investigations by Levi C. Turner and Lafayette C. Baker, 1861–66 (microfilm) (case file no. 2441), RG 94, Records of the Adjutant General's Office, 1780s–1917, War Department Division, National Archives, Washington, D.C.

52. For the ideas related to loyalty, duty, and the incomplete nature of loyalties, I draw upon George P. Fletcher, *Loyalty: An Essay on the Morality of Relationships* (New York: Oxford Univ. Press, 1993).

Chapter Four • *The Limits of Loyalty*

1. Louisa M. Whitney, *Goldie's Inheritance: A Story of the Siege of Atlanta* (Burlington, Vt.: Free Press Association, 1903), 149; Emory M. Thomas, *The Confederate Nation* (New York: Harper & Row, 1979), 128.

2. *Atlanta Daily Intelligencer,* Mar. 16, 1862.

3. Deposition of Thomas G. Healey, Jan. 11, 1873, claim of Thomas G. Heal[e]y, Records of the Southern Claims Commission (Allowed Claims), Fulton County, Ga., RG 217, National Archives, Washington, D.C.; similar citations appear hereinafter as Records of the Southern Claims Commission, and unless otherwise indicated, the references to approved claims are to those that originated in Fulton County, Ga. Whitney, *Goldie's Inheritance,* 149.

4. *Atlanta Daily Intelligencer,* Mar. 16, 1862.

5. Deposition of Robert McCroskey, Apr. 9, 1869, in *Markham v. United States* (case file no. 11137), Court of Claims, RG 123, Federal Records Center, Suitland, Md.; deposition of Lewis Scofield Sr., Apr. 9, 1869, ibid. Not much is known about Lewis Scofield, a Connecticut native born in 1817 who lived for a time in Trenton, New Jersey, before moving to Georgia with his Rhode Island–born wife. By 1858, Scofield and a partner had purchased the "unfinished [rolling] mills of L. A. Douglas" and soon put them into operation. Although Scofield had little capital in 1858, he had a good knowledge of the foundry business and a reputation for being active and industrious. By mid-1859, William Markham had acquired a one-third interest in the rolling mill, and Scofield and Markham successfully sought to eliminate Scofield's first partner from the business. By 1861, Scofield had acquired a three-acre lot assessed at $4,000. *Census of the United States,* 1860, Fulton County, Ga.; Georgia, vol. 13, p. 164, R.G. Dun & Co. Collection, Baker Library, Harvard University Graduate School of Business Administration; Franklin M. Garrett, *Atlanta and Environs: A Chronicle of Its People and Events,* 2 vols. (Athens: Univ. of Georgia Press, 1954), 1:629, 736, 846, 863.

6. James Michael Russell, *Atlanta, 1847–1890: City Building in the Old South and New* (Baton Rouge: Louisiana State Univ. Press, 1988), 47.

7. The statement concerning the mill as a haven for those avoiding the draft is based on an analysis of *Williams' Atlanta Directory, City Guide, and Business Mirror, 1859–1860* (Atlanta: M. Lynch, 1859) and published indexes to rosters of Confederate service.

8. "Proceedings of the Court of Inquiry upon the Fall of New Orleans," in *The War of the Rebellion: A Compilation of the Official Records of the Union and Confederate Army,* 130 vols. (Washington, D.C.: Government Printing Office, 1880–1902), ser. 1, 6: 625–27. Hereinafter cited as *OR.*

9. Deposition of James G. Minor, Feb. 5, 1868, in *Markham* v. *U.S.;* deposition of Lewis Scofield Sr., Apr. 9, 1869, ibid.

10. Deposition of Lewis Scofield Sr., Apr. 9, 1869, ibid.; deposition of James G. Minor, Feb. 5, 1868, ibid.

11. Wallace P. Reed, *History of Atlanta, Georgia* (Syracuse, N.Y.: D. Mason, 1889), 188.

12. Deposition of James G. Minor, Feb. 5, 1868, in *Markham* v. *U.S.*

13. Deposition of James Dunning, Apr. 19, 1869, in *Markham* v. *U.S.;* deposition of Jonathan Norcross, Apr. 8, 1869, ibid. For a briefer account and a different interpretation of the Atlanta Rolling Mill affair, see Mary A. DeCredico, *Patriotism for Profit: Georgia's Urban Entrepreneurs and the Confederate War Effort* (Chapel Hill: Univ. of North Carolina Press, 1990), 36–37. DeCredico concludes that "locals continued to distrust Scofield and Markham because of their Northern birth . . . [and] that factor may explain the sale of the Atlanta Rolling Mill to the Charleston firm of Trenholm & Frazier in 1863" (37).

14. *Atlanta Daily Intelligencer,* Apr. 1, 23, 1861.

15. Deposition of James Dunning, Jan. 11, 1873, claim of Thomas G. Heal[e]y, Records of the Southern Claims Commission (Allowed Claims); deposition of James Dunning, Apr. 19, 1869, in *Markham* v. *U.S.;* deposition of William Farnsworth, Jan. 13, 1873, claim of Thomas G. Heal[e]y, Records of the Southern Claims Commission (Allowed Claims).

16. Deposition of James Dunning, Apr. 19, 1869, in *Markham* v. *U.S.*

17. Deposition of C. P. Cassin, Nov. 2, 1866, in *McCroskey* v. *United States* (case file nos. 2513, 10137), Court of Claims, RG 123, Federal Records Center, Suitland, Md.

18. Deposition of W. S. Everett, Jan. 24, 1868, in *Markham* v. *U.S.;* deposition of Philip McIntire, Apr. 16, 1868, claim of Philip McIntire, Records of the Southern Claims Commission (Allowed Claims); deposition of Alexander M. Wallace, Apr. 16, 1875, ibid.

19. Summary, claim of David Young, Records of the Southern Claims Commission (Allowed Claims); deposition of David Young, Jan. 20, 1873, deposition of Austin Wright, May 21, 1872, both ibid. David Young, a North Carolina native, was born in 1808. Young had a reputation in the community for being obstreperous, independent, and radical in his thinking. He had real property in Atlanta assessed at only $3,000, but he appears to have had substantial amounts of cash and other property (perhaps as much as $20,000) which allowed him to invest heavily in cotton during the war. A recent arrival in the city, he had come from Columbus, Georgia, in 1859. *Census of the United States,* 1860, Fulton County, Ga.; summary, claim of David Young, Records of the Southern Claims Commission (Allowed Claims); Assessor's Book, City of Atlanta, 1861–62, Atlanta History Center; Georgia, vol. 13,

p. 20, R.G. Dun & Co. Collection, Baker Library, Harvard University Graduate School of Business Administration.

20. *Atlanta Daily Intelligencer,* May 13, 1862; Samuel Carter III, *The Siege of Atlanta, 1864* (New York: St. Martin's, 1964), 170.

21. Testimony of Anderson L. Scott, in *Report of the Treatment of Prisoners of War, by the Rebel Authorities, during the War of the Rebellion . . .* (Washington, D.C.: Government Printing Office, 1869), 885.

22. Louisa M. Whitney, *Goldie's Inheritance: A Story of the Siege of Atlanta* (Burlington, Vt.: Free Press Association, 1903), 151; "Miss Abby's Diary," Hargrett Rare Book and Manuscript Library, Main Library, Univ. of Georgia, Apr. 9, 1864; quotation on Mary Summerlin in William G. Le Duc, typescript draft of memoir, "Recollections of a Quartermaster," box 41, 223m–226m, William G. Le Duc Collection, Minnesota Historical Society, St. Paul. The draft of Le Duc's memoirs is much fuller and, for the purpose of this study, much more informative than the oft-cited and briefer published version: William Gates Le Duc, *Recollections of a Civil War Quartermaster: The Autobiography of William G. Le Duc* (St. Paul, Minn.: North Central Publishing, 1963).

23. Whitney, *Goldie's Inheritance,* 159–60, 164, 166–67, 179.

24. Deposition of Thomas G. Healey, Jan. 11, 1873, claim of Thomas G. Heal[e]y, Records of the Southern Claims Commission (Allowed Claims).

25. Whitney, *Goldie's Inheritance* 154, 155; quotation on p. 155.

26. *Atlanta Daily Intelligencer,* May 28, 1862.

27. Ibid., June 4, 1862.

28. Deposition of James Dunning, Jan. 11, 1873, claim of Thomas G. Heal[e]y, Records of the Southern Claims Commission (Allowed Claims).

29. *Atlanta Daily Intelligencer,* May 13, 1862; James R. Crew to Dear Wife, n.d., James R. Crew Collection, Atlanta History Center.

30. *OR,* ser. 2, vol. 4, 912; *Atlanta Daily Intelligencer,* June 18, 1862. Prentiss, Crittenden, and the others were transferred to the Confederate prison at Madison, Georgia, from which they sought to escape in early October 1862. Whether the escape was successful is unclear, but by mid-October Prentiss and his comrades were back in the North. They were not in good condition. Prentiss wrote to General Henry Halleck, seeking permission to proceed to Washington "to be provided for." "We are suffering," he told Halleck. Prentiss attracted the same sort of contumely from the Confederate officer in charge of the Madison Prison as he had from Atlanta citizens. "I look upon Prentiss as one among the most violent enemies of the South and an unprincipled scoundrel," wrote Captain W. L. Calhoun. W. L. Calhoun to Brig. Gen. John H. Winder, Oct. 7, 1862, in *OR,* ser. 2, vol. 4, 912; Benjamin Prentiss to Henry H. Halleck, Oct. 14, 1862, ibid., 621; William H. Ludlow to Adjutant-General Thomas, Oct. 13, 1862, ibid., 618.

31. Deposition of Robert Webster, May 31, 1872, in *Webster v. United States* (case file no. 13502), Court of Claims, RG 123, Federal Records Center, Suitland, Md.; Ben C. Yancey to Reuben Arnold, May 16, 1872, ibid.

32. Ben C. Yancey to Reuben Arnold, May 16, 1872, in *Webster v. U.S.;* Russell, *Atlanta 1847–1890,* 154; *Atlanta News,* Mar. 7, 1875; F[Frederick]. Ayer to Reverend Sam Hunt, June 2, 1866, Papers of the American Missionary Association (microfilm edition). American Missionary Archives, Amistad Research Center, New Orleans;

hereinafter cited as AMA Papers. Professor Russell's book provides the last two citations in this note. My interpretation of them as it relates to Webster differs from his reading.

33. F. Ayer to Reverend Sam Hunt, June 2, 1866, AMA Papers.

34. Irving H. Bartlett, *Daniel Webster* (New York: W. W. Norton, 1978), 284–86; Irving H. Bartlett to Thomas G. Dyer, January 27, 1995, in possession of Thomas G. Dyer. Professor Bartlett doubts that Robert Webster was Daniel Webster's son.

35. Deposition of Robert Webster, May 31, 1872, in *Webster* v. *U.S.;* statement of William Lewis, July 26, 1873, ibid.

36. Deposition of Thomas Crussell, May 31, 1872, ibid.; deposition of E. T. Hunnicutt, May 31, 1872, ibid.

37. Deposition of Robert Webster, May 31, 1872, ibid.; Gilbert E. Govan and James Livingood, *The Chattanooga Country* (New York: E. P. Dutton, 1952), 180–89, 240–41; Robert P. Rowland, undergraduate paper, University of Miami, in Clift Family Papers, Tennessee State Archives, Nashville.

38. Deposition of Robert Webster, May 31, 1872, in *Webster* v. *U.S.* The testimony regarding Clift comes from questions put by Webster to another witness, E. T. Hunnicutt, during Hunnicutt's testimony on the same day.

39. William D. Clift to Col. J. Merritt, Dec. 6, 1863; E[lizabeth] H. Clift to William D. Clift, Feb. 17, 1864; Robert H. Ramfery [?] to Mrs. Elizabeth H. Clift, Sept. 24, 1864; all in Clift Family Papers, Tennessee State Archives, Nashville.

40. Deposition of Robert Webster, in *Webster* v. *U.S.*

41. Deposition of Mary A. [Hinton] Davis, Sept. 17, 1878, claim of Martin Hinton, Records of the Southern Claims Commission (Allowed Claims).

42. Deposition of Samuel B. Houts, Jan. 17, 1872, ibid. Martin Hinton, an artist and photographer, came to Atlanta in 1860 from Montgomery, Alabama. Twenty-six years old in 1861, Hinton was born in New York of Irish immigrant parents. He operated a photographic studio in Montgomery, moving to Atlanta to open another, and bringing with him his mother and three sisters, the eldest of whom was twenty-two. *Census of the United States,* 1860, Montgomery, Ala.

43. Deposition of Samuel B. Houts, Jan. 17, 1872, in claim of Martin Hinton, Records of the Southern Claims Commission (Allowed Claims).

44. Testimony of Anderson L. Scott, in *Report on the Treatment of Prisoners of War,* 885.

45. James G. Bogle, "The Andrews Raid: A Sequel," *Atlanta Historical Bulletin* 16 (Summer 1971): 26–46.

46. Testimony of Anderson L. Scott in *Report on the Treatment of Prisoners of War,* 886.

47. James R. Crew to Dear Wife, June 18, 1862 (probable date), James R. Crew Collection, Atlanta History Center.

48. Whitney, *Goldie's Inheritance,* 157–58.

49. William Pittenger, *Capturing a Locomotive* (Washington, D.C.: National Tribune, 1884), 300.

50. Ibid.; Whitney, *Goldie's Inheritance,* 154–55.

51. Thomas, *The Confederate Nation,* 152–55. Also see Albert Burton Moore, *Conscription and Conflict in the Confederacy* (New York: Macmillan, 1924).

52. See chapter 7, "Exit and Espionage."

53. *Atlanta Daily Intelligencer,* Apr. 4, 1862.
54. Ibid., June 16, 27, 1862.
55. *Atlanta Southern Confederacy,* July 24, 29, 1862; all quotations from July 24.
56. *Atlanta Daily Intelligencer,* Aug. 2, 1862.
57. Deposition of James Dunning, Nov. 1, 1872, claim of Martin Hinton, Records of the Southern Claims Commission (Allowed Claims).

Chapter Five • *"A Perfect Reign of Terror"*

1. Paul D. Lack, "Law and Disorder in Confederate Atlanta," *Georgia Historical Quarterly* 66 (Summer 1982): 173–79.
2. Ibid., 181–82.
3. *Census of the United States,* 1860, Fulton County, Ga. Compiled Service Records of Confederate Soldiers from Georgia, microcopy 266, National Archives, Washington, D.C.; *Williams' Atlanta Directory, City Guide and Business Mirror, 1859–1860* (Atlanta: M. Lynch, 1859).
4. Thomas E. Lowe et al. to Joseph E. Brown, Jan. 25, 1861, box 38 (G. W. Lee folder), Incoming Letters to the Governor, Georgia Department of Archives and History, Atlanta; George W. Lee to Joseph E. Brown, Feb. 1, 1861, ibid.
5. Braxton Bragg to Joseph E. Johnston, Mar. 2, 1863, *The War of the Rebellion: A Compilation of the Official Records of the Union and Confederate Army,* 130 vols. (Washington, D.C.: Government Printing Office, 1880–1902), ser. 1, vol. 23, pt. 2, 656–67, hereinafter cited as *OR.* Whether Lee was illiterate is not clear. His letters are often well written but could have been composed by clerks. His signature takes different forms and varies markedly over time. It is possible, of course, that clerks signed for him. The fictional Cyrena Stone thought Lee "illiterate and uncommanding in appearance." See Louisa M. Whitney, *Goldie's Inheritance: A Story of the Siege of Atlanta* (Burlington, Vt.: Free Press Association, 1903), 217.
6. *Atlanta Daily Intelligencer,* July, 24, 1861.
7. Braxton Bragg to Joseph E. Johnston, Mar. 2, 1863, in *OR,* ser. 1, vol 23, pt. 2, 656–57.
8. Deposition of Thomas S. Garner, Apr. 19, 1869, in *Markham* v. *United States* (case file no. 11137), Court of Claims, RG 123, Federal Records Center, Suitland, Md.; G. G. Hull to Col. J. F. Gilmer, July 9, 1863, in *OR,* ser. 1. vol. 23, pt. 2, 910.
9. *Atlanta Daily Intelligencer,* June 3, 1862.
10. Lack, "Law and Disorder in Confederate Atlanta," 182, 192, n. 36, n. 37; Ralph Benjamin Singer, "Confederate Atlanta" (Ph.D. diss., University of Georgia, Athens, 1973), 123–25; Thomas Conn Bryan, *Confederate Georgia* (Athens: Univ. of Georgia Press, 1953), 95; J. A. Campbell to Maj. Gen. Samuel Jones, Oct. 27, 1862, in *OR,* ser. 1, vol. 16, pt. 2, 979–80.
11. Deposition of A. W. Stone, Mar. 20, 1869, in *Markham* v. *U.S.*
12. *Williams' Atlanta Directory;* quotation in David P. Conyngham, *Sherman's March Through the South, with Sketches and Incidents of the Campaign* (New York: Sheldon, 1865), 226; deposition of Mary A. [Hinton] Davis, Sept. 17, 1878, claim of Martin Hinton, Records of the Southern Claims Commission (Allowed Claims), Fulton County, Ga., RG 217, National Archives, Washington, D.C.; similar cita-

tions appear hereinafter as Records of the Southern Claims Commission, and unless otherwise indicated, the references to approved claims are to those that originated in Fulton County, Ga. Deposition of Julius Hayden, July 4, 1873, claim of Prince Ponder, ibid.

13. Deposition of E. T. Hunnicutt, typescript, n.d., in *Austell v. United States* (case file no. 13859), Court of Claims, RG 123, Federal Records Center, Suitland, Md.

14. G. W. Lee to G. W. Randolph, Aug. 9, Oct. 18, 1862, Letters Received by the Confederate Secretary of War, War Department Collection of Confederate Records, microcopy, RG 109, National Archives, Washington, D.C.; similar citations appear hereinafter as Letters Received by the Confederate Secretary of War.

15. Lee to G. W. Randolph, Nov. 11, 1862, Letters Received by the Confederate Secretary of War.

16. *Atlanta Southern Confederacy,* Aug. 29, 1862. Previous accounts of this incident are quite brief. See Ralph Benjamin Singer Jr., "Confederate Atlanta," 121, and Robert Gibbons, "Life at the Crossroads of the Confederacy," *Atlanta Historical Journal* 23 (Summer 1979): 32–33.

17. Deposition of James Dunning, Apr. 19, 1869, in *Markham v. U.S.;* deposition of Thomas G. W. Crussell, Nov. 20, 1872, claim of Martin Hinton, Records of the Southern Claims Commission (Allowed Claims). Five of the six men arrested are identified in a receipt accompanying N. J. Hammond to B. H. Hill, Jan. 14, 1863, Letters Received by the Confederate Secretary of War. They are identified as "Jas. L Dunning, Dr. Scott, Messrs Wilson, Manning and Sturgis." Samuel Richards confirmed the arrest of James Sturges: "Several of our citizens were arrested by the military authorities this week for supposed disloyalty or treasonable intentions; James Sturges was one!" Samuel P. Richards diary (typescript), Aug. 30, 1862, Atlanta History Center.

18. *Atlanta Southern Confederacy,* Dec. 3, 1862; testimony of Anderson L. Scott, in *Report on the Treatment of Prisoners of War, by the Rebel Authorities, during the War of the Rebellion . . .* (Washington: Government Printing Office, 1869), 885–86.

19. Bruce Manning to Thomas G. Dyer, Nov. 3, 1991, in possession of Thomas G. Dyer; *Atlanta Southern Confederacy,* Sept. 19, 1861; Samuel P. Richards diary (typescript), Aug. 30, 1862, Atlanta History Center; *Atlanta Daily Intelligencer,* Nov. 12, 1862.

20. *Atlanta Southern Confederacy,* Apr. 17, 1862.

21. Ibid., Aug. 30, 1862.

22. Ibid., Aug. 31, Sept. 3, 1862; *Atlanta Daily Intelligencer,* Sept. 3, 1862.

23. *Atlanta Daily Intelligencer,* Sept. 4, 1862.

24. J. Harford to Jefferson Davis, Oct. 4, 1862, Letters Received by the Confederate Secretary of War.

25. G. W. Lee to Hon. G. W. Randolph, Nov. 11, 1862, ibid.

26. William G. Le Duc, typescript draft of memoir, "Recollections of a Quartermaster," box 41, 223m–226m, William G. Le Duc Collection, Minnesota Historical Society, St. Paul. Louisa M. Whitney, *Goldie's Inheritance,* 164.

27. Deposition of Mary A. [Hinton] Davis, Sept. 17, 1878, claim of Martin Hinton, Records of the Southern Claims Commission (Allowed Claims); deposition of Sarah Hinton, ibid.

28. Deposition of Mary A. [Hinton] Davis, ibid.; *Atlanta Daily Intelligencer,* Oct. 4, 1862.

29. *Atlanta Daily Intelligencer,* Oct. 4, 1862.

30. Deposition of Mary A. [Hinton] Davis, Sept. 17, 1878, claim of Martin Hinton, Records of the Southern Claims Commission (Allowed Claims).

31. Whitney, *Goldie's Inheritance,* 168; A. W. Stone to E. M. Stanton, June 19, 1863, in Case Files of Investigations by Levi C. Turner and Lafayette C. Baker, 1861–66 (microfilm) (case file no. 2441), RG 94, Records of the Adjutant General's Office, 1780s–1917, War Department Division, National Archives, Washington, D.C.

32. Whitney, *Goldie's Inheritance,* 164–67.

33. Testimony of Anderson L. Scott, in *Report on the Treatment of Prisoners of War,* 885–86.

34. N. J. Hammond to B. H. Hill, Jan. 14, 1863, Letters Received by the Confederate Secretary of War. The information concerning Scott and habeas corpus is noted on a receipt accompanying the letter.

35. Deposition of James A. Dunning, Apr. 19, 1869, in *Markham* v. *U.S.*

36. N. J. Hammond to B. H. Hill, Jan. 14, 1863; deposition of James A. Dunning, Apr. 19, 1869, in *Markham* v. *U.S.;* James Michael Russell, *Atlanta: City Building in the Old South and New* (Baton Rouge: Louisiana State Univ. Press, 1988), 94.

37. Testimony of Anderson L. Scott, in *Report on the Treatment of Prisoners of War,* 885–86.

38. Ibid.; deposition of Martin Hinton, claim of Martin Hinton, Records of the Southern Claims Commission (Allowed Claims).

39. *Atlanta Daily Intelligencer,* Oct. 27, 1864; N. J. Hammond to B. H. Hill, Jan. 14, 1863, Letters Received by the Confederate Secretary of War; G. W. Lee to Hon. Jas. A. Seddon, July 10, 1863, ibid.

Chapter Six • *Amherst Stone's Mission*

1. Albert Burton Moore, *Conscription and Conflict in the Confederacy* (New York: Macmillan, 1924), 140–41.

2. Deposition of Amherst W. Stone, Nov. 9, 1867, in *Lynch* v. *United States* (case file no. 2502), Court of Claims, RG 123, Federal Records Center, Suitland, Md.; quotations in deposition of Amherst Stone, Mar. 20, 1869, in *Markham* v. *United States* (case file no. 11137), ibid. Stone even transferred some of his real estate, including, evidently, his and Cyrena's home property. It is clear, however, that he and Cyrena continued to live on the property, raising the possibility that he transferred it in order to protect it when he left the South. See Superior Court, Deed Records & Mortgages, Fulton County, Ga., vol. G, 1863, 304, Georgia Department of Archives and History, Atlanta.

3. Deposition of Amherst W. Stone, Mar. 20, 1869, in *Markham* v. *U.S.*

4. Samuel P. Richards diary (typescript), Mar. 22, 1863, 171, Atlanta History Center.

5. A. W. Stone to E. M. Stanton, June 19, 1863, in Case Files of Investigations by Levi C. Turner and Lafayette C. Baker, 1861–66 (microfilm) (case file no. 2441), RG 94, Records of the Adjutant General's Office, 1780s–1917, War Department

Division, National Archives, Washington, D.C.; hereinafter cited as Turner-Baker Papers.

6. Eric Heyl, *Early American Steamers,* 6 vols. (Buffalo, N.Y.: Eric Heyl, 1953–69), 6, 126 (source of "handy man" quotation); Stephen R. Wise, *Lifeline of the Confederacy: Blockade Running during the Civil War* (Columbia: Univ. of South Carolina Press, 1988), 9, 258, 301; "Steamer '*Gen. Clinch*'" Vessel Papers, RG 109, National Archives, Washington, D.C.

7. "Steamer '*Gen. Clinch,*'" Vessel Papers, RG 109, National Archives, Washington, D.C.; Register of Letters Received, Department of South Carolina, Georgia, and Florida, Alphabetical, October 1862–May 1863, RG 109, National Archives; endorsement, claim of Amherst W. Stone, Records of the Southern Claims Commission (Barred and Disallowed Claims), RG 233, National Archives, Washington, D.C.

8. Deposition of A. W. Stone, Nov. 9, 1867, in *Lynch v. U.S.;* deposition of A. W. Stone, Mar. 20, 1869, in *Markham v. U.S.*

9. Samuel Richards diary, Apr. 4, 1863, 171.

10. A. W. Stone to E. M. Stanton, June 19, 1863; A. W. Stone to General John A. Dix, June 28, 1864; both in case file no. 2441, Turner-Baker Papers. Deposition of A. W. Stone, Mar. 20, 1869, in *Markham v. U.S.*

11. A. W. Stone to E. M. Stanton, June 19, Turner-Baker Papers, 1863; Louisa M. Whitney, *Goldie's Inheritance: A Story of the Siege of Atlanta* (Burlington, Vt.: Free Press Association, 1903), 175.

12. Stone to Stanton, June 19, 1863; Stone to Dix, June 18, 1864; both in Turner-Baker Papers; Nat Brandt, *The Man Who Tried to Burn New York* (Syracuse, N.Y.: Syracuse Univ. Press, 1986), 97–98; Rolla Gleason to Secretary of War, Sept. 3, 1863, Main Series 1801–70 (microform), reel 106, register no. 116, RG 490, National Archives; hereinafter cited as Register, Letters Received by the Secretary of War. The cited document is a summary of a letter from Gleason to the Secretary of War.

13. Diary of Charles Birney Stone, Feb. 23, 1863, through Mar. 7, 1863, Special Collections Division, Bailey-Howe Library, University of Vermont, Burlington.

14. Quotation in *Burlington Free Press,* May 12, 1863; "A[.] O[.] Brainerd, Address to the Ladies—Wives of the Veterans in the G.A.R. Room, St. Albans, [April 15, 1895]," typescript, St. Albans Historical Museum, St. Albans, Vt.; Gleason to Secretary of War, Sept. 3, 1863, Register, Letters Received by the Secretary of War; John Sedgwick to Charles A. Dana, Sept. 14, 1864, case file no. 2735, Turner-Baker Papers.

15. *Burlington Free Press,* May 12 1863. Mark E. Neely, Jr., *The Fate of Liberty: Abraham Lincoln and Civil Liberties* (New York: Oxford Univ. Press, 1991), 68, 70, 72–74.

16. John A. Marshall, *American Bastile* (Philadelphia: T. W. Hartley, 1883), 553–54; Martin Burke to Colonel William Hoffmann, Feb. 3, 1864, *The War of the Rebellion: A Compilation of the Official Records of the Union and Confederate Army,* 130 vols. (Washington, D.C.: Government Printing Office, 1880–1902), ser. 2, vol. 6, 911; hereinafter cited as OR. Neely, *Fate of Liberty,* 135.

17. *Marshall, American Bastile,* 553–54; C. T. Alexander to Col. W. Hoffmann, June 25, 1864, in *OR,* ser. 2, vol. 7, 413–14.

18. *"Fort-La-Fayette" Life, 1863–64 in extracts from the "Right flanker," a manu-script sheet circulating among the southern prisoners in Fort-Lafayette, in 1863–64* (London: Simpkin, Marshall, 1865), 10–11, 69; hereinafter cited as *Fort-La-Fayette Life*.

19. Ibid., 10–11.

20. Stone to John A. Dix, June 28, 1864, case file no. 2441, Turner-Baker Papers; deposition of Amherst W. Stone, Mar. 20, 1869, in *Markham* v. *U.S.*

21. H. W. Halleck to Lieut. Col. Martin Burke, Nov. 18, 1862, in *OR*, ser. 2, vol. 4, 723.

22. Stone to E. M. Stanton, June 19, 1863, case file no. 2441, Turner-Baker Papers.

23. John Wool to Philip Marsh, July 11, 1863, Department of the East Letterbook, RG 393, pt. 1, entry 1394, vol. 1, National Archives; John A. Dix to John Wool, Nov. 9, 1863, ibid., 332–33; John A. Dix to Edwin Stanton, Mar. 25, 1864, ibid., vol. 21, 2, 98.

24. A. W. Stone to L. C. Turner, Aug. 24, 1863, case file no. 2735, Turner-Baker Papers.

25. A. W. Stone to L. C. Turner, Aug. 24, 1863; A. W. Stone to L. C. Turner, Aug. 31, 1863; both in case file no. 2735, Turner-Baker Papers.

26. L. C. Turner to W. S. Rosecrans, Sept. 12, 1863, ibid.; L. C. Turner to A. W. Stone, Sept. 12, 1863, ibid.

27. Stone to Turner, Sept. 16, 1863, ibid.

28. Turner to Dix, Nov. 25, 1863, ibid.

29. Stone to John A. Dix, June 28, 1864, case file no. 2441, ibid.

30. A. W. Stone to Charles A. Dana, Apr. 25, 1864, Letters Received by the Secretary of War, Main Series, 1801–70 (microform), reel 250, RG 490; hereinafter cited as Letters Received by the Secretary of War.

31. *Fort-La-Fayette Life*, 45.

32. Rolla Gleason to Secretary of War, Sept. 3, 1863, Register, Letters Received by the Secretary of War, reel 106, register no. 116.

33. L. C. Turner to Gen'l John A. Dix, Nov. 25, 1863, in case file no. 2735, Turner-Baker Papers.

34. "Miss Abby's Diary," Hargrett Rare Book and Manuscript Library, Main Library, Univ. of Georgia, Mar. 12, 1864.

35. John A. Dix to Edwin Stanton, Mar. 25, 1864; J. Holt, memorandum, Apr. 21, 1864, Letters Received by the Office of the Adjutant General (Main Series), 1861–70, RG 94 (microform), reel 667, 321 T, 1868, National Archives, Washington, D.C.

36. A. W. Stone to Charles A. Dana, Apr. 25, 1864, Letters Received by the Secretary of War; C. A. Dana to John A. Dix, Apr. 28, 1864, ibid.; Martin Burke to J. C. Dana, Apr. 25, 1864, ibid. On Charles A. Dana, see James Harrison Wilson, *The Life of Charles A. Dana* (New York: Harper & Brothers, 1907), 3. As a child, Dana lived in northeastern Vermont. See, also, Janet E. Steele, "From Paradise to Park Row: The Life, Opinions, and Newspapers of Charles A. Dana, 1819–1897" (Ph.D. diss., Johns Hopkins University, Baltimore, Md., 1985); and Roy Morris Jr., "A Bird of Evil Omen: The War Department's Charles Dana," *Civil War Times Illustrated* 25, no. 9 (1987): 20–29.

37. C. A. Dana to John A. Dix, Apr. 28, 1864, Letters Received by the Secretary of War.

38. Stone to John A. Dix, June 28, 1864, in case file no. 2441, Turner-Baker Papers.

39. Notation from John A. Bolles, July 22, 1864, in case file no. 2735, Turner-Baker Papers.

40. Benjamin Baily to Dear Sir, Aug. 19, 1864, in case file no. 2735, Turner-Baker Papers. William S. Pelletrau, *History of Putnam County, New York* (Philadelphia: W. W. Preston, 1886), 230–31; William J. Blake, *A History of Putnam County, New York* (New York: Baker & Scribner, 1849), 214, 226.

41. Charles A. Dana to John Dix (telegram) Aug. 20, 1864, Union Provost Marshal General's File (microform), National Archives, Washington, D.C.; Dana to Dix (telegram), Sept. 15, 1864, ibid.

42. John A. Sedgwick to Charles A. Dana, Sept. 14, 1864, in case file no. 2735, Turner-Baker Papers.

43. William Clapp to Major John A. Bolles, Sept. 19, 1864, Union Provost Marshal General's File, National Archives, Washington, D.C.

44. H. J. Raymond to Major General [John A.] Dix, Oct. 11, 1864, Letters Received by the Secretary of War.

45. *Leadville (Colorado) Herald-Democrat*, May 1, 1900.

46. Harold Hyman, *To Try Men's Souls: Loyalty Tests in American History* (Berkeley: Univ. of California Press, 1959), 232–33.

47. Merle Curti, *The Roots of American Loyalty* (New York: Columbia Univ. Press, 1946), 169.

Chapter Seven • Exit and Espionage

1. "Miss Abby's Diary," Hargrett Rare Book and Manuscript Library, Main Library, Univ. of Georgia, Feb. 14, 1864.

2. Deposition of Daniel Chaffee, Sept. 3, 1870, in *Markham* v. *United States* (case file no. 11137), Court of Claims, RG 123, Federal Records Center, Suitland, Md.; J.B. Devoe to Col. J. P. Sanderson, U.S. Army, June 17, 1864, in *The War of the Rebellion: A Compilation of the Official Records of the Union and Confederate Army,* 130 vols. (Washington, D.C.: Government Printing Office, 1880–1902), ser. 2, vol. 7, 355–56; hereinafter cited as *OR.* Ibid., ser. 2, vol. 2, 324.

3. Deposition of Thomas G. W. Crussell, Jan. 23, 1873, in *Crussell* v. *United States* (case file no. 10491), Court of Claims, RG 123, Federal Records Center, Suitland, Md.

4. Ibid. Thomas G. W. Crussell, a stonemason and contractor, was born in Washington, D.C. Thirty-nine years old at the outbreak of the war, he had been an early arrival in Atlanta and in 1842 built a log cabin on what is now Decatur Street. Crussell constructed a number of the more visible structures in antebellum Atlanta, including the stone depot of the Macon and Western Railroad and the state railroad shops. He also built several of the more notable residences in Atlanta, including the famous Calico House, and constructed a building at the University of Georgia in Athens, seventy miles away. Crussell owned property in Fulton County assessed at $3,000 in 1861. Franklin M. Garrett, *Atlanta and Environs: A Chronicle of Its People and Events,* 2 vols. (Athens: Univ. of Georgia Press, 1954), 1:199, 282, 400, 436, 481, 628, 634; Assessor's Book, City of Atlanta, 1861–62, Atlanta History Center.

5. Deposition of C. T. C. Deake, Jan. 23, 1873, in *Crussell* v. *U.S.*

6. Deposition of Thomas G. W. Crussell, ibid.

7. Deposition of Martin Hinton, Oct. 31, 1872, claim of Martin Hinton, Records of the Southern Claims Commission (Allowed Claims), Fulton County, Ga., RG 217, National Archives, Washington, D.C.; similar citations appear hereinafter as Records of the Southern Claims Commission, and unless otherwise indicated, the references to approved claims are to those that originated in Fulton County, Ga.

8. Deposition of Nedom L. Angier, June 23, 1877, claim of Nedom L. Angier, Records of the Southern Claims Commission (Allowed Claims).

9. James P. Hambleton to L. C. Turner, May 23, 1863, in Case Files of Investigations by Levi C. Turner and Lafayette C. Baker, 1861–1866 (microfilm) (case file no. 1123), RG 94, Records of the Adjutant General's Office, 1780s–1917, War Department Division, National Archives, Washington, D.C. Hereinafter cited as Turner-Baker Papers.

10. James P. Hambleton to L. C. Turner, Nov. 18, Oct. 15, 1863, ibid.

11. L. C. Turner to Abraham Lincoln, Oct. 17, 1863, ibid.

12. James P. Hambleton to L. C. Turner, Oct. 21, 1863; Hambleton to Lincoln, Oct. 17, 1863; both ibid.

13. James P. Hambleton to L. C. Turner, Nov. 18, 1863, ibid.; Margaret Leech, *Reveille in Washington* (New York: Harper & Brothers, 1941), 148.

14. James P. Hambleton to L. C. Turner, Nov. 18, Oct. 21, 1863, in Turner-Baker Papers.

15. Deposition of Nedom L. Angier, June 23, 1877, claim of Nedom L. Angier, Records of the Southern Claims Commission (Allowed Claims). John Erskine, an Irish immigrant and lawyer, practiced law in Newnan, Georgia, until either just before the war or shortly after it began—precisely when is uncertain. Erskine was considered a Unionist, but he appears to have had little contact with the Atlanta group. An adroit politician, he was a close friend of Governor Joseph E. Brown, who appointed him to a minor political post during the war so that Erskine could avoid conscription. See *Memoirs of Georgia; containing historical accounts of the state's civil, military, industrial and professional interests, and personal sketches of many of its people,* 2 vols. (Atlanta: Southern Historical Association, 1895), 1: 769–75, and W. S. Northen, ed., *Men of Mark in Georgia,* 7 vols. (Spartanburg: South Carolina Reprint Company, 1974), 3:169–71.

16. Deposition of Nedom L. Angier, June 23, 1877, claim of Nedom L. Angier, Records of the Southern Claims Commission (Allowed Claims).

17. Intelligence Reports Received by General [George] Thomas, 1863–65, box 1, Department of the Cumberland and Division and Department of the Tennessee, 1862–70, entry 958, RG 393 (U.S. Army Continental Commands, 1821–1920), pt. 1, National Archives, Washington, D.C.

18. Deposition of William Le Duc, May 26, 1866, in *Markham* v. *U.S.*

19. Statement of M. O. Markham, Sept. 15, 1863, filed under Shandly, Ed, and Scott, Jas, "Scouts, Guides, Spies and Detectives," Office of Provost Marshal General, 1861–66, RG 110, Two or More Names, box 1, National Archives, Washington, D.C.

20. Statement of Joseph Scott, Sept. 22, 1863, ibid.; statement of M. O. Markham, ibid.; Henry A. Scheetz to Col. James B. Fry, Sept. 23, 1863, ibid.

21. Quotations in statement of M. O. Markham, ibid.; Lafayette C. Baker to Colonel James B. Fry, Sept. 18, 1863, ibid.

22. Statement of M. O. Markham, ibid.; General Orders no. 353, War Department, Adjutant General's Office, Oct. 31, 1863 (report of court-martial), ibid.

23. *Atlanta Daily Intelligencer,* Aug. 18, 1863; quotation in affidavit of Charles Bohnefeld, May 24, 1864, box 24, Letters Received, Governor Joseph E. Brown, Georgia Department of Archives and History, Atlanta.

24. Deposition of Thomas Jordan, Feb. 12, 1878, claim of Thomas Jordan, Records of the Southern Claims Commission (Allowed Claims); deposition of Philip McIntire, Apr. 16, 1875, claim of Philip McIntire, ibid.

25. Deposition of C. T. C. Deake, Jan. 23, 1873, in *Crussell* v. *U.S.*

26. Deposition of Thomas G. W. Crussell, Jan. 23, 1873, in *Crussell* v. *U.S.,* Federal Records Center, Suitland, Md.; Thomas Scrutchin to McNaught, Jan. 2, 1864, McNaught-Ormond Collection, Atlanta History Center.

27. Intelligence Reports Received by General [George] Thomas, 1863–65, box 1, Department of the Cumberland and Division and Department of the Tennessee, 1862–70, entry 958, RG 393 (U.S. Army Continental Commands, 1821–1920), pt. 1, National Archives, Washington, D.C.

28. James S. Thomas to Dear Sister, July 8, 1864, in James S. Thomas Collection, Indiana Historical Society, Indianapolis.

29. Testimony of Anderson L. Scott, in *Report of the Treatment of Prisoners of War, by the Rebel Authorities, during the War of the Rebellion . . .* (Washington: Government Printing Office, 1869), 885. James A. Stewart sold his Atlanta property in the winter of 1863, moved to Rome in March 1864, and in May 1864 found himself within the Union lines; James A. Stewart to Hon. Andrew Johnson, July 23, 1864, in LeRoy P. Graf, ed., *The Papers of Andrew Johnson,* vol. 7, 1864–1865 (Knoxville: Univ. of Tennessee Press, 1986), 49; deposition of Thomas G. Healey, Jan. 11, 1873, claim of Thomas G. Heal[e]y, Records of the Southern Claims Commission (Allowed Claims); Ben Kremenak, ed., "Escape from Atlanta: The Huntington Memoir," *Civil War History* 11 (June 1965): 164; deposition of Julius Hayden, Mar. 10, 1869, in *Hayden* v. *United States* (case file no. 2543), Court of Claims, RG 123, Federal Records Center, Suitland, Md.

30. Statement of Miss Carrie King, Apr. 27, 1864, "Scouts, Guides, Spies and Detectives," box 3, National Archives. For a brief but incisive summary of the motivations of female spies as they related to gender assumptions, see Drew Gilpin Faust, *Mothers of Invention: Women of the Slaveholding South in the American Civil War* (Chapel Hill: Univ. of North Carolina Press, 1996), 214–20. Ernest B. Furgurson, in *Ashes of Glory: Richmond at War* (New York: Knopf, 1996), recounts the spying activities of the Richmond Unionist Elizabeth Van Lew. For a recent general treatment of espionage and military intelligence from First Bull Run through Gettysburg, see Edwin C. Fishel, *The Secret War for the Union: The Untold Story of Military Intelligence in the Civil War* (Boston: Houghton Mifflin, 1996). Previous writers have only touched lightly on the movement of spies in and out of Atlanta. See Wilbur Kurtz, "A Federal Spy in Atlanta," *Atlanta Historical Bulletin* 10 (1957): 13–20, which recounts the activities of J. Milton Glass and J. C. Moore, two agents moving about Atlanta and environs in the weeks just prior to the Battle of Atlanta.

31. William G. Le Duc, typescript draft of memoirs, "Recollections of a Quartermaster," box 41, 223m, William G. Le Duc Collection, Minnesota Historical Society, St. Paul.

Le Duc asked Summerlin to write down her story, which he then incorporated into his manuscript, although he excised it before publication. According to Le Duc, General Sherman later rewarded Summerlin for her service to the Union.

32. Ibid. 223m–24m. I surmise that in the process of transcribing and typing Mary Summerlin's statement and his own memoirs, Le Duc misspelled Newsom's name or misread Summerlin's handwriting. Enough evidence exists in Summerlin's statement to clearly identify "Hewson" as Newsom. See J. Fraise Richard, *The Florence Nightingale of the Southern Army: Experiences of Mrs. Ella K. Newsom, Confederate Nurse in the Great War of 1861–1865* (New York: Broadway, 1914). Also see Faust, *Mothers of Invention,* 99.

33. Le Duc, "Recollections of a Quartermaster," 235m (misnumbered in manuscript, out of sequence).

34. Ibid., 235m, 226m.

35. Statement of Miss Carrie King, Apr. 27, 1864, "Scouts, Guides, Spies and Detectives," box 3, National Archives; Statement of John Moran, Scout, Aug. 11, 1864, ibid., box 4. Henry G. Cole was an extremely vocal Unionist. A special commissioner for the Southern Claims Commission commented that Cole was "an uncompromising & in some respects violent union man." The commission determined that Cole had given very valuable information to the Union command. General George Thomas characterized the information that Cole provided as having been "of inestimable value." When he was imprisoned in Atlanta, he was kept in a cage in the prison yard before being transported to South Carolina, where he was imprisoned on Sullivan's Island for several months. After the war, Cole donated the land used for the Marietta National Cemetery. See claim of Henry G. Cole, Record of the Southern Claims Commission (Allowed Claims), Cobb County, Ga.; Mimi Jo Butler, "Cole-Fletcher Families," in *Cobb County, GA, Genealogical Society, INC Quarterly* (Dec. 1992): 146; Applications for Appointments as Customs Service Officers, 1833–1910, box 050, RG 56, National Archives, Washington, D.C.; and Sarah Blackwell Gober Temple, *The First Hundred Years: A Short History of Cobb County in Georgia* (Atlanta: Walter W. Brown Publishing, 1935), 127.

36. James G. Brown to J. P. Willard, [no month] 14, 1864; in "Scouts, Guides, Spies and Detectives," box 1, National Archives.

37. Report of É[mile]. Bourlier, [1863], ibid., box 1.

38. Louisa M. Whitney, *Goldie's Inheritance: A Story of the Siege of Atlanta* (Burlington, Vt.: Free Press Association, 1903), 196–97.

Chapter Eight • *"The Red Waves of War"*

1. "Miss Abby's Diary," Hargrett Rare Book and Manuscript Library, Main Library, Univ. of Georgia, first quotation in May 30, reference to Ticonderoga in Mar. 12, second quotation in Mar. 13, Mar. 24, 1864; Louisa M. Whitney, *Goldie's Inheritance: A Story of the Siege of Atlanta* (Burlington, Vt.: Free Press Association, 1903), 227, 230.

2. "Miss Abby's Diary," Mar. 12, 1864 ("Welcome letter"), July 19 ("Alone on the hill"), July 21 ("with no husband").

3. Ibid., Jan. 1 ("earthly possessions," "without a Goverment"), Jan. 20 ("roll away," "step forth," "true loyalty," "dwarf[ed] the soul"), May 15 ("longed to clasp").

4. Ibid., Jan. 20, 1864.

5. "Miss Abby's Diary," Jan. 20, 1864; Whitney, *Goldie's Inheritance*, 220–21; Drew Gilpin Faust, *Mothers of Invention: Women of the Slaveholding South in the American Civil War* (Chapel Hill: Univ. of North Carolina Press, 1996), 41–44.

6. "Miss Abby's Diary," first quotation in Jan. 20, remaining quotations in Mar. 24, 1864; Whitney, *Goldie's Inheritance*, 229–30. The diary reference to Amherst's absences is excised from Whitney's fictionalized account of Cyrena's life in *Goldie's Inheritance*, indicating the author's inability to reconcile Amherst's activities with the idealized version of Cyrena's experiences. "Mr. Newman" was likely Thomas Newman, who lived a short distance southwest of the Stones.

7. "Miss Abby's Diary," Jan. 20, 1864.

8. Ibid., Mar. 20, 1864; Whitney, *Goldie's Inheritance*, 228.

9. "Miss Abby's Diary," Jan. 20, 1864; Whitney, *Goldie's Inheritance*, 221–22.

10. "Miss Abby's Diary," Jan. 20, 1864; Whitney, *Goldie's Inheritance*, 221–22, 239.

11. Whitney, *Goldie's Inheritance*, 192–93, 222, 236; "Miss Abby's Diary," May 21, 1864.

12. Whitney, *Goldie's Inheritance*, 193, 230–32; "Miss Abby's Diary."

13. "Miss Abby's Diary," May 6, 1864.

14. "Miss Abby's Diary," first quotation in May 19, 1864; remaining quotations in May 24, 1864.

15. Ibid., Apr. 9, 1864; Whitney, *Goldie's Inheritance*, 228–29.

16. "Miss Abby's Diary," Apr. 9, 1864.

17. Ibid., Feb. 14, 1864.

18. Ibid., Mar. 13, 1864.

19. Ibid., May 9, 1864; Whitney, *Goldie's Inheritance*, 232.

20. "Miss Abby's Diary," May 15, 1864; Whitney, *Goldie's Inheritance*, 232–33.

21. "Miss Abby's Diary," May 15, 1864; Whitney, *Goldie's Inheritance*, 233.

22. "Miss Abby's Diary," May 19, 1864; Whitney, *Goldie's Inheritance*, 234.

23. "Miss Abby's Diary," May 21, 1864.

24. Ibid., May 24, 1864; Whitney, *Goldie's Inheritance*, 234.

25. "Miss Abby's Diary," May 24 ("delirium of fear," "wild up-heaving"), May 27 ("faintest echo," "awakened the wildest joy," "the first notes"), May 28, 1864 ("Mrs. M——"); *Goldie's Inheritance*, 235.

26. "Miss Abby's Diary," first two quotations in May 30, remaining quotations in June 1, 1864; Whitney, *Goldie's Inheritance*, 237.

27. "Miss Abby's Diary," June 2, 1864; Whitney, *Goldie's Inheritance*, 237.

28. "Miss Abby's Diary," June 2 ("worn horses," "It makes no difference," "the fences"), June 6 ("in tears," "much rather"); Whitney, *Goldie's Inheritance*, 238.

29. "Miss Abby's Diary," June 7, 1864; Whitney, *Goldie's Inheritance*, 239–40.

30. Deposition of Olive M. Healey, Jan. 14, 1873, claim of Thomas G. Heal[e]y, Records of the Southern Claims Commission (Allowed Claims), Fulton County, Ga., RG 217, National Archives, Washington, D.C.

31. "Miss Abby's Diary," July 5, 1864.

32. Ben Kremenak, ed., "Escape from Atlanta: The Huntington Memoir," *Civil War History* (June 1965): 163.

33. Ibid., 163–64.
34. Ibid., 164–65.
35. Ibid., 165–67.
36. "Miss Abby's Diary," July 5, 1864.
37. Ibid., July 19, 1864.
38. Ibid., July 21, 1864. Numerous sources comment upon the heat on July 22. See, for example, Shelby Foote, *The Civil War, a Narrative: Red River to Appomattox* (New York: Vintage Books, 1986), 477.
39. Albert Castel, *Decision in the West: The Atlanta Campaign of 1864* (Lawrence: Univ. Press of Kansas, 1992), 390; "Miss Abby's Diary," July 21, 1864; Whitney, *Goldie's Inheritance,* 243.
40. "Miss Abby's Diary," July 21, 1864; Whitney, *Goldie's Inheritance,* 244.
41. "Miss Abby's Diary," July 21, 1864; Whitney, *Goldie's Inheritance,* 244.
42. "Miss Abby's Diary," July 21, 1864; Whitney, *Goldie's Inheritance,* 247.
43. "Miss Abby's Diary," July 21, 1864.
44. Ibid.; Castel, *Decision in the West,* 408; Whitney, *Goldie's Inheritance,* 245.
45. "Miss Abby's Diary," July 21, 1864; Whitney, *Goldie's Inheritance,* 246.
46. "Miss Abby's Diary," July 21, July 22, 1864; Whitney, *Goldie's Inheritance,* 248–49.

Chapter Nine • *"Like the Frozen Snake"*

1. William Tecumseh Sherman, *Memoirs of General W. T. Sherman,* 2 vols. (New York: Library of America, 1990), 548; Wilbur Kurtz, "The Augustus F. Hurt House," *Atlanta Constitution Magazine,* June 22, 1930; deposition of Osborne A. Lochrane, Dec. 3, 1875, claim of Augustus F. Hurt, Records of the Southern Claims Commission (Barred and Disallowed Claims), RG 233, National Archives, Washington, D.C.; similar citations appear hereinafter as Records of the Southern Claims Commission, and unless otherwise indicated, the references to approved claims are to those that originated in Fulton County, Ga.
2. Architectural plan for Hurt house, claim of Augustus Hurt, Records of the Southern Claims Commission (Barred and Disallowed Claims); deposition of Augustus F. Hurt, Dec. 2, 1875, ibid.
3. Sherman, *Memoirs,* 548; map of defense line, L. P. Grant Collection, Atlanta History Center.
4. Albert Castel, *Decision in the West: The Atlanta Campaign of 1864* (Lawrence: Univ. Press of Kansas, 1992), 411–12.
5. *Atlanta Daily Intelligencer,* Dec. 20, 1864; Lee Kennett, *Marching through Georgia: The Story of Soldiers and Civilians during Sherman's Campaign* (New York: HarperCollins, 1995). See the illustration of the Ponder House and accompanying caption following p. 178.
6. Deposition of Richard Mayes, Mar. 24, 1874 (Southern Claims Commission), in *Mayes* v. *United States* (case file no. 4618), Court of Claims, RG 123, Federal Records Center, Suitland, Md.
7. Castel, *Decision in the West,* 411–12.
8. Wallace P. Reed, *History of Atlanta, Georgia* (Syracuse, N.Y.: D. Mason, 1889), 206.

9. A. W. Reese, "Personal Recollections of the Late Civil War in the United States. With Scenes, Incidents, and Memories of Earlier Times. By A. W. Reese, M.D. Late Surgeon U.S.A. [1870]," photocopy of manuscript, Western Historical Manuscript Collection, University of Missouri–Columbia, 531.

10. Ibid., 532–35.

11. Testimony of Alfred Austell, typescript, n.d., in *Austell v. United States* (case file no. 13859), Court of Claims, RG 123, Federal Records Center, Suitland, Md.; deposition of Julius Hayden, Mar. 10, 1869, in *Julius A. Hayden v. U.S.* (case file no. 2543), ibid.; case summary, claim of Peter Huge, Records of the Southern Claims Commission (Allowed Claims); deposition of George Edwards, Jan. 18, 1872, claim of George Edwards, ibid.; deposition of Christian Kontz, Nov. 27, 1868, claim of Christian Kontz, ibid.; deposition of John Silvey, Oct. 29, 1867, in *Lynch v. United States* (case file no. 2502), Court of Claims, RG 123, Federal Records Center, Suitland, Md.; deposition of John Silvey, Sept. 28, 1875, in *Webster v. United States* (case file no. 13502), ibid.; summary of letter from Lewis Scofield, RG 393, vol. 125, pt. 1, entry 1100, Records of the Provost Marshal General, Army of the Cumberland, National Archives, Washington, D.C.; deposition of James Dunning, Jan. 8, 1870, in *Webster v. U.S.;* deposition of William Markham, Jan. 8, 1870, ibid.; testimony of Austin Wright (typescript), in *Austell v. U.S.;* deposition of Prince Ponder, May 31, 1872, in *Webster v. U.S.*

12. Ben Kremenak, ed., "Escape from Atlanta: The Huntington Memoir," *Civil War History* (June 1965): 167.

13. Reed, *History of Atlanta,* 208; deposition of James Dunning, Jan. 8, 1870, in *Webster v. U.S.*

14. Deposition of James Dunning, in *Webster v. U.S.*

15. Deposition of John Silvey, Sept. 28, 1875, ibid.; deposition of William Markham, Jan. 8, 1870, ibid.; deposition of William Lewis, July 26, 1873, ibid.

16. Deposition of Prince Ponder, May 31, 1872, ibid.; deposition of Thomas G. W. Crussell, May 31, 1872, ibid.

17. Deposition of E. T. Hunnicutt, May 31, 1872, ibid.

18. Louisa M. Whitney, *Goldie's Inheritance: A Story of the Siege of Atlanta* (Burlington, Vt.: Free Press Association, 1903), 251.

19. Sally Clayton Memoir, box 5, Nicolson Family Papers, Atlanta History Center.

20. Deposition of Amy Holley, Sept. 7, 1877, claim of William Dyer, Records of the Southern Claims Commission (Allowed Claims).

21. *Atlanta Daily Intelligencer,* Aug. 6, 1864; Whitney, *Goldie's Inheritance,* 251; Franklin M. Garrett, *Atlanta and Environs: A Chronicle of Its People and Events,* 2 vols. (Athens: Univ. of Georgia Press, 1954), 1:628.

22. A. A. Hoehling, *Last Train from Atlanta* (New York: T. Yoseloff, 1958), 324, 352, 364, 366.

23. Castel, *Decision in the West,* 509, 522; Henry Watterson to Rebecca, Sept. 1, 1864 (typescript), Watterson Papers, Filson Club, Louisville, Ky.

24. Reed, *History of Atlanta,* 195.

25. Deposition of Henry Ivy, Oct. 1, 1875, in *Webster v. U.S.*

26. See, for example, Garrett, *Atlanta and Environs,* 1:634; deposition of John Ficken, Oct. 1, 1875, in *Webster v. U.S.*

27. Deposition of Bridget Doyle, Oct. 9, 1875, in *Webster* v. *U.S.*
28. James M. Calhoun to Reuben Arnold, Nov. 27, 1875, ibid.
29. Reed, *History of Atlanta,* 166; Garrett, *Atlanta and Environs,* 1:634–35.
30. Quotation in affidavit of James M. Calhoun, claim of Timothy D. Lynes, Court of Claims, RG 123, box 1452, Federal Records Center, Suitland, Md.; Reed, *History of Atlanta,* 196; Garrett, *Atlanta and Environs,* 1:634; Calhoun to Reuben Arnold, Nov. 27, 1873, in *Webster* v. *U.S.*
31. Robert Bence to My Dear Mother, Sept. 6, 1864, Bence Collection, Indiana Historical Society, Indianapolis; William Le Duc to Mary [Le Duc], Sept. 5, 1864, Letterbook, box 24, William G. Le Duc Collection, Minnesota Historical Society, St. Paul; "Daily record of movements in Quarter Master's Department of 20th Army Corps. Recorded by Henry A. Monser[,] clerk for L'Col Wm G. LeDuc Quartermaster," Sept. 3, 1864, box 28, William G. Le Duc Collection; hereinafter cited as Le Duc, "Daily Record."
32. Angus Brucker to Dear Wife, Sept. 18, 1864 (translated from German), Brucker Collection, Indiana Historical Society.
33. Diary of Henry Hurter, Sept. 20, 1864, *Civil War Times Illustrated* Collection, United States Army Military History Institute, Carlisle, Pennsylvania; Reese, "Personal Recollections of the Late Civil War," 642.
34. Hugh D. Gallagher to Dear Brother, Sept. 12, 1864, Gallagher Collection, Indiana Historical Society, Indianapolis.
35. David P. Conyngham, *Sherman's March Through the South, with Sketches and Incidents of the Campaign* (New York: Sheldon, 1865), 224–25.
36. Arthur Reed Taylor, "From the Ashes: Atlanta during Reconstruction, 1865–1876" (Ph.D. diss., Emory University, 1973), 20; deposition of Robert Lowry, Sept. 26, 1903, *Markham* v. *United States* (case file no. 11137), Court of Claims, RG 123, Federal Records Center, Suitland, Md.; Whitney, *Goldie's Inheritance,* 253; "A[.] O[.] Brainerd, Address to the Ladies—Wives of the Veterans in the G.A.R. Room, St. Albans, [April 15, 1895]," typescript, St. Albans Historical Museum, St. Albans, Vt.
37. Quotation in Elizabeth H. Whitney to Louisa M. Bailey, Oct. 12, 1864; Louisa M. Bailey to Joel F. Whitney, Oct. 28, 1864; both in Francis L. Hopkins Collection, Bailey-Howe Library, University of Vermont, Burlington.
38. Julian Wisner Hinkley, *A Narrative of Service with the Third Wisconsin Infantry* (Madison: Wisconsin History Commission, 1912), 140–41; L. G. Bennett and William M. Haigh, *History of the Thirty-Sixth Regiment Illinois Volunteers During the War of the Rebellion* (Aurora, Ill.: Knickerbocker and Hodder, 1876), 623; John A. Wilkens to Dear Sister, Sept. 5, 1864, John A. Wilkens Correspondence, Indiana Historical Society (microfilm), Bloomington.
39. William Henry Newlin, comp., *A History of the Seventy-third Regiment of Illinois Infantry Volunteers* (Springfield, Ill., 1890), 365. Newlin is quoting from a comrade's diary in which Luther Faught is misidentified as "Fort" but correctly identified as a Maine native who had come to Atlanta seven years before to work as a foreman in the Winship and Company Machine Shop.
40. Rufus Mead to Folks at Home, Sept. 4, 1864, Mead Collection, Library of Congress; Mead to Dear Folks at Home, Sept. 8, 1864, ibid.

41. Affidavit of Myron White, Jan. 25, 1865, claim of David Young, Records of the Southern Claims Commission (Allowed Claims).

42. William Le Duc to Mary [Le Duc], Sept. 5, 1864, Letterbook, box 24, William G. Le Duc Collection, Minnesota Historical Society, St. Paul; deposition of William G. Le Duc, May 26, 1866, in *Markham* v. *U.S.;* Le Duc, "Daily Record," Oct. 3, 1864.

43. William G. Le Duc, typescript draft of memoirs, "Recollections of a Quartermaster," box 41, 227m–230m, William G. Le Duc Collection, Minnesota Historical Society, St. Paul.

44. Ibid., 224m, 226m.

45. William C. Armor diary, Sept. 8, 1864, Special Collections Division, Woodruff Library, Emory University; affidavit of William Markham, Jan. 10, 1865, claim of David Young, Records of the Southern Claims Commission (Allowed Claims); affidavit of James Dunning, Jan. 10, 1865, ibid.

46. Samuel P. Richards diary (typescript), Sept. 21, 1864, 17–18, Atlanta History Center.

47. Summary of letter from Lewis Scofield, RG 393, vol. 125, pt. 1, entry 1100, Records of the Provost Marshal General, Army of the Cumberland, National Archives, Washington, D.C.; list of properties dated Sept. 2, 1864, in *Markham* v. *U.S.*

48. Deposition of Olive M. Healey, Jan. 14, 1873, claim of Thomas G. Heal[e]y, Records of the Southern Claims Commission (Allowed Claims).

49. Deposition of Polly Beedles, July 5, 1873, claim of Henry Beedles, Records of the Southern Claims Commission; deposition of Henry Beedles, July 5, 1873, ibid.

50. Summary of letter from Major T. C. Fitzgibbon, Sept. 12, 1864, RG 393, vol. 125, pt. 1, entry 1100, Records of the Provost Marshal General, Army of the Cumberland, National Archives, Washington, D.C.

51. Thomas H. Bomar to My Dear Sister, Sept. 17, 1864, in Bomar Family Papers, Special Collections Division, Woodruff Library, Emory University.

52. *Atlanta Daily Intelligencer,* Sept. 10, 28 ("for the purpose of claiming satisfaction"), 1864.

53. Deposition of William Lowry, Sept. 26, 1903, in *Markham* v. *U.S.*

54. *Atlanta Daily Intelligencer,* Oct. 22, 1864.

55. Quotations in Wallace to My precious wife, Nov. 19, 1863; Wallace to My precious wife, n.d.; Wallace to "Dear Jesse," Nov. 19, 1863; all in Anne Wallace Howland Papers, Atlanta History Center.

56. Court of Inquiry, George W. Lee, Courts-Martial, box 1, RG 22, Georgia Department of Archives and History, Atlanta.

57. *Atlanta Daily Intelligencer,* Oct. 27, 1864.

58. William G. Le Duc to Mary [Le Duc], Sept. 9, 1864, William G. Le Duc Collection, Minnesota Historical Society, St. Paul.

59. Conyngham, *Sherman's March Through the South,* 225.

60. Stephen J. Young et al. to Brigadier General Whipple (true copy), Sept. 10, 1864, claim of Thomas Heal[e]y, Records of the Southern Claims Commission (Allowed Claims).

61. William T. Sherman, endorsement, n.d. (true copy), ibid.

62. James R. Crew to Dear Wife, Dec. 1, 1864, James R. Crew Collection, Atlanta History Center; RG 393, v. 125, pt. 1, entry T100, Provost Marshal General, Army of the Cumberland, National Archives, Washington, D.C.

63. Carrie Berry Diary (typescript), Sept. 9 ("the citizens"), 12 ("Papa says"), 13 ("heard that"), 1864, Atlanta History Center.

64. Joshua Hill to James R. Crew, Oct. 23, 1864, Crew Collection, Atlanta History Center.

65. A list of citizens going south is located in the National Archives. See "The Book of Exodus," RG 393, Records of the U.S. Army Continental Commands, Military Division of the Mississippi, Letters Received, Misc., box 2. This document was signed by Colonel William Le Duc. Le Duc may have also compiled a list of those sent north, but, if so, it has disappeared. Le Duc recalled in later years that he had been told that a list that he kept, which included names of persons who applied for transportation, had been sent to a public library in Detroit, Michigan. William G. Le Duc, typescript draft of memoirs, "Recollections of a Quartermaster," box 41, 222m, William G. Le Duc Collection, Minnesota Historical Society. A search by librarians at the Detroit Public Library uncovered no such document.

　　Professor Lee Kennett estimates that a total of thirty-five hundred persons left the city. The Storrs memoir, cited later in the note, reports that 446 families went north, likely an error because numerous sources report that 446 families went *south*. If thirty-five hundred persons were in Atlanta at the conclusion of the siege, it seems reasonable that at least fifteen hundred went north. William Le Duc believed that "the most of the people here" were Union people. Le Duc to Mary [Le Duc], Sept. 24, 1864, Letterbook, box 24, William G. Le Duc Collection; John W. Storrs, *The "Twentieth Connecticut": A Regimental History* (Ansonia, Ct.: Press of the "Naugatuck Valley Sentinel," 1886), 147; Kennett, *Marching through Georgia*, 210; deposition of Julius A. Hayden, Mar. 10, 1869, in *Hayden* v. *U.S.* Mark Grimsley, in *The Hard Hand of War: Union Military Policy toward Southern Civilians, 1861–1865* (Cambridge: Cambridge Univ. Press, 1995), reports only on those who went south. See p. 188.

66. Deposition of Alfred Austell, typescript, n.d., in *Austell* v. *U.S.*

67. Statement of E. Richmond, n.d., ibid. Richmond was an official of the Southern Claims Commission who had interviewed Whitaker, probably in the early 1870s. Whitaker stated that he did not want to be quoted publicly but would testify about Austell if summoned to do so. According to Richmond, Whitaker said that if he were summoned, "then his neighbors" could not "blame him for telling the truth no matter who" would be harmed by it.

68. William G. Le Duc to William T. Sherman, Sept. 29, 1864, Letterbook, box 24, William G. Le Duc Collection, Minnesota Historical Society, St. Paul.

69. *Atlanta Daily Intelligencer*, Nov. 15, 1864.

70. Testimony of Daniel Chaffee, Sept. 3, 1870, in *Markham* v. *U.S.*; testimony of James Dunning, Jan. 10, 1865, claim of David Young (Allowed Claims); deposition of Olive Healey, Jan. 14, 1873, claim of Thomas G. Heal[e]y, ibid.; William G. Le Duc to William T. Sherman, Sept. 29, 1864, William G. Le Duc Collection, Minnesota Historical Society, St. Paul; Christian Kontz business card in Kontz Family Collection, Atlanta Historical Society; deposition of James Dunning, Nov. 2, 1866, in *Robert*

H. McCroskey v. *United States* (case file no. 2573), Court of Claims, RG 123, Federal Records Center, Suitland, Md.; *New York Times,* Feb. 1, 1865.

71. *Leadville (Colorado) Herald-Democrat,* May 1, 1900.
72. William Cogswell Collection, J. D. Phillips Library, Peabody Essex Museum, Salem, Mass. The most in-depth account of the destruction of Atlanta is in Lee Kennett, *Marching through Georgia.*
73. Charles F. Morse to William Cogswell, Nov. 3, 1864, Cogswell Collection, box 1, folder 1, J. D. Phillips Library, Peabody Essex Museum, Salem, Mass.
74. William M. Walker to Colonel William Cogswell, Nov. 2, 1864, ibid.
75. "Plan of Destruction," ibid., box 1, folder 2.
76. Kennett, *Marching through Georgia,* 239–42.
77. Ibid., 240–41.
78. Hoehling, *Last Train from Atlanta,* 533; Reed, *History of Atlanta,* 208.
79. See Grimsley, *The Hard Hand of War.*

Chapter Ten • *The Loyalty of Reconstruction*

1. Arthur Reed Taylor, "From the Ashes: Atlanta during Reconstruction, 1865–1876" (Ph.D. diss., Emory University, 1973), 3–32; Wallace P. Reed, *History of Atlanta, Georgia* (Syracuse, N.Y.: D. Mason, 1889), 208–9; Carrie Berry diary (typescript), Nov. 17, 19, 1864, Atlanta History Center.
2. Stephen V. Ash, *When the Yankees Came: Conflict and Chaos in the Occupied South, 1861–1865* (Chapel Hill: Univ. of North Carolina Press, 1995), 111.
3. *Atlanta Daily Intelligencer,* Dec. 12, 1864; Franklin M. Garrett, *Atlanta and Environs: A Chronicle of Its People and Events,* 2 vols. (Athens: Univ. of Georgia Press, 1954), 1:655, 660–62; Taylor, "From the Ashes," 32–35.
4. *Atlanta Daily Intelligencer,* Dec. 20, 1864.
5. Carrie Berry diary, Dec. 26, 1864; Jan. 4, 5, 1865.
6. Deposition of John Silvey, June 9, 1873, claim of John Silvey, Records of the Southern Claims Commission (Allowed Claims), Fulton County, Ga., RG 217, National Archives, Washington, D.C.; similar citations appear hereinafter as Records of the Southern Claims Commission, and unless otherwise indicated, the references to approved claims are to those that originated in Fulton County, Ga.
7. Deposition of E. W. Munday, in *Munday* v. *U.S.,* Court of Claims, RG 123, box 1541, Federal Records Center, Suitland, Md.; deposition of W. W. Wells, ibid.
8. Deposition of Michael Lynch, July 5, 1872, claim of Michael Lynch, Records of the Southern Claims Commission (Allowed Claims).
9. *New York Times,* Feb. 1, 1865.
10. Ibid., Feb. 1, 17, 1865; all quotations from Feb. 17.
11. "A[.] O[.] Brainerd, Address to the Ladies—Wives of the Veterans in the G.A.R. Room, St. Albans, [April 15, 1895]," typescript, St. Albans Historical Museum, St. Albans, Vt.; RG 393, Records of the U.S. Army Continental Commands, pt. 1, entry 1414, vols. 72, 194, 195, National Archives, Washington, D.C.
12. H. Everett Russell to Andrew Johnson, May 27, 1865, Pierpont Morgan Library, New York.
13. *Atlanta Daily Intelligencer,* Feb. 2, 1865.

14. Dan T. Carter, *When the War Was Over: The Failure of Self-Reconstruction in the South, 1865–1867* (Baton Rouge: Louisiana State Univ. Press, 1985), 24.

15. Ibid., 28, 48, 55; Samuel P. Richards diary (typescript), Aug. 24, 1865, 29, Atlanta History Center.

16. H. Everett Russell to Andrew Johnson, May 27, 1865, Pierpont Morgan Library, New York; Alexander N. Wilson to Andrew Johnson, June 5, 1865, in Paul H. Bergeron, ed., *The Papers of Andrew Johnson*, vol. 8: *May–Aug. 1865* (Knoxville: Univ. of Tennessee Press, 1989), 186–87.

17. William Jennings to C. F. Benjamin, July 8, 1872, claim of Amherst W. Stone, Records of the Southern Claims Commission (Barred and Disallowed Claims), RG 233 (Stone filed his claim while living in Chatham County, Ga.); "Testimony of Colonel A. W. Stone, Jan. 8, 1869," in "Condition of Affairs in Georgia," 40th Congress, 3d Session, *House Miscellaneous Document No. 52*, 43; *Savannah Daily Herald*, Apr. 23, 1865; Thomas Conn Bryan, *Confederate Georgia* (Athens: Univ. of Georgia Press, 1953), 138–39; Works Progress Administration, *Annals of Savannah—1850–1937: A Digest and Index of the Newspaper and Record of Events and Opinions in Eighty-seven Volumes* (Savannah, Ga., n.d.), 16: iv; quotations in Ash, *When the Yankees Came*, 265.

18. In 1866, Stone boarded at the Marshall House in Savannah. In 1867, his law office was located on the second floor of the Express Office. *Purse's Directory of the City of Savannah* (Savannah, 1866); *N. J. Darrell & Co. Savannah City Directory* (Savannah, 1867); Cyrena Bailey Stone, "Out in the Woods," Nov. 10, 1865, clipping, *Savannah National Republican*, Bailey-Hopkins Scrapbook, Francis L. Hopkins Collection, Bailey-Howe Library, University of Vermont, Burlington.

19. Savannah *Daily Herald*, Apr. 23, 1865.

20. Ibid., Apr. 23, 24, 1865; Georgia, vol. 1, p. 100, R.G. Dun & Co. Collection, Baker Library, Harvard University Graduate School of Business Administration.

21. Savannah *Daily Herald*, Apr. 23, 24, 1865.

22. For details of Johnson's amnesty policy, see Jonathan T. Dorris, *Pardon and Amnesty under Lincoln and Johnson: The Restoration of the Confederates to Their Rights and Privileges, 1861–1898* (Chapel Hill: Univ. of North Carolina Press, 1953).

23. Numerous sources confirm the return of the Unionists. In particular, I have relied upon Garrett, *Atlanta and Environs*, and Wallace P. Reed, *History of Atlanta*, as well as the records of the Southern Claims Commission, the records of the United States Court of Claims, and newspaper sources. For the specific references to Unionists who were aided by the Freedmen's Bureau, see C. P. Cassin et al. to Andrew Johnson, May 15, 1865, Registers and Letters Received by the Commissioner of the Bureau of Refugees, Freedmen, and Abandoned Lands, 1865–1872, M752, roll 16, Letters Received, M–R, March–October, 1865, National Archives, Washington, D.C.; and Kontz Family Collection, Atlanta History Center.

24. Reed, *History of Atlanta*, 211; Taylor, "From the Ashes," 36.

25. Bergeron, *Papers of Andrew Johnson*, 8:51n; *Pioneer Citizens' History of Atlanta, 1833–1902* (Atlanta: Pioneer Citizens' Society of Atlanta, 1902), 356–57. I base the assertion concerning the Unionists' interest in federal appointments on the subsequent maneuvering for office discussed later in this chapter.

26. Alfred Austell to Andrew Johnson, June 16, 1865, in Bergeron, *Papers of Andrew Johnson,* 8:246; Alfred Austell to Joshua Hill, RG 60, Series 350, Appointment Files for Judicial Districts, 1853–1905, Georgia, Federal Judges, Marshals, and Attorneys, National Archives, Washington, D.C. Austell evidently saw the president on June 9, 1865. See *Washington Morning Chronicle,* June 10, 1865.

27. Historians differ over the level of resistance among former Confederates in the immediate postwar months and whether Andrew Johnson should have acted more decisively and punitively toward the South than he ultimately did. Cf. Carter, *When the War Was Over,* and Michael Perman, *Reunion without Compromise: The South and Reconstruction, 1865–1868* (Cambridge: Cambridge Univ. Press, 1973).

28. Quotations in *Savannah Daily Herald,* June 5, 1865; William Markham, James A. Dunning, A. N. Wilson, and Aaron Wilbur to Andrew Johnson, May 18, 1865, Andrew Johnson Papers (microfilm), ser. 1, reel no. 14, Library of Congress.

29. *Savannah Daily Herald,* May 31, 1865.

30. Ibid., June 15, 1865; Washington *National Intelligencer,* June 17, 1865; O. A. Lochrane to Andrew Johnson, June 16, 1865, Andrew Johnson Papers (microfilm), ser. 1, reel no. 15, Library of Congress.

31. Alexander N. Wilson to Andrew Johnson, June 5, 1865, in Bergeron, *Papers of Andrew Johnson,* 8:186–87.

32. O. A. Lochrane to Andrew Johnson, June 16, 1865, Andrew Johnson Papers (microfilm), ser. 1, reel no. 15, Library of Congress.

33. *Savannah Daily Herald,* July 4, 1865; Reed, *History of Atlanta,* 213; Garrett, *Atlanta and Environs,* 1:679; *New York Commercial Advertiser,* in *Savannah Daily Herald,* July 7, 1865.

34. A thorough search of the appointment files in RG 60 in the National Archives yielded no information concerning Stone's alleged appointment. The various registers of federal appointments have also been searched, as well as the records of the U.S. District Court for Georgia at the Federal Records Center in East Point, Georgia. There is no mention of an appointment for Stone as U.S. attorney in any of these sources. The successful appointee was Henry S. Fitch, an Indiana native and former Union army officer. See *Savannah Daily News,* May 5, 1866.

    After escaping from Atlanta in 1863, Nedom Angier remained in Massachusetts until the war's end, apparently developing close ties with the Lincoln administration. He claimed to have met with Lincoln on several occasions to argue for a conciliatory policy of Reconstruction. He appears to have been a frequent visitor to Washington during that period and likely continued to build his political network after Johnson became president.

35. Holcombe was appointed clerk of the U.S. District Court by John Erskine; James Dunning became a freedmen's bureau agent; and James A. Stewart was appointed postmaster at Rome, Georgia; *Savannah Daily News,* May 9, 1866 (Holcombe); Paul A. Cimbala, *Under the Guardianship of the Nation: The Freedmen's Bureau and the Reconstruction of Georgia, 1865–1870* (Athens: Univ. of Georgia Press, 1997), 44 (Dunning); *Rome (Ga.) Weekly Courier,* Nov. 9, 1865 (Stewart); Cimbala, *Under the Guardianship of the Nation,* 66 (Stone as Freedmen's Bureau agent); *Savannah Daily Herald,* Mar. 13, 1866 (Stone as judge of Freedmen's Court); *Savannah Daily News and Herald,* Oct. 29, 1869: "Testimony of Colonel Amherst

W. Stone, Jan. 8, 1869," in "Condition of Affairs in Georgia," 40th Congress, 3d Session, *House Miscellaneous Document No. 52* (Stone as U.S. Commissioner); A. N. Wilson to Andrew Johnson, June 16, 1865, in Bergeron, *Papers of Andrew Johnson,* 8:248–49. Wilson commented on a widespread belief that Joshua Hill would be named governor. Wilson did not know Hill personally, he told the president, but he feared that Hill could "play Brownlow," a reference to the vengeful spirit manifested by the Tennessean Unionist William G. Brownlow and an indication of Wilson's belief that with appropriate appointments to federal positions, order could easily be restored in the South.

36. Reed, *History of Atlanta,* 211–23.

37. James A. Stewart to Andrew Johnson, Aug. 12, 1865, in Bergeron, *Papers of Andrew Johnson,* 8:578–79.

38. *Atlanta Daily Intelligencer,* July 6, 1865.

39. Ibid.; David Young To whom it may concern, Aug. 3, 1865, Papers of the American Missionary Association (microfilm edition), American Missionary Association Archives, Amistad Research Center, New Orleans; hereinafter cited as AMA Papers.

40. James A. Stewart to Andrew Johnson, Aug. 12, 1865, in Bergeron, *Papers of Andrew Johnson,* 8:578–59; David Young To whom it may concern, Aug. 3, 1865, AMA Papers. Numerous references to the involvement of Stone and Wilson in interracial politics exist. See, for example, *Savannah Daily News and Herald,* July 3, 1867. For Dunning's involvements, see Taylor, "From the Ashes," 224, 231. For Markham, see ibid., 325.

41. James Dunning to Andrew Johnson, July 2, 1865, in Bergeron, *Papers of Andrew Johnson,* 8:339.

42. Alex. N. Wilson to Andrew Johnson, Oct. 25, 1865, in Bergeron, *Papers of Andrew Johnson,* 9:286.

43. Reed, *History of Atlanta,* 214; "Journal of the Proceedings of the Convention of the People of Georgia" (1865), in Allen D. Candler, *The Confederate Records of the State of Georgia,* 6 vols. (Atlanta: Chas. P. Byrd, State Printer, 1909–11), 4:135.

44. Reed, *History of Atlanta,* 214.

45. Alex. N. Wilson to Andrew Johnson, Nov. 25, 1865, in Bergeron, *Papers of Andrew Johnson,* 9:431–32.

46. *Rome (Ga.) Weekly Courier,* Nov. 9, 1865; quotation in James A. Stewart to Andrew Johnson, Oct. 13, 1865, in Bergeron, *Papers of Andrew Johnson,* 9:239; *Rome (Ga.) Weekly Courier,* Oct. 12, 26, 1865. As a candidate for Congress, Stewart took to the newspaper columns and, in language strikingly similar to that used by Plebian during the secession crisis, promoted a "broad reconciliation" of the South.

47. First and second quotations in *Rome (Ga.) Weekly Courier,* Dec. 29, 1865; third quotation in James A. Stewart to Andrew Johnson, July 22, 1866, in Bergeron, *Papers of Andrew Johnson,* 10:714–15.

48. Taylor, "From the Ashes," 262.

Chapter Eleven • Claims of Loyalty

1. Frank Klingberg, *The Southern Claims Commission* (Berkeley: Univ. of California Press, 1955), 20.

2. Thomas Scrutchin to William McNaught, Jan. 2, 1865, McNaught-Ormond Collection, Atlanta History Center.

3. See the affidavits of James Dunning, Jan. 10, 1865, William Markham, Jan. 24, 1865, and Myron White, Jan. 25, 1865, claim of David Young, Records of the Southern Claims Commission (Allowed Claims), Fulton County, Ga., RG 217, National Archives, Washington, D.C.; similar citations appear hereinafter as Records of the Southern Claims Commission, and unless otherwise indicated, the references to approved claims are to those that originated in Fulton County, Ga.

4. Alfred Austell to Henry Sherman, Apr. 19, 1869, Austell Letterbook, Atlanta History Center; Austell to Sherman, Apr. 28, 1869, ibid.; affidavit of J. M. Blair, Jan. 19, 1867, claim of David Young, Records of the Southern Claims Commission (Allowed Claims); A. W. Eaton to A. Rutherford, May 20, 1870, ibid.

5. Endorsement sheet dated October 20, 1866, ibid.; endorsement sheet, War Department Claims Commission, December 10, 1866, ibid.; Hugh McCulloch to Messrs. North and Primrose, Attorneys, July 31, 1867, ibid.; J. Bartram North to Hon. John Wilson, June 9, 1868, ibid.

6. Endorsement, Third Auditor to Commissary General, June 11, 1868, ibid.; Klingberg, *Southern Claims Commission,* 54.

7. A. W. Eaton, Commissary General, to A. Rutherford, Third Auditor, May 20, 1870, claim of David Young, Records of the Southern Claims Commission (Allowed Claims).

8. *Cases Decided in the Court of Claims of the United States in the December Term for 1866* (Washington: Government Printing Office, 1868), 2:533–34.

9. "Petition, United States Court of Claims, October Term, 1865, *William Markham* v. *United States,* Claim Under Act of March 12, 1863," in *Markham* v. *United States* (case file no. 11137), Court of Claims, RG 123, Federal Records Center, Suitland, Md. *Cases Decided*, 2:535.

10. *Cases Decided*, 2:535 (for amount of award); "Petition. United States Court of Claims. *Robert H. McCroskey* v. *United States,*" in *McCroskey* v. *United States* (case file no. 10137), Court of Claims, RG 123, Federal Records Center, Suitland, Md.

11. 4 *Court of Claims* 490–94; 7 *Court of Claims* 278–79.

12. 7 *Court of Claims* 305–51.

13. Quotations in 4 *Court of Claims* 533–36; 7 *Court of Claims* 204–5, 276–78.

14. 4 *Court of Claims* 475–78.

15. "Opinion of the Court," *Lynch* v. *United States* (case file no. 2502), Court of Claims, RG 123, Federal Records Center, Suitland, Md.

16. 7 *Court of Claims* 599–603.

17. The discussion of the procedures of the Southern Claims Commission is primarily based upon Klingberg, *Southern Claims Commission,* passim.

18. Affidavit of Bridget Doyle, October 9, 1875, in *Webster* v. *United States* (case file no. 13502), Court of Claims, RG 123, Federal Records Center, Suitland, Md.

19. James L. Dunning to Jas. H. Burton, July 25, Aug. 5, 1862, RG 109 (microcopy 346), Confederate Papers Relating to Citizens or Business Firms, National Archives, Washington, D.C.

20. Claim of Amherst W. Stone, Records of the Southern Claims Commission (Barred and Disallowed Claims), RG 233.

21. Claim of Nedom L. Angier, Records of the Southern Claims Commission (Allowed Claims).
22. Claim of John Silvey, ibid.
23. Claim of Martin Hinton, ibid.
24. Claim of Amy J. Holley, executrix of estate of William J. Dyer, ibid.
25. Claim of Prince Ponder, ibid.; claim of Henry Beedles, ibid.
26. The materials pertaining to Webster's claim before the Southern Claims Commission are found in *Webster* v. *U.S.*
27. Claim of David Young, Records of the Southern Claims Commission (Allowed Claims).
28. Claims of Michael Lynch, George Edwards, Christian Kontz, Amans Delphey, and Laurent J. DeGive, administrator of the estate of Peter Huge, ibid.
29. Statement of Thomas Healey, claim of Edward Jones, Records of the Southern Claims Commission (Barred and Disallowed Claims), RG 233; statement of Thomas Healey, claim of L. P. Peacock, ibid.; statement of James Dunning, claim of Thomas Hornby, ibid.; statement of James Dunning, claim of Henry Banks, ibid.; statement of John Silvey, claim of Pliney R. Oliver, ibid. Typically these "statements" are comments concerning the various claimants that are attributed to the Unionists in materials contained in the claims cited. Often the "statements" are brief quotations and appear to have been entered into the claims in question by investigators for the Southern Claims Commission. They are not usually dated.
30. Depositions of Thomas Crussell, Robert Webster, Austin Wright, Thomas Jordan, William Farnsworth, Thomas Healey, and Henry Holcombe, typescript, no dates; all in *Austell* v. *United States* (case file no. 13859), Court of Claims, RG 123, Federal Records Center, Suitland, Md.
31. Deposition of James Dunning, July 6, 1873, ibid.
32. Deposition of Joshua Hill, typescript, May 31, 1872, ibid.
33. Deposition of Benjamin H. Hill, typescript, Dec. 20, 1876, ibid.
34. Summary of case, ibid.
35. "Extract from the testimony of E. T. Hunnicutt, in the case of Mr. Crussell," n.d., in *Crussell* v. *United States* (case file no. 10491), Court of Claims, RG 123, Federal Records Center, Suitland, Md.
36. Summary of claim of Thomas G. Crussell, "Extract from the testimony of E. T. Hunnicutt," ibid.
37. Claim of William Markham, Records of the Southern Claims Commission (Barred and Disallowed Claims).
38. *Markham* v. *U.S.*

Postscript

1. Dorothy Hemenway Ashton, *Sheldon, Vermont: The People Who Lived and Worked There* (St. Albans, Vt.: Regal Art Press, 1979). The inside cover of Ashton's book contains a plat of Sheldon, which shows that the Stones owned property there. Persis Lorette Hopkins to Louisa Bailey, Dec. 22, [1868], Francis L. Hopkins Collection, Bailey-Howe Library, University of Vermont, Burlington. The record of Cyrena's death in the office of the Sheldon town clerk lists the cause of death as

cancer. See "Marriage, Birth, Death Register," book 3, 1. Also see Enna Bates, "A Vermont Spring and a Cure for Cancer," in *News and Notes* (Montpelier: Vermont Historical Society, Mar. 1952): 49–52.

2. Persis Lorette Hopkins to Louisa Bailey, Dec. 22, [1868], Hopkins Collection, Bailey-Howe Library, University of Vermont, Burlington.

3. "Testimony of Colonel A. W. Stone, Jan. 8, 1869," in "Condition of Affairs in Georgia," 40th Congress, 3d Session, *House Miscellaneous Document No. 52,* 44; *Census of the United States,* 1870, Chatham County, Ga.; I. W. Avery, *The History of the State of Georgia from 1860 to 1881, Embracing the Three Important Epochs: The Decade Before the War of 1861–5; the War; the Period of Reconstruction, with Portraits of the Leading Public Men of this Era* (New York: Brown and Derby, 1881), 502.

4. *Savannah Morning News,* Sept. 2, 1873; Frank Hall, *History of the State of Colorado* (Chicago: Blakely Printing, 1890), 2:535; *Rocky Mountain News,* Mar. 19, 1911; Carlos W. Lake, "The Kidnapping of Judge A. W. Stone," *Colorado Magazine* 17 (Jan. 1940): 19–26; *Leadville (Colorado) Daily Herald,* Mar. 28, 1882; ibid., July 17, 19, 1900.

5. *Atlanta News,* Mar. 7, 1875.

6. John W. Pattillo, "William Markham," in Kenneth Coleman and Charles Stephen Gurr, eds., *Dictionary of Georgia Biography,* 2 vols. (Athens: Univ. of Georgia Press, 1983), 2:684–85; Wallace P. Reed, "Markham, Colonel William," in "Biographical," *History of Atlanta, Georgia* (Syracuse, N.Y.: D. Mason, 1889), 93–95.

7. There are numerous newspaper sources for James A. Stewart in the postwar years, primarily in the Rome, Georgia, newspapers. See, for example, *Rome (Ga.) Weekly Courier,* Sept. 12, 1867. An advertisement in J. A. Stewart, *Conservative views. The government of the United States: what is it? Comprising a correspondence with Hon. Alexander H. Stephens, eliciting views touching the nature and character of the government of the United States, the impolicy of secession, the evils of disunion, and the means of restoration* (Atlanta: Franklin Printing House, 1869) announced his preparation of a manuscript dealing with the Civil War.

8. Alexander St. Claire Abrams, *Manual and Biographical Register of the State of Georgia for 1871–72* (Atlanta: Plantation, 1872), 4–6; *Memoirs of Georgia; containing historical accounts of the state's civil, military, industrial, and professional interests, and personal sketches of many of its people* (Atlanta: Southern Historical Association, 1895), 1:702–3.

9. Dozens of articles concerning Alexander N. Wilson appear in the Savannah newspapers during the 1860s, 1870s, and 1880s. For a comprehensive listing, see Works Progress Administration, "Annals of Savannah, 1850–1937: A Digest and Index of the Newspapers and Record of Events and Opinions in Eighty-seven Volumes" (Savannah, Ga., n.d.).

10. The sources I have used to track the Unionists mentioned in the preceding paragraphs are too numerous to cite. I have leaned heavily on Franklin Garrett's "Necrology," on deposit at the Atlanta History Center.

11. James Michael Russell, *Atlanta 1847–1890: City Building in the Old South and the New* (Baton Rouge: Louisiana State Univ. Press, 1988), 201; Jerry J. Thornbery, "The Development of Black Atlanta, 1865–1885" (Ph.D. diss., University of

Maryland, College Park, 1977), 131; Daniel E. Sutherland, *Confederate Carpet-baggers* (Baton Rouge: Louisiana State Univ. Press, 1988), 162.

12. *Atlanta Constitution,* Jan. 12, 1893.

13. Journal of the Proceedings of the Constitutional Convention of the People of Georgia (1867), in Allen D. Candler, *The Confederate Records of the State of Georgia,* 6 vols. (Atlanta: Chas. P. Byrd, State Printer, 1909–11), 6:207; Royce Shingleton, *Richard Peters: Champion of the New South* (Macon, Ga.: Mercer Univ. Press, 1985), 156–57.

14. George P. Fletcher, *Loyalty: An Essay on the Morality of Relationships* (New York: Oxford Univ. Press, 1993).

15. The term *nationalism* has achieved widespread usage only in the twentieth century, and throughout this century the term has greatly expanded, becoming fully freighted with multiple connotations that evoke modern imperialism and the internecine conflicts that have occurred among aggressive nation-states. It may be obvious that it is extremely unlikely that any Civil War–era Atlantan understood the term *nationalism* as twentieth-century scholars conceive it. In fact, it is virtually impossible that any Southerners *or* Northerners were aware of or used the term in a way that approximates contemporary usage.

For most of the antebellum period, a reader would have searched in vain for *nationalism* in an American dictionary. Not until 1858 did it enter Webster's dictionary, and then the definition differed substantially from the modern understanding of the term. Nineteenth-century dictionaries did not capture contemporary usage precisely, of course, but other linguistic sources confirm that *nationalism* appeared in American English only very late in the antebellum period, and they suggest that no comprehensive formal concept of nationalism had widespread currency. Words such as *nation, nationality,* and *country* did find common usage and definition in the discourse of the day. Americans thought and talked about the meanings of those words and what they connoted. But discussions of nationalism per se did not take place. That is not to say, of course, that Americans, in the North and South, did not think on many of the same topics that collectively compose the elements of a latter-day nationalism. They did, at least in part. But if we take the era literally on its own terms, we quickly realize that the construct of "nationalism," strictly speaking, did not have currency in the Civil War era.

Historians rarely distinguish between patriotism and nationalism, but other scholars do. For a psychological perspective, see Daniel Druckman, "Nationalism, Patriotism, and Group Loyalty: A Social Psychological Perspective," *Mershon International Studies Review* 38 (1994): 43–68. For a highly suggestive philosophical, linguistic, and historical perspective, see Maurizio Viroli, *For Love of Country: An Essay on Patriotism and Nationalism* (Oxford, England: Clarendon, 1995).

16. James M. MacPherson, *For Cause and Comrades: Why Men Fought in the Civil War* (New York: Oxford Univ. Press, 1997). In the section that follows, I have drawn liberally on Clement Eaton, *The Freedom-of-Thought Struggle in the Old South* (New York: Harper & Row, 1964), 406–7.

17. For a discussion of religion and "folk loyalty," see James H. Moorhead, *American Apocalypse: Yankee Protestants and the Civil War 1860–1869* (New Haven, Conn.: Yale Univ. Press, 1978), 129–72.

18. David M. Potter, *The South and the Sectional Conflict* (Baton Rouge: Louisiana State Univ. Press, 1968), 40–41.

Appendix A • *In Search of Miss Abby*

1. Wallace P. Reed, *History of Atlanta, Georgia* (Syracuse, N.Y.: D. Mason, 1889), 187.
2. James M. Russell, "Atlanta, Gate City of the South, 1847 to 1885" (Ph.D. diss., Princeton University, Princeton, N.J., 1971).
3. Stephen J. Young et al. to Brigadier General Whipple (true copy), Sept. 10, 1864, claim of Thomas Heal[e]y, Records of the Southern Claims Commission (Allowed Claims), Fulton County, Ga., RG 217, National Archives, Washington, D.C.

Appendix B • *Miss Abby's Diary*

There are persons, places, and literary allusions throughout the diary that I have been unable to identify. Those that I have identified are noted. Many, if not most, of the persons mentioned in the diary were given pseudonyms or were referred to by initials, for example, "Mrs. I." In some instances, the initials match the last names of the persons mentioned; in others they do not.

The reader will find seven brief sections from the diary included in these notes. These are, with the exception of the material in notes 3 and 16, comments added by Cyrena Stone after the war. It seems likely that she or someone else was preparing the diary for publication or distribution and was adding annotations. That person used a star or an asterisk to mark these sections; I have used superscript numbers. It also seems likely that Cyrena purposely obscured the identities of the persons mentioned in the diary and thus adopted, perhaps piecemeal or inconsistently, pseudonyms and initials for them.

1. A church for blacks was located to the southwest of Cyrena's home.
2. During early 1863, *Harper's New Monthly Magazine* published a series of three travel articles on Iceland. Cyrena was clearly reading one of these issues.
3. The following passage has been added to the document at the bottom of a manuscript page, separated from the main portion of the diary: "Two Southern men have died in this city recently, who thought and talked of nothing else, but the coming of the Union Army. It was said the Act of Secession literally broke the heart of one of them. He was a man of worth and intelligence—but said he did not wish to live—only to see the triumph of his Goverment. Another lawyer of eminence, died suddenly in 1861, while making a Union speech. His last words were for his country." The latter reference is likely to Charles Murphey of Decatur. See Franklin M. Garrett, *Atlanta and Environs: A Chronicle of Its People and Events*, 2 vols. (Athens: Univ. of Georgia Press, 1954), 1:494.
4. *H* stands for "husband" and refers to Amherst Stone.
5. Poppy was a slave girl, approximately five years old, whom Cyrena had apparently purchased in order to protect her. See Louisa M. Whitney, *Goldie's Inheritance: A Story of the Siege of Atlanta* (Burlington, Vt.: Free Press Association, 1903), 211–12.
6. Henry Wadsworth Longfellow, "The Old Clock on the Stairs," *The Complete Poetical Works of Henry Wadsworth Longfellow* (Boston: Houghton Mifflin, 1899), 85.

7. "Mrs. F——h" was Emily Farnsworth, wife of William Farnsworth. Cyrena regarded Mrs. Farnsworth as the most courageous of the Unionist women. In 1864, she was thirty-six years old.

8. The following passage was added to the document after the war and kept separate from the main body of the text, likely in order to preserve the chronology: "These are but a few extracts from a long article, that would read strangely by the side of those eloquent eulogiums which were poured forth by a weeping Nation over the grave of its Martyr—and the answering notes of sympathy and sorrow that swept over the sea from all the crowned of Europe."

9. The following passage was added after the war: "Two of them [the prisoners] recovered—were sent to Andersonville—lived through those horrible scenes, & since peace has come, have written to their benefactor—telling her that under God, they owed their lives to her & little Nelly."

   Nelly and Mollie (mentioned in the diary paragraphs that follow) may be pseudonyms for Mrs. Farnsworth's two daughters, Helen, 14, and Emma, 6; *Census of the United States,* 1860, Fulton County, Ga.

10. The following passage was added after the war: "This prisoner was soon after sent to Andersonville, where he remained nearly a year; but the letters were safely kept through all that wretched life, and when he was exchanged—they reached their destinations, though somewhat worn."

11. This entry appears out of chronological order in the diary.

12. Likely Thomas Newman, who lived on the corner of Houston and Collins Streets, a short distance to the southwest from the Stones.

13. Arthur is the pseudonym for Chester Able Stone, Amherst's brother, who lived in the Stone household before and after his service in the Gate City Guard. Cyrena refers to him as her brother, not brother-in-law. Her only surviving brother, Keyes Bailey, lived in New York City during the war.

14. Tom is Thomas Lewis, the white servant who lived with his wife and five-year-old son in the Stone household; *Census of the United States,* 1860, Fulton County, Ga. Dan is a slave who was leased from a man who is referred to in the diary as "Mas' George." See the entry for May 21, 1864. Jerry is another of the Stones' slaves.

15. The following passage was added at this place in the document after the war: "During the long fearful seige that followed—this noble women lost her health–her home–her property, and every thing save her devotion to God and her country."

16. Apparently adapted from Henry Wadsworth Longfellow, "A Psalm of Life," *Complete Poetical Works,* 3.

17. The following section has been added to the diary: "It is a custom, when a person dies, to place the body at once upon a board—which has the horribly suggestive name of *cooling board.*"

18. David placed Uriah at the head of his legions in battle so that he would be killed and so that David could then marry Uriah's wife, Bathsheba. II Samuel 11.

19. Joe Brown's Pets refers to the state troops raised by Governor Joseph E. Brown, who were thought to have favored status. See William Harris Bragg, *Joe Brown's Army: The Georgia State Line, 1862–1865* (Macon, Ga.: Mercer Univ. Press, 1987). I am unable to identify the "New Issue."

20. The date of this entry cannot be determined. June 7, 1864, the date of the previous entry, fell on a Tuesday. The entry that follows the Sabbath entry is June 10, which was a Friday. The Sabbath entry therefore appears to be out of order. When material from the Sabbath entry is referred to in the text, I have cited it as June 7, 1864.

21. Margy was one of the slaves, perhaps Jerry's wife.

22. I Kings 27: "And it came to pass at noon, that Elijah mocked them and said Cry aloud: for he is a god; either he is talking, or he is pursuing, or he is in a journey, *or* peradventure he sleepeth and must be awaked."

23. Dreams of Cyrena's contemporaries are insightfully analyzed in Jean Friedman, *The Enclosed Garden* (Chapel Hill: Univ. of North Carolina Press, 1985), 39–53. Ossian was a legendary Gaelic hero of the third century.

24. "Mrs. I" is Martha Huntington. See chapter 8.

25. The following passage was added after the war: "The question soon became so important—how to secure their own safety of these Jesuitical officials—that no arrests were made of the Union flag makers."

26. Bess and Robert were likely Robert Webster and his wife, who lived quite near the Stones, only a few hundred feet down Houston Street toward the city.

27. The Washington Artillery was active in and around the Stones' house during the battle. See chapter 8. Also see Nathaniel Cheairs Hughes Jr., *The Pride of the Confederate Artillery: The Washington Artillery in the Army of Tennessee* (Baton Rouge: Louisiana State Univ. Press, 1997).

28. "Mr. Y——" may have been the black Unionist Robert Webster, also known as Robert Yancey.

Thomas G. Dyer is University Professor of Higher Education and History at the University of Georgia. His books include *Theodore Roosevelt and the Idea of Race; "To Raise Myself a Little": The Diaries and Letters of Jennie, a Georgia Teacher;* and *The University of Georgia: A Bicentennial History, 1785–1985.*